FLORIDA STATE
UNIVERSITY LIBRARIES

NOV 17 1999

TALLAHASSEE, FLORIDA

This study fills a major gap in the mainstream narrative of Irish history by reconstructing political developments in the year before the restoration of Charles II. It is the first treatment of the complex Irish dimension of the king's return.

The issue of the monarchy did not stand alone in Ireland. Entangled with it was the question of how the restoration of the old regime would affect a Protestant colonial community which had changed in character and fortune as a result of the Cromwellian conquest, the immigration that had accompanied it and the massive transfer of land that followed. As the return of Charles became increasingly probable, Cromwellian and pre-Cromwellian settlers were united in their determination to ensure that the restoration of Charles did not deprive them of their gains. This account discloses how the leaders of the Protestant establishment protected its interests by managing the transition back to monarchy.

AIDAN CLARKE is Erasmus Smith's Professor of Modern History, Trinity College, Dublin, and a former president of the Royal Irish Academy.

PRELUDE TO RESTORATION IN IRELAND

The end of the commonwealth, 1659–1660

AIDAN CLARKE

CAMBRIDGE
UNIVERSITY PRESS

PUBLISHED BY THE PRESS SYNDICATE OF THE UNIVERSITY OF CAMBRIDGE
The Pitt Building, Trumpington Street, Cambridge CB2 1RP, United Kingdom

CAMBRIDGE UNIVERSITY PRESS
The Edinburgh Building, Cambridge, CB2 2RU, UK   http://www.cup.cam.ac.uk
40 West 20th Street, New York, NY 10011-4211, USA   http://www.cup.org
10 Stamford Road, Oakleigh, Melbourne 3166, Australia

© Aidan Clarke 1999

This book is in copyright. Subject to statutory exception and to the provisions of relevant collective licensing agreements, no reproduction of any part may take place without the written permission of Cambridge University Press.

First published 1999

Printed in the United Kingdom at the University Press, Cambridge

Typeset in Dante Regular 10.5/14 pt [VN]

A catalogue record for this book is available from the British Library

Library of Congress Cataloguing in Publication data

Clarke, Aidan, 1933–
Prelude to restoration in Ireland: the end of the Commonwealth,
1659–1660 / Aidan Clarke.
p. 00 cm.
Includes bibliographical references.
ISBN 0 521 65061 5
1. Ireland – History – 1649–1660. 2. Protestants – Ireland – History – 17th century. I. Title.
DA944.4.C53   1999
320.9415'09'032 – dc21   98-36968   CIP

ISBN 0 521 65061 5 hardback

*To Oisin, Caoimhe,
Subhanora and Ceasan*

Contents

Acknowledgements [viii]
Conventions and abbreviations [ix]
Map: Representation in the General Convention [xii]

1. A kind of colony [1]
2. Commissioners and submissioners: May to June [21]
3. The rule of the rump: July to October [56]
4. The threefold cord: October to December [92]
5. Setting up for themselves: January to February [131]
6. The election returns [169]
7. The General Convention of Ireland: March to April [243]
8. Without expectation of resurrection: May to June [292]

Appendix: Members of the General Convention [321]

Select bibliography [326]
Index [346]

Acknowledgements

I have accumulated the familiar debts and obligations which add to the pleasures of research and I would like gratefully to acknowledge the financial assistance provided by the Royal Irish Academy/British Academy exchange scheme and the Arts and Social Sciences Benefaction at Trinity College Dublin; the hospitality of the Fellows of Hertford College, Oxford, and of James Welsh at King's College, London; and the courtesy and professionalism of the staffs of the libraries and archives in which I worked and with which I dealt by correspondence. My particular thanks are due to Toby Barnard, who would have done this better, for much kindness and a good deal of information; to Sarah Barber, Bob Hunter, Brid McGrath, Jane Ohlmeyer, Kevin O'Herlihy, Micheal O Siochrú and Harold O'Sullivan who have supplied me with references, copies of documents or odds and ends of information; to Matthew Stout who prepared the constituency map; to Ciarán Brady who commented on the text with disconcerting honesty and James McGuire who, among other things, saved me from an egregious error on the first page; to Linda Montgomery who helped me with pagebreaks, spreadsheets, tabs and other such mysteries; to Maija and Dylan whose morning walks gave me time to think; to Mary, for everything. 'And for the rest', in the words of Daniel Burston, 'I do everywhere (to the best of my Remembrance) acknowledge my debt to my Creditors, from whom I have borrowed them, and with whose stock I have traded.'

Conventions and abbreviations

For the most part I have used the standard term New English to describe the pre-1641 Protestant colonists and 'settler' or 'newcomer' to refer to those who came after the outbreak of rebellion. These later arrivals rendered the term New English ambiguous, of course, and contemporaries learned to avoid confusion by speaking of Old and New Protestants. I have adopted this usage where the context required it.

Dates are given in old style except that the year is treated as beginning on 1 January. For the sake of clarity, continental dates have been adjusted to conform to the Julian calendar.

Full bibliographic details of works referred to are given at the first citation: thereafter, short titles are used. The following abbreviations have been employed throughout.

Acts and ordinances	Firth, C. H. and Rait, R. S. (eds.), *Acts and ordinances of the Interregnum, 1642–1660.* 3 vols., London, 1911
Add. MSS	Additional Manuscripts
Anal. Hib.	*Analecta Hibernica, including the reports of the Irish Manuscripts Commission,* Dublin, 1930–
Arch. Hib.	*Archivium Hibernicum: or Irish Historical Record,* Maynooth, 1912–
BIHR	*Bulletin of the Institute of Historical Research*
BL	British Library
Cal. Clarendon SP	O. Ogle, W. H. Bliss, W. D. Macray and F. J. Routledge (eds.), *Calendar of the Clarendon state papers preserved in the Bodleian Library.* 5 vols., Oxford, 1869–1970
Cal. SP, Adventurers	*Calendar of state papers, Adventurers, 1642–59.* London, 1903

Cal. SP, Dom.	Calendar of state papers, domestic series
Cal. SP, Ire.	Calendar of state papers relating to Ireland
Cal. SP, Ven.	Calendar of state papers and manuscripts, relating to English affairs, existing in the archives and collections of Venice
CJ	Journals of the House of Commons
CJ Ire.	Journals of the House of Commons of the kingdom of Ireland
Clarendon State Papers	Scrope, R. and Monkhouse, T. (eds.), *State papers collected by Edward, earl of Clarendon*. 3 vols., Oxford, 1767–86
Cork HAS jn.	Journal of the Cork Historical and Archaeological Society
DNB	Dictionary of National Biography
EHR	English Historical Review
HMC	Historical Manuscripts Commission
IMC	Irish Manuscripts Commission
'Inedited letters'	Meyer, Joseph (ed.), 'Inedited letters of Cromwell, Col. Jones, Bradshaw and other regicides', *Transactions of the Historic Society of Lancashire and Cheshire*, new series, 1 (1860–1)
IRC	Irish Record Commission
Kildare AS jn.	Journal of the County Kildare Archaeological Society
LJ	Journals of the House of Lords
Louth HAS jn.	Journal of the County Louth Historical and Archaeological Society
Montgomery MSS	Hill, George (ed.), *The Montgomery MSS (1603–1706): compiled from the family papers by William Montgomery of Rosemount, Esquire*. Belfast, 1869
NLI	National Library of Ireland
PRONI	Public Records Office of Northern Ireland
PRO	Public Records Office of England
Regimental history	Firth, C. H. and Davies, G., *Regimental history of Cromwell's army*. 2 volumes paged as one, Oxford, 1940
RIA trans.	Transactions of the Royal Irish Academy
RIA proc.	Proceedings of the Royal Irish Academy

RSAI jn.	*Journal of the Royal Society of Antiquaries of Ireland*
SP	State Papers
TCD	Trinity College Dublin
TSP	Birch, Thomas (ed.), *A collection of the state papers of John Thurloe, esq.* 7 vols., London, 1742
UJA	*Ulster Journal of Archaeology*

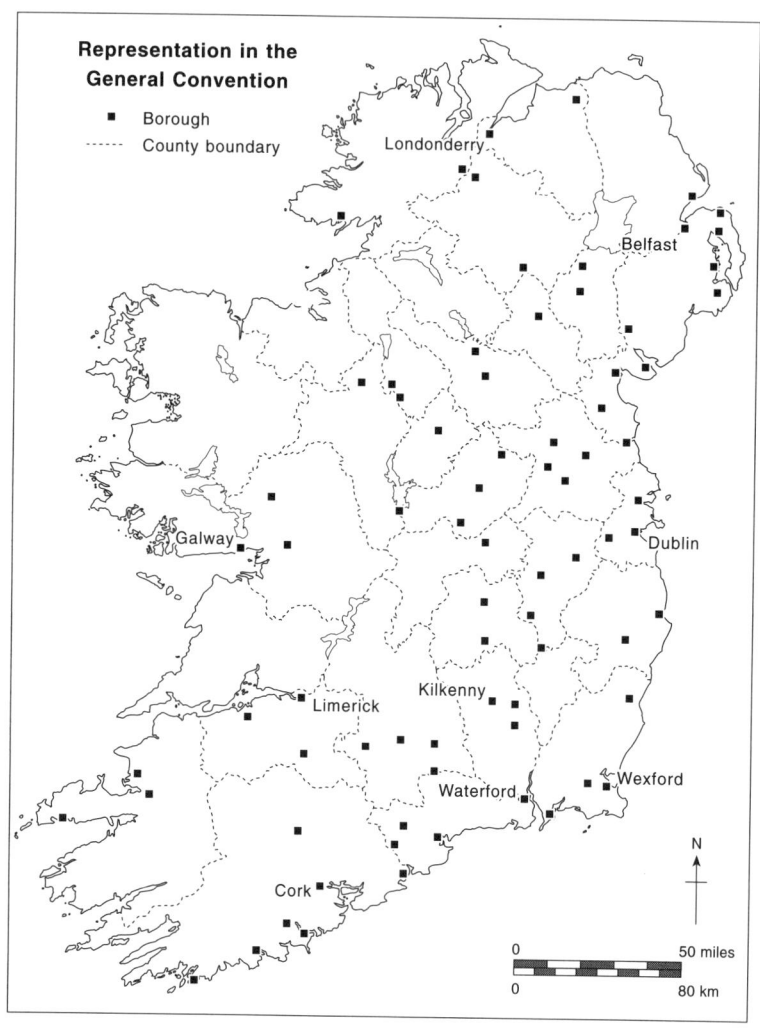

Representation in the General Convention

1

A kind of colony[1]

On the afternoon of Tuesday, 13 December 1659, two veterans of the Irish wars, visiting the capital from their homes in County Kilkenny, walked together in the garden of Dublin Castle. Both were Englishmen. Colonel William Warden had been in Ireland since the 1640s when he had fought with Inchiquin and Broghill in Munster; Captain John Joyner, lately mayor of Kilkenny, had been in the domestic service of King Charles before coming to Ireland with Cromwell's expeditionary force in 1649. They may have reminisced, but that was not the purpose of their meeting. At about 5 o'clock they called upon the sentinel to let them out through the postern gate, recently reinforced against surprisal by the erection of an inner gate. As he did so, some thirty or forty soldiers thrust him aside, overpowered the castle guard and marched them out of the castle precincts with their hands in their pockets. Shots from the roof of the castle announced success and horse troops at once rode through the town with drawn swords, crying 'a parliament, a parliament'. At their head were two more veterans, of a different stamp. Both were Irish born. Sir Theophilus Jones, second son of the bishop of Killaloe and younger brother of the bishop of Clogher, had been cashiered from the captaincy of the lord lieutenant's life-guard in the summer; Major Edward Warren, whose father was dean of Ossory, was a serving officer of republican principles and radical religious opinions. Their objective was to secure both the commissioners who had been appointed to govern Ireland by the English parliament in the previous June and the commanders of the Dublin garrison. Captain Robert Fitzgerald, the earl of Kildare's son and Lord Broghill's nephew, seized three of these men in the council chamber in the new custom house and the other two at a religious meeting in South Werburgh Street. The first stage

---

[1] ''Tis true, we are but a kind of colony', Henry Cromwell to Fauconberg, April 1658. Thomas Birch (ed.), *A collection of the state papers of John Thurloe, esq.* (7 vols., London, 1742), vii, 101.

of the coup was complete. No blood had been shed. It remained for fellow conspirators and sympathizers to follow suit throughout the garrison towns of Ireland.

This is, in the words of a contemporary royalist historian, 'one of the Curtain-Stories that cannot be pryed into as yet, as are the other abstruse contrivances of the King's restitution'.[2] Outwardly, the episode is easily explained. Two months earlier, to the day, the English army had expelled the parliament that ruled all three of the former Stuart kingdoms and taken control. In Ireland, both the army leaders and the civil governors were thought to be in sympathy with the military takeover and as resistance mounted in England and Scotland a group of old and new settlers came together to help to reverse it by seizing power in parliament's interest. Behind the curtain, there was not so much a different story as a number of possible stories, each with different beginnings and with endings which depended upon events that were not under local control, if they were under control at all.

There were both irreconcilable royalists and implacable republicans among the Protestant community in Ireland, but the rule of the Cromwells, whose policies had proved less repugnant than their usurpation, had served the interests of many sufficiently well to lead them to regret the overthrow of the lord protectorship by the alliance of army officers and republicans in May 1659 which had restored its predecessor, the 'rump' of the Long Parliament. The rule of the 'rump', more doctrinaire and less responsive than that of the Cromwells, brought the unacceptable features of the commonwealth back into renewed prominence. Its replacement in October by a military junto which was still more doctrinaire may have given it some retrospective attraction, but among those who called for parliament's restoration in December were many who had neither welcomed its recall in May nor been reconciled to what it had done since. A greater antipathy towards military rule served to account for that anomaly. But the catchcry of the horsemen was ambiguous. For Edward Warren and others it meant the reinstatement of the 'rump' but that was far from being its only possible meaning, in Ireland or England. Already, some were arguing for the readmission to parliament of the members

---

[2] James Heath, *A Chronicle of the late intestine war in the three kingdoms* (London, 1661), p. 432.

who had been purged by Colonel Pride eleven years earlier, so that the 'rump' that had executed the king would be reconstituted as the House of Commons that had fought the civil wars. Others called for fresh elections to a 'free parliament'. In both cases, the intended outcome was usually a return to monarchy. How complete that return should be was a vital point of difference, but only those who wished to preserve the gains that had been fought for in the civil wars were at liberty to state their position plainly.

In retrospect, the December *coup d'état* became the defining moment when Protestants in Ireland 'declared for the Happy Restoration of his Majestye'.³ At the time, its purposes were more circumscribed. The capture of the castle, the government and the army leaders was not the work of a close group united behind a political programme, but of a consortium of men with different interests and different preferences, practising different degrees of pragmatism and dissimulation. What they had in common was a determination to seize the opportunity to wrest power from extremists, recreate acceptable governmental and political processes and find a way of allowing the political nation to arrive at decisions. Once they had done that, they competed with one another to influence the decisions that were to be made. Their disagreements, however, were contained by their realization that the large decisions, which extended to England and Scotland as well as Ireland and ultimately embraced the relations of the king with all three, would be made elsewhere. They could hope to influence what happened, but not to determine it. They concentrated on keeping control of the local situation in their own hands by 'remodelling' the command of the army, establishing an executive and summoning a representative convention to legitimate the initiative that they had taken. While in England the 'rump' gave way in February to a reconstituted Long Parliament, with the purged members in the majority, and this gave way in its turn in April to an elected parliamentary convention which restored the king in May, the dominant group in Ireland paced their response to the emerging possibilities and extended the range of local political activity and choice in rough step with developments elsewhere. They kept a watching brief on the 'abstruse

³ Public Record Office, State Papers, Ireland, 63/305. 6a. S. J. Connolly, *Religion, law, and power: the making of Protestant Ireland, 1660–1760* (Oxford, 1992), pp. 5–6.

contrivances' of others and individually engaged in some of their own, but their common concern was to police the Irish boundaries of the political flux which was beyond their control.

It cannot be claimed that their activities contributed directly to the king's return. But there is a local story to be told, because the central issue of the kingship did not stand alone in Ireland. Entangled with it was the question of how the restoration of the monarchy would affect a Protestant community which had changed fundamentally in character and fortune as a result of the recent conquest, the immigration that had accompanied it, and the massive transfer of property that followed. As the return of Charles became increasingly probable, old and new colonists alike were united in their determination to ensure that the restoration of the old regime did not entail the restoration of the old Catholic proprietors and upset the land settlement fashioned by the usurpers in the 1650s. The political means that they had improvised to protect themselves against the king's enemies were adapted to preserving their new estates against the possibility of royal reprisal for the disloyalty or collusion to which their gains testified. Their achievement, before normal decision-making procedures were formally resumed on 18 June, when the king granted an audience to a delegation from the Irish Convention and negotiations commenced, was unity. Although the established Protestant colonists and those who joined them in the 1650s had little enough in common, in the last year of the commonwealth both learned to understand that they must subordinate their differences to their shared interests and cooperate to meet the challenge of the restoration 'all as one body'.

The collective stake that Protestant political action was designed to preserve in 1660 had its origins eighteen years earlier when investors were invited in February 1642 to contribute to the cost of subduing the Irish rebellion in return for a share in the land that would become available through forfeiture when it was over. Some £300,000 was subscribed by about 1500 'adventurers', geared up to a liability of £360,000 by the terms of a special offer made to investors in a doubling ordinance in 1643.[4] Later, when the English civil wars were over and the new republic turned its attention to establishing its authority in Ireland, it was decided to meet the

---

[4] Karl Bottigheimer, *English money and Irish land* (Oxford, 1971), pp. 55, 121–2, 143.

pay costs of conquest in the same way. Arrears were allowed to accumulate and officers and soldiers were paid in Irish land to the value of the services they had given, an arrangement which enhanced the security of both countries by ensuring that the soldiers were not demobilized in England. After the conquest, the distribution of confiscated estates amounting to more than half of Ireland in fulfilment of these obligations transformed the political and social geography of the country. The framework of the settlement was established by an initial decision that landownership in the provinces of Ulster, Leinster and Munster should be reserved to Protestants and, accordingly, that Catholics who were able to establish their innocence should be required to surrender their estates in return for land in Connacht and County Clare.

In the Act of Satisfaction, passed in 1653 by 'Barebone's parliament', a nominated assembly convened by the army after it had forcibly dissolved the purged parliament – the 'rump' – which had abolished the monarchy, the land forfeited in the ten counties of Antrim, Armagh, Down, Meath, Westmeath, King's County, Queen's County, Tipperary, Limerick and Waterford was designated as the resource from which the state's debts were to be met. One half of the baronies in each county was to be set aside to satisfy the claims of the adventurers and the other allocated to meeting army arrears.[5] The baronies were sorted into two groups by lottery in January 1654 and a preliminary survey of the extent and location of the forfeited land in each county was made. It was on the basis of this information that the claims of the adventurers, or in many instances those to whom they had assigned the benefit of their investment, were dealt with in the first instance. Lots were drawn and entitlements were conveyed to a total of 1,043 individuals, but the difficulty of the task and the inadequacy of the survey prolonged the business; an exact match between the amount of land allocated to adventurers in particular counties and the amount of confiscable profitable land actually available proved impossible to achieve, and perhaps 10 per cent of the total value of the adventurers'

---

[5] The amount of forfeited land in these counties varied: the Ulster counties were to meet 12.5 per cent of the adventurers' claims, the Munster counties 30.5% and the Leinster counties the remainder. In total, these claims amounted to about 17% of the debt to be discharged, and this is approximately the proportion of the available land that was assigned to meet them. Bottigheimer, *English money and Irish land*, pp. 143, 153.

claims was left unsatisfied, or 'deficient'.[6] In mid-1657 their spokesmen were still complaining that 'few or none of them can to this day find any such settlement as will admit them with security to build plant or bestow their industry upon their proportions'.[7] In an effort to expedite the business, they agreed late in 1658 that the details of their settlement should be redrawn in accordance with the later and more sophisticated survey directed by William Petty, which had been used to allocate land to the soldiers, but the business was still unfinished when the Cromwellian protectorate was overthrown and the 'rump' was recalled to its duties in May 1659. The adventurers' settlement had not been at a standstill: some had established themselves on their property, while others had realized their assets or remained at home as absentees, but many waited with increasing impatience for the completion of the administrative process and the final confirmation of their new holdings.

In the meantime, the claims for arrears owing to some 35,000 officers and soldiers, most of them demobilized in the successive disbandments of army units between 1653 and 1656, proved larger and more complicated than the original scheme could contain. The original allocation of forfeited land in the ten counties designated for this purpose had been intended to meet the payments due for service in Ireland after 5 June 1649, which was the accounting date for the commencement of Cromwell's expedition. Disbandment began in June 1653, however, with men who had accumulated arrears for service in Ireland before that date. Additional resources were needed to satisfy these supernumeraries, among whom were many established settlers who had fought on parliament's side as well as members of earlier expeditionary forces from England. The land forfeited in County Cavan and in selected baronies in Fermanagh, Monaghan, Louth, Longford, Kilkenny, Cork and Sligo was assigned to the payment of these '49 arrears, as they came to be known, with the intention of settling those involved, so far as was practicable, in the areas in which they had been stationed, which were also in many cases the places where they had formerly resided. Thus a rough distinction between two categories of military claimant, the pre-Cromwellian and the Cromwellian, was incorporated into the geography of the settlement. As the disbandment of large

---

[6] Ibid., pp. 143–52.
[7] *Calendar of state papers relating to Ireland,1647–60*, p. 640. PRO, SP Ire., 63/ 287. 45.

numbers of men who had come with or after Cromwell got under way in 1655, the land which had been assigned to them in the ten counties proved to be insufficient to meet the amounts due, which had grown incrementally since the original calculations had been made.[8] The forfeited land in Londonderry, Tyrone, Wexford and Kerry and in assorted baronies in Fermanagh, Monaghan, Kilkenny and Sligo was added to the pool. There were also obligations to some of these men arising out of unpaid arrears due for previous service in England: parts of County Mayo were appropriated to these.

The reality of the settlement in the 1650s was not as tidy as the paperwork envisaged. This was partly due to technical deficiencies. There were innumerable disputes arising from challenges to the classification of individual liability to forfeiture, from the redemption of confiscated property by the payment of composition fines or from the shortcomings of the surveys on which the distribution was based. A more fundamental reason was the untidiness of human behaviour. Many of the original adventurers had sold their interest before the settlement began, and most of those who received land under this heading never came to settle in Ireland. Likewise, it had not been unknown for army men recalled to England to sell their arrears.[9] Above all, the great majority of the demobilized officers and soldiers converted their entitlements into as much capital as they could realize and went home, most at the first opportunity, others after they had inspected their new property. 'They have high expectations till they see the country', explained one of the many established colonists who looked forward to expanding their holdings at bargain prices.[10] Perhaps one in five of the army beneficiaries stayed in Ireland, and by no means all of these retained the property assigned to them.[11] There was a lively buyer's market in land, in adventurers' lots and in the greatly depreciated soldiers' debentures, as the instruments which conveyed entitlement to forfeited land of a stated value were known. Army officers were particularly well

---

[8] After Henry Cromwell's arrival in July 1655, thirty-six companies of foot and fifteen companies of horse were disbanded. *Calendar of state papers, Adventurers, 1642–59* (London, 1903), p. xxxiii.

[9] *Cal. SP, Ire., 1647–60*, p. 496.

[10] *Cal. SP, Ire., 1647–60*, p. 625. SP Ire., 63/287. 9.

[11] It was reckoned that of those who remained in the army 'not one in fifty of them hath one foot of land in Ireland'. Memorandum on the north of Ireland. SP, Ire., 63/305. 113.

[7]

placed to accumulate soldiers' portions, 'being well stored with money, and the soldiers greatly wanting the same',[12] but purchases were made by old colonists as well as by newcomers. As a result, involvement in the arrangements was far from being confined to the nominal beneficiaries and vested interest was spread widely throughout the older Protestant community. The pattern of settlement was disturbed by these uncontrolled variables, while its density was not only uneven but random, depending as it did both on variations in the amount of forfeited land available in different areas and on the totality of the decisions made by individuals, to come or to stay as the case might be. None the less, a significant number of newcomers did settle in Ireland. Most of these acquired relatively small amounts of land and the number of proprietors increased sharply as estates were subdivided into soldiers' portions. A significant number of officers, however, availed of the opportunity to assemble cut-price estates which were inestimably larger than the realizable value of their arrears would have purchased for them in England. The configuration of the scheme, though greatly modified in application, provided the structure of the new colonial Ireland. There were differences of interest between those who had been disbanded and those who remained in arms, but the ex-army component of this settlement process was by no means fully differentiated from the army itself. Those officers who remained in service had shared in the distribution of lands, though their claims had not been met in full. Many of them had received temporary grants of land from government reserves, known as custodiams, to provide for their support and some had received grants as security for their unpaid arrears.[13] Conversely, disbanded officers and soldiers remained as an essential reserve force in the security system.

Formally, the army in Ireland had been reduced to eighteen regiments by 1659, six of horse, one of dragoons and eleven of foot, but, in real terms, the military establishment was not clearcut in either composition or structure. The arrangements were complicated by a proliferation of 'loose' companies and troops, free from regimental associations, and often commanded by senior officers. In some instances these were dedicated to

---

[12] F. R. Bolton, 'Griffith Williams, bishop of Ossory (1641–72)', *Journal of the Butler Society*, 2 (1984), p. 329.   [13] *Cal. SP, Ire., 1660–2*, p. 243.

a specific purpose, usually garrison duty under the command of a formally disbanded officer who had settled in the vicinity; in others, they served as appendages to prominent individuals whose status and influence they both signified and upheld. Structurally, moreover, the operational deployment of the army diluted the impact of the nominal lines of command. Policy dictated that the soldiers should live in quarters and security demanded the presence of force everywhere. There was a minimum of fifty-seven garrisons to be manned,[14] and fifteen administrative precincts to be serviced. In these conditions few if any of the regiments, horse or foot, existed as a coherent entity. As a matter of course, the various troops or companies were dispersed over the area of the regiment's responsibility, if it had one, and often beyond, for units and officers were routinely detached for special duty in distant places, so that Carrickfergus, for example, was governed by the lieutenant-colonel of a regiment stationed in north Munster. Some regiments were literally nominal in character: they consisted of unrelated companies grouped together for administrative purposes, and had neither territorial base nor corporate identity. Senior officers commonly combined garrison commands with their regimental duties, and many carried out onerous local, regional or national administrative functions as well. The interests that most had acquired in landed property absorbed some of their energies and some spent a good deal of time in the political centres of Dublin or London. In these circumstances, the degree of devolution was large and the real distribution of authority might bear little relation to the simple pyramid of military line management.

With the implementation of the land settlement and the institution of regular machinery for the government of the country came the elaboration of a bureaucracy. Although many of the administrative and executive tasks were carried out by army officers, the train of ancillary officials and administrators who came to assist in the administration of Ireland in the 1650s constituted a further element in the new population, alongside the 'adventurers and debenturers' whose interests they came to share,

---

[14] *Cal. SP, Ire., 1647–60*, pp. 687–8. This was an assessment of the strategic requirements: it was alleged that in reality the garrisons were 'most partially placed, not according to the Commonwealth's interest but as relations or friends can procure them'. HMC, *Report on the manuscripts of the earl of Egmont* (3 vols., London 1905–23), i, 560.

partly because a portion of their salary was often paid in debentures and partly because opportunities to acquire property were readily available.¹⁵ A motley collection of opportunists and job seekers, merchants, lawyers, ministers and other professionals among them, contributed to the profile of the new colonists.

The predicament of the old colonists in 1659, in wishing to be rid of the usurping regime while preserving some of its works, had been adumbrated in the confusions of the 1640s. When civil war in England had impeded the suppression of rebellion in Ireland after 1642, Protestant loyalty to King Charles I had been strained by the fact that his policy of arranging a truce and coming to terms with the rebels in order to concentrate on winning the civil war was less attractive than parliament's policy of containing the rebels while it lasted and defeating them after it was over. At various times and places, circumstances or inclination led Protestant colonists to cooperate with the king's enemies against the Confederate Catholics.¹⁶ This posture briefly received implicit official sanction in the aftermath of the king's defeat in England when his lord lieutenant, the marquess of Ormond, made the same choice and surrendered Dublin to the victorious parliament before leaving Ireland in 1647.¹⁷ When he returned late in the following year and brought the royalist cause into an incongruous coalition with that of the Catholics, the issue was less clear than it seemed because the Irish and English dimensions of royal policy were in conflict. The question for Protestants in Ireland could not be confined to whether they were for or against the king; they had also to determine whether it was proper or wise to join with Irish Catholics against English Protestants in an effort to prevent the decisive conquest of Ireland and secure the free exercise of the Catholic religion and the retention of Catholic political influence. In that dilemma, some followed Ormond and some did not. It was not until after August 1650, when Charles II restored the rebellious status of the Catholics in arms by repudiating the terms on which the coalition was based and Ormond once

---

¹⁵ Civil List, 1654–55. British Library, Add. MS 19,833.

¹⁶ In 1660, Captain Fulke Rokely claimed to have been the only commissioned officer under Sir Charles Coote's command in Connacht who had remained consistently loyal to the king. *Cal. SP, Ire., 1660–2*, p. 65.

¹⁷ Ormond to Charles, 17 March 1647. Bodleian Library, Oxford, Carte MS 29, f. 153.

again withdrew, leaving the country without the vestige of a royal presence, that it became possible for Protestants to concentrate with a clear conscience on the primary local priority of bringing the rebellion forcibly to an end in cooperation with the only force capable of doing so. In this task there was ready collaboration with the usurping regime, but for most of those involved it was subject to the same reservation that had accompanied collaboration with parliamentary forces and their Scottish allies in the 1640s: that to combine with the king's enemies against the Catholic forces in Ireland was an act of preservation rather than an act of rebellion, a necessity not a choice.

The way in which the members of the established Protestant colony had conducted themselves in the 1640s determined how they were dealt with in the settlement of the 1650s. Broadly, they were sorted into two categories. One consisted of those who had remained loyal to the crown throughout all the vicissitudes of the war years until the royalist cause ceased to have substance. The other comprised those who had shown 'good affection' to parliament. In the Act for the Settling of Ireland, passed in August 1652 by the 'rump' of the Long Parliament, those who belonged to the first group were made liable to the forfeiture of one-fifth of their estates. Those who qualified for the second not only escaped this penalty but were rewarded by the state's acceptance of the obligation to pay arrears due for military service against the rebels in the same way as it paid those of its regular soldiers, in debentures. The sorting process was not simple. Those who claimed to have shown 'good affection' had done so in a wide variety of ways and circumstances. Many benefited from the fact that the confused manner in which the war had developed in most parts of the country lent itself to simplified judgements of what constituted a transfer of allegiance to parliament. Those who had accepted parliamentary authority after Ormond's departure in 1647 and continued to do so after his return were accorded equal status with those who had not observed the 1643 Cessation of hostilities between the king and the confederates. So also were the regiments supported from 1642 by parliament in Ulster, despite the fact that they had not only been raised and deployed with the king's ostensible approval but had at least nominally recognized Ormond's authority.

Simplification could go only so far, however, and the complexities of the war in Munster gave rise to a further distinction. Many of those who had followed the earl of Inchiquin into the parliamentary camp in 1644 in defiance of the Cessation had also followed him back to the king in 1648. Some made handsome amends when they defected to parliament after Cromwell came to Ireland, preferring, in the later words of parliament's general of horse for Munster, Lord Broghill, 'the hazard of their lives once more before the Servitude of their Country'.[18] The terms of the Act of Settlement nonetheless made them liable to partial forfeiture. This was attended to by an ordinance made in June 1654 which gave indemnity to 'all persons British and Protestant' in the province but distinguished between those who had come to parliament's support before and after 1 December 1649 by imposing composition fines on the latter. A few months later, this concession was extended by an ordinance which allowed Protestants in the rest of Ireland to avoid confiscation by paying a fine of not less than twice the 1640 income from the property, though it did not similarly confer indemnity.[19] Arrangements to meet '49 arrears for the absolved Munstermen were incorporated into the scheme of settlement and the forfeited land in Donegal, Wicklow and the unassigned baronies in Longford was allocated to these claimants.[20] Placed as they were at the end of a lengthy queue, they had received nothing by 1659.

The case of the Scots settlers in Ulster, who greatly outnumbered their English fellow colonists, perhaps by as much as fifteen to one, was more problematic still.[21] There were unswerving royalists among them, as there were in Scotland also, but many had been drawn into the convolutions of Scottish opposition politics. They had sympathized with Covenanter resistance to royal policy in the late 1630s, welcomed the Scottish army which had come to their defence in 1642, supported the alliance of the Scots with the English parliament in 1643, approved the design to impose Presbyterianism on England and Ireland which moti-

---

[18] *The Irish colours displayed in the reply of an English Protestant to a late letter of an Irish Roman Catholique* (London, 1662), p. 14.

[19] C. H. Firth and R. S. Rait (eds.), *Acts and ordinances of the Interregnum, 1642–1660* (3 vols., London, 1911), ii, 1015–16.

[20] *Acts and ordinances*, ii, 933–7.

[21] Shortly after the restoration, it was estimated that Ulster contained 80,000 Scots 'able to beare Armes' and 'not 5000 English'; 'both towne and Country in a manner swarme with the Scotch'. SP, Ire., 63/305, 113.

vated it and subscribed to the Solemn League and Covenant which cemented it. When the Scots government divided its supporters by changing sides and invading England in the king's cause during the second civil war in 1648, the response of Scots in Ireland was similarly divided, but they were numbered among parliament's enemies when Cromwell brought the New Model Army to Ireland in 1649 and the subsequent conquest of Scotland placed them firmly among the unreconciled. As Ormond observed in July 1649, 'I understand not perfectly the submission of that province, that fatal ingredient of the covenant having still some mixture in it.'[22] In the 1650s there were degrees of intransigence among them. At one end of the spectrum, there were some who renounced the covenant; at the other, there were a good many who were sufficiently disenchanted with the Stuarts to cooperate with those who had overthrown them. All, however, remained suspect to the regime because their close connections with Scotland and their outspoken commitment to Presbyterianism or monarchy, or both, made them potentially dangerous.[23] A scheme to transplant them to parts of Ireland more remote from Scotland was formulated, but dropped, and the act of settlement and the ordinance which ameliorated it protected their position. Almost all of them, however, remained somewhat apart from their fellow colonists because their loyalty to the crown was defined by their Presbyterian principles and was predicated upon Charles II's adherence to the terms of the covenant of 1643, which he had taken at his coronation in 1651 and which called for the English and Irish churches to be reformed along Scottish lines.

Few Protestants who remained in Ireland in the 1650s remained uncompromised in some degree. As the republican commonwealth established after the execution of Charles I in 1649 and the Cromwellian protectorate which replaced it in 1653 successively went about the business of arranging a settlement designed to make Ireland safe for Protestantism, they could

---

[22] T. Carte (ed.), *A collection of original letters and papers concerning affairs in England, from 1641–1660* (2 vols., London, 1739), ii, 391.

[23] Anthony Morgan informed parliament in 1656 that 'in the North, the Scotch keep up an interest distinct in garb and all formalities, and are able to raise an army of 40,000 fighting men at any time, which they may easily carry over into the Highlands upon any occasion'. T. K. Lowry (ed.), *The Hamilton Manuscripts* (Belfast, 1867), p. 69n.

count on local Protestant cooperation. From the outset, leading members of the old community played a willing part as members of the commissions of revenue and sequestration of delinquents' estates established in each precinct, and there seems to have been little reluctance to undertake the usual chores of local government and administrative office thereafter. That acquiescent tendency was reinforced after the mid-1650s when the severity of the regime was significantly softened in the lord deputyship of Oliver Cromwell's son Henry who cultivated the support of the established Protestant communities and sought to restore normal civilian routines in an effort to counterbalance the predominant military and radical influence. Composition fines unofficially ceased to be enforced, the law courts were reinstated, new town charters were issued, sheriffs and justices of the peace were appointed to carry out their familiar functions and office holders in the central administration resumed their duties. The traditional elite was brought comfortably into complicity with the usurping regime. But the framework of administration remained the new military precincts into which the counties had been grouped and the reality was that power in Ireland had changed hands and was sustained by an army of occupation, partly under arms and partly settled on the land. The Irish parliament had been replaced by token representation in a union parliament at Westminster, where members from Ireland and Scotland were outnumbered, almost seven to one, by the representatives of English and Welsh constituencies. Moreover, while Henry Cromwell displayed a welcome conservatism in religious matters and gradually curtailed the influence of the radical extremists imported with the army and encouraged by his predecessor, Charles Fleetwood, the fact remained that the Church of Ireland had been abolished and a non-episcopal church imposed.

Collaboration with the regime in securing Protestant Ireland was qualified not only by disapproval of its political principles but also by disagreement about what Protestantism itself properly was and what the relationship between the church and the community should properly be. Though members of the formerly established Church of Ireland and their Presbyterian rivals differed in their views on church government and liturgy, and English and Scottish Presbyterians were also at odds, all shared the conviction that the only acceptable ecclesiastical system was an established church, uniform in belief and practice, to which everybody was obliged to belong. By contrast, the religious purposes with which the anti-royalist movement was suffused were novel and diverse. A pragmatic mainstream Presbyterianism had been influential for some time, and had proved acceptable to many who, though they would have preferred Episcopalianism, believed that God had enjoined conformity but had not ruled on church government. However, the political calculus which led first to the purging of parliament and the abolition of the monarchy and later to the expulsion of the parliament itself placed power in the hands of men who respected variety, within puritan limits. The ecclesiastical arrangements which evolved were based on two novel principles. The first was an acceptance of the responsibility of the state to provide and pay for religious services for the community at large without prescribing their precise form, so that the system which evolved was made up, in James McGuire's words, of 'autonomous congregations served by licensed ministers of various theological positions'.[24] The second and even more obnoxious principle was that those who wished to come together to worship outside this framework should be free to do so. The religion prescribed by law was not grossly offensive, except in so far as it restricted admission to communion, nor need it even be oppressively prescriptive in practice. Moreover, only those who took the extreme view that episcopacy was divinely ordained objected passionately to its absence. But the licence given to the Independents and the extremist sectaries and the iconoclastic influence that they were able to exercise through the authority of zealous army officers were deeply disturbing. It was intolerable that a local commander could deprive the local congregation of their place of worship by removing the roof of the church and replacing it with 'a speaking-house in a bog for his soldiers to take their turns of speaking in', as Major John Desborough did in Ballinasloe, or by demolishing it to build a house in Kildare and pave his kitchen in Dublin, as Captain Aland did in Tallaght.[25] For a time, under the rule of Fleetwood at the beginning of the

---

[24] 'The Dublin convention, the Protestant community and the emergence of an ecclesiastical settlement in 1660', Art Cosgrove and J. I. McGuire (eds.), *Parliament and community: historical studies XIV* (Belfast, 1983), p. 128.

[25] T. W. Moody and J. G. Simms (eds.), *The bishopric of Derry and the Irish Society* (2 vols., IMC, 1968–83), i, 346. W. D. Handcock, *The history and antiquities of Tallaght* (Dublin, 1991), p. 14.

protectorate, the Baptists in particular seemed irresistible and not the least of the virtues of Henry Cromwell (a man, it was said in Ireland, who deserved to be the son of a better father)[26] was that he increasingly favoured the relatively conservative ministers, moderated the influence of the radicals and seemed to accept the arguments in favour of a uniform national church urged upon him by collaborationist clergy. Nonetheless, different religious values divided most of the established settlers from most of the newcomers.

By contrast, the degradation and expropriation of the Catholic communities and the associated redistribution of their property, which together conferred both direct and indirect benefits, was widely approved and deeply compromising. The Munster settler, Vincent Gookin, argued that 'the confiscation of lands in Ireland is soe generall, the setters and sellers soe many, the buyers and takers soe few, except [the old Protestants] that it is certain, within a year or two, all these men will have too great interests in forfeited lands to give them up to Charles Stuart'.[27] Moreover, property acquisition was not the only common ground between old and new settlers. Members of both groups objected to the level of taxation, which was significantly higher than in England. In 1657, it was reported to Henry Cromwell that a motion had been proposed in parliament 'that the members serving for Ireland might be sent to the tower for their contest about the apportioning the assessment twixt England and Ireland' and a year later Henry himself protested that the levies for the army were '10 times more than in due proportion they ought to be'.[28] Likewise, both resented the failure to fulfil undertakings to allow Ireland to trade freely with England and Scotland. They also shared a unifying interest in guarding against a Catholic counter-offensive and both were concerned that government in England should maintain the stability and authority to enable it to provide the defence that the colony in Ireland required. Representatives from both sections were prominent among the members of the union parliament at Westminster who promoted the proposal to replace the

---

[26] Richard Baker, *A chronicle of the kings of England* (London, 1665), p. 704.
[27] *TSP*, v, 646.
[28] Anthony Morgan to Henry Cromwell, 16 June 1657, BL, Lansdowne MS 822, f. 92. *TSP*, vii, 72.

protectoral constitution and offer the kingship to Oliver Cromwell in 1657. The same fear of diminished security encouraged widespread civilian acceptance of Richard Cromwell's succession as lord protector on his father's death in September 1658.

When 'the lion was forced to quit his prey', as an Irish parliamentarian glossed Oliver's passing, the balance of political forces in England was significantly altered.[29] On the surface, the change offered little hope to royalists, but one of the consequences of the increasing instability that followed was the remodelling of the organization of royalist resistance in England. For some years royalist strategy had been based on the Treaty of Brussels which committed Spain to bringing an invasion force to the assistance of a royalist rising, and Charles himself had built up a small expeditionary force, largely composed of Irish soldiers who had transferred from French regiments. It became clear, however, that nothing could be done unless the sequence was inverted: the invasion was needed to trigger the rising, because England was effectively policed and English royalists were divided. There had been differences of opinion from the outset. Some favoured a united front which would bring together all opponents of the regime, particularly those former parliamentarians, typically Presbyterian, who had never intended or approved the abolition of monarchy. The argument in favour of this course was that committed royalists were too few and too disadvantaged to rise on their own. The arguments against were, first, that these allies would require conditions that would preserve what they had fought for against the king's father in the civil war, usually presumed to be the terms of the Newport treaty which had been aborted by Pride's purge of parliament and the regicide, and second, that true hearted royalists might be unwilling to ally with their former enemies. The alternative view, based on the unwavering belief that the king must be restored on his own terms, was that conspiracy should be confined to royalists and that patience would provide an opportunity sooner or later when the victors fell out among themselves. Both the king's chief advisors on the continent – Lord Chancellor Hyde, Secretary Nicholas and the marquess of Ormond – and the accredited putative leaders of English royalists, organized in the Sealed Knot, took

[29] 'England's confusion', Walter Scott (ed.), *Somers tracts* (13 vols., London, 1809–15), vi, 513–29.

the cautious long-term view and were fitfully challenged by more impatient men who wanted quicker results and were prepared to canvass wider support to achieve them. In the aftermath of Oliver's death, as circumstances seemed to become increasingly favourable, the opinion of the court itself began to change. Early in 1659, the Knot was effectively superseded in the court's confidence by a fresh organization under the direction of John Mordaunt, the Great Trust, which aimed to organize a more broadly based rising with the support of Presbyterians and others. This revised approach was not accompanied by a new willingness to compromise. It was founded on the belief that there existed a growing number of men who were so far alienated from the regime and so emboldened by the signs of its vulnerability that they would no longer insist upon terms for their support.

The instability that gave this sense of opportunity to royalist conspirators was created by a combination of the determination of the army leaders to recover lost influence, the strivings of the republicans to revive the 'good old cause' that Cromwell was thought to have betrayed and the growing confidence with which men of more moderate opinion confronted both. In due course both the officers and the republicans seized their chance, spurred on in part by the fact that the parliament that Richard convened at the beginning of 1659 proved so conservatively inclined in matters of both religion and constitutional form as to seem to endanger everything that had been accomplished. For those newcomers to Ireland who were committed to the commonwealth and who supported one or other of its competing factions the choice that now fell to be made between the continuation of the protectorate, the recall of the 'rump' and the rule of the army leaders was an important one. Some were 'Cromwellians' who believed in the protectoral formula of rule by 'a single person and parliament'. Some were republicans, ideologically opposed to the 'single person' and committed to the reinstatement of legitimacy through the return to government of the members of parliament expelled in 1653. Some were indifferent to governmental forms and believed that the army alone could uphold what had been achieved and that it must not be prevented from doing so, either by opposition from without or dissent from within. Few of the established settlers belonged to this ethos. Some had certainly adopted republican or commonwealth

[18]

principles and some had embraced religious innovation, but these were small minorities. For the majority who had done neither, the issue was nonetheless significant and those who had come to terms with the regime took sides as it became destabilized. Some of them were no doubt acting within the system only to subvert it, as they afterwards maintained, but others were pragmatically concerned with the need to ensure the most favourable immediate outcome, and not all of these were wholly uncommitted in terms of post civil war factional politics. They belonged to that spectrum of royalism which consisted of unrepentant parliamentarian supporters who believed that the wrong turn had been taken as late as 6 December 1648, when parliamentary authority had been subverted by the army in the purge which had brought peace negotiations to an end and prepared the way for the execution of the king.

Most fundamentally, what old and new settlers discovered in common as the survival of the riven commonwealth became increasingly unlikely was the predicament created by the interests that they had acquired in the 1650s. The old were faced with the problem of reconciling a genuine desire for the return of monarchy with a recognition that Charles I would never have done what parliament and Cromwell had done to secure and enrich Protestants in Ireland, and that his son might not be willing to uphold a settlement which was neither legal nor just. As the usurping regime began to crumble, their concern was to find a way to ensure that if it proved possible to restore what had been lost they did not thereby lose what had been gained. The new settlers, by contrast, could not hope to have the best of both worlds. Their difficulty was to decide whether their stake in Ireland was detachable from the cause that had brought them there and, if so, to find the strategy that would allow them to keep it if the regime were overturned. Thus, between established Protestants who did not wish to have to choose between the king and their gains and new ones who were increasingly ready to settle for both, there was a sound basis for cooperation. In May 1660, Charles II was confronted by a unified demand from the enlarged Protestant settler community for the preservation of their gains. Before that point was reached, however, in the twelve months which followed the overthrow of Richard Cromwell, the alternative to monarchy was destroyed by the obstinately conflicting purposes of those who had created it. The collaboration which developed in Ireland, as new and old settlers sought to control the local consequences of what was happening elsewhere, in Scotland and among the royalists on the continent as well as in England, shaped the social and political relationships of restoration Ireland.

2
Commissioners and submissioners: May to June

On the night of 21 April 1659 the parliament that Richard Cromwell had convened in January was dissolved on the insistence of the leading army officers. There followed a quick purge of his supporters in the army command. Otherwise, there was uncertainty, both as to what form of government was to prevail, and as to whether the separately commanded armies in Scotland, Ireland, Flanders and the fleet would accept what had been done in London. In the London area itself, there was little agreement. The leaders of the *coup d'état* had no more ambitious plan than to take over control of the administration with Richard as their figurehead. Others saw the situation as an opportunity to undo the whole Cromwellian initiative, which had reintroduced 'the single person' to English government, and revert to the 'good old Parliament'. The need for money, support and some kind of legitimation weakened the resolve of the Wallingford House group, as the officers were called, and before long negotiations were in train to restore the old alliance of army and parliament that had brought the commonwealth into existence and was now needed to preserve it. There was disagreement on the form of a parliament, for the officers hoped for a two chamber arrangement with a senate to balance the representative house, but they seem to have felt too isolated to insist on the point and may have feared that the uncertainty might open the way for counter-revolutionary plotting on behalf of Richard Cromwell. By 5 May, they had agreed to the restoration of the Long Parliament on minimal terms and on the next day they announced that they had invited the members of parliament who had continued sitting until 20 April 1653 to reconvene and resume their trust. On the following day, forty-two members assembled and declared their intention to settle the commonwealth without king, single person or lords, to carry on the reformation, and to secure a godly magistracy and ministry. A committee of safety was appointed to serve until a council of state could be constituted and the wider effects of change were softened by the passage of an act providing that legal proceedings should be carried on in the name of the keepers of the liberties of England by the authority of parliament and empowering justices of the peace and sheriffs to continue to exercise their functions. Fleetwood was made commander in chief of the land forces in England and Scotland and a committee appointed to deal with military appointments. A bid to resume their seats by some members who had been excluded from parliament by Pride's Purge more than ten years earlier was rebuffed, and the speaker canvassed qualified persons to attend, with some success: on 14 May, 78 members were present; by 1 June, it was reported that 114 had made an appearance. By that stage, a council of state had been established, assurances of obedience and support had come from the armed forces in both Scotland and Dunkirk and Richard had formally accepted the authority of the new government and relinquished his position on 25 May. There was no need to abolish the protectorate because it had never legally existed.

In normal circumstances the time required for letters, news and people to travel between Dublin and London was of little political significance. One of the achievements of the duke of Ormond, still worth recalling after his death fifty-six years later, was to have left London at 4 o'clock one Saturday morning and sat down to dine in Carrick at 3 o'clock on Monday afternoon.[1] Youth, panache, good horses, fair weather and a favourable tide were the ingredients of this feat. Prudent men conducted business on the assumption that an exchange of letters was very unlikely to be completed within two weeks and in the knowledge that communications would be interrupted at irregular intervals by unfavourable winds and other adverse weather conditions.[2] In the 1650s a weekly pacquet – The Harp – plied between Holyhead and Ringsend, small trading boats made the crossing daily, and government shipping was available to meet exceptional needs. The tendency for Irish business to be pushed to one side in

---

[1] 'Some domestic informations', Carte MS 69, ff. 49v–50.
[2] When the pacquets were rescheduled in 1666 to enable letters to be answered by return post, six days were allowed for transit in each direction. *Cal. SP, Ire., 1666–9*, pp. 150–1.

London was less easy to cope with, but an agent could be retained to push it back again and important business could be entrusted to a messenger empowered to lobby for prompt attention. Delay was part of the routine. In abnormal circumstances, time acquired a different value. The information on which to make decisions was needed quickly in a crisis, but it was usually out of date when it arrived; silence and procrastination had now to be assessed for their possible political significance; rumour confused judgement; and action was inhibited by ignorance and uncertainty.

Henry Cromwell had been out of Dublin, 'taking his pleasure', and the first detailed news of the forced dissolution is said to have been brought to him by Sir Charles Coote, who had represented Galway and Mayo in the parliament. Somewhat later this was supplemented by inside information from Lord Broghill.[3] Long before, in 1651, the earl of Clanricarde, a hostile but shrewd observer, had identified these two men as the leaders of the party of 'the Presbyterian and the old Protestant'.[4] These were the people whose support Henry had assiduously cultivated as he weaned himself from dependence upon the army and Coote and Broghill were still the most prominent among them. Both were ambiguous figures. Coote, who was formidably influential in Ulster, where he had campaigned vigorously, as well as in Connacht, of which he was titular lord president, had collaborated actively with the regime but was widely suspected of reserving his loyalties. Henry, however, had trusted him with the delicate task of conveying his objections to the composition of the council of state.[5] Broghill, whose elder brother's circumspect royalism left him largely free to deploy the vast Munster influence of his late father, the 'great earl' of Cork, had been deeply involved in the protectorate.[6] In Ireland, he held the post of general of the ordnance and was a close associate of

---

[3] P. Beresford Ellis, *Hell or Connaught!* (London, 1975), p. 217. Catterall, 'Two letters', *AHR*, 8, pp. 87–8. Before he left England, Broghill wrote a full account for Henry Cromwell which he entrusted to Thomas Stanley who did not forward it until 11 May, from Clonmel. Stanley to Cromwell, 11 May 1659, BL, Lansdowne MS 823, f. 316.

[4] HMC, *Calendar of the manuscripts of the Marquis of Ormonde*, new series (8 vols., London, 1902–12), i, 239.

[5] Coote to Henry Cromwell, 29 March 1659, BL, Lansdowne MS 823, ff. 271–2.

[6] T. Barnard, 'Land and the limits of loyalty: the second earl of Cork and first earl of Burlington (1612–98)', in T. Barnard and J. Clark (eds.), *Lord Burlington: architecture, art and life* (London, 1996), pp. 180–4.

[23]

Henry.[7] In the wider arena, he had served as president of the council in Scotland where he had attempted to modify the regime by encouraging Scots to become involved,[8] played a leading part in the scheme to persuade Oliver to accept the crown in 1657, and been appointed a member of the 'Other House' of parliament established under the new constitution of that year. He had not only attended the aborted parliament but argued Richard's case in the army council itself.[9] By his own account, it was he who had suggested to Richard the provocative last ditch strategy of 18 April, of using parliament to control the army by restricting its right to hold general councils while arranging to find money to pay it.[10] About 29 April, the day after the army council stripped Richard and his supporters of their commands,[11] Broghill left London and made his way to Minehead where he was collected by a boat from Kinsale and landed in Waterford on 10 May.[12] He was, it was later said, when useful myths were being constructed, under suspicion of being involved in a plot against the army and was followed by an order for his arrest.[13] But in reality he had been given permission to leave and the army officers seem not to have doubted that his intention was to do what he could to secure a peaceful settlement.[14]

Both men figured prominently in Henry's unofficial reaction to his brother's virtual deposition. He dispatched Coote to Connacht and Lieutenant-Colonel Henry Flower to Ulster with instructions to gather their most reliable troops and be prepared to bring them to Dublin, and

[7] *Cal. SP, Ire., 1647–60*, p. 685.

[8] Keith Brown, *Kingdom or province? Scotland and the Regal Union, 1603–1715* (London, 1992), pp. 138–9.

[9] R. Hutton, *The restoration: a political and religious history of England and Wales, 1658–1667* (Oxford, 1987), p. 36. At a meeting of the Army Council on 14 April at which Desborough proposed an oath applauding the execution of Charles, Broghill, in alliance with Goffe and Whalley, proposed an oath of loyalty to the protectorate instead. Both proposals were dropped. T. Morrice, *A collection of the state letters of Roger Boyle, the first earl of Orrery* (2 vols., Dublin, 1743), i, 27–9.   [10] Hutton, *The restoration*, p. 37.

[11] Catterall, 'Two letters', *AHR*, 8, p. 87. Hutton, *The restoration*, p. 39.

[12] *Egmont MSS*, ii, pt. 2, p. 604. Robert Boyle, *Works* (6 vols., London, 1772), vi, 126–7.

[13] Morrice, *State letters of the first earl of Orrery*, i, 60. K. M. Lynch, *Roger Boyle, the first earl of Orrery* (Knoxville, 1965), p. 97. James Ware, *His works concerning Ireland*, ed. W. Harris (2 vols., Dublin, 1739–46), ii, 173–4.

[14] *Cal. SP, Dom., 1659–60*, pp. 12–13. In the recent parliament, Broghill had been characterized as 'a cavalier, a presbyterian, an independent; for a republic, for a protector, for everything, for nothing, but only that one thing, *money*'. *Somers Tracts*, vi, 469.

requested Broghill to do likewise in Munster. Flower was not altogether an odd man out in this company. Though he had fought in England in the 1640s and come to Ireland as a major with Cromwell's foot in 1649, he too was of New English provenance: his family was settled in Kilkenny and his grandfather had been governor of Waterford fort. William Petty, Henry's secretary, paid him the backhanded compliment of allowing that he was 'no Anabaptist, because of his too loose Conversation for any church at all'.[15] At the same time, Henry sounded out the army officers. At best, he seems to have found them disposed to await events in England rather than to commit themselves to supporting the Lord Protector.[16] But not all were of this mind, and a group, identifying themselves as 'the old Officers', wrote to England on 4 May with an assurance of their resolve 'to own and stand by and with the Army in England, having an high Affection to the good Old Cause; and hoping, that it is now reviving; and those that are Back-Friends to it, think it their best Posture to be silent'.[17] Henry's official response was none the less unequivocal. On 9 May, he ordered the officers to their posts and required both civil and military authorities to forbid unlawful assemblies, suppress seditious papers and prevent the circulation of tests, engagements or declarations 'which may tend to divide the good People of this land or alienate them from obedience to his Highnesse and the present Government'.[18] The rationale, real or feigned, was both the fear that 'the Common Enemy' – the royalists – might exploit English divisions, and the possibility that encouragement might be given to that 'more dangerous, numerous and exasperated people, the

---

[15] C. H. Firth and G. Davies, *Regimental history of Cromwell's army* (2 vols. paged as one, Oxford, 1940), p. 647. R. Dunlop, *Ireland under the commonwealth: being a selection of documents relating to the government of Ireland, 1651–59* (2 vols. paged as one, Manchester, 1913), p. 366n. John Lodge, *The Peerage of Ireland*, ed. M. Archdall (7 vols., Dublin, 1789), v, 283–4. William Petty, *Reflections upon some persons and things in Ireland* (London, 1660), pp. 88–9. Compare the explicit abuse of Flower in T. A. Larcom (ed.), *The Down survey by Dr William Petty, 1655–1656* (Dublin, 1851), p. 267.

[16] C. H. Firth (ed.), *The memoirs of Edmund Ludlow* (3 vols., Oxford, 1894), ii, 72. G. Davies, *The restoration of Charles II* (Oxford, 1955), p. 243.

[17] *Journals of the House of Commons*, vii, 647.

[18] By the lord lieutenant of Ireland, 9 May 1659. B.L. 669 f. 21 (38). The proclamation was printed in London, misleadingly, at the end of May. *Calendar of state papers and manuscripts, relating to English affairs, existing in the archives and collections of Venice, 1659–61* (London, 1931), p. 28.

Irish Natives and Papists'.[19] On the following day the sheriffs were ordered to return the names of those who had been convicted at assizes for failing to move to the lands assigned to them west of the Shannon.[20] At the same time, for the same reasons, Henry formally requested that the city of Dublin be put in a posture of defence against the 'Irish papists and other common enemies' and encouraged a group of prominent citizens to requisition an extraordinary meeting of the city council to make the necessary arrangements. On 13 May, the council not only approved the formation of two regiments, one for the city and one for the suburbs, but granted the request of the petitioners that they be entrusted with command of these forces.[21] Henry, in short, was both attempting to keep the army in check and exploring the possibility of finding countervailing support for Richard from outside the military establishment.

Henry's prime needs were for sure knowledge of what was happening in England in the aftermath of the coup and clear instructions from his brother. Common rumour and private information brought some news, but Irish visitors to London were not allowed to return and his brother's silence made everything uncertain.[22] What news there was, was discouraging. Writing on 5 May on his way back to Ireland, Petty reported that 'People take the late transactions very patiently.'[23] He had been 'fuly instructed' by Richard before he left London and carried a letter from Fleetwood urging Henry to return to England, but both had been overtaken by events before he reached Dublin.[24] At what stage Henry learned of the recall of the Long Parliament is unknown. Official notice of its reinstatement was conveyed in a letter from Fleetwood, written on 10 May on behalf of the committee of safety. Writing on the same day, Major

---

[19] Baker, *A chronicle*, p. 704. *TSP*, vii, 683–4. *Cal. SP, Ven., 1659–61*, p. 25. The quotation is from Henry's letter of resignation, *TSP*, vii, 684–5.

[20] The King's Inns, Dublin, Prendergast Papers, i, 547.

[21] J. T. Gilbert (ed.), *Calendar of ancient records of Dublin in the possession of the municipal corporation* (17 vols., Dublin, 1885–1916), iv, p.162.

[22] *Cal. SP, Ven., 1659–61*, p. 25.

[23] Petty to Henry Cromwell, Lansdowne MS 823, f. 310.

[24] Catterall, 'Two letters', *AHR*, 8, pp. 87–8. Petty, who had been in parliament as a member for West Looe in Cornwall, had initially been ordered to stay in England. Lord Edmond Fitzmaurice, *The life of Sir William Petty* (London, 1895), p. 87. He arrived in Dublin on 12 May. Petty, *Down survey*, p. 301.

Anthony Morgan, an officer friendly to Richard who had represented the Louth–Meath constituency in parliament, confirmed that Petty's impression remained valid after the reappearance of 'the Old new parliament', observing that he could 'not say here is a generall satisffaction but all men seem so or at least strangely indifferent who governs'.²⁵ Henry received Fleetwood's news without comment, replying flatly on 18 May that he would do his best to secure the peace of the nation, and would report what the officers decided.²⁶ It was not until 12 May that his brother finally wrote to him, indicating that he could do nothing without 'a diversion from the forces at the distant places', indecisively expressing hopes of support from Scotland, Dunkirk and the fleet as well as Ireland, but admitting that the news from Scotland was discouraging and that he had heard nothing from the others. A week later, he dispatched the Coleraine and Londonderry MP, Dr Ralph King, to brief Henry, with a covering letter reporting that Monck's response had been 'a poore one', and that his remaining hopes rested on the fleet and Lord Broghill.²⁷ It seems likely that Henry had not received either letter by 23 May, when he wrote formally to Richard as head of state, protesting that he had received no letters from him since the dissolution of parliament and describing himself and his officers as still 'in a waiting frame to see what God or our superiors should command us', though it is just possible that he had received the first and was signalling as plainly as he could in a public communication that Richard could count upon support in Ireland.²⁸ The same implication was perhaps contained in the phrasing of a companion letter to Fleetwood in which Henry explained that the officers had decided not to write, 'thinking that their so doing might look too like a capitulation', and had instead authorized Henry to assure Fleetwood that they would 'continue in a peaceable disposition' and would in due course let him know what needed to be done to give satisfaction.²⁹

The impression given by people in London who were not privy to

²⁵ Morgan to Henry Cromwell, Lansdowne MSS 823, f. 314.
²⁶ *TSP*, vii, 674. *CJ*, vii, 663.
²⁷ Catterall, 'Two letters', *AHR*, 8, pp. 88–9. John A. Butler, *A biography of Richard Cromwell, 1626–1712, the second protector* (New York, 1994), pp. 122–7, 217–18.
²⁸ *TSP*, vii, 674.
²⁹ *TSP*, vii, 674. C. H. Firth (ed.), *Selections from the papers of William Clarke* (Camden Society, 4 vols., London, 1891–1901), iv, 11.

official information, but who made it their business to try to find out what was going on, in other words by royalist informants and diplomats, was one of uncertainty and confusion about reactions in Ireland, Scotland and the navy. As one phrased it at the end of April, 'Tis too young daies with us to guesse what the Irishe Harry, the Scottes Munck or the Sea Mountague will doe.'[30] The forces controlled by Henry and Monck were significantly larger than those in England itself,[31] so that there was sound reason for the assumption that the success of the coup depended upon what happened in Scotland and Ireland, but it was not easy to get hard information.[32] Royalist rumours were sensationalist at first: in the first week of May, fragments of news suggested that a plan to seize Henry at the same time as Richard, led by the Baptist Colonel Hierome Sankey, had been thwarted and Henry had 'hanged up 2 or 3 of the chief designers and so spoiled their game there',[33] and there was a 'stronge report' that two members of the Irish Council, Lord Chancellor Steele and Lord Chief Baron Corbet, were among those executed or, variously, imprisoned.[34] In fact, Sankey was in England 'beeing now a very great man and one of the Committee of Safety', in the words of his long time adversary Petty.[35] The alternative version, reported by the French ambassador, was that Henry 'was in the same condition as the Protector, that is, under a sort of arrest'.[36] The story that reached Paris by royalist channels was that Henry was conducting a military and civil purge of 'all such persons as be Anabaptistical or of the now prevailing faction in England'.[37] A London

[30] G. F. Warner (ed.), The *Nicholas papers, 1657–60* (Camden Society, London, 1920), iv, p. 123. Edward Montague, general-at-sea, a close associate of the Cromwells, was in command of a fleet in the Baltic.

[31] The Irish army comprised a core of 11 foot, 1 dragoon and 6 horse regiments: in Scotland there were 11 foot, 1 dragoon and 5 horse regiments. The English army was made up of 8 foot and 9 horse regiments. There were also 3 regiments of foot and 1 of horse in Dunkirk. *Regimental history*, pp. xxix–xxx.

[32] F. Guizot, *History of Richard Cromwell and the restoration of Charles I* (2 vols., London, 1856), i, 392.

[33] *Nicholas Papers*, iv, p. 126. *Calendar of the Clarendon state papers preserved in the Bodleian Library*, ed. O. Ogle, W. H. Bliss, W. D. Macray and F. J. Routledge (5 vols., Oxford, 1869–1970), iv, 194–5, 198.

[34] *Nicholas Papers*, iv, pp. 135, 140. Broderick to Hyde, 6 May 1659, Bodleian Library, Oxford, Clarendon MS 60, f. 503.

[35] Fitzmaurice, *Petty*, p. 86.   [36] Guizot, *Richard Cromwell*, i, 380.

[37] *Nicholas Papers*, iv, p. 138.

correspondent believed that Broghill's return to Ireland was cause for optimism, 'if his hearte dare walke with his tongue',[38] while another reported that 'Henry playes the very tyrant & is an arch Rebell. He hangs & spoils Townes & people that oppose him as they say.'[39] As time passed, however, most observers based their expectations on the inference that the lack of information meant that Henry was consolidating his position against the new regime,[40] and might yet 'turn these Jugglers out of their Box, as his father did'.[41] The prime royalist conspirator, John Mordaunt, speculated to Hyde that 'you might find a doore open there if Money could be procured'.[42] The Catholic bishop of Meath reported to Rome from London that Henry would not submit 'et sic erit regnum adversus regnum'.[43] The French ambassador, whose delicate task it was to decide whether and when to recommend the recognition of the new government, was perhaps reflecting its hopes when he discounted the Irish officers: 'they have too much interest in retaining possession of that country, where all their property is situated, to be easily persuaded to leave their goods at the mercy of the inhabitants, and come to make war in England'.[44] The corollary was that they had nothing to gain from the king except confirmation of their estates, which would be 'more fully secured to them if they submit to the Parliament'.[45] When Henry's reply to Fleetwood came to hand, on 23 May, the newsbooks (which were dependent upon government favour) reported that the Irish officers 'are unanimously resolved upon a compliance'. Mordaunt assumed that Henry had resigned and the French ambassador concluded that 'nothing remains in that quarter likely to disturb the public tranquillity'.[46] But some saw the phrasing of Henry's letter as encouragingly ambiguous, 'full of

---

[38] Ibid., p. 140.
[39] S. S. to Hyde, 22? May 1659, Clarendon MS 61, f. 1v.
[40] R. Scrope and T. Monkhouse (eds.), *State papers collected by Edward, earl of Clarendon* (3 vols., Oxford, 1767–86), iii, 202, 204, 206, 207, 208, 209.
[41] *The acts and monuments of our late parliament* (London, 1659), p. 13.
[42] On 16 May. Clarendon MS 60, f. 555. He also wrote encouragingly of Ireland to the king three days later. Ibid., f. 560.
[43] Archives of the Jesuits in Ireland, HMC, *Rep. 10*, pt. v (London, 1885), p. 359.
[44] Guizot, *Richard Cromwell*, i, 382.   [45] Ibid., 384.
[46] *Mercurius Politicus*, 19–26 May; *Publick Intelligencer*, 23–30 May. M. Coate (ed.), *Mordaunt Letter Book* (Camden Society, London, 1945), p. 15. Guizot, *Richard Cromwell*, i, 400.

condescension, but with a subterfuge of wordes like Monkes'.⁴⁷ With Broghill's support, Henry might yet rebel.⁴⁸ There were those who thought that both had already done so and were in arms with Coote 'against the new republic': fact or rumour, one thing at least was both sure and reassuring to the regime's opponents: 'The faithful Lenthall hath not yet (as in the daies of old) told his fellow members againe, 'Gentlemen, I have received letters out of Ireland, and shall tell you what great services God hath donn for you there.'' '⁴⁹

In fact, the only hint of public defiance in Ireland was the doubtful case of a kinsman of the Cromwells, Colonel Henry Ingoldsby, who had come to Ireland with Oliver in 1649, served as governor of Limerick since 1653, and represented the combined south-western counties in Richard's parliament. Boasting that 'he would to the warring out of his ould shoes withstand this Government', he left London before 2 May and evaded the embargo by travelling to Ireland by way of Dieppe, but there is no clear evidence that he made his gesture.⁵⁰ To the immediate fear of the reaction of Cromwellian diehards, however, was added the anxiety that the 'common enemy' might seize its opportunity. If this was justified, the threat had no public face. There is later, but first-hand, testimony that after Richard's deposition Sir Charles Coote prepared his officers 'that they might be ready upon any sudden occasion', took soundings in the north, and assured two Scots settlers, his brother-in-law Sir Francis Hamilton and Sir Arthur Forbes, 'that he would espouze the king's interest, and that whatsoever he did should tend that way'.⁵¹ Although this is probably an alternative version of Coote's mission on behalf of Henry Cromwell, it

---

⁴⁷ Broderick to Hyde, 23 May 1659, 'An account of Affaires written in the character of a friend to the Government', Clarendon MS 61, ff. 15–16. It was suspected that Monck had deliberately left it unclear whether he supported the Long Parliament in its purged or unpurged form. ⁴⁸ *Clarendon State Papers*, iii, 210. ⁴⁹ *Nicholas Papers*, iv, 146.

⁵⁰ *Cal. SP, Dom., 1659–60*, p. 19. French Newsletter [30 June], Clarendon MS 61, f. 360. *TSP*, vii, 666. Ingoldsby, who was Waller's son-in-law, had been created a baronet by Oliver Cromwell in 1658. He was a younger brother of the (perhaps reluctant) regicide, Richard Ingoldsby, who was becoming involved with royalist conspiracy at this stage. Henry had served with the king at the beginning of the civil war. R. K. G. Temple, 'The original officer list of the New Model Army', *Bulletin of the Institute of Historical Research*, 59 (1986), pp. 57–8.

⁵¹ Forbes to Ormond, undated, Granard Papers, PRONI H/1/5/1. Hamilton had married Coote's sister.

may also be an accurate enough indication of the basis upon which he canvassed support. Forbes was a Presbyterian who had served with Montrose in the 1640s and taken part in armed resistance to the regime in Scotland in the 1650s and Coote may have known that he and Hamilton had been engaged in 'making a partie' for the king's restoration in the previous year.[52] The chief suspicion fell upon the Scots and the assumption, in both Ireland and England, was that they were disaffected and likely to respond to a royal call. The distance that Henry had placed between himself and the English regime by his efforts to secure the support of local Protestants is reflected in the fact that there were those who thought that he too might take the king's side. When he sent Colonel Flower to Ulster, he was suspected of collusion rather than concern by one side and urged to declare for the king by the other. Among the persuaders was Mark Trevor, a second-generation Welsh settler in Down, who had fought on the royalist side in the civil war and was reputed to be the man who had wounded Oliver Cromwell at Marston Moor: he had joined Ormond in 1649, but ingratiated himself with Henry in the 1650s, persuading him that he had resolved 'to live as becomes an honest man under the present government'.[53] The difficulties of reconstructing what took place are suggested by the fact that the most direct evidence consists of an account later conveyed to the marquess of Ormond by Sir Edward Hyde of what the earl of Ossory's secretary, Thomas Page, had reported of what Lady Ormond had said of what she had heard from Trevor himself.[54] He 'came one night to your Wife and told her all was done': Henry had promised to declare, Dublin had undertaken 'to stand to him', and Viscount Montgomery had pledged to 'draw twenty thousand men

---

[52] Statement by Forbes on behalf of Sir James Wyart. Carte MS 31, f. 606. Forbes, who had inherited estates in Longford and Leitrim, returned to Ireland in 1655 and was restored to his lands under the provisions of the articles of surrender between Monck and Lorne. John Forbes, *Memoirs of the House of Granard* (London, 1868), pp. 30–6, 69. Monck thought him a 'man of Honour' who would not wrong those who had gone surety for his good behaviour. Monck to Henry Cromwell, 15 December 1657, Lansdowne MS 822, f. 294.

[53] Harold O'Sullivan, 'The Trevors of Rosetrevor: a British colonial family in 17th century Ireland' (M.Litt., University of Dublin, 1985), p. 155. *TSP*, vii, 410.

[54] The marchioness of Ormond lived at Dunmore House in Co Kilkenny throughout the 1650s. C. N. Russell and J. P. Prendergast, *An account of the Carte collection of historical papers* (London, 1871), pp. 70–1, 181.

together in the North'. The next day, 'that wretched fellow' Henry received letters from England, and withdrew.[55] Hugh Montgomery, lord of the Ards, had been commander in chief of the king's forces in Ulster by commission from Charles II in 1649. The contemporary historian of his family recalled that Henry 'had fair offers to stand for himself, and might have prospered (as Monck did) and played the game which Orrory and Coote won', and intimated obliquely that the offers were from Trevor, Montgomery and Lord Cromwell, who were 'secretly consulting... what to do to advance the King's cause'.[56] Seeking favour after the restoration, Sir Robert Sterling, who had been in Ireland since 1641 and joined Charles in Scotland in 1651, claimed to have offered Henry 5,000 horse and foot 'as did the Lord of Ards [and] Col Trevore, but that unworthy wretch refused those good offers'.[57] Like Trevor, Montgomery and Sterling had remained loyal to the royal cause until forced into submission and both had been imprisoned during the 1650s.[58]

+ Whether the possibilities that Henry quietly explored involved taking up the royal cause rather than coming to the aid of Richard seems extremely doubtful. The indications are that in canvassing the availability of support from outside the army, he inevitably made indirect contact with men who hoped to use the situation to the king's advantage, but there is no firm evidence to suggest that he saw his role as more than supportive of his brother. He was preparing to play his part in a concerted resistance, not to act alone, and like everybody else he understood that it was the combined response of the forces outside England that would determine what happened. The reaction of his own command was not encouraging, but might be overcome by drawing on alternative sources of support. Through George Monck's cousin Henry, who was a cornet in his own regiment of horse, he set out to discover how the commander in chief of the English forces in Scotland viewed the situation. When Henry Monck left Ireland, however, the issue was between Richard and the

---

[55] *Clarendon State Papers*, iii, 588–90.
[56] George Hill (ed.), *The Montgomery MSS (1603–1706): compiled from the family papers by William Montgomery of Rosemount, Esquire* (Belfast, 1869), pp. 217–19. Wingfield Cromwell, Viscount Lecale and earl of Ardglass, succeeded in 1653, aged 29. Broghill later became earl of Orrery.   [57] *Cal. SP, Ire., 1669–70*, p. 394. PRO, SP, Ire., 63/344. 101 (I).
[58] *Cal. SP, Ire., 1647–60*, pp. 580–91.

colonels: by the time he left Scotland on the return journey the Long Parliament had taken over, and his mission yielded no encouragement. General Monck merely forwarded copies of letters of 12 May in which he and his officers had, a little ambiguously, expressed their joy 'at your anticipating our desires in recalling members of the long parliament' and given assurances of their willingness to comply with its authority.[59] What private message he conveyed through his cousin is unrecorded, but there is no reason to suppose that it qualified his public stance in any substantial way. With Monck collaborating with the change of government, with Richard supinely relying on others to take the initiative rather than offering leadership, and with some officers in Ireland welcoming the revival of the good old cause and others cautiously reserving their position, Henry's scope for action was very limited and became more so. The political calculations which suggested the tactical feasibility of defying the army officers on 9 May were irrelevant to the broader issue involved in seeking to uphold the protectorate itself against the parliament whose authority it had usurped.

The parliamentarians had their own special sources of advice, information and prompting about Irish affairs. At least five colonels of Irish regiments were implicated in the coup: Thomas Cooper, John Clarke, John Hewson, Henry Pretty and Hierome Sankey. They were not the only officers of the Irish army in London at the time, but it is likely to have been they who served as the channel through which the encouraging assurances of the affection of the 'old Officers' in Ireland reached the commons as early as 9 May.[60] Presumably in response to lobbying from both the inner and the wider group, which included Henry Cromwell's dissident, Quaker major of horse, Peter Wallis, parliament took notice of 'the whole business touching the settling the lands of Ireland' on 18 May, and directed the council of state to prepare an act confirming the estates of adventurers and soldiers.[61] This was not, of course, a matter of exclusively Irish concern: many of those who had acquired Irish land had remained in England, among them a number of members of parliament, and two days earlier, in anticipation of developments, the London Committee of Adventurers, which had been keeping an active interest in Irish affairs on

---

[59] Baker, *A chronicle*, p. 704. *TSP*, vii, 669–70.   [60] *CJ*, vii, 647.   [61] *CJ*, vii, 657.

behalf of investors and speculators since the early 1640s, had announced that it intended to approach parliament on behalf of unsatisfied claimants and invited all concerned to make known 'where, and how much, they are deficient'.[62] On 23 May, the council of state deputed five of its members to prepare the required legislation:[63] of these, John Jones, Edmund Ludlow and Robert Reynolds had extensive experience of Irish government in the 1650s, and Algernon Sidney, whose father and brother had both been lord lieutenants, had been involved in Ireland in the 1640s.[64]

The lands of Ireland were also, of course, one of the principal matters that concerned those who met together at about the same time in Ireland to compile a schedule of requests for presentation to parliament, but it was far from being the only one. The authors of this working document, which contained no formal courtesies and conveyed no deference, are not recorded.[65] Henry Cromwell described them as acting on behalf of both 'people and army here, whose case and concernments are very different from those of England and Scotland',[66] and the scope of the seventeen recorded requests that were agreed confirms the breadth of the constituency that framed them. The immediate problem posed by the end of the protectorate was, of course, the same in Ireland as elsewhere: everything that had been done in the name of public authority since 19 April 1653 was illegal in the eyes of the restored parliament, and everybody who had exercised or obeyed authority since then was culpable. The first requirement therefore was the indemnification of all concerned by a general act of oblivion, and the validation of all laws, ordinances, orders, judgements and decrees deriving from 'the late public authority'.[67] In Ireland a particular difficulty arose from the fact that while the preparatory measures dealing with the forfeiture of Irish land had been enacted in August 1652 the subsequent arrangements for its disposal and management had been made after the expulsion of the parliament. Thus, none of

---

[62] *Mercurius Politicus*, 12–19 May; *Public Intelligencer*, 16–23 May. The committee undertook to sit in Grocers' Hall each Thursday afternoon to receive submissions.

[63] Bodleian Library, Rawlinson MS C, 179, f. 10.

[64] The odd man out was Bulstrode Whitelock who had, however, acquired property in Ireland. [65] TCD, MS 808, ff. 160–2.

[66] *The Tanner letters. Documents of Irish affairs in the sixteenth and seventeenth centuries extracted from the Tanner collection in the Bodleian Library, Oxford*, ed. Charles McNeill (IMC, 1943), pp. 391–3. [67] Articles 1, 2, 9.

the grants which had been made, either to repay the adventurers who had advanced money for the suppression of the rebellion or to meet the arrears of payment of the soldiers who had fought to suppress it, were valid. Similarly, contracts by which the land retained by the government had been leased out were without legal effect. The second requirement, therefore, was that all grants and leases should be 'made good firme effectuall and inviolable against the Commonwealth to all intents and purposes'.[68] This general provision, however, did not satisfy all interests because the state's responsibilities had not yet been fully discharged. Although liability had been acknowledged for military service rendered in Ireland before 5 June 1649 and debentures for these arrears had been given, in many cases no grants had actually been made, most particularly in respect of services in Munster. In addition, there were cases in which satisfaction for arrears which had accrued later had been given in part only. The completion of these transactions 'out of the forfeited lands or houses in Ireland, or in some such other way as shall be thought fit' was the third requirement.[69] Vested interest in the confirmation of estates and the satisfaction of arrears was not, of course, confined to the categories of grantees nominally involved. Because of the active market in both adventurers' shares and soldiers' debentures, those who stood to gain were in many cases not the original recipients but those to whom the benefit had been assigned by purchase.

In addition to outlining the steps that were needed to rectify the anomalies created by the recent 'intrusion', the petition addressed a variety of both general and specific 'concernments'. The opportunity was taken to raise the longstanding issue of the conditions of trade between Ireland and the rest of the commonwealth. The failure to fulfill an undertaking to remove duties had been a source of constant grievance and though the legal requirement was that trade between Ireland and England was liable to full custom, 'in like manner as to any foreign part of the world', the Dublin Grand Jury had recently instituted proceedings against the custom farmers for the offence of collecting duties.[70] The petitioners now urged that Ireland should be permitted to trade with both England and Scotland on the same terms as the two traded with each other.[71] They

[68] Article 3.   [69] Article 6.   [70] *Cal. SP, Ire., 1647–60*, pp. 678–9.   [71] Article 5.

[35]

also pressed that the courts of justice, which had been seriously undermanned since they were restored in 1655, should be brought back to their customary staffing level of three judges in each of the four courts.[72] The requests reflecting special interests were more numerous. The professional grievances of the army were concisely expressed in two demands: for the payment of current arrears (which were officially calculated to have stood at about £371,000 on 29 March)[73] and for the provision of a subvention to bring pay levels in Ireland up to those prevailing in England and Scotland.[74] The favours requested on behalf of the established colonists amounted to a comprehensive attempt to retrieve their position by removing the disadvantages that had accrued over the preceding twenty-five years. They asked that rent increases and alterations of tenure imposed by the defective titles commission during Wentworth's viceroyalty in the 1630s should be voided,[75] and that inquisitions taken at that time to prove crown title as a prelude to plantation in Roscommon, Sligo, Mayo, Limerick, Tipperary and Clare should be disregarded in so far as they had affected Protestant estates.[76] For the 'encouragement of Protestants and for the better enabling them to replant their estates', they requested that the commonwealth should write off outstanding rents due on crown and church lands and remit future rents for so long as the adventurers and soldiers were remitted theirs.[77] Most pointedly, observing that general acts of oblivion had been passed for England and Scotland, and a special act for the Protestants of Munster, and that even those who had been transplanted to Connacht and Clare had received an indulgence, they requested an act of oblivion 'for all the Protestants that doe nowe preserve their Estates in Ireland'.[78] This bid to achieve parity for those who had not shown 'good affection' was supplemented by requests that parliament should make good all compositions made with delinquents,

---

[72] Article 12   [73] *CJ*, vii, 660.   [74] Article 7.

[75] Article 10. The 'Second Ormond Peace' (1649) had included a similar provision.

[76] Article 15.

[77] Article 8. Adventurers and soldiers had been freed of quitrent for five years or until such time as the Irish assessment was brought into line with that of England, *Acts and ordinances*, ii, 926. In February 1657, the former clerk of the Irish council, Sir Paul Davis, had been charged by 'the antient Protestant inhabitants' to present a similar request to Oliver Cromwell. *TSP*, vi, 71.

[78] Article 13.

allowing local discretion to reduce the amounts to be paid,[79] and that it should confirm all articles of war.[80] Finally, the petition requested the suspension of the 1657 act against recusancy, on the grounds that it was unworkable in the prevailing conditions. The act required justices of the peace and other local officials to present the oath of abjuration to 'all persons suspected of being Popish recusants': the desire to have it formally suspended arose from the inconvenience of certain penal provisions which stipulated fines for those who neglected their duty and rewards for those who informed upon them.[81]

As a hostile pamphleteer concluded, the petition from Ireland was evidently designed to unite 'discording parties and factions'.[82] The treatment of religion, however, though it also sought common ground, did not attempt to accommodate the extreme. What was required was, first, 'a course whereby Godly faithfull orthodox learned and Gosspell preaching Ministers may be speedily settled in all parts of Ireland' and, second, provision 'for the better education of the youth in piety and learning'. Nuances have been detected in the use of the word orthodox which, it has been suggested, 'certainly represents a departure from commonwealth practice'.[83] The second protectoral constitution, however, had stipulated that there should be a Confession of Faith to which publicly maintained ministers must subscribe,[84] and Irish practice had been moving steadily in that direction.[85] The challenge of the petition's conservatism was not to official policy, but to the radicals who rejected both the notion of orthodoxy and the elitist association of religion with learning. Inopportunely, however, the coup had opened the way for a revival of radical influence

[79] Article 14. [80] Article 16.
[81] Article 17. *Acts and ordinances*, ii, 1170–80. The petition ascribed the act, which was passed on 26 June 1657, to 1656.
[82] *Ambitious tyranny clearly demonstrated in Englands unhappy and confused government*. [London?] 1659, p. 8.
[83] By James McGuire in 'The Dublin Convention, the Protestant community and the emergence of an ecclesiastical settlement in 1660', in Cosgrave and McGuire (eds.), *Parliament and community*, p. 125, who assumes that the petition was prepared in December, following F. M. O'Donoghue, 'Parliament in Ireland under Charles II' (MA, University College Dublin, 1970), p. 6.
[84] The Humble Petition and Advice, May 1657, article 11. S. R. Gardiner (ed.), *The constitutional documents of the puritan revolution, 1625–1660* (Oxford, 1962), pp. 454–5.
[85] T. C. Barnard, *Cromwellian Ireland* (Oxford, 1975), pp. 114–32.

and the newly powerful were to prove unsympathetic to the old policy. Three commissioners were appointed to present these requests to parliament. Characterized by Henry Cromwell as 'three worthy persons of this nation', they aptly represented the combination of interests that the document reflected. The administration's representative, Sir William Bury, was a relatively conservative parliamentary activist from Lincolnshire with Presbyterian inclinations, 'a religious sober man' in the estimation of a severe judge:[86] he had been a member of the Irish council since 1656 and was closely identified with Henry who had knighted him in 1658. He was specially charged by his fellow councillors to reinforce the petition by emphasizing 'how needful it is that timely care and provision be made for the proceedings of justice in this nation'.[87] The army's representative, Colonel Richard Lawrence, had come to Ireland as marshal general of horse with Oliver Cromwell in 1649. He had commanded a foot regiment throughout the 1650s, become heavily involved in administrative work and, in a celebrated controversy, vigorously promoted a policy of comprehensive transplantation against the more restrained approach of a spokesman of the established settlers. Distrusted by Henry Cromwell as an extremist in religion, his political connections were with his father-in-law and fellow Baptist, the regicide John Hewson, who had also come to Ireland with Oliver. Hewson, who combined commands of both English and Irish regiments and had been closely involved in Richard's overthrow, was regarded by Henry as the leader of his extremist critics. The third member of the delegation was Dr Henry Jones, eldest son of the bishop of Killaloe and brother of both Michael, the late parliamentarian commander to whom Dublin had been surrendered in 1647, and the veteran Theophilus who had acted as advance agent for Oliver in Dublin in 1649 and commanded Henry's life guard in 1659.[88] Jones had achieved prominence as head of the clerical commission which had gathered influential evidence of the massacre of Protestants in the early 1640s and had been appointed bishop of Clogher on the recommendation of Ormond in 1645. A ready collaborator with the regimes of the 1650s, to which he acted successively as scout master general and official

---

[86] P. Adair, *A true narrative of the rise and progress of the Presbyterian Church of Ireland, 1603–70*, ed. W. D. Killen (Belfast, 1866), p. 236.

[87] Dunlop, *Commonwealth*, p. 696.   [88] Ludlow, *Memoirs*, ii, 105.

historian and information gatherer, his reservations were nonetheless plainly expressed in his refusal to abandon his episcopal style until commanded to do so late in 1651 and in his avoidance of clerical duties throughout the interregnum.[89] Though his compliance was unique as well as disedifying in one of his status, in other respects he personified those Protestants who had suppressed their principles in the hope of preserving both personal and collective interests against the greater threat of popery. Writing to Richard to introduce this trio when they left Ireland about 25 May,[90] Henry reminded him that he already knew Lawrence and assured him, in an understated contrast in an open letter, that Jones and Bury were 'my very good friends'.[91]

The arrival of the commissioners in London, 'some say to expostulate, others to treat and submitt',[92] both aroused interest and produced confusion. If hearsay is to be credited, the commissioners were snubbed by parliament. Both the Venetian ambassador and a royalist informant reported that they had been received only as messengers, and neither admitted nor conferred with,[93] and Viscount Conway likewise reported that parliament 'would not look upon any proposals of theirs'.[94] The Venetian ambassador's explanation was that parliament was affronted by a request from Henry that he be confirmed in his position, and no changes made. The more closely informed French ambassador understood, however, that although the demands were 'rather harsh', the agents were 'willing to forego those which concern the interest' of Henry.[95] There can be no doubt that Henry's position was not part of the commissioners' official brief, if only because Lawrence would certainly not have been associated with the promotion of his interests. There may have been an unofficial brief as well, but parliamentary hostility to the commissioners seems not to have needed so specific a cause: their presumption in

---

[89] Joseph Meyer (ed.), 'Inedited letters of Cromwell, Col. Jones, Bradshaw and other regicides', *Transactions of the Historic Society of Lancashire and Cheshire*, new series, 1 (1860–1), pp. 181–2.

[90] Dunlop, *Commonwealth*, p. 696.   [91] *TSP*, vii, 674.

[92] Cooper to Hyde, 3 June 1659, Clarendon MS 61, f. 97.

[93] *Cal. Clarendon SP*, iv, 231. Slingsby to Hyde, 10 June 1659, Clarendon MS 61, ff. 170v–171. *Cal. SP, Ven.*, 1659–61, p. 33.

[94] E. Berwick (ed.), *Rawdon Papers* (London, 1819), pp. 195–6.

[95] Guizot, *Richard Cromwell*, i, 408–9.

presenting terms may have been a sufficient provocation in itself, coming as it did from Oliver's beneficiaries. This reaction was publicly expressed in an extreme form by an anonymous republican who launched a double-barrelled attack, by publishing the same pamphlet under two distinct titles, warning members of parliament that the Irish commissioners were proposing a Saturnalian feast, 'where servants shall sit at the Table and you (their absolute Sovereign Lords and Masters) with trenchers in your hands, attend and wait upon them'. He believed that they were seeking four acts of parliament: for indemnity, for union, for the payment of arrears and for the settlement of estates, and he briskly disposed of each. There could be no indemnity for high treason and 'Tyrannical Apostasy'; there could be no question of entering into union with 'guilty servants' in parliament's 'own Mercenary Army'; there could be no arrears without repentance, and if there were repentance arrears would have been foregone in the hope of pardon. Most disturbingly, while he acknowledged the justice of confirming estates granted before April 1653 as 'their due wages and proper hire', he opposed the ratification of grants made thereafter, 'there being a Right neither in the Donor to grant, nor in the Donees to receive, and both apparently guilty of high Treason, only the greatness of their power hath prevented the justness of their attainder'.[96] The author, who was not the only one to pick up the rumour that an act of union was being sought,[97] was not fully informed,[98] but that did not diminish the significance of what he had to say. The plain fact is that the request for the confirmation of estates, though lengthily discussed and never refused, was never granted. As the pamphleteer shrewdly inferred, the Irish requests were designed to overcome divisions by drawing a 'more common and effectual interest upon the stage'.[99] So long as they were unattended to, they continued to serve that purpose.

The council of state, which never formally received the commissioners, had made its dispositions in advance. On 31 May, Henry's letter, which

---

[96] *Ambitious tyranny clearly demonstrated* (London, 1659); *Irelands ambition taxed* (London, 1659) passim.

[97] Mordaunt included an act of union in an otherwise accurate list of the main points sent to Hyde on 6 June. *Clarendon State Papers*, iii, pp. 482–3.

[98] He did not know, for instance, whether the commissioners had been sent to parliament or to Fleetwood. *Ambitious tyranny*, p. 2.   [99] Ibid., p. 8.

had been referred to it by parliament, was read and the council decided to recommend that 'the affaires of Ireland be for the present carryed on by Commissioners'. They also agreed to nominate one of their number, Colonel John Jones, together with the incumbent lord chancellor of Ireland, William Steele. They went on to appoint a fifteen-man committee for Irish affairs with a quorum of three.[100] There is hearsay evidence to suggest that these proposed arrangements became the subject of political manoeuvring. Some welcomed an end to 'the single person' in Irish government in the form of deputies and lord lieutenants, but others believed that the special circumstances called for the concentration of authority in a single commander. Some thought it should be Major General John Lambert, who was thought by others more worthy to be tried for high treason: Lambert himself was said to favour Ludlow for the position, as a way of removing 'soe obstinate a Comonwealthman', while Ludlow's 'ffriends labour his stay as a Check to Lambert and his designes'.[101] In the upshot, the recommendation of the council of state was accepted on 7 June when parliament resolved, 'with some passion' in the words of the Venetian ambassador, that the administration of Ireland should cease to be entrusted to a single person, and should revert to a commission, and Henry was ordered to return to report on the state of the country.[102]

Once made, the decision was quickly amplified. Henry's place was to be taken by a commission of five men, appointed in the first instance for a period of three months. The two men nominated by the council were accepted without demur. Steele, a radical activist in London and the city's first recorder under the commonwealth, had been prevented by illness from assisting in the prosecution of the king but had taken a leading role in a number of state trials, including those of the duke of Hamilton and the earl of Holland. He was a leading Independent who had been in Ireland as lord chancellor and councillor since 1656 and had consistently opposed Henry Cromwell, particularly his religious policy which he deemed insuf-

---

[100] Rawlinson MS C, 179, f. 34. The members were Whitelock, Sidney, Reynolds, Ludlow, Jones, Salway, Vane, Walton, Fleetwood, Lambert, Desborough, Berry, Wariston, Honeywood and Barners.
[101] Broderick to Hyde, 3 June 1659, Clarendon MS 61, ff. 104–104v.
[102] CJ, vii, 674. TSP, vii, 684–5. Mercurius Politicus, 16–23 June.

ficiently attentive to the godly.[103] Jones was a regicide member of parliament and zealot who had seen his appointment as one of the original commissioners for Ireland in 1650 as an opportunity to drive out antiChrist. He had remained in post until 1654. Since then, he had married Oliver Cromwell's sister Catherine, become a member of the council and been appointed to the upper house.[104] The other nominees, whose names had not been discussed by the council of state though they may well have been proposed by its Irish committee, proved problematic. Robert Goodwin, who had first gone to Dublin as a parliamentary agent in 1642, acquired 875 acres in Leinster as one of the original adventurers, and served as a member of the Irish council from 1654 to 1657 when he was dropped as unsatisfactory, met with some opposition before being approved.[105] William Basil, whose family had acquired the Bingley estates in Lifford in County Donegal in the 1630s,[106] who was married to the daughter of a prominent Fermanagh planter, Sir William Caulfield, and who had recently been elevated to the upper bench (as the former King's Bench was now known) after serving for ten years as attorney general, was rejected out of hand. The Irish exchequer court judge, Miles Corbet, a regicide member of parliament and religious Independent who had collaborated with Steele and the London radicals in the 1640s, had been continuously involved in Irish government as commissioner or councillor since 1650, and had combined with Steele in opposing Henry, was rejected on a vote of 39 to 32.[107] The council's Irish committee, reinforced by an MP with long Irish associations, Henry Wallop,[108] responded energeti-

---

[103] DNB. Robert Brenner, *Merchants and revolution: commercial change, political conflict, and London's overseas traders, 1550–1653* (Cambridge, 1993), pp. 547, 549, 567, 574. TSP, vii, 198–9, 243.

[104] DNB. R. L. Greaves and R. Zeller (eds.), *Biographical dictionary of British radicals in the seventeenth century* (3 vols., London, 1982–4), sub John Jones.

[105] TSP, vi, 599, 633. Henry Cromwell believed that he 'was not laid aside for his own faults, but rather to make me fit to be chastised', ibid., vii, 145.

[106] R. J. Hunter, 'Plantation in Donegal', in *Donegal: history and society*, ed. William Nolan, Liam Ronayne and Mairead Dunlevy (Dublin, 1995), p. 301.

[107] The tellers for the opposing majority were Sidney and Haselrig; for the minority, Ludlow and Marten. *CJ*, vii, 674. DNB. Brenner, *Merchants and revolution*, pp. 408, 520, 552, 573, 606–7.

[108] Rawlinson MS C, 179, ff. 51–2. Wallop's family had had interests in the Enniscorthy area of County Wexford since the 1580s.

cally: the commissioners' instructions were drafted, plans were laid, and two days later the business was completed when the councillors, exploiting a stipulation that at least two of those chosen should already be in Ireland, renominated Corbet, who had secured substantial property in County Dublin, and brought forward the name of Colonel Matthew Thomlinson, who had been in charge of King Charles during his trial and was, though presently in England, a sitting member of the Irish council and another opponent of Henry Cromwell. Both were accepted.[109]

The net effect of these decisions was that all three of the men who had recently constituted the opposition to Henry within his five-man council were elevated in power,[110] that the new commission was composed of men with extensive experience of Irish government, and that the only group represented was the new class of proprietors, officers and officials of the 1650s. The political implications of what was happening were succinctly conveyed by Lord Conway who wrote from London to tell his brother-in-law in County Down how much he feared 'the innudation of Anabaptists again amongst us'.[111] One of Henry Cromwell's early achievements had been the elimination of the largely military Baptist influence in Irish government. His removal provided an opportunity to reassert it. Another result of his rule had been the alienation of the mainly civilian Independents who, under the leadership of the provost of Trinity, Samuel Winter, had at first welcomed Henry but turned against him when he began to work towards an inclusive ecclesiastical policy acceptable to local Irish Protestants: they had, Henry observed, 'thought they should ride when they had thrown the Anabaptist out of the saddle'.[112] They too saw his removal and the confirmation of Steele and Corbet in office as an opportunity to reintroduce to the conduct of government a concern for godliness in which they thought it recently lacking. In short, the end of the protectorate signified more than a change in the form and personnel of government. There were also important policy implications, particularly in the reopening of opportunities for the influential expression of religious unorthodoxy.

Although neither the parliament nor the council of state took official

---

[109] *CJ*, vii, 678.
[110] The two who had supported him were Bury and Richard Pepys, chief justice of the upper bench, who had died on 2 January 1659.
[111] *Rawdon Papers*, p. 198.   [112] *TSP*, vii, 162.

cognizance of the Irish demands, the indications are that there was a fairly encouraging response from the council's Irish committee, which intimated that most of the matters raised either were or could be incorporated in the act for the confirmation of estates, the instructions to the new commissioners or the act of general oblivion that was already before parliament. Those who dealt with the business, however, baulked at the notion of overturning the plantation inquisitions, dismissing the request as 'impracticable', would go no further than to promise to consider the related request to wipe out Wentworth's rent and tenure changes, and professed to be unable to understand the request for a particular act of oblivion for Irish Protestants.[113] Above all, the Irish stipulations on religion found no favour. The instructions prepared for the parliamentary commissioners directed them to give encouragement and maintenance to both 'such Godly and able Ministers and other persons (of Pious life and Conversation) as they shall find qualified with Gifts for the preaching of the Gospell, and instructing the people there'. Moreover, they were to do this 'by way of stipend' from the tithe revenues.[114] Both the instructions and the bill empowering the commissioners to act, which were reported to the council of state by Sidney and to the house by Salway,[115] were referred to a Commons committee on 9 June.[116] Five days later a note of urgency was imparted when it was reported that those of the commissioners who were presently in England would not be able to set out for Ireland for some time, which meant that Henry could not be replaced at once by a quorate commission. There was no obvious reason for the delay and royalists sardonically conjectured that the commissioners were deterred by the belief 'that venomous beasts cannot live in the Irish ayre'.[117] On the advice of the council of state the House resolved the difficulty by confirming Henry's recall and authorizing the two men on the spot, Steele and Corbet, to act together until they were joined by one or more of the others.[118] Both the goodwill of some members of parliament and its

---

[113] TCD, MS 808, ff. 160–2. [114] Instructions, Article 2. Carte MS 67, ff. 307–10.
[115] Rawlinson MS C, 179, ff. 53, 57. Jonathan Scott, *Algernon Sidney and the English Republic, 1623–1677* (Cambridge, 1988), pp. 88, 126n.
[116] C.J., vii, 678. [117] *Nicholas Papers*, iv, p. 157.
[118] Rawlinson MS C, 179, f. 69. CJ, vii, 683. Cal. SP, Ire., 1647–1660, p. 862. The quorum had been set at three.

insufficiency were demonstrated in the House on 22 June when an attempt was made to insert a proviso into an act dealing with the collection of customs and excise. The effect would have been to allow horses, cattle and native goods and commodities to be traded freely in both directions between England and Ireland, 'as those that go from port to port in any other part of this Commonwealth'. The proposal, which had been supported by the Irish army officers in London as well as urged by the Irish commissioners, was rejected, and the instructions approved for the new commissioners on 1 July empowered them to raise the rates, provided that trade was not prejudiced.[119]

While the regime attended to its Irish concerns, and evidently in some measure disagreed about them, the official newsbooks carried reassuring reports of quiet concurrence in Ireland and extravagant rumours were again circulating in royalist circles.[120] An attempt 'at surprizal' was reported to have been made on Henry Cromwell, who 'pistolled the officer that layd hold of him';[121] from Beaumaris came news that the army in Ireland had declared for Henry 'and are resolved to live and die with him';[122] the contrasting word from Ireland was that Coote, 'Newgent and some others' were 'in the head of an army of 10 thousand men, declaring the Scotts Kings interest, and that Montague is daily expected there with his fleet'.[123] Despairing of leaders who had done nothing but wait for something to happen and were now waiting for 'my Lord Harry', an anonymous correspondent wrote to tell the king that 'the playne truth of the matter is this, that there is yet no certain accompt of the Condition Ireland is in at present'.[124] The most considered treatment of the conundrum of Henry was dispatched on 21 June by the royalist informant, John Barwick, conveying the opinion of Lord Meath who was passing through London on his way from Ireland to France. His argument was that Henry was neither submissive nor defiant: 'he hath

---

[119] *Rawdon Papers*, p. 197. *CJ*, vii, 691. Article 9, Carte MS 67, ff. 307–10.
[120] *Mercurius Politicus*, 9–16 June; *Publick Intelligencer*, 13–20 June.
[121] *Cal. Clarendon S.P.*, iii, 220.   [122] *Nicholas Papers*, iv, 152.
[123] Ibid., 156. Nugent is presumably Richard, second earl of Westmeath, who had fought with Ormond in the 1640s, acted as general of the Leinster forces in 1650–2 and been transplanted to Connacht.
[124] *Clarendon State Papers*, iii, 491. Anon to King, 17 June 1659, Clarendon MS 61, ff. 221–2.

hitherto stood in equilibrio taking no notice at all of the Parliament as the Supreme Authority (as they call it) but proceeding on his former course, as if his brother were still Protector. He is neither so active as he might be to play his own game, or so plyable as they would have him here to comply with theirs.' Meath reported that the nobility and gentry had offered to make up the army to 20,000 and that Dublin alone had offered to pay 2,000 of them: he thought that 'a good game may there be played if things be well managed though he should do as his brother did', the only obstacle being 'some great officers in that Army who have got into estates there'.[125]

In fact, Meath's opinions were out of date before they were reported, let alone received, for shortly after he left Ireland on 9 June Henry ceased to be 'very pendulous which way to take'. Still without firm information of what was taking place in England and in ignorance of his recall,[126] he prepared a 'letter of acquiescence' which he dispatched on 16 June in the care of two 'submissioners': Colonel Edmund Temple, captain of a troop in his regiment of horse, and William Petty whom he entrusted with negotiating the practical details of his withdrawal from public life.[127] Henry gave a brief, formal account of his handling of affairs since the coup, stressing his lack of information and instructions, before intimating that since he understood that Richard had acquiesced in the new arrangements, he wished to do likewise, as one who believed rather in 'the worthiness of governors than forms of government'. He concluded flatly

---

[125] Barwick to Hyde, 21 June 1659, Clarendon MS 61, f. 289. *TSP*, vii, 686–7. Edward Brabazon, second earl of Meath, had been dismissed from the Irish council in 1646 for opposing the peace: his lands had been first sequestered, then in part restored, in the 1650s. *Cal. SP, Ire., 1647–60*, pp. 389–90. G.E.C., *Peerage*, sub Meath. Henry Cromwell had recommended him to Thurloe when he was going to England in August 1657, but disclaimed any real knowledge of him. *TSP*, vi, 466. On Barwick, see Alan Marshall, *Intelligence and espionage in the reign of Charles II, 1660–1685* (Cambridge, 1994), p. 19; P. Barwick, *The life of John Barwick* (London, 1728).

[126] *TSP*, vii, 684–5.

[127] George Thomlinson to [Hyde], 24 June 1659, Clarendon MS 61, f. 325. Petty, *Down survey*, p. 301. *Mercurius Politicus*, 16–23 June. *Cal. SP, Ire., 1647–1660*, p. 700. Temple had been closely associated with William Jephson, who had first mooted the proposal to crown Cromwell, and had connections with Lord Wharton, Lord Say and Richard Norton of the old 'middle-group' in England. Fleetwood had obstructed his appointment to Henry's regiment. Temple to Henry Cromwell, 13 December 1658; 1 January [?], Lansdowne MS 823, ff. 168, 366.

by declaring that he was unwilling to continue to serve.[128] His letter crossed that from the speaker which ordered him to transfer authority to Corbet and Steele and on 22 June he formally notified the speaker that he had complied.[129]

It is sufficiently clear that the options discarded by Henry had not included an alliance with Charles, despite the misleading claim of Edward Hyde, the king's lord chancellor and chief coordinator of royalist action, who later alleged that Henry had given an assurance that he would declare for the king, but backed down at the last moment.[130] The record suggests that although the royalists on the continent were deeply interested in what was going on in Ireland and anxious to take advantage of it to supplement evolving plans for widespread risings in England, their attempts to do so were inept. The timing seemed opportune, but was not. Since 1656, Charles's dependence had been upon Spain while the English protectorate was allied to France. In May 1659, however, Spain and France agreed upon a truce and prepared to conclude a treaty. Charles believed that this development, combined with the overthrow of the protectorate, might bring the Anglo-French alliance to an end and that France and Spain might be persuaded to include a declaration of support for his restoration in their treaty. Direct action was always attractive and Charles did not relinquish the hope that he might soon have the opportunity to go to England to lead his supporters against the new regime, but he had always worked on the assumption that foreign assistance was essential to success and his chief preoccupation was to secure support for the joint declaration.[131] Hyde's initial response to the belated news of English and Irish developments had been quite rapid: by 13 May he had already identified the opportunity and was assuming that if Richard were overthrown Henry would probably seek the king's protection.[132] But he was in no position to make even the most rudimentary of plans. All that could be done was to hope 'that some discret Persons in Ireland who are faithfull to the King, and

---

[128] *TSP*, vii, 684–5.   [129] *Mercurius Politicus*, 23–30 June.
[130] *Clarendon State Papers*, iii, 589 (cf. p. 500); *Cal. Clarendon SP*, iv, 575.
[131] F. J. Routledge, *England and the treaty of the Pyrenees* (Liverpool, 1953), pp. 15–20, 47–52.
[132] *Clarendon State Papers*, iii, 500; 23 May, according to the Gregorian calendar. For clarity's sake, continental dates are given in old style.

[47]

are not as we hear unacceptable to [Henry], may propose of themselves what is reasonable, and proceed accordingly, for it is not easy for us to send any proper person from here nor have we any kind of correspondence in that Kingdom'. His advice, from the royalist adventurer and agent Nicholas Armorer, was that Mark Trevor would be the most appropriate person to approach Henry and that Sir Charles Littleton, organizer in Worcestershire of the secret royalist grouping known as the 'Great Trust', who had recently been in Ireland and intended to return, was well acquainted with Trevor.[133] He arranged, therefore, for Littleton to ask Trevor to convey to Henry a royal offer that he might make his own terms for himself and his family in return for his support.[134] Frustrating silence ensued, and an exasperating conflict of information: 'letters at the Same time contradicting what another of the same date affirmes'.[135] By another channel, Hyde extended the offer of satisfactory terms to be made to Henry by Littleton to 'his frendes' as well, but still without response.[136] Over a period of some three weeks, during which two steady streams of equally confident assertion reached the court, one affirming Henry's submission to the successive changes and the other his determination to resist them, the king's mother in Paris explored the possibility of raising money to finance an initiative in Ireland. By 2 June she had reported that a promise of men, money and arms could be made to Henry,[137] and this was confirmed on 10 June, however optimistically.[138] The reality was that Cardinal Mazarin, as yet undecided how to deal with the English dimension, was concerned only to play for time.

In the meantime, another possibility opened, more promising because it seemed to link with the plans that were being made in England. From

---

[133] David Underdown, *Royalist conspiracy in England* (New Haven, 1960), pp. 74, 242. Eva Scott, *The travels of the king: Charles II in Germany and Flanders, 1654–1660* (London, 1907), p. 55. *Clarendon State Papers*, iii, 483, 490, 559.

[134] *Cal. Clarendon SP*, iv, 202. Hyde to Rumbold, 13 May 1659, Clarendon MS 60, f. 535. Rumbold had been secretary of the 'Sealed Knot'. Philip Aubrey, *Mr Secretary Thurloe; Cromwell's secretary of state* (London, 1990), p. 102.

[135] Hyde to Barwick, 12 June 1659, Clarendon MS 61, f. 78.

[136] Hyde to Barwick, 2 June 1659, Clarendon MS 61, f. 77.

[137] King to Jermyn, 2 June 1659, Clarendon MS 61, f. 76.

[138] Queen Mother to King, 10 June 1659, Clarendon MS 61, f. 146. *Cal. Clarendon SP*, iv, 228.

the outset, there had been hopes of Broghill, who seems to have been approached indirectly by English royalists before the dissolution of parliament. They believed that they had made 'some progres in discoursing at distance' with him at that stage, and the open hostility to the new regime of his brother Francis, Lord Shannon, who was in The Hague, seemed to hold out promise of his support.[139] On 3 June, Broghill's brother-in-law, Thomas Howard, wrote to Charles from The Hague to say that Broghill had asked him to come to Ireland and given an assurance of his willingness to 'doe all things that may advance your service'. Howard requested approval to undertake the journey and promised to report quickly either in person or through Shannon.[140] It was not until a little later that Charles discovered that Howard was an occasional spy, but he already knew him to be untruthful,[141] and the approach to Broghill was instead entrusted to the man who claimed to have had him discreetly canvassed in April, Edward Villiers, one of the six members of the original royalist leadership group, the 'Sealed Knot'. Villiers and Broghill had married sisters and Villiers, who was the son of a former lord president of Munster, was requested by letter on 10 June to hasten to Ireland to assure both Broghill and Henry Cromwell that the king would supply men, money and arms if they declared for him, 'by which they may promise themselves all the advantages they may desire'. Hyde explained that the uncertainty about Henry's position was thought to be immaterial, for 'if there be any formall complyance it cannot hold long especially if any changes happen at home', while Broghill was thought not to 'have any aversenesse to it when the season shall be proper'.[142] English royalists, a nervously distrustful group, seem to have been piqued at the introduction of an Irish dimension,[143] but there were obvious advantages to a scheme by which, in concert with a

---

[139] Lynch, *Orrery*, p. 98, citing Clarendon MSS 60, f. 340. Villiers to Hyde, 11 April 1659, Clarendon MS 60, f. 19.

[140] *Cal. Clarendon SP*, iv, 219. Howard to King, 3 June 1659, Clarendon MS 61, f. 87v. Howard to Daniel O'Neill, 3 June 1659, ibid., ff. 85–6. Broghill married Margaret Howard, daughter of the [late] earl of Suffolk and sister of Tom, in 1641.

[141] *Cal. Clarendon SP*, iv, 245. Scott, *The travels of the king*, pp. 154, 386–7. Aubrey, *Mr Secretary Thurloe*, p. 125.

[142] Underdown, *Royalist conspiracy*, pp. 75, 81–2. *Clarendon State Papers*, iii, 500–2.

[143] 'it is a work that cannot be overdone', Hyde soothingly assured Belasyse as he revealed Villiers's mission, 10 June 1659, Clarendon MS 61, f. 156.

rising in England, Henry would land a force in Chester or Liverpool while his 'friendes in Munster' landed one in Bristol.¹⁴⁴

Hyde was satisfied that everything had been done that could be done to promote the king's cause in Ireland¹⁴⁵ and reassuring news continued to arrive, but the reality was that nothing was done. Littleton's apparent familiarity with Mark Trevor's proceedings had been gained 'from discourse that he had with my Ld Ormond's Lady': he did not know Trevor or any one else in Henry's confidence and did not 'thinke himself fitt' to go to Ireland, nor did it prove possible to find a substitute.¹⁴⁶ For his part, Villiers claimed to have been advised by his friends against approaching Broghill, whom they regarded as 'a very great villain', and he insisted that if Broghill 'had a minde to act, he hath soe far bin treated with as that Villiers would certainly ere now have heard from him': he too stayed in England.¹⁴⁷ Hyde knew nothing of this setback until 10 July, and found it difficult to reconcile this characterization of Broghill with that of his friends, who 'always magnified his interest to serve the Kinge in a proper season, and sure he never can finde a more proper one'.¹⁴⁸ In short, because of the absence of any lines of communication between either the exiled court or the English royalists and Ireland, and perhaps also as a by-product of the tendency of English royalists to promise more than they could deliver, the long-drawn-out royal approaches were never actually made. It was not a time for delay, and the reality seems to have been that Broghill had sought an accommodation with the new regime early on: on 29 May, Bulstrode Whitelock, who was a member of the council of state, recorded the arrival of letters from him about the state of affairs in Ireland 'and of my Lord's joining with this Parliament'.¹⁴⁹

While Henry was composing his valediction to public life, the officers in council were preparing their long promised address, independently of Henry who thought it important, or so he professed, that 'the parliament should have the true knowledge of them'. The delay was elegantly

---

¹⁴⁴ *Cal. Clarendon SP*, iv, 221.   ¹⁴⁵ Ibid., 236.
¹⁴⁶ Rumbold to Hyde, 20 June 1659, Clarendon MS 61, f. 262. It seems likely that Littleton had heard the story later relayed by Hyde to Ormond. See pp. 31–2 above.
¹⁴⁷ *Cal. Clarendon SP*, iv, 247, 269. Villiers to Hyde, 24 June 1659, Clarendon MS 61, f. 314. The coded portions of letters were commonly written in the third person.
¹⁴⁸ Hyde to Villiers, 11 July 1659, Clarendon MS 62 f. 54.
¹⁴⁹ B. Whitelock, *Memorials of the English affairs* (4 vols., London, 1853), iv, 350.

accounted for, inasmuch as 'by reason of our distance, we could not attain as much light as might give forth to such early resolutions' as their brethren in England and Scotland had been able to produce. They acknowledged that they had 'reaped the fruit of your earlier Government', and declared their 'humble, hearty and free submission to your Authority'. Their compliance, however, did not extend to a repudiation of the protectorate. Noting the provision that had been made for Richard, they asked that Henry too might receive such favour 'as may be suitable to a branch of the stock whom God had made so eminently instrumental in the service of these Nations'. They concluded by observing that the 'state of your affairs in this Nation at present, and our Interests under you, doth call upon us to minde you of a Union with England, and other great concernments'.[150] Others displayed a greater enthusiasm: a group of Independents under the leadership of Samuel Winter and Samuel Mather were also preparing an address, as were the Dublin Baptists, under the name of the Church of Christ, who conveyed their desire for 'the welfare of Syon, and the True Happiness of the Nations'.[151]

The first concern of Corbet and Steele, assuming their role as acting commissioners shortly after the army had agreed upon its statement, was to undo Henry's military dispositions. The story relayed by Edmund Ludlow, who arrived in Ireland about a month later, was that after the news of his recall, Henry had retired to the chief governor's house, 'The Phoenix', leaving Dublin Castle under the command of Colonel Thomas Long, who had been in Ireland since taking a regiment of foot from Somerset to Michael Jones's assistance twelve years earlier.[152] The commissioners, suspecting that he intended to keep the Castle, surprised it.[153] The record shows only that on 21 June the senior officer in Ireland, Sir Hardress Waller, major general of foot since 1650, who was both the only New English senior officer in the original New Model Army and the only New English regicide,[154] was ordered to rescind all movements of troops

---

[150] *Mercurius Politicus*, 23–30 June.   [151] *CJ*, vii, 695.
[152] *Regimental history*, pp. 598, 650.   [153] Ludlow, *Memoirs*, ii, 94.
[154] Temple, 'Original officer list', *Bulletin of the Institute of Historical Research*, 59, p. 55n. He was also one of the five officers appointed to 'consider of the time and place for the execution of the sentence against the king'. C. V. Wedgwood, *A coffin for King Charles* (New York, 1964), p. 189.

and companies made since 2 April and, in particular, to secure Dublin Castle by replacing the garrison with Colonel Hewson's foot company and what other forces he thought necessary. On the following day, the halberdiers in the Castle were sent back to their dragoon regiment and the absentee Hewson's major, Henry Jones, was ordered to move his company into their place.[155] There was more to this than symbolism, and early in July the repair of the Castle gates and the blocking of access were put in train.[156] The private concerns of Waller, a Kentish man who had come to Ireland when he married a Dowdall heiress in County Limerick in 1629, were of a different order. On the day the Castle guard was changed he wrote to his cousin, William Lenthall, speaker of the English House of Commons, protesting his fidelity to 'the good old cause', justifying his adherence to the protectorate and asking permission to present his case in person.[157] On the face of it, although he was under the immediate disadvantage of being Henry Ingoldsby's father-in-law, his credentials were better than most. He was an Independent in religion, 'very well esteemed by the godly people, being one of dr Winter's congregation',[158] and a veteran who had stood at the door of the Commons when the present parliament was being fashioned by Pride's Purge. But he had also been a follower of Oliver and had voted for kingship in parliament in 1657. He was a man, it was said, who 'had complied with every party that had been uppermost':[159] now he judged the time right to do it again.

On the day that Steele and Corbet received the speaker's order to assume temporary responsibility for the conduct of government, they issued licences to Henry Cromwell's party to leave Ireland.[160] Henry took ship on Monday, 27 June, after 'The university condoled the departure of their Chancellor in an excellent speech presented by their orator.'[161] On the same day, his letter of 22 June was read to the House of Commons and the petition of the officers was presented by Colonel Robert Phayre, a man

---

[155] Dunlop, *Commonwealth*, pp. 696–7. Prendergast Papers, ii, 468, 469.
[156] Dunlop, *Commonwealth*, p. 699.   [157] *Tanner Papers*, pp. 394–5.
[158] According to Henry Cromwell, who did not trust him. Making arrangements to visit England in 1658, he planned to take Waller with him 'and such others as cannot so safely be left there'. *TSP*, vi, 773; vii, 492. Ingoldsby married Anne Waller in 1653. H. F. Berry (ed.), *The register of the church of St Michan, Dublin 1636 to 1685* (Parochial Record Society of Dublin, 1907), p. 13.   [159] Ludlow, *Memoirs*, ii, 122–3.
[160] Dunlop, *Commonwealth*, p. 697.   [161] *Clarke Papers*, iv, 23.

of unimpeachable credentials in these circumstances: the son of a Cork clergyman, but a patron of the Quakers, he was a veteran of the New Model Army as well as the Munster wars, had signed the order for the king's execution, and returned to Ireland with Oliver to become governor of his county town.[162] The house returned its formal thanks, but the petition had not struck the right note. Not alone was its praise for the Cromwells wholly at variance with the political climate, but its language was interpreted by some as implying that the first allegiance of the officers was to their 'employment and estates' rather than to the parliament.[163] The response was immediate. On the following day the absentee officers, whose political dependability was so much greater, were ordered to return to their duties and soon after the Commons set about remodelling the Irish command, a matter that a sub-committee of the council of state had been considering for some weeks.[164]

For some days, it had been common knowledge in London that 'Henry of Ireland hath laied downe the cudgells there',[165] but rumour was not stilled and hope was not dispelled. The rumours were familiar: Coote and Broghill were leading 6,000 men 'declaring against this present government';[166] disturbances had broken out in Ireland, and the king's party had greatly increased there.[167] The hope stemmed from two sources. The first was the news that Henry's 'late harbinger and scout', Colonel Temple, had gone back 'very dissatisfied', which gave rise to the possibility that Henry might not hazard his 'polletic noddle' by obeying parliament's summons.[168] Though the government issued assurances that all was well in Ireland, Henry's delayed return left room for doubt.[169] Further ground for hope was found in an optimistic reading of the address from the Irish officers, which seemed to suggest that they were not entirely well affected

---

[162] J. C., 'Colonel Phaire, the regicide', *Journal of the County Cork Historical and Archaeological Society*, 2nd series, 20 (1914), 146–50, 199–203; 21 (1915), 46–9. W. H. Welphy, 'Colonel Robert Phaire, 'regicide'', ibid., 29 (1924), 76–80; 30 (1925), 20–3. In 1658, Phayre had, incongruously, married the daughter of Sir Thomas Herbert, who had attended Charles on the scaffold.

[163] *CJ*, vii, 695. *Mercurius Politicus*, 23–30 June. *Cal. SP, Dom, 1659–60*, p. 19. *Cal. Clarendon SP*, iv, 247–8. Rawlinson MS C, 179, f. 57.   [164] *CJ*, vii, 696.

[165] *Nicholas Papers*, iv, 160–1. *Cal. Clarendon SP*, iv, 247–8, 248, 250, 255.

[166] *Nicholas Papers*, iv, 162.   [167] *Cal. SP, Ven., 1659–61*, p. 35.

[168] *Nicholas Papers*, iv, 164.   [169] *Cal. SP, Ven., 1659–61*, p. 39.

'to this side', and might well have been in correspondence with their colleagues in Scotland, where the outwardly compliant Monck was showing signs of rebuffing parliament's attempts to interfere with his army.[170] A review of the situation sent to the French government surmised that the 'nameless officers... did not vallew much henry Cromwells interest as to struggle for him but they will not quitt their imployment, estates, or subiect their fortunes to the power and will of this parliament'.[171] Henry's arrival in London on 2 July, formally conveyed by Fleetwood to parliament on 4 July, when Henry was ordered to report to the council of state, ended both the speculation and the rumours.[172] Although Hyde found cause for hope in 'some new Revolutions, which probably may be at hand', nearer home it was no longer possible to doubt that the situation in Ireland was under control.[173] Thereafter, there was 'no noyse of Scotland or Ireland, nor much talk of the navy'.[174] Worse still, as only initiates and government spymasters realized, there would be no Irish dimension to the coordinated revolts which were intended to take place shortly in many parts of England. Indeed, as was quickly perceived by Sir George Booth, who had engaged to rise in Cheshire 'upon presumption that Ireland would not submit', the freedom to use the Irish army against them shifted the odds decisively in the government's favour: 'if he should stirr', he was reported to have said, 'he is liable to be suppressed from there in foure houres'.[175]

Strategically, the point was a sound one. Politically, as the rulers of England were uneasily aware, there remained genuine doubt as to whether the apparatus of military power in Ireland was in wholly reliable hands. The imputation that the army was infected with Cromwellianism

---

[170] Ibid., p. 35. *Cal. Clarendon SP*, iii, 247–8. Geo. Thomlinson to Hyde, 24 June 1659. Clarendon MS 61, ff. 247–8. *The parliamentary or constitutional history of England from the earliest times* (24 vols., London, 1751–62), xxi, 426–7.
[171] Clarendon MS 61, f. 360.
[172] *Mercurius Politicus*, 30 June–7 July. *CJ*, vii, 702. He reported on 6 July. Rawlinson MS C, 179, ff. 143–4.
[173] Barwick, *Life of Barwick*, p. 434. *Cal. SP, Ven., 1659–61*, p. 42.
[174] *Nicholas Papers*, iv, 171.
[175] *Clarendon State Papers*, iii, 516, 517. Mordaunt and Titus to Hyde, 6 July 1659, Clarendon MS 61, f. 390. The Gloucestershire leader, John Howe, took the same view. Underdown, *Royalist conspiracy*, p. 249.

had been confirmed both by the way in which it awaited Henry's submission before making its own and by the studied recalcitrance of its respect for Oliver's memory. To the ideologues who had disempowered those who had disempowered Richard, the pragmatic willingness of the officers to protect their estates by accepting the authority of the restored parliament was an inadequate substitute for enthusiastic allegiance. Although there were pressing needs in Ireland, not least to settle estates and reverse the conservative religious drift, the immediate priority was to 'remodel' the army.

3
The rule of the rump: July to October

The initial task of the restored parliament was to consolidate its position. At first, that was a matter of securing the support of all of the armed forces – in England, Scotland, Ireland, Dunkirk and the navy. Once that had been done, it was a matter of ensuring that parliament was master in its own house. There were some members who thought otherwise, and who argued that parliament and army should work in partnership to achieve their common purposes, but the council of state appointed on 19 May contained a majority whose determination to relegate the army and its leaders to an appropriate subordination to the parliament set the immediate priorities of the regime. The issue of principle was given practical expression in decisions to withhold from the new commander in chief the right to commission and promote officers and to refuse the demand that officers should be cashiered only after court martial. A commission of seven, including Fleetwood, systematically reviewed the officers and those who passed muster were recommissioned by the speaker in a formula which required them to obey parliament and the council of state before their superior officers. Just as the commissioners were particularly concerned to be rid of those who had been too close to the Cromwells, as well as those judged morally deficient, so they paid special attention to reinstating those who had lost their positions through opposition to the protectorate. The scrutiny was neither rigorous nor well informed: the assumption that hostility to Cromwell was proof of devotion to parliament was ingenuous, and the intention of ensuring that those who commanded the army would show 'Faithfulness and Obedience' to the 'Parliament and Commonwealth'[1] was not achieved. A series of measures exacerbated the hostility of the officers. An act of indemnity, which finally passed after protracted debate on 12 July, fell short of the

---

[1] *CJ*, vii, 10 June.

[56]

army council's demands, and bills for the reform of the militia enacted in the same month gave rise to intense suspicions of a design to create an alternative force. The confidence with which the republicans outfaced the army command was founded upon their knowledge that the army was divided. The junior officers, whose influence over the rank and file was more immediate and greater than that of the 'Grandees', had enthusiastically supported the recall of parliament. That support was not rewarded, however. Nothing was done to pay the arrears; an early, liberal resolution on religious toleration was soon qualified by a house vote in favour of the continued payment of tithes for the support of godly ministers; and although the parliament resolved to terminate before 7 May 1660, it took no steps to decide what form of government would follow. While the restored members thus antagonized their allies, alienated their friends and conciliated no one, the 'common enemy' plotted to overthrow them and set the beginning of August as the time to do so.

The arrangements for the government of Ireland were formally completed on 7 July, when the commissioners of the Parliament for the Affairs of Ireland were appointed, for a period of three months, by an act of parliament which also declared 'severall Laws, Ordinances, and Acts of Parliament to be in force in Ireland'. They were those which dealt with treason, priests, Jesuits, delinquents, pluralists, scandalous ministers, felony, drunkenness, adultery, fornication, incest, the abolition of episcopacy, the Book of Common Prayer, and the abolition of the kingly office.[2] Although particular legislation was specified in only a few cases, all of the designated areas were ones in which the law had been significantly altered by enactments of the Long Parliament: the act was an explicit exercise of English legislative supremacy over Ireland. The point was reinforced by the commissioners' instructions, which directed them to govern Ireland 'according to the laws and Constitutions of England, so far as the present Constitution of the Country will admit'.[3] Parliamentary authority had been conceded by the petition carried by Bury, Jones and Lawrence, and the measure that had then been chiefly desired, an act for settling estates,

---

[2] *CJ*, vii, 699–700, 707. *Acts and ordinances*, ii, 1298–9.
[3] Instructions, Article 5. Carte MS 67, ff. 307–10. The instructions were approved on 1 July.

was brought forward at the same time and twice read. On the previous day, in anticipation of this development, a petition had been presented on behalf of the adventurers by one of the most substantial of them, the London merchant-tailor, William Hawkins. The petition and the bill were referred to the same committee.[4]

Side by side with these civil preparations, revised military arrangements had also been under way, involving changes which extended from the position of commander in chief right down through the command structure. The first step appears to have been taken on 16 June when the seven commissioners appointed to deal with the nomination of English officers reviewed those officers of the Irish army who were in England. Their instructions were to replace all officers suspected of hostility to the republic, immorality or doubtful religious opinions. Four of the Irish officers passed muster and were confirmed in their commands:[5] the agent, Richard Lawrence; his fellow Baptist, Hierome Sankey, sometime Fellow of All Souls and honorary doctor of Dublin University, who had come to Ireland in Cromwell's double regiment and served as governor of Clonmel; Thomas Cooper, a Scot who had been in effective command in Ulster since 1656 and is credited with having persuaded Henry Cromwell that the presbyterian ministers there 'may with more ease be led than driven';[6] and John Clarke, who had an English regiment also, and had not served in Ireland for some considerable time. The last three of these men had been involved in Richard's overthrow,[7] as had Henry Pretty who had been independently confirmed in his command by parliament three days earlier.[8] Pretty, who was also a Baptist and had also been a major in Cromwell's double regiment, had served as governor of Carlow since 1652.[9] In addition, Alexander Brayfield, a Baptist who had been court martialled and cashiered from his position as lieutenant-colonel of Henry Cromwell's foot in 1657, was reinstated as colonel of a foot regiment. Brayfield, who had served with Hewson and was closely associated with

---

[4] *CJ*, vii, 706, 707, 709. *Mercurius Politicus*, 30 June–7 July. Bottigheimer, *English money and Irish land*, p. 155.   [5] Davies, *The restoration*, p. 106.

[6] J. S. Reid, *History of the Presbyterian church in Ireland*, ed. W. D. Killen (3 vols., Belfast, 1867), ii, 225–7.

[7] Baker, *A Chronicle*, pp. 692, 699.   [8] *Clarke Papers*, iv, 6. *CJ*, vii, 684.

[9] Barnard, *Cromwellian Ireland*, p.103n. Dunlop, *Commonwealth*, p. 5n.

[58]

him, had unsubtly compared his commanding officer to Absalom, the traitorous son of David with whom Oliver was sometimes eulogistically identified.[10] Once these initial decisions had been made, the process was formalized. In consultation with Fleetwood, whose appointment as lord general and commander in chief of the land forces of England and Scotland had been confirmed by act of parliament on 7 June,[11] a committee loosely referred to as 'the officers of Ireland here in town' drew up recommendations.[12] This advisory subcommittee consisted of Sankey and Lawrence, their fellow Baptist Edward Roberts, auditor of the Irish exchequer,[13] Major Peter Wallis, a Quaker sympathizer who had risen from corporal in Oliver's horse troop in 1644 to major in Henry's regiment in 1650 and who was in origin the son of a settler on Raleigh's seignory in County Cork,[14] and Edmund Ludlow who was responsible for presenting their recommendations to the committee for nominations for transmission to parliament.[15]

Formally, the army in Ireland consisted of eighteen regiments, six of horse, one of dragoons and eleven of foot. There were normally twenty-four officers in a horse regiment, while dragoon and foot regiments had a complement of thirty-four. It was with the forty-eight regimental command posts, however, consisting of colonels and majors in the horse and lieutenant-colonels as well in the foot, that the committee concerned itself in the first instance. The assertion of effective control, as the subcommittee well knew, would require more than alterations at the top of the regular establishment, but both the lower echelons – the troop and com-

---

[10] *TSP*, vi, 505–6, 599. Oliver thought Henry had misjudged Brayfield and suggested that he be 'handsomely restored'. W. C. Abbott (ed.), *The writings and speeches of Oliver Cromwell* (4 vols., Cambridge, Mass., 1937–47), iv, 646–7.

[11] *Acts and ordinances*, ii, 1283–4.

[12] *Cal. SP, Dom., 1659–60*, p. 12.   [13] Barnard, *Cromwellian Ireland*, p. 210.

[14] *Regimental history*, pp. 6n, 591. Barnard, *Cromwellian Ireland*, pp. 110n, 149n. Henry Cromwell sent him to Ulster in Cooper's absence in March 1657, on the principle that he could be trusted against the Scots. *TSP*, vi, 143. He was the second son of Thomas who settled at Curraglass (near Tallow), in 1595. *Burke's Irish family records* (London, 1976).

[15] *Cal. SP, Dom., 1659–60*, pp. 12–13. Ludlow, *Memoirs*, ii, 94; *CJ*, vii, 651. It was later alleged that the sub-committee had consulted Dr John Harding, a former vice-provost of Trinity who had become a leading Baptist minister in Ireland. John Bridges, A. Warren and E. Warren, *A perfect narrative of the grounds and reasons moving some officers of the army in Ireland to the securing of the Castle in Dublin for the parliament* (London, 1659[60]), p. 4.

pany captains, lieutenants, cornets, ensigns and quartermasters – and the irregular units – the unregimented garrison commanders and troop and company captains – were left for later treatment.

The task of ensuring ideological and political soundness in the higher echelons, and the associated aim of redressing past injustices in doing so, was facilitated both by the vacancies created by the removal of the Cromwell brothers and by Fleetwood's decision to stand down. So far as the horse was concerned, replacements were required in half of the six regiments. Henry Cromwell's was given to its major, Wallis,[16] and Joseph Deane was promoted from captain to fill his place:[17] both were not only veterans of the Irish service but part-time entrepreneurs who had been jointly involved in a loss-making project to supply Irish soldiers to the Spanish army in 1657.[18] Richard Cromwell's regiment was reserved for the new commander in chief: his major, Henry Owen, who had come to Ireland in 1649 and taken his support of the Cromwells so far as to ridicule Major Pride in a speech in support of the proposal to crown Oliver in the 1657 parliament, was cashiered.[19] His replacement, Henry Kempson, was a Quaker who had not seen Irish service since the 1640s but was married to Edmund Ludlow's sister and leased state property in County Dublin.[20] Thomas Cooper, who had been confirmed in his foot regiment at the outset,[21] was subsequently given command of Fleetwood's horse, with Edward Warren replacing its unlikely major, the doctor of medicine and amateur scientist, Anthony Morgan, who had received permission to dissect the corpse of a hanged prisoner in 1652. Morgan, who was one of Henry Cromwell's confidants, had supported kingship in 1657.[22] Warren, one of three soldier sons of the dean of Ossory, had moved some distance from his origins and had written against Baptist doctrines from an avowedly Fifth Monarchist position in the mid-1650s.[23] In two of the

[16] On 9 July. *CJ*, vii, 710, 712. *Cal. SP, Ire., 1647–60*, p. 700, has a list of officers.
[17] *Cal. SP, Ire., 1647–60*, p. 700. The remaining captains were John Friend, William Meredith, Sam Shere and Edmund Temple.   [18] *Regimental history*, p. 591.
[19] Anthony Morgan to Henry Cromwell, 12 May 1657, BL, Lansdowne MS 822, f. 71.
[20] Richard Bagwell, *Ireland under the Stuarts* (3 vols., London, 1909–16), ii, 364. Davies, *The restoration*, p. 245. Barnard, *Cromwellian Ireland*, p. 111n. *Cal. SP, Ire., 1647–60*, p. 673.
[21] *CJ*, vii, 696.
[22] *DNB*. Barnard, *Cromwellian Ireland*, p. 223. Prendergast papers, i, 41.
[23] [Edward Warren], *In Canaan: by grace, not works* (London, 1655), The Epistle.

remaining regiments the senior positions were left unaltered: Pretty and Sankey kept their commands and their respective majors, Francis Bolton, who had come to Ireland with Abbott's dragoons in 1649,[24] and Elias Greene, who seems to have come with Horton in the same year.[25] Colonel Daniel Redman, however, who had replaced Sankey as major in Oliver's regiment in 1650 and been given his own command in 1657, was removed because of 'his zeal to the usurpation of Cromwell'.[26] The committee was somewhat behind the game in this case, for Redman was already in touch with royalist agents.[27] He was replaced by a prime instigator of the recent coup, William Allen, a prominent Leveller in the 1640s, a Baptist, and one of a group who had jointly resigned their Irish commands in protest against Henry's religious policy in 1656.[28] Redman's major, John Godfrey, who had come to Ireland as one of Sankey's captains, was left in place.[29]

Both Henry Cromwell and Fleetwood had also commanded foot companies, so that two changes were unavoidable. In the event, the entire command of Henry's regiment was altered. The colonelcy was reserved for the new commander-in-chief. Lieutenant-Colonel John Gorges, one of Waller's captains in the original New Model Army, former governor of Londonderry and eldest brother of Henry's secretary, was replaced by Solomon Richards, formerly governor of Clonmel, while Major John Read made way for William Rawlings: both of the new appointees were civil war veterans with extensive Irish experience.[30] Fleetwood's regiment was given to Daniel Axtell, a Baptist who had commanded the guard at Westminster Hall during the king's trial and governed Kilkenny from 1650 until he

[24] *Regimental history*, p. 621.   [25] Ibid., p. 85.   [26] Ludlow, *Memoirs*, ii, 203.

[27] *Regimental history*, p. 594. Barwick, *Life of Barwick*, p. 420. Underdown, *Royalist conspiracy*, p. 309. He was brother-in-law to John Otway, an excluded fellow of St John's who was closely in contact with the royalist agent John Barwick who was also an excluded fellow of St John's: another of Otway's brothers-in-law was Col. John Clobery, one of Monck's most trusted officers. Ibid., p. 309.

[28] R. L. Greaves and R. Zeller (eds.), *Biographical dictionary of British radicals in the seventeenth century* (3 vols., London, 1982–4), sub William Allen.

[29] *Regimental history*, pp. 613–14. He had, Petty alleged, been 'left in the lurch by his own dear Colonel' Sankey, who had misappropriated an estate which he was supposed to have secured as an agent. Petty thought well of him. *Reflections*, p. 90.

[30] *CJ*, vii, 716. Temple, 'Original officer list', *BIHR*, 59, p. 56. Commonwealth records, *Archivium Hibernicum*, 6 (1917), 202; 7 (1918–21), 29.

resigned in protest with Allen in 1656 and returned to England.[31] Lieutenant-Colonel Henry Flower, who had been in effective command in Fleetwood's absence,[32] was displaced by the promotion of Major Bryan Smith, governor of Carrickfergus, who was himself replaced by Captain John Barrett.[33] All three had been with the regiment since Fleetwood inherited it after Ireton's death.[34] Amidst some confusion, the regiment commanded by the absentee John Hewson, who was also colonel of an English regiment, was given to Henry Markham on 13 July: five days earlier, the subcommittee had proposed that Hewson should act as commander in chief of the foot while he was in Ireland. The confusion was compounded by the fact that Markham, a captain of horse at the foundation of the New Model Army, who had performed a variety of important administrative tasks in Ireland throughout the 1650s, was also an absentee.[35] Effective command devolved upon Henry Jones, a 'busie Anabaptist' in Henry Cromwell's estimation, who had been major to Hewson since 1651 and now displaced William Arnop as lieutenant-colonel.[36] Jones, who had, like Lawrence, married one of Hewson's daughters, was a brother of the recently appointed commissioner, John Jones.[37] His place as major was taken by John Bennett, one of Pretty's officers.[38] It was the command of Cooper's regiment, which became vacant on his transfer to Fleetwood's horse, that was given to Alexander Brayfield.[39] Cooper's lieutenant-colonel, John Duckenfield, seems to have moved to Hewson's English regiment

---

[31] Regimental history, pp. 628–31. Barnard, Cromwellian Ireland, p. 101. CJ, vii, 712.

[32] Dunlop, Commonwealth, p. 366n.

[33] Regimental history, pp. 647, 648. Cal. SP, Ire., 1660–2, pp. 650–60. CJ, vii, 716.

[34] Regimental history, p. 647.

[35] CJ, vii, 716. Cal. SP, Dom., 1659–60, p. 12. Regimental history, pp. 164–5. Dunlop, Commonwealth, pp. 162n, 459, 538, 615, 648, 665.

[36] There had been an intermission in Jones's service when he had been reduced to captain and received full satisfaction for his arrears, as against the 'little more than one half' that he would have received if he had remained in the army. He subsequently secured a new commission from Oliver Cromwell and was found to have drawn full pay for the period of about ten months when he was reduced. TSP, vi, 142.

[37] Regimental history, pp. 409–11, 629. TSP, vi, 94. Greaves and Zeller, Biographical dictionary of British radicals, sub John Jones.   [38] Dunlop, Commonwealth, pp. 90n, 434.

[39] The initial recommendation agreed by the committee on 16 June, and reported to the Commons on 28 June, was that he should be given Richard Cromwell's foot regiment, with Arnop as lieutenant-colonel. In fact, Richard did not have a foot regiment. Cal. SP, Dom., 1658–99, p. 375. CJ, vii, 696.

and was replaced by William Keane who transferred from England and whose associations are suggested by the fact that he had the backing of Colonel Lawrence.[40] William Lowe, who had been cashiered by Henry Cromwell in 1658, ostensibly for neglect of duty, 'peevishness and perverseness', but in reality for his opposition to the protectorate, recovered his position as major, displacing his successor Alexander Staples who had represented the north-west in the 1659 parliament.[41]

The command which Henry Ingoldsby had abandoned on his flight from Limerick was an extreme example of Irish regimental arrangements, for it was no more than a notional unit created by the nominal amalgamation of loose companies dispersed in garrisons in 1655.[42] It was given to the Baptist Robert Barrow, yet another of those who had collectively resigned in 1656, and yet another of those who were involved in the unseating of Richard. He had come to Ireland in 1649, campaigned vigorously in Ulster, and served as governor of Carrickfergus after his regiment was disbanded in 1653.[43] William Purefoy, who had come to Ireland as major of Castle's regiment in 1647 and been lieutenant-colonel of Ingoldsby's since its formation, remained in place.[44] Samuel Bonnell, a captain in Hewson's English regiment, was appointed major.[45] Thomas Sadler, a veteran of the earl of Manchester's Eastern Association army who had come to Ireland as adjutant general of foot with Cromwell and had served as governor of Galway since 1655, retained his regimental command, surviving a challenge in the Commons by 48 votes to 22 on 28 June.[46] He too was a Baptist. What happened to his officers is not entirely clear: it is probable that John Brett, who had supported kingship as member for the Galway/Mayo constituency in 1657, was continued as lieutenant-colonel in the first instance,[47] and the Baptist William Walker was appointed major in place of

---

[40] *CJ*, vii, 682, 684, 710, 716. *Regimental history*, pp. 260, 668, 670–1. Duckenfield represented Belfast and Carrickfergus in the 1659 parliament and did not return to Ireland.

[41] *TSP*, vii, 142. Lowe had been a captain in Venables' foot. *Cal. SP, Adv.*, p. 398.

[42] *Regimental history*, pp. 644–5.

[43] Ibid., pp. 333, 595, 629, 637–9. Barnard, *Cromwellian Ireland*, p. 103n.

[44] *Regimental history*, pp. 633–4, 638, 644–5.

[45] *CJ*, vii, 682,684. He was commissioned as sergeant major on 14 July, ibid., p. 718.

[46] *CJ*, vii, 696. The opposing tellers were Mildmay and Neville, the proponents Ralegh and Salwey. *Regimental history*, pp. 582–3, 612. Barnard, *Cromwellian Ireland*, p. 103n.

[47] *Clarke Papers*, iv, 252. *Cal. SP, Dom.*, 1659–60, p. 12.

someone unknown.[48] Within a few months, however, Walker replaced Brett and Isaac Dobson, who 'had been used ill by Oliver, and unjustly removed from his command' became major.[49]

The regiment of John Clarke, like Ingoldsby's, was made up from loose companies in 1655 when his original regiment was disbanded and Clarke, who was one of the Admiralty commissioners in London, was not in Ireland during its entire existence.[50] The committee allowed him to retain his nominal command, but the lieutenant-colonelcy was removed from John Cole, member of a New English settler family in Fermanagh and colonel of a regiment in Ulster from 1650 to 1653.[51] Arnop, who had protested vigorously at being forced out of Markham's regiment, 'being unconscious of wrong', was given his place.[52] The incumbent major, whose name is not recorded, was replaced by a newcomer to Ireland, George Owen, an officer in Colonel Gibbon's English foot regiment.[53] Richard Lawrence retained his regiment and his officers, both of whom were well established: Richard Tonson seems to have been with him from the outset and had been promoted to major by 1656; Simon Finch had come to Ireland after the battle of Worcester as a lieutenant-colonel with reinforcements for Sir Hardress Waller's regiment, and had transferred to Lawrence's with the same rank by 1656.[54] Robert Phayre's regiment was also left undisturbed, with Francis Wheeler and John Dennison, both New Model veterans, retaining the places that they had held since 1651 and 1650 respectively.[55]

---

[48] Kevin Herlihy, 'The Irish Baptists, 1650–1780' (Ph.D. thesis, University of Dublin, 1992), p. 267.

[49] SP, Ire., 63/287, 183. *Regimental history*, p. 583. The comment on Dobson is Ludlow's, *Memoirs*, ii, 151. Dobson, formerly a lieutenant-colonel, had been appointed as one of the original Athlone Commissioners in 1654, Dunlop, *Commonwealth*, pp. 469–71. He had an appointment in the court of common pleas, *Cal. SP, Ire., 1647–60*, p. 664.

[50] *CJ*, vii, 722. Clarke came to Ireland with a regiment in 1652, served as an Irish MP in Barebone's Parliament in the following year, and seems never to have returned. He was put in command of Dunkirk in August 1659. *Regimental history*, pp. 634–5.

[51] *Regimental history*, pp. 50–3. He was a signatory of the controversial articles for the surrender of Galway. Dunlop, Commonwealth, pp. 163–6.

[52] *CJ*, vii, 717; *Cal. SP, Dom., 1659–60*, pp. 12–13.

[53] *CJ*, vii, 718. *Cal. SP, Dom., 1659–60*, p. 30.

[54] *CJ*, vii, 716. *Regimental history*, pp. 357–8, 446. Ludlow, *Memoirs*, i, 323. 1656 officers list, BL, Add MS 35,102, f. 56.   [55] *CJ*, vii, 716.

Phayre's fellow New English foot colonels were treated with less favour, but also with a significant lack of assurance. The recent conduct of Sir Hardress Waller was severely criticized in committee but the decision on his case was postponed, apparently indefinitely. He was neither confirmed in his place nor superseded, he did not take the oath of engagement, and his position remained ambiguous.[56] The same could not be said of his second in command John Nelson, a Baptist who had been a halberdier at the trial and execution of Charles and was reputed to have declared that he 'would have gone a 1000 miles to have the honour of doing it himself'. He had accompanied Phayre as major on his return to Ireland in 1649, transferred to Reeves's regiment as lieutenant-colonel in the same year and become commander in Kerry and Desmond.[57] Nelson was left in place, but without a new commission, the colonelcy 'not being agreed on'.[58] In the first instance, so too was the regimental major, Ralph Wilson, who had succeeded Ingoldsby as governor of Limerick, but he was subsequently removed. Sir Charles Coote was also subject to criticism in committee, where Lawrence spoke on his behalf, reporting that Coote had said that 'all the favour he ever had was from Parliament, and he would be faithful to them to the uttermost'. He retained his regiment, but he too was not formally confirmed and did not subscribe to the oath.[59] His lieutenant-colonel, William Moore, who was a Baptist, was left in place.[60] Moore's Irish service had earlier been interrupted by a turn of duty in Jamaica where his performance had led his commanding officer to plead for officers from England or Scotland in future 'for those in Ireland onely minde theire great estates there': Moore did indeed have some 2,000 acres in Meath.[61] Major Thomas Davis, who had been stationed in Connacht throughout the 1650s and was listed as a member of a Baptist congrega-

[56] Ludlow, *Memoirs*, ii, 122.
[57] *Cal. SP, Dom., 1659–60*, pp. 12–13. *Cal. SP, Ire., 1647–60*, p. 690. Prendergast papers, iv, 57. *Regimental history*, pp. 447, 655–6, 658. Dunlop, *Commonwealth*, p. 309n. Commonwealth State Accounts, *Analecta Hibernica*, 15, pp. 299–300. Herlihy, 'Baptists in Ireland', p. 257.
[58] *Cal. SP, Dom., 1659–60*, p. 20.
[59] Ibid., pp. 12–13. Coote's horse regiment had been disbanded in 1655. *Regimental history*, p. 617.   [60] Herlihy, 'Baptists in Ireland', pp. 257, 266.
[61] *Regimental history*, pp. 726–7. Commonwealth State Accounts, *Anal. Hib.*, 15, pp. 291–2, 299, 300. TSP, vi, 455. R. Caulfield (ed.), *The council book of the corporation of Kinsale* (Guildford, 1879), pp. 21–2.

tion in Galway in 1653, also retained his post.[62] The regiment of dragoons was left unchanged, with Daniel Abbott, who had commanded it since it came to Ireland in 1649, as colonel and John Desborough, who had been with it for as long, as his major.

In addition to the five changes arising from the replacement of the Cromwells and Fleetwood, thirteen of the remaining forty-three regimental command positions were altered. In the cases of Hewson and Duckenfield, both of whom were heavily involved in England, this was a matter of redeployment rather than displacement: the turnover remains, however, close to 40 per cent, with a quarter of the incumbent senior officers losing their positions. Of the five new colonels appointed (apart from the commander in chief), one was an absentee replacing an absentee in peculiar circumstances, which may reflect English politics: the other four were reinstated Baptist opponents of Henry Cromwell. So far as the army's internal stability was concerned, taking account of the two transfers and four promotions, half of the command positions changed hands. The arrangements were completed by the appointments of Benjamin Worsley as commissary general of musters,[63] Edward Roberts as auditor,[64] Richard Kingdon as judge advocate,[65] Waldine Lagoe as adjutant general,[66] Edward Tomlins as comptroller of the train,[67] Henry Porter as provost-marshal general and, most significantly, Thomas Patient as chaplain to the general officers. Patient, one of the most influential Baptist ministers in Ireland, had been similarly employed when Fleetwood was in control.[68]

---

[62] Herlihy, 'Baptists in Ireland', pp. 257, 265. Ludlow, *Memoirs*, i, 407. Commonwealth records, *Arch. Hib.*, 6, p. 197.   [63] *CJ*, vii, 710.

[64] *CJ*, vii, 710. Roberts was a Baptist. Herlihy, 'Baptists in Ireland', p. 258.

[65] *CJ*, vii, 710, 716. Roberts and Kingdon, with Henry Markham, were commissioners-general of the assessments. Dunlop, *Commonwealth*, p. 459.

[66] *CJ*, vii, 722. He was appointed lieutenant-colonel of Charles Fairfax's foot two weeks later and did not come to Ireland. Greaves and Zeller, *Biographical dictionary of British radicals. Regimental history*, pp. 486–7, 503–4.

[67] Tomlins, who had been a member of a Baptist congregation in Wexford in 1653, had held this post since at least 1656. Commonwealth State Accounts, *Anal. Hib.*, 15, p. 303. Herlihy, 'Baptists in Ireland', p. 266.

[68] Barnard, *Cromwellian Ireland*, pp. 101–12, 146; St John D. Seymour, *The Puritans in Ireland 1649–1661* (Oxford, 1921), pp. 33, 59–60, 88, 125, 127,141. B. R. White, 'Thomas Patient in England and Ireland', *Irish Baptist Historical Society Journal*, 2 (1969–70).

As early as 11 June a newsletter had reported that the 'officers of Ireland' in London had signed a petition requesting that Edmund Ludlow, a leading member of the council of state, should be appointed commander in chief.[69] Ludlow, who had served as a commissioner in Ireland from 1650 to 1654, when he had resigned in protest against the protectorate, and as commander in chief from 1651 to 1655, had joined a Baptist congregation in Dublin in 1654.[70] Formally, his appointment (together with a related appointment as lieutenant general of horse) was recommended by the sub-committee and his name was put to parliament by Arthur Haselrig on behalf of the committee of safety, and approved on 4 July.[71] On 7 July Henry Marten's proposal that Ludlow should be added to the governing commission was defeated by 26 votes to 22.[72] Two days later, Ludlow received his commission from the speaker, together with permission to return to settle his private affairs when army affairs were in good order.[73] A further proposal, made by Haselrig for the council of state on 16 July, that Ludlow be deputed to commission those officers who were unable to receive their commissions from the speaker was also opposed: an amendment giving the responsibility to the civil authority in line with policy in England was accepted, and the commissioners were substituted.[74] On 18 July, Ludlow was formally invested with his new authority by the speaker.[75] No appointment as commander in chief of the foot was made, which left Waller in incongruous occupation of the post.

Ludlow travelled to Ireland with John Jones: on their way, at St Albans on 19 July, they wrote jointly to the speaker to emphasize the importance of the bill for the regularization of land titles: it was, they insisted, 'very much for your service that it be sent over with all possible speed'.[76] In Dublin they were greeted ceremonially by 'the guard that formerly attended Col Cromwell' under the command of Sir Theophilus Jones, who had been major of Ludlow's regiment when it was disbanded in 1655.

[69] *Clarke papers*, iv, 19.
[70] Barnard, *Cromwellian Ireland*, p. 101.   [71] *CJ*, vii, 703.
[72] *CJ*, vii, 707. The tellers for the proposal were Salwey and Neville: against, Haselrig and Reynolds.
[73] Ludlow, *Memoirs*, ii, 94. Ludlow's letter of appointment is in BL, Stowe MS 142.
[74] *CJ*, vii, 721. St Patrick's College, Maynooth; Russell Library, O'Renehan MSS, ii, f. 644 (Richard Bagwell's transcripts from the Commonwealth Records).
[75] *CJ*, vii, 722.   [76] Ludlow, *Memoirs*, ii, 446–7.

The arrival of John Jones made up the quorum and placed the commissioners on a regular footing: they decided to rotate the chairmanship on a monthly basis and arranged for the clerk of the army, John Vernon, at one time an active member of the Baptist community in Ireland, to act as their London agent.[77] For his part, Ludlow convened a meeting of the officers, at which he extolled the parliament and gave assurances that the act dealing with their estates would pass speedily.[78] There was to be no settling in period: almost at once the new regime was plunged into urgent business, for intelligence arrived of problems in the north-west of England, where resistance to the parliament was being mounted by Sir George Booth.

'Booth's rising', which broke out in Lancashire and Cheshire on 1 August, was the only dangerous manifestation of a far more widespread plot, of which the government had ample forewarning, which linked some royalists and presbyterians in an uneasy alliance against the regime, under the direction of the 'Great Trust'. The hope had been to involve Cromwellian officers dismissed in the recent purge, but the only notable convert was Henry Ingoldsby's regicide brother Richard. The strategy did not command a general support: the Sealed Knot itself did not believe (in Manchester's words) in 'restoration by tumult' and was content to wait upon events. The plot's purposes were confused; the partners shared a distaste for the present government, fear for the social and political consequences of its instability, and a conviction that the way was being left open to Baptist and Quaker extremists; but there was no clearcut agreement as to what they wanted to achieve. Though there was little doubt that a successful rising would lead to a restoration, the monarchy did not feature in Booth's public declarations. The unresolved question was what terms would be required of Charles. There was to be no resolution. Booth's rising had never been viable in itself: the success of the scheme had depended upon a multiplicity of outbreaks. On 19 August his troops were defeated with ease by Lambert at Winnington Bridge, four days later he was captured, and the rest was mopping up.

[77] Ibid., 105. Dunlop, *Commonwealth*, p. 700. *TSP*, iv, 314, 327. Vernon had been quartermaster-general in Ireland and retained an estate in Clontarf.
[78] *Memoirs*, ii, 106.

The initial need in Ireland was to guard against related or opportunistic disturbances. Though favoured Dubliners were encouraged to undertake military training and a volunteer force under Captain Stopford was enlisted and armed with pistols, pikes lent to the Dublin militia forces were recalled, a number of people were placed in preventive detention, horses, saddles, arms and ammunition were sought out and secured in the city and its suburbs and vagrants and beggars were expelled.[79] Major Deane was sent to take command of the horse troops in Ulster where the Scots were thought to be the chief royalist security risk.[80] Colonel Cooper was instructed to send Hugh, Viscount Montgomery, who had served as commander in chief in Ulster under Ormond after the second peace, as a prisoner to Dublin.[81] Sir Charles Coote, who had defeated Montgomery at Derry in 1649, was forbidden to leave Dublin. Sir Arthur Forbes was imprisoned in Athlone.[82] Mark Trevor, Francis and Hans Hamilton, Vere Cromwell and Daniel Munroe were ordered to present themselves in person at Dublin.[83] On 5 August the life guard commanded by Theophilus Jones was disbanded, ostensibly and unconvincingly 'for the lessening of the public charge'.[84] Connacht was, of course, the area of greatest danger and orders were issued on 6 August for the arrest of the earls of Clanricarde and Westmeath and more than thirty local and transplanted

[79] Dunlop, *Commonwealth*, pp. 701, 703, 705. *Arch. Hib.*, 7, pp. 34–5. Allen Library, Dublin, Jennings MSS, Box J2, Notebook E. 'Extracts from the Cromwellian Council Books'. BL, Egerton MS 212, A/17, Orders in 1659.
[80] Ludlow, *Memoirs*, ii, 107.
[81] *Montgomery MSS*, pp. 206n, 219. Dunlop, *Commonwealth*, p. 701. Montgomery had been exiled, allowed to return, gaoled, confined to Dublin in 1656 and allowed to compound in 1657. Ibid., pp. 590–1. Commonwealth State Accounts, *Anal. Hib.*, 15, p. 288. He was, in Barnard's words, 'a fervent Royalist who relieved his despondency at the sorry turn in the King's affairs by taking to the bottle'. 'Settling and unsettling Ireland: the Cromwellian and Williamite revolutions', in J. H. Ohlmeyer (ed.), *Ireland from independence to occupation* (Cambridge, 1995), p. 226.
[82] Forbes to Ormond, Granard Papers, PRONI H/1/5/1.
[83] Jennings MSS, Box J2, Transcripts of the Commonwealth records, Notebook E. The arrest of Jeremy Taylor on 11 August may be another instance. He had been summoned to Dublin in June after being delated upon by a Presbyterian rival: 'The greatest scandal being that he christened Mr Bryer's child with the sign of the Cross.' He was soon released and did not go to Dublin until December, when he was dismissed at once. M. H. Nicolson (ed.), *Conway letters* (London, 1930), p. 120. *Rawdon Papers*, p. 196. Reid, *Presbyterian Church*, ii, 236n.   [84] Prendergast papers, ii, 469.

gentlemen in the province.⁸⁵ Two weeks later, Colonel Sadler was instructed to expell 'all the Irish papists' from Galway town and its liberties and the governors of Limerick and Athlone were reminded of the need for a strict enforcement of the licensing controls on those wishing to leave the province.⁸⁶ Proclamations announcing that priests, including those in prison, would be allowed one month in which to leave the country if they gave an undertaking that they would not return were issued on 19 and 23 August.⁸⁷ Some of the government's anxieties may have been well founded. The story that Forbes later told was that during his confinement in Athlone Coote sent his eldest son, Charles, 'to bring me out of prison'. Charles revealed that his father was intending to escape from Dublin, join his forces, which were ready to receive him under the command of Francis Gore, and 'declare something in order to the king's restoration'. Booth's defeat put an end to this plan, and Coote withdrew to Connacht where he consulted with his friends, both at home and further afield, for the promotion of the king's service.⁸⁸ Less dramatically, it was later reported by William Montgomery that when 'Sr Geo. Booth was up in Lancashire, Colo Cromwell (afterwards earl of Ardglass) and Colo Trevor were secretly consulting with our Visct what to do to advance the King's cause'.⁸⁹ Wingfield Cromwell, the earl of Ardglass, was closer to the action: after the rising, he was imprisoned in Staffordshire on suspicion of complicity, 'being a frequent companie Keeper of grand caveleires'.⁹⁰

[85] Dunlop, *Commonwealth*, pp. 702. Westmeath was on the continent, where he was conspiring with the French general Schomberg to have Dunkirk (which was in English possession) delivered to King Charles. *Mordaunt Letter Book*, pp. 39, 64n, 103–4.
[86] Dunlop, *Commonwealth*, pp. 702–3. Hardiman, *The history of the town and county of the town of Galway* (Galway, 1926), p. 144. M. D. O'Sullivan, *Old Galway: the history of a Norman colony in Ireland* (Galway, 1983), p. 344n. Egerton MS 212, A/17.
[87] *Arch. Hib.*, 7, pp. 33–4.
[88] Forbes to Ormond, Granard Papers, PRONI H/1/5/1. Forbes identified Coote's confidants in Connacht as his son Charles, his brother Richard, his cousins Oliver and George St George, Francis Gore and James Cuffe, another cousin, 'with whom he constantly advised', and reported that he corresponded with his brother Chidley, Henry and Theophilus Jones and Dr Ralph King in Dublin 'to the same effect'. The only Irish ex-officer known to have been with Booth, Captain Richard Edmonds (sheriff of Longford and Westmeath in 1656) had been an officer in Chidley Coote's regiment. Dunlop, *Commonwealth*, pp. 633, 705. *Regimental history*, p. 619.
[89] *Montgomery MSS*, pp. 217–19. Vere Cromwell succeeded his nephew Thomas as earl in 1682.   [90] A list of prisoners, Clarendon MS 62, ff. 222–3.

Munster presented different problems. Though Coote's influence in Connacht was considerable, it owed more to his personality and achievement than to his lord presidency and foot regiment and was qualified by the presence of large numbers of malcontent Catholic gentlemen whose potential for trouble may have dictated prudence and certainly attracted close government attention to the affairs of the province. Broghill, though he held no office and commanded only a 'loose company', was the acknowledged master of Munster. His biographer believed that the commissioners were instructed 'to have a particular eye upon Lord Broghill, and to take any occasion of securing him: he being the only person they imagined might practise against their government',[91] and described an encounter, sometime after the arrival of Jones and Ludlow, between Broghill and the commissioners, who told him that they had 'orders to secure him either by confinement or special bonds' and said that if he would not give an assurance that there would be no 'commotions' in Munster he would be held in Dublin Castle. Broghill replied that he could not undertake to prevent disorder unless he was given the authority to preserve peace, and was allowed to return home on his promise to live quietly.[92] When the Booth crisis broke, Ludlow immediately sent for him and two of his officers, Majors Warden and Purdon, 'to require them to give satisfaction touching their acquiescence under the present government',[93] as he later expressed it, passing silently over the unlikely anomaly of a single company staffed by a colonel and two majors. Warden and Purdon had indeed been joint majors in Broghill's horse regiment in the exceptional circumstances of late 1649, an arrangement approved by Oliver Cromwell himself. Warden had subsequently transferred to Ludlow's own regiment, been disbanded in 1653, and settled in Kilkenny.[94] The two men were linked, however, in a warrant issued on 5 August which ordered their arrest on suspicion of having 'been active in a late dangerous design against the Commonwealth and present Government'.[95] Since the proceedings were connected with the arrest of John

---

[91] Morrice, *State letters of the first earl of Orrery*, i, 60.
[92] Ibid., 61–3.   [93] Ludlow, *Memoirs*, ii, 107.
[94] R. Caulfield (ed.), *The council book of the corporation of Youghal* (Guildford, 1878), p. 559. *Regimental history*, pp. 587, 602–4.
[95] Dunlop, *Commonwealth*, p. 701.

Hodges of Kilkenny on a similar charge,[96] ordered almost three weeks earlier, the 'design' evidently had to do with the defence of the protectorate rather than with Booth's rising. It seems likely that they had been associated with Broghill in Henry Cromwell's canvass for support and that Ludlow was both satisfied that the three could be trusted in this crisis and reluctant to challenge the informal apparatus of influence by which Broghill sustained his control over the province. In the event, there were no commotions.

Hyde had some hopes that Booth's action would give rise to 'some stirr in Ireland', but no attempt had been made to promote concerted action and there was little continental control over what happened in England.[97] On 19 August, Ormond confessed to Hyde that he knew 'no more than the Council of State gives their printer licence to tell me'.[98] There had been poorly organized intentions of reinforcing the local risings with the king's troops in Spanish service in Flanders and Charles had left Brussels en route for Brest and, if all went well, Cheshire.[99] Booth's defeat and, more importantly perhaps, the failure of his fellow conspirators to appear 'according to honour given and taken'[100] compelled a reconsideration of the royalist strategy. Charles determined upon a personal intervention in the peace negotiations between France and Spain at Fuenterrabia and made his way to Spain. He did not return to Brussels until Christmas, after the treaty had been concluded without anything to his advantage, and in the meantime the royalist cause busied itself with recrimination.

The Irish dimension did not impinge as dramatically on Booth's rising as he had feared, but only because the main government forces were not otherwise engaged, as they would have been if all had gone according to plan. On 6 August, after a report from a frigate sent to Holyhead in search of information, a foot company was sent to reinforce Beaumaris.[101] Notice, dispatched from London on 30 July, of the requisitioning of a

---

[96] Ibid., p. 699.
[97] Hyde to Samborne, 19 August 1659, Clarendon MS 63, f. 247.
[98] Clarendon MS 63, f. 250v.
[99] Routledge, *The treaty of the Pyrenees*, pp. 52–8. Hyde to Wright, 19 August 1959, Clarendon MS 63, f. 248.   [100] *Clarendon State Papers*, iii, 483, 490, 559.
[101] Dunlop, *Commonwealth*, pp. 701–2. Ludlow, *Memoirs*, ii, 107. Commissioner Jones was still trying to have them returned in December. 'Inedited letters', p. 287.

contingent of 1,000 foot and 500 horse met with reservations, however, partly for the obvious reason that it would reduce protection at a time of possible threats from the Irish and Scots, but also, more rhetorically than persuasively, because of 'the condition of our own forces, who had been debauching for some years for the interest of the commonwealth', and were more in need of relief than fit to give it.[102] Once the political point had been scored, however, the response was efficient. The required numbers were recruited on a voluntary basis, with a promise of two months' pay, half at once, and half on landing in England, as the inducement.[103] On the instructions of Fleetwood overall command was given to Colonel Sankey, who had served in the area during the civil war in the dual roles of captain of horse and chaplain under Sir William Brereton.[104] Axtell, who was anxious to return to England, took charge of the foot regiment. The horse were accompanied by two majors, Godfrey and Bolton, and the foot by three, Rawlings, Bonnell and Walker. Shipping was embargoed to clear the way for transport and the men left in three batches over ten days, the first consisting of 400 men under Walker, the rest following with Sankey and Axtell. Bolton and Rawlings, with 30 soldiers, were drowned on route.[105] The rest of the 'Irish Brigade' had passed through Holyhead before 20 August on their way to north Wales, where Chirk Castle fell to Sankey in the last action of the rising.[106] Informal news of Booth's defeat reached Ireland on 29 August and was confirmed officially on 3 September.[107]

The imperative need to apply all the energies of government to the management of the internal and external demands of the crisis had already led to the adoption of a style of government that was at variance with

---

[102] *Cal. SP, Dom., 1659–60*, p. 54. Dunlop, *Commonwealth*, p. 700. Ludlow, *Memoirs*, ii, 110. The number sent constituted roughly 9% of the foot and 25% of the horse in Ireland, assuming the regiments were at full strength.

[103] *Cal. SP, Ire., 1647–60*, p. 686 [S.P. Ire., 63/287. 168] is a listing of the officers and the numbers of horse [474] and foot [845] sent into England with Sankey and Axtell.

[104] J. S. Morrill, *Cheshire, 1630–1660* (London, 1974), p. 164. J. E. Auden, 'Sir Jerome Zanckey of Balderstone', *Transactions of the Shropshire Archaeological Society*, 1 (1940).

[105] Ludlow, *Memoirs*, ii, 110–13. HMC Portland MSS (10 vols., London, 1891–1931), i, 685–6. *CJ*, vii, 796, 686.

[106] *Clarke Papers*, iv, 43. Davies, *The restoration*, p. 246. Morrill, *Cheshire*, p. 309.

[107] Dunlop, *Commonwealth*, pp. 708–9, 709.

parliament's intention. When the Commons turned down the proposal that Ludlow should deputize for the speaker in the commissioning of officers and rejected the move to make him a commissioner they were following the principle that was at the heart of their policy in England, that the civil authority must have primacy. In fact, Ludlow himself was one of those who had reservations about this hardline approach: he had opposed the transfer of commissioning authority to the speaker in England on the grounds that collaboration between parliament and army was more appropriate than confrontation.[108] Lenthall's letter appointing him lieutenant general of horse and commander in chief, however, made his subordinate position plain, requiring him 'to observe and follow orders and directions' not only from parliament itself and the council of state, but also from the commissioners in Dublin.[109] These English niceties had little relevance to Ireland, where the interdependence of government and army had become very close since Henry's departure, and the practice did not honour the intention. Soon after his arrival, the commissioners invited Ludlow to join them informally to facilitate the management of the crisis, which was prolonged in Ireland by fears of imminent invasion from Spain and by the heightened activities of tories.[110] Rumours of a plot to massacre the English in Wicklow led to the disarming of the local Irish in early September and were followed by alarms and disturbances in Kildare, Kilkenny, Wexford and Waterford.[111] Limerick became a particular cause of concern, as a bulwark between the Catholics of Clare and the Protestants of Munster: a proclamation required the expulsion of Catholics from the town by 20 October and orders were issued to repair the city gates, change the locks and demolish neighbouring castles.[112] The corporation of Fethard in Tipperary was suspended and the corporation of Dublin was ordered to choose godly and loyal men for municipal office.[113] In October, Pretty, Deane and Nelson were given special three-month commissions authorizing them to raise and arm local forces to seek and destroy tories in

[108] Scott, *Algernon Sidney and the English Republic*, p. 127.
[109] BL, Stowe MS 142, 12 July 1659.
[110] Ludlow, *Memoirs*, ii, 105. Dunlop, *Commonwealth*, p. 710. Egerton MS 212, A/26. O'Renehan MSS, ii, f. 652.
[111] Prendergast papers, ii, 445, 453, 454–5, 455–6, 464.
[112] Prendergast papers, ii, 465. Jennings MSS, Box J2, Notebook E.
[113] Egerton MS 212, A/17.

Carlow, Kilkenny, King's County and Queen's County.[114] In short, crisis conditions continued and normality proved unattainable. The legitimacy of authority remained at issue, with the courts of justice in suspension, the legal basis of local administration unsure, the equity of recent parliamentary taxation in dispute, and the discontent of recently cashiered officers adding dangerously to the ranks of the disaffected. With symbolic aptness, the government even lacked an official seal to validate its transactions.[115] Inexorably, civil and military authority became indistinguishable and the role of the commissioners was largely confined to assisting Ludlow to maintain security.

The emergency created by Booth's rising had impeded Ludlow's intention to continue with 'new modelling', and it was not the only distraction. The routine professional side of his duties also interfered with his political purpose. When he arrived, he found the army more than a year in arrears of pay,[116] and the musters some five months out of date.[117] Figures given to the English parliament had indicated that the arrears due when the commissioners took over in June amounted to some £262,000 and that a further £150,000 would be needed to meet charges falling due before 1 December. The former estimate proved optimistic, if not politically motivated, and it was quickly revised upward, to £333,000: that figure, which represented thirteen months' pay, was roughly accurate.[118] It was a simple matter to order new musters, and this was done on 2 August.[119] The financial problems were less tractable. Though Ludlow himself had been canny enough to request that the responsibility for pay should be attached to the commissioners, rather than to himself as commander in chief, the problem was not one that he could avoid.[120] On the eve of his departure

---

[114] Prendergast papers, ii, 451.

[115] Dunlop, *Commonwealth*, p. 710. The act of 14 May 1659 had legislated only for the Great Seal of the Commonwealth of England. *Acts and ordinances*, ii, 1271. The question of the Irish seal was not dealt with until February 1660. Ibid., 1421.

[116] Ludlow, *Memoirs*, ii, 448.

[117] The musters used for the Cheshire expedition dated from the previous spring.

[118] *CJ*, vii, 678, 737. An earlier estimate had put the arrears at £371,000 at the end of March. The pay budget was £25,608 per month, ibid., pp. 660, 737. Expenditure in Ireland annually was £346,000 and the income £208,000.

[119] Dunlop, *Commonwealth*, p. 701.

[120] Ludlow, *Memoirs*, ii, 102, 103. *CJ*, vii, 721. Rawlinson MS C, 179, f. 146. Instructions to the commissioners, Article 15. Carte MS 67, ff. 307–10.

for Ireland the council of state had decided to subvent the pay budget by two instalments of £8,000 from English resources, the first to be paid at once and the second in October.[121] Cash flow problems were eased by a warrant to draw £30,000 from the treasurers of war in England and the commissioners and the council of officers agreed that one month's pay should be issued on both the old and the new musters. Ludlow was unwilling to waste precious resources on men who were no longer in service and insisted that only those presently under arms should be paid. The officers were prepared to consent on condition that parliament give assurances that church, crown and other lands would be allocated to paying the arrears, but the condition seems not to have been sanctioned and the matter remained unresolved.[122] Ludlow was busy also with making sure that the regiments were properly equipped and restocking garrisons with provisions and ammunition.[123] In September, he and the commissioners turned their attention to implementing the council of state's advice that, as in England, so in Ireland, militia forces should be organized in each county.[124] County committees were established to enlist and arm volunteers, in Wicklow with arms taken from the Irish, elsewhere from government stores, and Ludlow later claimed to have created a body 'as considerable as the army itself', consisting for the most part of experienced army men who were willing to make the declaration of fidelity to the commonwealth, 'without a single Person, King-ship, or House of Peers', known as the 'engagement'.[125] The indications are that Ludlow was less successful than he supposed. The captain of horse in Wexford, Robert Thornhill, was a cashiered officer, lapsed Baptist and author of a congratulatory petition to Richard Cromwell in which he had asserted that Oliver 'is canonized in Heaven for his works sake'.[126]

Ludlow's first priority had been to continue the purge that had begun in London, by scrutinizing the captains and lower commissioned officers and

---

[121] Rawlinson MS C, 179, ff. 189–90.   [122] Ludlow, *Memoirs*, ii, 105–6, 447–8.
[123] Ibid., 116. Dunlop, *Commonwealth*, pp. 707, 708–9. Jennings MSS, Box J2, Notebook E.
[124] Ludlow, *Memoirs*, ii, 116. CJ, vii, 764. Cal. SP, Dom., 1659–60, p. 157. Dunlop, *Commonwealth*, pp. 709–10.
[125] Prendergast papers, ii, 464. Dunlop, *Commonwealth*, p. 713. Jennings MSS, Box J2, Notebook E. The Engagement was the oath required of beneficiaries of the act of indemnity and general pardon. *Acts and ordinances*, ii, 1304.
[126] Prendergast papers, ii, 457–8.

making recommendations to the committee.[127] He was reinforced in his resolution by what he observed of his new command: the officers fell below his moral standards and he believed that some were withholding their soldiers' pay. Above all, he found them 'debauched in their principles by the late usurpation of the Cromwells'. With the assistance of some members of the subcommittee for nominations who had joined him in Ireland, he busied himself with drawing up fresh lists which incorporated the established policy of getting rid of those regarded as incorrigible and replacing them where possible with men who had previously been cashiered because of their attachment to parliament.[128] The alternative view was that he was 'preferring men of parboild & hare-braind principles & layeing aside persons of knowne integritie and faithfullnesse, without soe much as giving them a reason for it'.[129] A simple test had been laid down by parliament, which required both newly commissioned and recommissioned officers to subscribe to the engagement. Those who refused to do so were to be removed. Those who were affected by the purge described a rather different procedure, involving the use of 'several persons in every corner of the Nation, to pick up informations against them, without hearing them speak for themselves, or acquainting them by whom, or for what they were accused'.[130] That this was not an entirely fanciful rendering of what took place is suggested by a certificate submitted in September by the sheriff of Tipperary and the mayor and officers of Clonmel, defending a locally based lieutenant against the charge of being a common tippler, and affirming that he was 'a person of very civil deportment and a constant frequenter of the public worship of God'.[131] The evidence does not allow any estimate to be made of the numbers cashiered, though a total of 200 was later alleged, but it is clear that the purge was a wide-ranging one. It probably began with the members of the expeditionary force to England, since the quarter-master who died when the *Sea Flower* was lost had just been reinstated after dismissal from the life guard

---

[127] *Cal. SP, Ire., 1647–60*, p. 690.
[128] Bridges et al., *A perfect narrative*, p. 4. Ludlow, *Memoirs*, ii, 117.
[129] *Cal. SP, Ire., 1647–60*, p. 712. S.P., Ire., 63/303. 13. The accuser was Thomas Scot.
[130] *The declaration of Sir Charles Coot Lord President of Connaught, and of the Officers and Souldiers under his command* (London, 1660).
[131] *Cal. SP, Ire., 1647–60*, p. 691.

'for refusing to address the late Single Person'.[132] It extended from the systematic replacement of garrison commanders,[133] many of whom had escaped the original scrutiny because they were unregimented, to the dismissal of a lieutenant for 'deboistness' and the impolitic ousting of Monck's cousin in favour of the cornet whose place he had taken, who had been put out for disrespect towards Richard Cromwell.[134] In legal form, the victims of the purge were merely suspended, for parliament had reserved the power of dismissal to itself, but the distinction was without practical significance and may not have been fully understood.[135] Ludlow's particular brief had been to review the junior officers, but the process went further: on 7 September, an inquiry was initiated into 'the principles and practices of private soldiers'.[136] The professed aim was to discover soldiers who had married Irish papists or who 'having formerly been Popish Recusants (notwithstanding that they pretend to be Protestants) may justly be suspected to continue Papists', but it was later alleged that private soldiers had also been cashiered for political reasons.[137]

The purge seems not to have been confined to the military. Opponents later traced the steps by which an extremist group had allegedly 'gained almost a Supremacie of power in Ireland', taking control of the principal garrisons, the county militias, 'and even the management also of civil things, as to sheriffs, justices of the peace &c'.[138] Just as Ludlow was later said, with some justice, to have appointed 'Annabaptists, and persons of the like fanattique spiritts',[139] Steele was said to have used his office as lord chancellor to discountenance ministers, and even the ministry itself, by

[132] Ludlow, *Memoirs*, ii, 447.
[133] Ludlow's intrusions included Arnop in Enniskillen, Brayfield in Athlone, Desborough in Drogheda, Nelson in Limerick, Aland in Passage, Skinner in Duncannon, Puckle in Ross and Richards in Wexford.
[134] *Cal. SP, Ire., 1647–60*, p. 700, i.e. debauchery: the noun form is not in OED. The dismissed officer was related to the Cromwells, but the fact that 'his wayes are such as are not well pleasing to the Lord and good men' had come to his father's attention some months previously. Henry Whalley to Henry Cromwell, 15 March 1659, Lansdowne MS 823, f. 253. [135] Instructions to the Commissioners, Carte MS 67, f. 310.
[136] Ludlow, *Memoirs*, ii, 117. Dunlop, *Commonwealth*, pp. 711–12.
[137] *Declaration of Sir Charles Coot*.
[138] Bridges et al., *A perfect narrative*, pp. 3, 4. Cf. *HMC Portland MSS*, i, 688–9.
[139] *The declaration of Sir Charles Coote and the rest of the Council of Officers*. Feb 16 [1660] (London, 1659[60]).

casting out 'honest men' from the commission of the peace and putting in Baptists and Quakers instead.[140] The rationale offered by parliament's agents was indignantly repudiated on the grounds that those who had 'once adhered to the Single Person' were not enemies of parliament: all that they had done in 'the owning that power' was what everyone had done 'in the generality of the three Nations'.[141] Ludlow himself, indeed, was quoted as having told a meeting of the officers in Dublin 'that, of all parties, he knew none more guilty, nor more to be blamed for that defection, then the Anabaptists'.[142] Though these things were said after the event, there is little reason to doubt their testimony to the prevalence of change and the reactions it provoked.

The commissioners themselves were profoundly worried by the widespread interruption of the administration of justice. As early as 25 May, when Bury was leaving for London, Henry Cromwell and his council had warned Fleetwood 'how needful it is that timely care and provision be made for the proceedings of justice in this nation'.[143] Parliament had already sought to remedy this on 11 May by passing a general act authorizing justices of the peace and sheriffs in post to continue to function.[144] In Ireland this proved to be neither wholly effective nor sufficient to deal with the wider problem: in some parts of the country the justices of the peace ceased to act, and the courts of justice did not open for the Midsummer Term, so that private suits could not be pursued, wills could not be proved nor letters of administration issued, the trial of felons could not proceed, and certain kinds of public business could not be processed.[145] The situation provoked a practical protest against the lack of 'means for the recovering of their just debts and estates' and a sharper edged demand that the courts should be 'continued according to law, the birthright of every Englishman'.[146] The situation was, at the least, embar-

---

[140] *HMC Leyborne Popham MSS* (London, 1899), p. 141.

[141] Bridges et al., *A perfect narrative*, pp. 2–3.

[142] *Ireland's fidelity to the parliament of England, in answer to a paper, entitled The petition of the officers and soldiers of Duncannon* (London, 1660).

[143] Dunlop, *Commonwealth*, p. 696.

[144] *Acts and ordinances*, ii, 1270.

[145] *Cal. SP, Ire., 1647–60*, pp. 691–2. S.P., Ire., 287.182. Instructions to Lieutenant General Ludlow, Stowe MS 142, f. 136. Dunlop, *Commonwealth*, p. 710.

[146] *The humble petition and representation of the despoiled Protestants of Ireland*.

rassing: a government which insisted that those who claimed that its orders infringed their property rights must proceed 'by due course of law' and at the same time 'layd aside' the means of doing so could not easily defend itself against the charge of arbitrary conduct.[147] Some minor alleviation was offered in August, when parliament approved the form of various commissions requested for use in Ireland, for Oyer, Terminer, Gaol Delivery and the determination of civil causes, and dispatched them under the new great seal of England.[148] A well-informed contemporary, however, believed that those named in the commissions 'did not think fit to act thereupon'.[149] At the urgent request of the commissioners, a committee made up of the leading members of the English council of state considered the larger problem and recommended on 5 September that parliament should be asked to deal with it.[150] It was not until 5 October that this was done, and the response was entirely predictable. The house simply referred the matter back to the council for a specific recommendation, and asked particularly that nominations to judgeships be brought forward.[151] The result was that when Michaelmas Term came round the courts remained closed and the commissioners decided to suspend payment of judicial salaries until instructions from parliament were received.[152] By that time, a further inconvenience had been disclosed. The commissions for determining disputes arising from the division of land among the soldiers, which derived from powers conferred upon the commander in chief by an act of parliament 'made since the interruption',

---

[147] Dunlop, *Commonwealth*, p. 699. *Declaration of Sir Charles Coot.*   [148] *CJ*, vii, 764.

[149] *A sober vindication of Lieutenant General Ludlow, and others. In answer to a printed letter sent from Sir Hardress Waller in Ireland, and other non-commissioned Officers at Dublin to Lt. General Ludlow at Duncannon, Commander in chief of all the Parliament's forces in Ireland* (London, 1659[60]), p. 8.

[150] The special committee (for Irish and Scottish affairs) was appointed by the council of state on 29 August to consider matters raised in a letter of 17 August from the commissioners: it consisted of Harrington, Thompson, Morley, Scot, Wariston, Fleetwood, Vane, Lambert, Walton, Salway, Barners, Haselrig and Desborough, or any three of them. The committee also recommended that officers should return to their posts in Ireland, that troops and companies should be filled up and that a militia should be raised. *Cal. SP, Dom.*, 1659–60, p. 157; Dunlop, *Commonwealth*, pp. 709–10; Ludlow, *Memoirs*, ii, 116n.   [151] *CJ*, vii, 791–2.

[152] Dunlop, *Commonwealth*, pp. 708, 709–10, 710. *Cal. SP, Ire.*, 1647–60, pp. 691–2. W. H. Hardinge, 'Manuscript census returns of the people of Ireland', *RIA trans.*, 24 (1873), p. 322.

were void: it required an act of the present parliament to enable them to resume.[153]

A few days before the commissioners assumed power in Ireland, on 18 June, parliament had ordered that the collection of the monthly assessment 'already imposed by pretence of parliamentary authority' should go ahead from 24 June, but with the major modification that half of the entire annual sum should be raised before 1 August and the remainder before 10 October. Ireland's share of the £50,000 required each month was set at £9,000 and the commissioners were instructed to oversee the levy.[154] These arrangements were not merely unwelcome in themselves, but raised an important and politically sensitive point of principle. An ordinance of 23 June 1654, giving effect to assurances contained in the 1653 act of settlement, had undertaken that after 24 June 1659 the level of tax assessments in Ireland would be the same as those in England.[155] It could not now be claimed that the promise had force, though it was argued by self-styled 'despoiled Protestants of Ireland' that the original act had been based 'upon the Ground-work of a Bill prepared by this present Parliament'. In a petition dated 1 September, which was prompted by a proposal to double the assessment in the following year,[156] they protested inability to pay, requested either a return to collection by monthly instalments or acceptance of payment in kind, and spelled out the present 'unequal measure' in detail. The city of Dublin paid £720 a quarter, while Norwich, Bristol and Gloucester together paid only £780 'whereas the worst of the three is near as good as Dublin': at a total of £6,899 a quarter, Antrim, Down, Galway and Tipperary together paid more than ten English counties, 'whereas Rutland or Durham exceeds the best of those four in Ireland'. Indeed, they thought 'it easy to name fourty parishes in England not including London of more value than the thirty two counties in Ireland'. They feared that an increase to £21,600 a month was imminent, 'which would even swallow up the whole rent of Ireland', and

[153] Judge Santhy to Ludlow, 17 October 1659, Stowe MS 185, f. 141.
[154] *Acts and ordinances*, ii, 1284–6.
[155] Ibid., 925. The 1654 ordinance had been modified by an assessment ordinance of June 1657 which had reduced the Irish contribution to £9,000. Ibid., ii, 1243–5. In April 1658 Henry Cromwell had described the assessments as '10 times more than in due proportion they ought to be'. *TSP*, vii, 72.
[156] A bill to that effect received its first reading on 29 August. *CJ*, vii, 770–1.

pleaded, in the same words from the Book of Genesis that had been used by the Irish parliament in a petition to the English parliament in 1640, that 'that poor Nation, who are now generally English, bone of your bone, and flesh of your flesh', should be taxed proportionately.[157] All five of the predominantly Dublin based office-holding group associated with the organization of the petition had been members of that parliament. Their solicitation of subscriptions 'for defraying the charges of Mr Annesley's agency in England for the Protestants' indicates that they were using the services of Arthur Annesley, Lord Mountnorris's son, to press their case.[158] The attendant organization had included an authorization to Annesley by a group of Protestants in Cork in July 'to supplicate reliefe in the several petitions already transmitted to him, or to be transmitted to him'.[159] In one sense, the choice was an obvious one: in the last protectorate parliament, Annesley, representing Dublin, had spoken forcefully against the inequitable taxation of Ireland and reminded the members that those he represented 'are your own flesh'. Politically, it was less apt: as one of the ten secluded members who had noisily asserted their right to sit in parliament in May, another of whom was Sir George Booth, Annesley was far from being well regarded by the members of the rump.[160] There is no record of the petition having been received by parliament.

The commissioners, who had appointed a commission to consider the public revenue, identified three ways in which it might be improved.[161] The first and most promising was in the collection of excise and customs taxes, but they were under the disadvantage that the system was admin-

---

[157] *To the Parliament of the Common-wealth of England, Scotland and Ireland. The humble petition and representation of the despoiled Protestants of Ireland* (London, 1659). For related petitions, see SP, Ire., 63/287. 192; BL, Add. MS 32,471, f. 83v.

[158] *Egmont MSS*, ii, pt. ii, 610. The five were Lord Ranalagh, William Ussher, Paul Davis, John Bysse and William Dixon. Mountnorris, Ulster planter, sometime secretary of state for Ireland and vice-treasurer, was famously sentenced to death by the Irish council of war in 1635.   [159] Prendergast papers, xiii, 477–8.

[160] Annesley, who had joined the Long Parliament as recruiter member for Radnorshire in 1647, was one of the parliamentary commissioners to whom Ormond handed over Dublin in 1647 and had signed the order replacing the Book of Common Prayer with the Directory of Worship. Russell and Prendergast, *Account*, p. 104. When he petitioned for his father's former place as secretary of state in 1658, Henry Cromwell testified that he was well affected to Oliver, 'as also very friendly to myself'. TSP, vi, 777.

[161] Dunlop, *Commonwealth*, pp. 698–9.

stered under contract by a financial consortium and they had no authority to regulate it.[162] For political reasons, they favoured both a reduction in the duty on cattle from 6/8d to 2/- or 2/6d, which 'would exceedingly help the plantacion' and probably not affect the returns because of increased trade, and the introduction of an equitable appeal procedure against the decisions of the farmers. For financial reasons, they wanted a system of staple towns to prevent the illegal export of wool, a reduction in the rates on textile manufactures imported from England,[163] and the setting of fixed rates for commodities not listed in the book of rates. The second possibility was to eliminate 'the subtilties and delayes' of the traditional system of revenue collection by introducing 'receivers' to perform the role of the sheriffs and other county officers. The third was to try to make good the revenue lost since 1653 as a result of the undervaluation of land and the conferring of grants without an adequate return to the state by insisting that the 'Disposition of all lands' should be reviewed before they were confirmed, except 'what hath been duly sett out to Adventurers and soldiers or their assigns'. It took time to develop these ideas, all of which required parliamentary action, and the commissioners did no more than make them ready for submission when the time came.[164] In the meantime, protestors asked rhetorically 'is it not very hard that whilst one Commonwealth with England we are reputed as foreigners to our native country's trade?'[165]

Parliament continued to set aside time for the transaction of Irish business. The bill dealing with the lands of the adventurers and soldiers was reported upon, twice read, extensively discussed, and effectively recommitted in the last weeks of August.[166] This protracted treatment did not arise

---

[162] The custom on tonnage and poundage and the excise on all native and foreign commodities in Ireland had been leased in 1658 for seven years, for £70,000 a year, to William Dodson, John Drury and Thomas Morrice. *Cal. SP, Dom., 1657-8*, p. 113. *Cal. SP, Ire., 1647-60*, p. 678.

[163] Free trade in these goods (provided they were not reexported) was introduced by parliament in March 1660, but in the interests of English manufacturers rather than of Irish consumers. *Acts and ordinances*, ii, 1416-17, 1423-4.

[164] 'Instructions to Lieutenant Generall Ludlow', Stowe MS 142, ff. 136-8.

[165] Arguments against increasing the assessment of Ireland and for continuing supplies from England for support of the army in Ireland, PRO, SP, Ire., 63/287. 192.

[166] *CJ*, vii, 752, 759, 761, 763, 767, 770.

from reservations about confirming what had been done, but from the need to protect the interests of adventurers and creditors whose outstanding claims had been referred to the Commons committee early in July, and perhaps also from the intense lobbying by which it was accompanied.[167] An enabling clause, with a proviso that the unsatisfied should have satisfaction after the adventurers and soldiers had been dealt with was agreed on 29 August.[168] On 3 September, the powers of the commissioners were continued for a further six months 'and no longer',[169] and over the following two weeks the estates bill was before the House again on four occasions. These continued discussions concerned special cases rather than matters of substance, and the bill was referred back to be prepared for engrossment on 17 September.[170] Petitions continued to arrive, however, and the House entertained them. Further delay was assured when they were referred to the committee for consideration on 5 October.[171]

The atmosphere created by the new administration, whose assault on political deviance was associated with a rejection of the relatively conservative religious arrangements instituted by Henry Cromwell, imparted renewed energy to the religious radicals and revived the influence of the Independents. After Henry Cromwell's disengagement from the Independents in the previous year, Samuel Winter, the provost of Trinity College and acknowledged leader of the Independents, had busied himself with the organization of a 'brotherly association' of Independent churches in Dublin and Leinster which reached terms of agreement in February 1659. These envisaged a system of regular meetings of ministers and elders to maintain unity and resolve differences, and decreed that ministers were not to become involved in civil and commonwealth affairs. Following the example of English Independents, who had adopted a Declaration of Faith in the previous October, both the Westminster Confession (allowing, as their English fellows had not, for some difference of opinion about 'a few

---

[167] *Mercurius Politicus*, 30 June–7 July. Colonels Barrow, Lawrence and Sankey took an active interest in the act, according to Petty, *Down Survey*, p. 81. One of its clauses, dated 16 July, validating decrees and judgements on claims issued by the court of claims, the exchequer and the council table, together with compositions entered into on foot of the ordinance of indemnity for Irish Protestants of September 1654, is in Clarendon MS 62, f. 140. Since it is Annesley's copy, the implication is that he was lobbying on this issue as well as on taxation.

[168] *CJ*, vii, 770   [169] *CJ*, vii, 773.   [170] *CJ*, vii, 774ff.   [171] *CJ*, vii, 792.

expressions touching Discipline') and the Westminster catechisms were approved. The approach was in one respect providentially circumspect: although the agreement both affirmed the validity of infant baptism and condemned an assortment of heresies (including Socinianism, Seekerism, Quakerism, Antiscripturism and Erastianism as well as Popery, Prelacy and Arminianism), Anabaptism was not among them. It was later claimed that fear was the reason for this omission, and the tone of the agreement is certainly defensive, the work of men who 'saw themselves as the elect of God living in the midst of enemies'.[172] On the other hand, there was little reason to fear the Baptists in the spring of 1659 and it is likely enough that the reticence of the Independents reflected some sort of general *modus vivendi* in the face of conservative advance. With Henry's departure, the policy returned dividends. An Independent minister, Edward Jenner, was appointed chaplain to the Irish Brigade in August and Winter was entrusted with finding his replacement in Drogheda.[173] When a Kildare minister was discharged for malignity to parliament at the end of August, he was replaced by a New England minister whose point of contact was Samuel Mather.[174] When an order was issued for a day of prayer and fasting on 31 August, Winter, Mather and their associate Enoch Grey were deputed 'to carry on the work'.[175] And when Winter was ordered by parliament in the same month to attend the pleasure of the House, apparently in connection with the affairs of the university, Ludlow requested that the order should not take effect, invoking not only 'the earnest desire' of Winter's congregation and 'many other Christians in this place', but also 'the knowledge I have of his usefulness here'.[176]

---

[172] *The agreement and resolution of the ministers of Christ associated within the city of Dublin and the province of Leinster* (Dublin, 1659); A. G. Matthews (ed.), *The Savoy declaration of faith and order* (London, 1959); Phil Kilroy, *Protestant dissent and controversy in Ireland* (Cork, 1994), p. 90. The copy of *The agreement* in the National Library of Ireland contains annotations by John Brereton, a prebend of St Patrick's, who had heard it read from the pulpit in Waterford, where it was presented as an instrument to reconcile Presbyterians and Independents: noting the failure to condemn Anabaptism, he commented that 'truely at that time the Anabaptists had gott the Masterie almost over both'. Title page, verso, and p. 3.   [173] Dunlop, *Commonwealth*, p. 704.

[174] Seymour, *Puritans in Ireland*, p. 175. Greaves and Zeller, *Biographical dictionary of British radicals*, sub William Aspinwall.   [175] Jennings MSS, Box J2, Notebook E.

[176] Seymour, *Puritans in Ireland*, pp. 215, 175–6. Dunlop, *Commonwealth*, p. 704. *CJ*, vii, 757. Ludlow to Lenthall, 14 September 1659, Carte MS 67, ff. 283v–84.

The regime had more intimate allies than Winter, however. At a meeting in Chichester House on 12 September, the Church of Christ, whose welcoming address to parliament had been received on the same day in June as that of the Independents, approved Thomas Hickes as a person fully qualified to preach and to dispense the gospel. Though Hickes had been on the civil list since 1655, serving first in Drogheda and then in Ballinasloe, it was specifically on foot of this approval from the headquarters of the Dublin Baptists that the commissioners appointed him to preach in Stillorgan and throughout the barony of Rathdown, 'as often as the Lord shall enable him and in such places as the Lord shall make his Ministry most effective'.[177] The implication seems plain: a new mechanism for the screening of ministerial appointments was being employed, at least for insiders, of whom Hickes was undoubtedly one. He was, it was alleged, one of Edmund Ludlow's closest confidants,[178] while Colonel Desborough had been his patron in Ballinasloe and Stillorgan was in the possession of Commissioner Jones's brother, Major Henry Jones.

The regard in which Winter was held by the commissioners did not extend to his provostship. Throughout the decade, the college had been close to the centre of the religious policy of a regime which valued a learned ministry and needed a seminary to create it. Winter had been provost since 1651, and Henry Cromwell had been installed as chancellor in place of Ormond in 1654. Though Winter had done much to revitalize the college, not least by introducing a competent staff, and it had recovered steadily from the collapse of the 1640s, the entire thrust of his policy had been the promotion of Independency. At first, that had been somewhat against the grain, because of resistance from within and lukewarm official favour from a regime which was more radically inclined, but after 1655 Winter had had a free hand for some years, during which he acted in effect as the official leader of government religious policy, and was able to pack the fellowship body with congenial members. His displacement from influence in 1658, when Henry Cromwell transferred his patronage to the alliance between conservative presbyterians and former episcopalians led by Edward Worth in Cork, had threatened his position in Trinity, but failed to unseat him.[179] The commissioners, who

---

[177] Prendergast papers, ii, 704, 706.   [178] See p. 134 below.
[179] Barnard, *Cromwellian Ireland*, pp. 198–206.

shared the radical distrust of universities, represented a different kind of threat to his position, but as great a one: they took the firm view that those who managed the College needed to be called to account and that the act of 1649 which had reconstituted its government needed to be revised both to allow that to be done and because it was not 'suitable or sufficient for carrying on the intent of the Parliament therein'.[180]

In England, the suppression of Booth's rebellion gave parliament and army the confidence to pursue their previously muted disagreements to the point of crisis. On 22 September the victorious army presented parliament with the menacing 'Derby petition' (drafted by a committee of three, of whom Hierome Sankey was one) which protested against both the arrangements for the command of the army and the failure to prepare for dissolution. In Scotland, Monck declined to support this petition and wrote to the speaker encouraging the house to resist it. Parliament rejected the petition and ordered Fleetwood to admonish the officers for their behaviour. The army response was delayed until 5 October when an intransigent second petition was delivered. Parliament's discussion of the matter was heavily informed by a sense of the probability that a further expulsion was contemplated: to obstruct this, and to construct a framework of total illegality for a new regime, a bill was passed on 11 October which both made it high treason to levy a tax without parliamentary consent and voided all 'patents, grants, acts and ordinances' issued since 19 April 1653, except those that had been specifically approved by the present house. Mordaunt believed that the decision to confront the army was influenced by the fact that Ludlow 'was supposed to have settled Ireland so well to their purpose' and certainly Ireland was not forgotten: the bill included a proviso that the voiding clause should not be taken 'to interrupt the Possession of any Soldier or Adventurer, or any Purchaser, their heirs or assigns, in Possession of any lands or Hereditaments in Ireland'.[181] Learning that the army leaders were soliciting further signatures to their petition, the house then cashiered the nine officers involved, annulled Fleetwood's commission, and placed control of the army in the hands of seven commissioners, including the officers in command in each

[180] 'Instructions to Lieutenant Generall Ludlow', Stowe MS 142, f. 137.
[181] Carte, *Collection*, ii, 246. *Acts and ordinances*, ii, 1352.

of the three countries: Fleetwood, Ludlow and Monck. Confrontation resulted: on 13 October the army prevented the House from meeting. The council of state stayed in defiant existence until 25 October. By that time, the army council had proposed a committee of safety to replace it, which sought to bring into partnership with the army those who were prepared to work with it to achieve a settlement. The new government took office on 26 October. Among those invited to join it were Commissioner Steele and Edmund Ludlow.

The Derby petition reached Ireland in late September, sent by Sankey, and almost certainly by Axtell also, with the request that it be submitted to the officers for their concurrence.[182] A meeting of the officers from the Dublin area unanimously rejected it and passed a resolution acknowledging that the supreme authority of the nation lay in the parliament. This was sent at once to Haselrig, with the promise of a fully developed declaration to follow, 'to encourage our friends, as to discourage our enemies in England'.[183] Ludlow had already been given leave by parliament to return to England,[184] and news of what was happening in London quickened his preparations. There were several difficulties to resolve, and he cut corners in dealing with them. In the first place, he had not completed his 'new modelling' arrangements, which had been further complicated by the need to find acting replacements for the two colonels and five majors who had left with the Irish Brigade.[185] He had a 'black List', as a critic called it,[186] ready for the committee for nominations to present to parliament, but he was unwilling to await the legalities and acted on his own authority to cashier those who 'gave the greatest cause of suspicion' and substitute others 'in whom I might best confide, and who had given evident proof of their affection to the public'.[187] Second, he needed to find a deputy to fill

[182] The officers inviting Monck's support included Axtell as well as Sankey. *Clarke Papers*, iv, 67–8.

[183] Ludlow, *Memoirs*, ii, 119–21. Though it has not survived, the declaration seems to have been sent. Ibid., ii, 124.

[184] *Cal. SP, Ire., 1647–60*, p. 691. SP, Ire., 63/287. 181, 182. Bramble to Hyde, *c.* 9 Oct. 1659, Clarendon MS 65, ff. 3–4.

[185] For practical purposes, the establishment was also short of the four colonels, one lieutenant-colonel and one major who had not come to Ireland.

[186] *Ireland's fidelity*.   [187] Ludlow, *Memoirs*, ii. 121.

his own position. That raised problems, because the senior officer was Sankey, who was neither in Ireland nor politically reliable, and next in line came Waller, whom Ludlow believed to be an opportunist and who in any event had not been confirmed in his command. His own inclination had been to empower the commissioners to act for him, but Fleetwood was opposed and after consulting 'with sundry officers of the army now at the head Quarters' Ludlow compromised by recommending that his command should be delegated to Commissioner Jones.[188] He took the trouble to mollify Waller by telling him that Jones had been chosen so that Sankey could be by-passed. Significantly, the other man who was singled out for special attention was Sir Charles Coote, and Ludlow was well pleased with the outcome. Coote's only concerns seemed to be that he should retain his presidency of Connacht, and be confirmed in both his commands, for he had a 'loose company' of horse as well as his foot regiment. He promised elaborately to serve the parliament,

> all that he enjoyed being derived from their authority; and that as he had opposed the late king in his arbitrary designs, so he would continue to act in conformity to those actions, well knowing that if the son should happen to prevail, the English interest would be lost in Ireland, and the Irish restored to the possession of their lands, according to an agreement passed between them.

Ludlow undertook to do his best in Coote's interests, and he went back to his charge.[189]

A letter from Fleetwood, written in formal compliance with parliament's order to prevent promotion of the Derby petition, revealed the increasing gravity of the situation and Colonel Lawrence urged Ludlow to make haste, arguing that Ireland was secure, and he might do more good in England. In retrospect, Ludlow was in no doubt that Lawrence was in league with the officers in England and wanted him out of the way. There were still some awkward difficulties to be overcome. Commissioner Thomlinson opposed the transfer of authority to Jones as *ultra vires*, and was outvoted. Steele wanted to accompany Ludlow, but was dissuaded. Finally, having ceremonially inspected the Dublin militia, 1,200 foot and

[188] SP, Ire., 63/287. 181.
[189] Ludlow, *Memoirs*, ii, 122–4.

120 horse, all of whom had taken the engagement, Ludlow was seen off by Jones, Waller, and 'my good friend' Chief Justice Cook on 18 October.[190]

Ludlow carried with him a set of instructions in which the commissioners reviewed the difficulties that they had encountered in conducting their duties and proposed courses of action. The need for something to be done about the administration of justice featured once again and the need to do something about Trinity College was broached; the possibilities for improving the revenue were outlined and power to require wider subscription to the oath of engagement was requested. The chief focus, however, was on deficiencies in the areas of law and security. The former could be dealt with easily, and the commissioners forwarded the draft of a statute, roughly modelled on a clause in Poynings' Act, providing for all public acts of the English parliament enacted since 1495 to be 'deemed and judged good and effectuall and accepted used and executed in Ireland'. With this was conjoined the request that 'the Justice of the Nation' should in future 'be dispenct and regulated in like manner as in England'.[191] The matter of security was more complex because it arose from their discovery of the inadequacy of the existing means of controlling the native Irish. Part of what was required was summarized in a second draft statute, 'for the better security of Ireland', which had three purposes: to legalize the recent extension of the English militia system to Ireland; to reintroduce the principle of community liability for the payment of damages for crimes committed by tories and rebels, which had been discontinued in 1634;[192] and to authorize the levy of reward money at quarter sessions for the 'discoverey and apprehension' of both tories and the priests by whom their crimes were 'usually fomented'.[193] More generally, however, they fell back upon the need for wide discretionary powers which would allow them to impose a system 'whereby each person may become surety for one another', to compel the 'Popish Irish' to live in 'townshipps', to move them either 'out of the Nation' or from place to place within it, and to send 'into forraine plantacions' children whose parents would not 'suffer

---

[190] Ibid., 125–7. *Cal. SP, Ire., 1647–60*, p. 691. Egerton MS 212, A/17.

[191] Stowe MS 142, f. 139.

[192] 'An act for the following of hue and cry' (10, 11 Car I, cap. 13) had significantly curtailed powers derived from English statutes of Edward I and Edward III.

[193] Stowe MS 142, f. 140.

them to be educated so as to learne to reade, and speake the English Tongue'. The towns presented special problems because their chartered privileges enabled them to resist intrusion, and the commissioners outlined a scheme to abolish the smaller corporations and restrict the jurisdiction of the larger ones by incorporating a sufficient number of justices of the peace to 'answer the end of Magistracy, and carry on Reformacion'.[194]

It was not until Ludlow landed in Beaumaris that he learned that the army had once again expelled the 'rump'. At Conway, on his way to London, he met the absentee Colonel Robert Barrow, who had been chosen by the general council of officers to deliver their request for support to his commander in chief. Ludlow, unshaken in his determination to go on to London,[195] wrote to warn Jones that he must 'take all possible care, that the common enemy might not be able to take advantage of this sad conjuncture to disturb the public peace'.[196] It may be that he was anxious that the fundamental priorities should be maintained in Ireland, or it may be that he thought it imprudent to advise on Irish reactions to English developments in a letter carried by Barrow. At all events, the hint of equivocation conveyed by his reticence was ill judged, for his deputy was a man of simple principles who placed little value on human institutions.

[194] Stowe MS 142, ff. 136–40.
[195] He arrived on 29 October. Ludlow, *Memoirs*, ii, 131–2.
[196] Ibid., 129.

4

The threefold cord: October to December

The army's attempt to put a government in place was unsuccessful. Though a few members of parliament cooperated, the majority refused to compromise and nine members of the council of state, with Thomas Scot as president, claimed authority. An assurance from Monck that he would bring his army from Scotland to their support if necessary both confirmed them in their resistance and forced Lambert to march north to counter the threat. Parallel attempts to resolve the Anglo-Scottish disagreements and to arrive at a constitutional settlement led to a conference at which the representatives from Scotland were mandated to insist that the rump should sit until 6 May 1660 and be charged with determining the future constitution. In fact, on 15 November, they agreed to an arrangement by which a special general council of the whole army composed of two commissioned officers from each regiment in England, Scotland and Ireland would convene on 6 December and alone determine the form of a future parliament: in addition, a special committee would decide on qualifications for membership.[1] The council in Edinburgh sent new commissioners to reinforce the existing ones and renegotiate the treaty, but without success: the disagreements could not be reconciled, Monck repudiated the treaty on 24 November and the army in England proceeded without Scottish support. On the day after the treaty, two of the 'Nine' met Monck's commissioners. Claiming that they had support in the army around London and in the fleet, that Portsmouth would declare for them, and that Ireland would be secured by Sir Charles Coote,[2] they urged that Monck should stand firm. Shortly afterwards, they issued a commission,

---

[1] Ludlow, *Memoirs*, ii, 158–9. Three of the members of the committee were connected with the army in Ireland: Ludlow, Dobson and Barrow.

[2] W. D. Christie, *A life of Anthony Ashley Cooper, first earl of Shaftsbury* (2 vols., London, 1871), i, 195–6.

making him commander in chief in England and Scotland and authorizing him to act against forces hostile to parliament.

As the members of the rump divided, Ludlow went with the minority who sought compromise. At first he associated himself with Vane and attended a meeting late in October at which Lambert and other officers tried to persuade the civilians to attend the committee of safety, and promised 'great things for the public good'. It ended inconclusively, but both Vane and Ludlow agreed to serve on a subcommittee 'to prepare a form of government' and Ludlow took the task seriously. To fellow members of the rump he explained that the army and parliament were bound up with one another, and that neither must prevail: one must vote taxes to pay the other, the other must help to establish a new government. His chief opportunity to influence events lay in the unfolding discussion of new constitutional proposals. It is clear that he hoped to persuade the proposed general council of officers to recall the rump, but his close identification with the army's plans exposed him to suspicions of active collaboration with parliament's enemies.

Some six years before, from the same vantage point that he again occupied in Ireland, Commissioner Jones had accepted the establishment of the protectorate philosophically: 'if the government be soe Established as may produce the fruits of Righteousness, peace and love to the Saints', he had written, 'I am not solicitous what forme or shape it hath.'[3] This indifference to issues about which others felt deeply and quarrelled violently qualified him poorly to cope with an emerging crisis which was largely concerned with the form that government should take. It may indeed have coloured his impression of local reaction to the news that the 'rump' had been expelled once again, which reached Dublin in private letters two days after Ludlow sailed. Certainly Ludlow, for one, did not credit his deputy's assessment of the prevailing attitude among the officers as one of resigned willingness to 'acquiesse in the acting of the Lord's Providence', coupled with concern 'for a speedie Establishment of Power for administration of Justice and government'.[4] The dominant feeling, however, does seem to have been that the integrity of the army must be preserved, at

[3] 'Inedited letters', pp. 219–20. His authority was Proverbs, 29. 2.
[4] 'Inedited letters', p. 263.

whatever cost. Writing to Fleetwood on 22 October, Jones reported that 'wee, the Commanders and Officers of the army, keepe together to seeke the Lord for councell and guidance to our ffreinds in England, that you may be lead by his blessed Spirit (and not your owne) to bring forth things as eminently gloriouse in holinesse and justice as your late actings have been eminently strange and unparalleled'. The conclusion, that the bloodlessness of the coup showed that God 'seemes to promise some such fruict' was his own.[5] The outcome of a further meeting, convened after Barrow's arrival on the following day, was a carefully non-committal acceptance of the *fait accompli* in the interests of unity. Though the officers professed astonishment at the recent turn of events, they accepted that those involved had acted under 'necessity and sense of duty', and hoped that the result would be a 'more firme establishment of Peace and Righteousness in our Lord'. They promised to do their best both to preserve the public peace of Ireland and to resist efforts to 'devide us in interest or affection from our Brethren in the army of England or Scotland which is the grande designe of the Common Enemy of mankinde': everything depended upon that brotherly love and union, 'that soe we may be in the hand of the Lord as a threefold cord not easily broken'.[6] This statement, sent to Fleetwood for the general council 'in the name and by the consent of the Council of Officers', was signed by eight colonels,[7] four lieutenant-colonels[8] and three majors,[9] representing between them three of the six regiments of horse, seven of the eleven foot regiments, and the dragoons. On the conclusion of this business, they dispersed to their commands 'to prevent any practice of the common enemy upon us'.[10]

The statement was not published. By contrast, no attempt was made to conceal knowledge of the overtures that had been made. Allegedly because failure to comply would have been open to 'misunderstanding' in both England and Ireland, the meeting agreed that the material brought by Barrow from the general council should be distributed to the regiments

---

[5] Ibid., pp. 263–4. Ludlow, *Memoirs*, ii, 142.
[6] 'And if one prevail against him, two shall withstand him; and a threefold cord is not easily broken.' Ecclesiastes, 4. 12.
[7] Waller, Cooper, Wallis, Brayfield, Lawrence, Abbott, Pretty, Sadler.
[8] Nelson, Arnop, Jones, Moore.
[9] Deane, Davies, Warren.   [10] 'Inedited letters', pp. 264–6.

[94]

at once as requested, accompanied by an injunction to 'maintain love and union amongst us'.[11] The alternative view of this compliance was that the circulation of the papers was preemptive and Ludlow claimed that they had been accompanied by a warning from Jones that parliament would not vote the soldiers' pay.[12] The arrival by special messenger of further letters from the general council to the commissioners applied fresh pressure. Enclosed were packets addressed individually to the 'Chief Officers' containing copies, for distribution to the regiments and garrisons, of the army's Representation of 5 October, the subsequent petition to parliament and parliament's answer (that is, the vote of the Commons on it) and the general council asked that the first two should be 'signed by as many as shall be free to subscribe to the same'.[13] The commissioners recommended that Jones should consult with 'such Field officers as are now in Dublin' and they convened on 30 October with Barrow in attendance.[14] Their response was complaisant to a degree, in as much as their reiterated priority was to strengthen and maintain union and love between them and the army of England, but they proved unwilling to commit themselves. They justified this in two ways. One was the dangerously unstable condition of their own forces in the aftermath of Ludlow's remodelling: 'many officers discharged of their commands without a court marshiall, and very many more expecting the like measure; and how to prevent these persons appeareing with their commands, and attempting a discomposure amongst the fforces, is matter of seriouse advise'. The other was that they had yet to receive the promised declaration in which the army's intended settlement was to be outlined, and therefore lacked the information they needed to reach a decision. This deficiency provided them with grounds to resolve upon a week's adjournment. Their determination to withhold judgement made at least some of the officers uneasy about the efforts of the English officers to involve them in canvassing support in Ireland and a decision about the distribution of the papers for signature had not been agreed when the meeting concluded. At the resumed meeting it was agreed without debate to make no collective

[11] Ibid., p. 267. [12] Ludlow, *Memoirs*, ii, 151–2.
[13] Baker, *A chronicle*, p. 717. *TSP*, vii, 766. The letter itself does not survive, but it was presumably the same as that sent to Monck in Scotland. *Clarke Papers*, iv, 67–8.
[14] Dunlop, *Commonwealth*, p. 715.

decision on what should be done with these, leaving each officer to make up his own mind.[15]

Though it was reported in London that Barrow had come back from Ireland 'with the concurrency of the Officers and Army there',[16] his mission had not been fulfilled, and Ludlow noted with satisfaction his failure to 'obtain any public approbation from them of the proceedings of the army in England'.[17] If the press was misled, the council of officers was not. On 4 November Barrow represented the situation in Dublin fairly, reporting that the officers had postponed a decision for a further week while they considered how to achieve 'full unanimity' and 'remove scruples', and that their chief hope of doing this was that the army's declaration, which had been adopted (in Barrow's absence) on 24 October, would prove, in the words of Jones, to 'bee soe comprehensive of good things, and soe suitable to the spirit of an army of ffreeborne Englishmen and Gospell professors, that it will give universall satisfaction'.[18] Privately, Barrow was undoubtedly in a position to give greater comfort by disclosing the existence of influential sympathizers. Certainly Henry Monck, who had been reassured by the inclination towards 'a general neutrality' shown at the 30 October meeting, was dismayed when he subsequently learned of the letter of 26 October and concluded 'that all that are inclinable to Anabaptism do declare against the parliament'.[19] The impression of approval at the highest level in Dublin must have been strengthened by the conduct of Isaac Dobson, the recently promoted lieutenant-colonel of Sadler's regiment, who was chosen on 26 October to represent the army in London. He had been cashiered by Henry Cromwell and owed his reinstatement to Ludlow and his sole briefing was that he should take Ludlow's advice as to what it would be proper for him 'to appeare in and insist upon in the behalf of this army'.[20] He did not follow these instructions. Instead, he associated himself with the Wallingford

---

[15] 'Inedited letters', pp. 270–1, 282.

[16] *Occurrences from Foreign Parts*, 1–8 November. Whitelock formed the same impression, noting letters from Ireland 'of the forces there concurring with them here'. *Memorials*, iv, 369.   [17] Ludlow, *Memoirs*, ii, 142.

[18] *A true narrative of proceedings in parliament, councell of state, general councell of the army, and committee of safety* (London, 1659), pp. 63, 66. 'Inedited letters', pp. 271. *Mercurius Politicus*, 3–11 November.

[19] *Clarke Papers*, iv, 95.   [20] 'Inedited letters', pp. 267.

House group and became, in Ludlow's words, their creature rather than the agent of those who sent him.[21] Dobson's dereliction may have been compensated in some measure by the presence in London also of Commissioner Steele, whose opportunity to leave Ireland had come with the news that he had been nominated to the committee of safety.[22] He responded at once, and travelled over with Barrow, but this apparent enthusiasm was belied by the fact that he never actually attended the committee. Comfort was given to the army's opponents by an assurance 'of six thousand men out of Ireland upon the first notice' which Sir Anthony Ashley Cooper later remembered to have been given in person by Sir Charles Coote 'who was sent over on purpose to us'. Without that assurance, he wrote, 'we should have hardly ventured to have made our opposition to the Committee of Safety'.[23] Ludlow made a connection between Steele's departure and demands from Cooper, Waller and others that he should return himself, because 'those who had the management of affairs' in Ireland were imposing upon them.[24] There may be some force in the view that Steele had been a moderate and restraining influence in the response of the commissioners to the crisis, though there is no evidence that they treated it as anything other than the army's business, but there was no real inconsistency in the reaction of the leading officers in Ireland to an alarming indication that the 'threefold cord' was unravelling.

The cause for alarm was a letter from George Monck, commander in chief of the army in Scotland, to his counterpart in Ireland.[25] Trenchantly declaring his support for the expelled parliament 'against ambition and tyranny', he asked Ludlow as a fellow member of the parliamentary commission for the control of the army to do likewise. The intransigence with which he spoke of going on 'to the last drops of my blood' to restore parliament raised precisely those fears of disunion and division which had become the main preoccupation of the men in charge in Ireland, and

---

[21] Ludlow, *Memoirs*, ii, 151.   [22] Ibid., 152–3.
[23] Christie, *A life of Anthony Ashley Cooper*, p. 210. There is no evidence to confirm that Coote was in England at this time.
[24] Ludlow, *Memoirs*, ii, 142.
[25] Ibid., 449. Somewhat similar letters to Fleetwood, Lambert and the speaker had been sent on 20 October.

seemed to compel a committed response. But it is evident that they were not confident that their reaction would be widely shared. The answer sent on 4 November was signed by John Jones and Colonels Cooper, Waller, Lawrence and Phayre, together with Lieutenant-Colonel Henry Jones[26] and Major Kempson. This group was not only small, but oddly composed. John Jones participated as acting commander in chief. Of the others, only his brother Henry, Cooper and Waller had been associated with the reply to the English officers, Lawrence was suspected of collusion with them, Phayre was a Baptist normally stationed in Cork, and Kempson was a Quaker who had only recently rejoined the army in Ireland. It was later claimed that two officers who had been summoned to the meeting had refused to sign the letter and that Waller had done so only in order 'not to incapacitate himself from laying hold on the first opportunity to appear for the Parliament'.[27] The reply showed none of the relative circumspection which the larger group had exercised in dealing with the English officers. The subscribers professed themselves 'very much troubled and startled' by Monck's attitude, put it to him that he was 'opening a sure way for the comon enemy to destroy oure common Interest as men and Christians', declared that they could not approve of anything that would engage 'any part of the Armyes or fforces of these Nations against their brotheren', urged him to desist, and offered to mediate between him and the army in England if necessary.[28] Major John Barrett took the letter to Scotland, together with a copy of the statement previously sent to England. His reception was unwelcoming: indeed, Monck found his behaviour so unacceptable that he 'thought fit to confine him to his chambers'. It appears that Monck had already been assured by his cousin Henry that Sir Charles Coote, Sir Theophilus Jones 'and a very considerable part of the army, were resolved to assist him', and that they hoped to gain the support of Waller.[29] These men were well known to Monck: when he had commanded parliament's forces in Ulster, Jones had been one of his officers and Coote had been his counterpart in the west of the province. Primed with the knowledge that the army in Ireland was not of one mind, he severely rebuked Barrett and sent him back with a more measured

---

[26] Bagwell was mistaken in assuming that this was Dr Henry Jones. *Ireland under the Stuarts*, ii, 364.   [27] *Ireland's fidelity*.   [28] 'Inedited letters', pp. 272–3, 274.

[29] Baker, *A chronicle*, p. 726. *Clarke Papers*, iv, 95–6n.

request for joint action 'that this Parliament may be restored, and put a legal period to their sitting; and settle such expedients as may be for the securing of these Nations, against the common enemy'.[30] Apart from the doubt about Waller, it seems likely that his fellow signatories were not of one mind either, for Cooper joined Major Warren in writing to Ludlow to complain of the 'breach, and of the hardships put upon them by those in command of forces'. Ludlow denounced the letter to Monck as a 'great alteration' in attitude and a 'great defection' from duty, for 'they manifestly took part with the army'. He warned Cooper and Warren not to 'join themselves to a faction in opposition to the civil authority of the nation' and ordered Cooper ('a good officer, and very acceptable to the best sort of people in the Northern parts') to return to his command in Ulster.[31] John Jones, who scarcely troubled to disguise his opinion that Ludlow's failure to return to his own post was itself a defection from duty, was not disposed to think so well of Cooper: he suspected that both he and Warren were Cromwellians unreconciled to the fall of the protectorate.[32]

It seems obvious that the reluctance of the officers to discuss the substantive issues at their meeting on 30 October was well founded. Their hope that the English army's declaration on a future settlement would help to reconcile their differences proved illusory.[33] Only when it arrived did the army in Ireland learn the lengths to which their English brethren had gone in declaring the acts passed by parliament in its last three days to be 'invalid, null, and void to all intents and purposes'.[34] Commissioner Jones reported disconsolately to Axtell and Barrow that 'sober men' thought that this part of the declaration 'might have been better worded': in particular, they believed that it ought not to have purported to repeal acts of parliament, but rather to have shown 'the Lawe declared against to be destructive to the Navy our Bullworke against forreigne Nations, to the Army our Strenght and Security against our home and comon Enemy, to

---

[30] Baker, *A chronicle*, p. 726. Ludlow, *Memoirs*, ii, 150. George Monck, *A letter to the commissioners of the parliament in Ireland, touching his present acting*. London, 1659. *Mercurius Politicus*, 24 November–1 December.

[31] Ludlow, *Memoirs*, ii, 147.   [32] 'Inedited letters', pp. 280–3.

[33] There were two army statements: *The Army's plea for their present practice* was issued on 24 October and was followed by an abridged version, *A declaration of the general council of the officers of the army agreed upon at Wallingford House, 27 Octob. 1659*.

[34] *A declaration of the general council*, p. 17.

the people in opening a doore for free Quarters and sword powere immediately to returne upon them'. A reference to the abolition of tithes was 'conceived not seasonably inserted, nor thorroughly satisfactory to any'. Even the parts that were approved failed to give full satisfaction because they were 'wrapped in Generalls'. Jones was careful to emphasize that he was expressing the opinion of others: his own view, characteristically, was that substances were more important than 'fformes and fframes' – 'righteousnesse itselfe and holynesse itselfe will never decay'. Nonetheless, while he recognised that the declaration was not persuasive, he was disposed to blame the unpersuaded. Disquiet, he believed, was mostly felt by people who had also been dissatisfied with the recall of parliament in May. His meaning became plain as he rehearsed the depressing consequences of the failure of the declaration to command support. The Cavaliers 'of all sort' were 'much raised in their Spirite and hope for good newes for their King from Scottland'. Though the various papers sent to England and Scotland were to be printed for widespread distribution, and Cooper had gone to the north to take command, the prospects were gloomy. There was still no 'power to putt lawes in execution for preservation of the peace', not least because the proclamation continuing justices, sheriffs and other officers in post, which had been published by the 'Committee of Safety of the Commonwealth of England, Scotland and Ireland, etc.' on 31 October, referred only to England and Berwick: 'noe man layeth our condicion to heart', he complained.[35] One of the consequences of neglect, as he also protested, was that 'Wee have noe exact Intelligence how Affaires goe in England, nor what to declare for if there were need.'[36] What they did have were rumours that opinion in England was moving towards a full restoration of the Long Parliament with the excluded members and the lords readmitted. Jones dispatched information of royalist intrigues in Ireland to help to prevent this development by showing that it was part of a plot for the restoration of Charles Stuart 'for there are noe greater friends to a single government than the excluded members of both Houses'.[37]

Although Jones assured Barrow that he had found no one 'opening his

---

[35] 'Inedited letters', pp. 275–6. The proclamation is in the Thomason Collection, E. f. 669, 21 (97). *A true narrative*, pp. 54–5. [36] 'Inedited letters', p. 277.
[37] Ibid., p. 278.

mouth for restoreing the Long Parliament as they last mett', he was actually in correspondence with a former officer, Thomas Scot, who had expressed disquiet at the legality of the situation and insisted that the present parliament should be restored to 'their just Rights and priviledges'. Jones affected to find this unclear. On the one hand, he could not believe that Scot wished for the return of the 'rump', 'wherein you had noe satisfaction': if, on the other hand, a full restoration was intended, 'that is but a faire umbridge devised by the common Enemy to disguise a wicked designe to bring in Charles Stuart'.[38] The misconstruction is unlikely to have been as ingenuous as it was made to appear, for the upbraided officer's political position was not in doubt: he was both a son of the republican regicide who was president of the recalcitrant 'Nine' and a consistent critic of the protectorate who had dared to question the legality of the distribution of land in the absence of an act of parliament and been jailed by Henry Cromwell for 'seditious and revileinge expressiones against the gouvernment'.[39]

The condition of the army had been a source of anxiety from the outset. Initially, the fear had been that the cashiered officers would try to regain their commands. To this was shortly added the fear that many of the officers were 'unfixed' by suspicions that a fresh purge was intended.[40] There may have been some foundation for this unease. Certainly, Ludlow later claimed to have dissuaded Fleetwood from severe measures lest officers should resign and be replaced by worse.[41] At all events, the result was that many of the officers were 'very much incensed and yet continue in the head of their comands, and this is the condition of some of our chief Guarrissons'.[42] For want of a more practical way of dealing with army divisions and disagreements, and mindful of the fact that 'the name of a Saint is become a reproach unto too too many in our land', a weekly day of humiliation and prayer was proclaimed on 8 November, beginning on 11 November, 'being the sixth day of this week, commonly called Friday': 'all the Churches and People of the Lord' were particularly asked to

---

[38] Ibid., pp. 279–80.
[39] *Regimental history*, pp. 603–4. Scot, who had represented Westmeath, Louth and King's County in the first protectorate parliament, had been in Ireland since he contracted to bring a cavalry troop in 1647. *Cal. SP, Ire., 1647–60*, pp. 747–8.
[40] 'Inedited letters', pp. 278–9.   [41] *Memoirs*, ii, 148.   [42] 'Inedited letters', pp. 278–9.

remember Fleetwood 'and to be earnest and incessant with the Lord on his and our other friends in Englands behalves; that they may not be left of him, but that he may be their sun and shield'. The opportunity was taken to give a public assurance that the misunderstanding with Monck was 'in some way of composure'.[43] Before long, Jones and his colleagues had altered their title to 'Commissioners of the Commonwealth', arranged for a ship to be sent to control movement between Ireland and Scotland, and set about attending to their immediate defences.[44] Orders were issued to search out and secure dangerous persons in Dublin and its port and work was begun on the repair of the platform on the gun towers of Dublin Castle and the construction of an inner gate to reinforce its postern gate.[45] By the end of the month, Jones was beginning to refine the categorization which had been implicit in some of his earlier reports. He now positively identified a group within the army with two characteristics: they were formerly 'Cavalleeres or New Royallistes' (by which he meant those who had been associated with the kingship party) and they had been opposed to the restoration of the Long Parliament. They were now

> for dividing of us, and setting us in opposition to the Army in England, under the Notion of being for a parliament the sence whereof and the scope of the Designe is in all probability but the same that Sir George Booth and his confederats indeavour to Carry on, which although Crushed in England is kept intyre in Ireland, wayteing for an opportunity by reason that none of the Instruments which probabley were to Carry it on have beene incapacitated or cleereley discovered.[46]

Undependable officers were only part of the problem. The other part concerned the operational logistics of the army's task. At a time of opportunity for the 'common enemy', when general defection was possible, the army was scaled only to garrison duty and local control: to assemble another body of the proportions of the Irish Brigade anywhere in Ireland would endanger the areas from which they were drawn. It became increasingly desirable, however, to be able to deploy concentrated force in

---

[43] *Publick Intelligencer*, 14–21 November. [44] Ludlow, *Memoirs*, ii, 153.
[45] Dunlop, *Commonwealth*, p. 716. Prendergast papers, ii, 470.
[46] 'Inedited letters', p. 281.

both Connacht and Ulster. In the former, this seems to have proceeded from prudence rather than from suspicion of any specific threat, and anxiety still focused on the city of Limerick, where the order to clear Catholics out of the city was repeated on 11 November.[47] In Ulster by contrast the signs were ominous: the sheriffs had ceased to collect the assessment (as had the sheriff of Queen's County)[48] and 'Scottish papers' were being 'industriously scattered'. During the first week of December, two incidents were taken to show that Scottish influence was gaining ground dangerously. In the first, two companies in Carrickfergus mutinied and were forced to their quarters with naked swords and pistols by Cooper and his officers. In the second, a 'rising out' of some 240 horse was organized by the British in east Fermanagh, ostensibly in defence against the Irish.[49] A sinister background to these events was provided by reports that during November a series of meetings involving Viscount Montgomery, Mark Trevor, Dr Gorges and many others had begun at the Hill residence of Hillsborough in County Down and moved from house to house over a period of about a fortnight. This was a menacing coalition. Montgomery's royalist sympathies were not in doubt; Gorges and Trevor had been close associates of Henry Cromwell; outwardly, Arthur Hill had collaborated actively with the regime, but the bishop of Down and Connor, Henry Leslie, lived under his protection and his household was one in which, in the words of Jeremy Taylor, 'the publick Liturgy of the Church is greatly valued, and diligently us'd'.[50]

Ludlow had been too preoccupied to pay much attention to Irish matters, though the Irish Brigade proved an embarrassing aspect of his responsibilities.[51] It was at Chester on its way back to Ireland when the October coup took place, but because it had supported the Derby petition

---

[47] Prendergast papers, ii, 465.
[48] 'Inedited letters', pp. 278–9. An order to collect arrears in Dublin was issued in early November. Egerton MS 212, A/17.   [49] 'Inedited letters', p. 290.
[50] Hillsborough was the residence of Hill and his son William, by his second wife, Mary, daughter of Sir William Parsons. Henry Leslie, *A discourse of praying with the Spirit and with the Understanding preached in two sermons at Hillsborough* (Dublin, 1659?), Epistle by Jeremy Taylor, p. 1. W. A. Maguire, *The Downshire estates in Ireland* (Oxford, 1972), pp. 2–4. Gorges and Arthur Hill had worked together as auditors-general. J. T. Gilbert (ed.), *Facsimiles of the national manuscripts of Ireland*, iv, pt. 2 (London, 1884), Plate lxix.
[51] Ludlow, *Memoirs*, ii, 154–7.

it was ordered to London as reinforcement instead. Ludlow met the regiment on his journey and found that, with the sole exception of Captain Winckworth, 'a creature of Col Sankey',[52] the officers were unhappy with the turn of events, particularly Lieutenant-Colonel Walker. Ludlow exhorted them to keep faith with parliament and journeyed on.[53] Subsequently, despite Sankey, they resolved that they would not engage against Monck. When Lambert blamed Ludlow for this decision, he wrote to ask them to be more circumspect.[54] The care with which he sought to occupy the middle ground in England did not prevent him from roundly accusing Commissioner Jones of having deserted the parliament. Although Jones denied the charge, a hint of his real position was contained in his protest that the letter to Monck had contained nothing that 'disrespects the Parliament, or publique safety which is above Parliaments'. He found Ludlow insensitive to the difficulty of the situation in Ireland and insufficiently appreciative of the absolute necessity of preserving unity: for the armies to fall out was the 'grande designe of our Comon Enemy'. With an unusually subtle touch he congratulated Ludlow on being 'freed from the Snare of such a Turne as this' and reminded him that on his departure he had said that 'if those now in power would resolve to establish honest righteouse things you would with them, if not you would take your Retirement. I have had noe other intimation from you which might be an example for me to follow.'[55] This was an oblique comment on Ludlow's object in writing, which had been to deal with the Anglo-Scottish articles of agreement and, more particularly, to instruct the Irish army to send representatives to the extraordinary general council of the army of the three nations on 6 December.

The instruction, delayed by cross winds, arrived on Saturday, 26 November.[56] On the Monday, each commander was sent a copy of the agreement and a schedule of times and places at which the commissioned officers of the operationally scattered regiments were to meet to choose

---

[52] Winckworth's treatment by Petty had formed the substance of one of the charges brought against him by Sankey in parliament earlier in the year. J. P. Prendergast, *The Cromwellian settlement of Ireland* (Dublin, 1922), pp. 237–8.

[53] Ludlow, *Memoirs*, ii, 130–1. The order for the Brigade's return to Ireland had been made on 3 September. O'Renehan MSS, ii, f. 658.

[54] Ludlow, *Memoirs*, ii, 153–4.

[55] Ibid., 147. 'Inedited letters', pp. 282–3.   [56] 'Inedited letters', p. 280.

two agents to attend the general council.⁵⁷ A covering letter pointed out that it would not be possible for anyone from Ireland to reach the council meeting in time and suggested that officers presently in England should be chosen: it also urged the officers to select those with the 'largest portion of a meeke, loveing, peaceable, healing spirit' and a willingness to tolerate the consciences of others.⁵⁸ Relatively few of the regiments seem to have complied with the order. Ludlow's horse met at Athy on 6 December and selected Ludlow himself and Nicholas Kempson: three days later at Trim his foot regiment also nominated him, together with Colonel William Allen who had yet to take up his Irish command. The other five regiments from which returns were certified by Jones on 10 December were commanded by Baptists. On 6 December the regiments of Lawrence and Markham (for whom Major Jones substituted) had convened at Carlow. Lawrence's regiment had chosen Dr William Stanes, the muster master general of England and Scotland, and Richard Kingdon, the Irish judge advocate: Markham's had chosen Lawrence's son-in-law, Dr Philip Carteret, the judge advocate of England, a Baptist who had previously been a commissioner of claims and advocate general in Ireland, and Captain Thomas Shepherd who was with the Irish Brigade.⁵⁹ On the following day, the regiments of Sankey, Wallis and Brayfield met at Cashel, Clonmel and Ardee. Sankey and Wallis were both chosen, with Captain Thomas Aske, another member of the Irish Brigade, and Captain Samuel Sheers respectively. Brayfield's officers chose Captain John Blackwell, treasurer at war, and Benjamin Worsley, the commissary general.⁶⁰ There may have been other nominations, and even participants. Captain Sampson Toogood, formerly an officer in the regiment of the Baptist

---

⁵⁷ Ibid., pp. 283–5.   ⁵⁸ Ibid., pp. 284–5.

⁵⁹ Herlihy, 'Irish Baptists', p. 258. Shepherd had been with the regiment since at least 1654 (*Arch. Hib.*, 6, 186; vii, 57) and had served as a regimental agent in 1657 (Petty, *Down survey*, pp. 180–1).

⁶⁰ BL Stowe MSS 142, f. 68. Blackwell's co-treasurer was a cousin of Major Joseph Deane of Wallis's regiment, which may explain the choice; he was an original adventurer who had drawn some 3,000 acres in Tipperary, acquired extensive property in County Dublin and was associated with the Wallingford House Party. G. Aylmer, *The state's servants* (London, 1973), pp. 242–6. *Cal. SP, Ire., 1647–60*, p. 643. Arnold, *The restoration land settlement in County Dublin*, pp. 34, 35, 93. For Worsley, see Aylmer, *The state's servants*, pp. 270–2; Barnard, *Cromwellian Ireland*, pp. 219–22.

Henry Pretty, later related in evidence his confused recollection that the commissioners had summoned county meetings at which disbanded soldiers like himself as well as serving soldiers were required 'to chuse two out of a regiment that might be the rulers of the people, legislators I think they called them'.[61] There is, moreover, an authentic ring to the accusation that after his selection, Captain Henry Aland, a Baptist and former officer in Pretty's regiment, who had been brought back from civilian life by Ludlow to command the fort at Passage, had been 'soe zelouse to promote the worke [that he] began his jorny on the Lords day from this place'.[62] But it is quite clear that the issue was a divisive one and that only the more radical officers cooperated. A hint of the conservative response is provided by Broghill who knew of the Anglo-Scottish agreement before Jones did and suggested to him that he should honour its spirit by restoring suspended officers to their commands.[63] Since Broghill was in correspondence with Monck, it seems likely that this proposal was disingenuous.[64] By the time the first regimental meetings took place, the news that Monck had repudiated the agreement had reached Ireland, Jones's position had hardened correspondingly and he had divined 'the hopes and Expectations of the Wicked', which were to restore the parliament, lay aside the army and raise a new one 'of other principles, and those wilbee such as Countenanced Sir George Booth's designe (vizt) Cavaleeres under the maske of a Presbyterian Interest, such as would have the peace established on the concessions at the Isle of Weight'.[65]

When the general council met on 6 December there were no representatives from Scotland and Ireland was represented only by those chosen by

---

[61] Ludlow, *Memoirs*, ii, 153. T. B. Howell, *Collection of state trials and proceedings for high treason* (33 vols., London, 1809–26), v, 1189, 1194.

[62] *Cal. SP, Ire., 1647–60*, pp. 710, 711. S.P., Ire., 63/303. 12. Aland had settled in Waterford after his disbandment in 1655. Dunlop, *Commonwealth*, p. 35; Prendergast, *Cromwellian settlement*, p. 218. *Regimental history*, p. 597.

[63] 'Inedited letters', pp. 286–7.

[64] The letter from Monck to Broghill assigned by Ms Lynch to 23 November 1659 was written a year previously, when Broghill was still lord president of the Scottish council. Harvard, Orrery MSS: MS 218. 22. Lynch, *Orrery*, p. 100. That the correspondence continued, however, seems to be confirmed by the state of Broghill's information.

[65] 'Inedited letters', pp. 288–9. Disagreement over the terms offered by the king at Newport in the Isle of Wight in 1648 had been the occasion of Pride's Purge.

the Irish Brigade, of whom Ludlow was one.⁶⁶ The circumstances were not propitious, and they became less so. Three days earlier, the army's most resolute enemy, Sir Arthur Haselrig, and two others, had established themselves on behalf of the 'Nine' in Portsmouth where they declared for the parliament and set about assembling an alternative government to challenge the authority of the army which they claimed to control as parliamentary commissioners. On 5 December, blood had been shed in the suppression of an apprentice riot against the army in London. On 12 December an attempt by the 'Nine' to take the Tower of London was foiled. On the following day, Lawson and his captains wrote from the fleet in the Downs to London demanding the renewed sitting of the rump and indicating that they were prepared to use force to make this happen. The fleet then sailed towards London with members of the 'Nine' on board.

Ludlow had spoken forcefully for the recall of the rump, but unavailingly. The general council had gone on to discuss the outline of a new constitutional arrangement and Ludlow did his best to influence its form. It was on 13 December that preliminary arrangements were published in the newspapers. A bi-cameral parliament was to meet on 24 January, though decisions on voting qualifications were postponed; there was a set of seven 'unalterable fundamentals' and a body of 'conservators of liberty' which was to adjudicate differences in their interpretation between parliament and the army. Ludlow claimed to have originated the conservator group, but when its members were chosen his suggestions were disregarded, and the officers appointed themselves – intending 'to carry on a faction, and govern the nation by the sword' – and Ludlow left the council. Its members continued their discussions, and were debating whether Irish and Scottish representatives should sit in the new parliament when they heard on 21 December that soldiers sent to besiege Portsmouth had changed sides. On 23 December they brought the meeting to an end, and the members of the council of state asserted their authority over the forces in London. On 24 December General Fleetwood sent the keys of the parliament house to the speaker with an assurance that there was no longer anything to impede the members from sitting. It

---

⁶⁶ Ludlow, *Memoirs*, ii, 163. Walker and two others were also chosen. According to the Venetian ambassador, the council grew daily in numbers as officers arrived from the garrisons of England and Ireland. *Cal. SP, Ven.*, 1659–61, p. 102.

was on that day that the London newsbooks received word that a *coup d'état* had taken place in Dublin on 13 December.⁶⁷

According to the principal actors in the coup, in a justificatory 'Narrative of the dealings of God with the Irish Nation', their enterprise had originated with 'some dissenting Officers about Dublin' who had become increasingly alarmed by the way in which the restoration of the Long Parliament in May had been used by a group which was not loyal to parliament to gain 'almost a Supremacie of power in Ireland' through the remodelling of the army and the 'management also of civil things'. When their suspicions were confirmed by the expulsion of the members in October, plans were laid. These revolved around a petition demanding that a general council of officers should meet to discuss the situation, which Major General Waller, who was unaware of the ulterior design, undertook to present. There was an authentic purpose to the petition, for they believed that it would constrain Jones who would recognize the implied opposition yet find the request difficult to ignore. At the same time, however, the preparation and management of the submission provided cover for private meetings and for the canvassing of support throughout the army.⁶⁸ Jones resolved his dilemma by preemption, they alleged: he proposed to have the issues discussed instead at a meeting of the 'Juncto of Officers' elected to attend the general council of the army in England. The 'dissenting Officers' discovered from an intercepted letter that this was to be accompanied, with the approval of Fleetwood, by their arrest and the disarming of 'all others in the Nation not of their party'. On 12 December, therefore, they decided to execute on the following day 'what had bin before resolved', which was the capture of Dublin Castle and the commissioners.⁶⁹ Among those directly involved in carrying out this plan were Major Edward Warren and his brothers John (a former

---

⁶⁷ *Mercurius Politicus*, 22–29 December. The newly launched *Parliamentary Intelligencer*, in its first issue (19–26 December) commented, unfairly, 'better late then never'. Whitelock, *Memorials*, iv, 383.

⁶⁸ Bridges et al., *A perfect narrative*, pp. 2, 3, 4–7. In mid-November, Jones reported to Barrow his apprehension of 'some designe supposed to be on foot for the restoreing of some friends to comand that which I dare not menton without further light. Private meetings give cause for suspicion.' 'Inedited letters', p. 279.

⁶⁹ Bridges et al., *A perfect narrative*, pp. 7–8.

lieutenant-colonel) and Abel (a former captain, a halberdier at the king's execution, and recently mayor of Kilkenny);[70] John Joyner who had been in the king's domestic service, and 'did wait upon him' during his trial, before he took arms and was settled in Kilkenny; Colonel John Bridges, who was closely associated with Winter, had supported the kingship petition in 1657 (when he represented the Roscommon–Sligo–Leitrim constituency) and had been stripped of his English regiment in April after the forced dissolution of parliament;[71] Sir Theophilus Jones, William Warden, Captain Daniel Lisle and Lieutenant John Thompson. The identity of their associates is a matter for conjecture. There is no doubt that Broghill and Sir Charles Coote were among them, Lord Montgomery was certainly privy, and credit was contemporarily claimed for Mark Trevor, Oliver St George, Sir Audley Mervyn and Dr Henry Jones.[72] The way in which events unfolded, however, tends to confirm the claim of the conspirators themselves that by the time they acted complicity was widespread. Knowledge of what was afoot may have been wider still. The lawyer Jerome Alexander, who lived close to the Castle, claimed to have been told of the plot by a client a month before it was carried out and to have been warned 'to remove the weomen kinde to some place els least any combustion should fall out in the action, to affright them'.[73]

The forces in Dublin, which consisted of five foot companies, four of them from the regiment commanded by Richard Lawrence, supplemented by three troops of horse brought in for greater security by Henry Jones, governor of the Castle, were not privy to the plot.[74] The plan of action was suggested by the coincidence that Joyner had formerly been captain of one of the foot companies and his successor, Captain Bond, proved

[70] His petition to Henry Cromwell to be appointed to the rank of major had been unsuccessful. 30 September 1658, Lansdowne MS 823, f. 118.
[71] Baker, *A chronicle*, p. 699. Richard Baxter, to whose congregation at Kidderminster Bridges belonged for a time, thought him 'truly and judiciously religious', *Autobiography* (London, 1931), p. 83.
[72] H. R., 'A letter to the author', in Richard Cox, *Hibernia Anglicana* (London, 1679), p. 2. Edmund Borlase, *The history of the execrable Irish rebellion, 1641–1662* (London, 1680), p. 316. Dr Henry Jones was actively involved in drafting material for the council of officers in the weeks after the coup. TCD MS 844, ff. 185–9.
[73] Alexander to Sir Edward Massey, post October 1661, Gloucester County Record Office, Sherborne Muniments, D 678, Barwick MSS, No. 3.
[74] Bridges et al., *A perfect narrative*, p. 8.

amenable.⁷⁵ According to the Dublin correspondent of *Mercurius Politicus*, Warden and Joyner went into the Castle in the afternoon of Tuesday, 13 December, and walked for a while before calling upon the sentinel, at about 5 o'clock, to let them out through the back gate. As he did so, some thirty or forty foot soldiers of Bond's company, 'then upon an outgard' but 'of late quartered in the yard', thrust him aside, fell upon the hundred-strong guard, disarmed them, and forced them to march out with their hands in their pockets. Their success was signalled by shots from the top of the Castle, whereupon horse troops rode through the town with drawn swords, 'scouring the streets hindering the Anabaptists to get to a body' and crying 'a parliament, a parliament'.⁷⁶ Some surrounded the new custom house, where the Council Chamber was situated, and there they captured John Jones and the two local army commanders, Lawrence and Henry Jones: others secured the civil governors Corbet and Thomlinson 'at a conventicle in South Werburgh Street'.⁷⁷ Contemporary report attributed the former captures to Theophilus Jones and the latter to Edward Warren.⁷⁸ Credit for both was later given to Broghill's nephew, Captain Robert Fitzgerald of Ballymartyr in County Cork, who was in command of one of the horse troops quartered in Dublin and brought his men over to the conspirators. Fitzgerald, the earl of Kildare's son, had formerly served as a cornet under Warden.⁷⁹ A hint of the preliminary organization of this second phase is provided by William Montgomery's account of Lord Montgomery, who was still confined to Dublin, and who 'was covertly active, for though he staied in his lodgings, he sent myself and his servants in messinges, and allowed his horses and mine to a friend, called George

---

[75] An earlier plan to force entry under cover of supplying the garrison with bread came to light, rather mysteriously, at the time of the 1663 plot, which it may have influenced. *Cal. SP, Ire., 1669–70*, pp. 454–5. Connolly, *Religion, law, and power*, p. 25.

[76] *Mercurius Politicus*, 29 December 1659–5 January 1659[60]. *Montgomery MSS*, p. 219.

[77] John Nicoll, *A diary of public transactions* (Bannatyne Club, 1836), p. 263. 'A letter to the author', Cox, *Hibernia Anglicana*, p. 2.

[78] *Mercurius Politicus*, 29 December–5 January.

[79] *Cal. SP, Ire., 1660–2*, pp. 114, 316; *1663–5*, p. 472; *1665–7*, pp. 475, 491. Russell and Prendergast, *Account*, p. 206. T. U. Sadleir, 'Kildare members of parliament', *Kildare AS jn.*, 6 (1911), p. 472. He was described in 1663 as 'wholly my Lord Orrery's'. Prendergast papers, iv, 248.

Wiulton, who mounted himself and others on them, joining Theos Jones'.⁸⁰ Ludlow's major, Kempson, who was in the Castle, joined the conspirators, and they at once sought and gained the support of Waller, on whom the position of commander in chief now devolved, 'he having some weeks before prepared by some general discourse concerning it'. The citizens of Dublin, it was reported 'all made bonfires and offered their assistance'.⁸¹ The government had been overthrown, the only magazine in Dublin, replenished by 500 barrels of powder from England as lately as the previous Monday, was in the hands of the conspirators, and no blood had been shed.⁸²

On the following day, a group describing itself as the council of officers issued a declaration in the form of a broadsheet for countrywide distribution. This was not an apologia for the events of the previous day. It made no reference whatever to the seizure of the Castle and the commissioners. The occasion invoked was the larger one of the 'sinfull interruption' of parliament by the 'disturbers of the peace of this our Israel' which had moved the officers to seek the Lord and adopt six resolutions which it was the purpose of the declaration to announce. The first was to remain firm in obedience to the trust reposed in them by parliament and affirmed by them through Ludlow 'as it were but yesterday'. The second was not to allow themselves to be divided from one another, from those of their brethern of the armies who remained faithful, or from those who returned to their obedience. The third was to work for 'the setling and maintaining a Godly, learned and faithful Ministry in these three Nations, with due encouragement to the Universities and Schools of good literature, that they may be Nurseries of Piety, Learning and Godliness'. The fourth was to suppress those who disturbed the peace, either by attempting to set up 'the interest of any single person whatsoever' or by fomenting confusions 'through turbulency of spirit'. The fifth was not 'to impose upon any tender Consciences, being otherwise sound in the fundamentals of relig-

---

⁸⁰ *Montgomery MSS*, 219. Jones and Lord Montgomery were former companions in arms. Ibid., pp. 164, 167, 223. Wilton was a grandson of the 1st Viscount. Ibid., 219n. He was among a petitioning group of regimental agents in 1657 which included Jones and John Thompson. Petty, *Down survey*, pp. 180–1.

⁸¹ *Mercurius Politicus*, 29 December–5 January. Bridges et al., *A perfect narrative*, p. 9.

⁸² Bridges et al., *A perfect narrative*, pp. 8–9. *Mercurius Politicus*, 29 December–5 January. *Cal. SP, Dom.*, 1659–60, pp. 316–17. Jennings MSS, Box J2, Notebook E.

[111]

ion'. The last was to protect their adherents and to 'endeavour that due encouragement may be given to such whether Officers or Soldiers formerly of the Army, who either have or will joyn with us in this undertaking'.[83] Copies of this declaration were taken at once to all of the garrisons by 'parties' charged to secure answering declarations in favour of parliament, and presumably to elucidate the immediate circumstances in which it had been issued.[84] It went formally over the name of Sir Hardress Waller, but the names of twenty-one other assenting officers were subjoined. Nine of these had been directly involved in the Castle coup,[85] one was Nicholas Kempson, and a further six were junior officers of small significance,[86] but William Moore was Coote's lieutenant-colonel, Sir Maurice Fenton was Broghill's cousin (as well as Waller's son in law),[87] John Cole and Edmund Temple were cashiered colonels and Henry Whalley was a Nottinghamshire cousin of Cromwell who was both a former judge advocate of the army in all three countries and an adventurer with large interests in County Galway.[88]

On the same day, an extraordinary meeting of the corporation of Dublin took place in response to a petition from 'certain of the commons' requesting consideration of the danger from 'Irish papists and other common enemies' in the present 'unsettledness' of affairs. It was agreed to call out the two regiments raised in the previous May, and, significantly, that these should be commanded by individuals nominated by the petitioners and commissioned by the mayor as commander in chief.[89] It was reported that this militia force, 2,000 foot, as well as horse, was on duty within eight hours.[90]

The officers' declaration was dispatched to both the parliamentary commissioners at Portsmouth and Speaker Lenthall, ostensibly on the day

---

[83] *A declaration of several officers of the army in Ireland, on behalf of themselves and those under their commands, holding forth their stedfast resolutions to adhere to the parliament in defence of its privileges; and the just rights and libertyes of the people of these nations as men and Christians* (Dublin, 1659[60]).

[84] *Cal. SP, Ire., 1647–60*, p. 716.   [85] That is, all but Captain Bond.

[86] Theo Dancer, Theoph Sandford, James Hand, Tho Hopkins, Ri Nun, Robert Cook.

[87] Berry, *Register of the church of St Michan*, p. 13.

[88] *HMC Rep. 10* (London, 1885), p. 502. *Cal. SP, Adv.*, p. 23. Mark Noble, *Memoirs of the protectoral house of Cromwell* (2 vols., London, 1787), ii, pp. 154–5.

[89] Gilbert, *Records*, iv, 171.   [90] Baker, *A chronicle*, p. 738.

it was signed, but in reality only after news of favourable reaction in the rest of the country had begun to arrive.[91] It was accompanied by an account of the overthrow of the army regime in Dublin.[92] There was no suggestion that the coup was in any way related to the activities of the opponents of the army outside Ireland: on the contrary, it was presented as having been intended for some time and as being entirely contingent in its timing. The tone of the letter to Lenthall was one of strident religiosity: characterizing the interruptions of parliament in both 1653 and 1659 as a sin, the writers claimed that 'our Religion and our liberties, as Englishmen and Protestants, were subjected to the Lusts of Men', offered their services 'against Apostatized Usurpers', and expressed suspicions of their 'apostatized Commander in Chief': 'what his Civils allow, his Consiontials destroy', they observed. Theophilus Jones was the leading signatory of the letter, which was subscribed only by those who had surprised the Castle and led the horse.[93] By the time that it was written, the officers had already turned their attention to the need to engage the wider politics of the situation. On 16 December, they wrote to Monck, regretting that it not been possible to join him in his defence of parliament earlier, 'the power of this Army running violently the contrary way', and announcing the capture of Dublin Castle and the concurrence of the lord president of Connacht and the city of Dublin.[94] On the same day, Waller wrote privately to Monck apologizing for his association with the previous letter of 4 November and protesting that he had signed it only after insisting upon the deletion of 'some sharper expressions'. Affirming his belief that what had happened in Dublin 'must undergo the hazard to be judged much by your success', he now engaged himself to Monck, professing

---

[91] The newsbooks received it on 28 December. *Publick Intelligencer*, 26 December 1659–2 January 1659[60].

[92] *An account of the affairs of Ireland in reference to the late change in England; with a declaration of several officers of the army in Ireland, holding forth their steadfast resolution to adhere to the parliament* (London, 1659).

[93] Assuming that J. Trevor, of whom there is no other record, should read J. Joyner. *A letter to Sir William Lenthall, 15 December 1659* (London, 1659). The other signatories were Jones, the three Warrens, Bond, Warden, Thompson, Lisle, Bridges and Temple.

[94] *Parliamentary Intelligencer*, 9–16 January. The signatories were Waller, Bridges, Theo Jones, Edward and John Warren, Cole, J. Frearer, J. Hand, Will Ward, Lisle, A. Ware, Fenton, Sanford, Dancer, Tho Hopkins and Whalley.

himself confident that he would 'neither deliver up the English interest to the Scottish nation nor betray this good old cause to the Cavalier party'.[95] Monck's 'old servant Capt John Campbell' was sent to Scotland to deliver these letters and apparently to seek advice and directions as to how to proceed.[96] He was also entrusted with a letter to the Irish Brigade, which Monck duly forwarded.[97]

In the wake of the overthrow of the government, direct action was mounted against Carlow Castle, which was taken from Colonel Pretty by Edmund Temple with a force of five horse troops which had been placed under his command on the evening of the coup.[98] Captain Lisle likewise went from Dublin to seize Drogheda from Lieutenant-Colonel Desborough.[99] Elsewhere, the reactions fell a little untidily into three categories: in some places garrison commanders were surprised by rivals whose complicity in the Dublin plot may safely be assumed; in others the commanders retained control and either cautiously concurred with the declaration or sought to reserve their position, not, it was claimed, 'out of dislike to the cause but out of dislike to those that were active in the declaration';[100] in others, conflict ensued.

The provinces of Leinster and Ulster seem to have proved largely unproblematic. The preemptive strikes against Drogheda and Carlow suggest that the centres of probable resistance in Leinster had been identified in advance and the change of control seems to have been otherwise quietly accomplished except in Kilkenny, where Ludlow's recent appointee was 'frighted out of his government' and replaced by Humphrey Hurd, a former lieutenant-colonel who had been removed on the standard grounds of an allegedly vicious life and disaffection to the public.[101] In Ulster also, recorded incidents were few. Colonel Cooper was

---

[95] *Clarke Papers*, iv, 202–3.

[96] *Clarke Papers*, iv, 227–8. Campbell 'stuck to me in Ireland when most of the forces left me', Monck recalled. Ibid., pp. 225–7. The messenger was in fact Charles Campbell, a cousin of Lord Montgomery. He and William Montgomery, who wrote an account of the Montgomery family, represented Newtownards in the 1661 Irish parliament. *Montgomery MSS*, p. 249.

[97] *Clarke Papers*, iv, 228–9. *Parliamentary Intelligencer*, 2–9 January.

[98] Bridges et al., *A perfect narrative*, p. 9.

[99] Ludlow, *Memoirs*, ii, 189.   [100] *Cal. SP, Ire., 1647–60*, p. 716.

[101] Ludlow, *Memoirs*, ii, 191.

ill and responsibility devolved upon Lieutenant-Colonel Brian Smith, governor of Carrickfergus since the previous August, who first ordered the garrisons to keep close to their quarters and maintain 'quietness' and then, on 19 December, summoned them to rendezvous at Belfast.[102] In the event, this mobilization seems not to have taken place. Cooper died 'in his Chair' two days later and Smith was seized by a number of his own soldiers and taken to Dublin: the mainsprings behind this coup seem to have been the mayor, John Davis, and one Charles Twigg, who made several journeys, 'day and night', to Dublin and was rewarded with the command of a foot company.[103] John Gorges, the displaced lieutenant-colonel of Henry Cromwell's foot, secured the city of Londonderry, where he had been governor some years previously, apparently without opposition.[104] Within a few weeks of the coup in Dublin, only Arnop in Enniskillen remained undeclared.

In Connacht, Sir Charles Coote is said to have invited the governor of Galway, Thomas Sadler, and his officers to drink a cup of wine at his country seat at Tyrellan, where he enticed the colonel away from his officers and returned secretly by boat to Galway to open the castle gates and admit a new garrison amidst cries of 'A Coote, a Coote' and 'a free parliament'.[105] Coote, having 'clapt up' a number of 'Anabaptists, or other Phanatiques', including the mayor, one of the sheriffs and Major Ormsby, who enjoyed Ludlow's approval and was presumably substituting for Dobson, went on to assemble 'a considerable body both of horse and foot, consisting chiefly of the English-Irish', with which he surprised Colonel Brayfield and took control of Athlone, the only place in Connacht to show resistance.[106] The term 'English-Irish' was used to denote those who had settled in the 1650s and the declaration issued by Coote 'and the Officers and Souldiers under his Command', in which they affirmed their determi-

---

[102] Dunlop, *Commonwealth*, p. 706. HMC, *Hastings MSS* (4 vols., London, 1928–47), ii, 362.
[103] *Cal. SP, Ire., 1660–2*, pp. 32, 33. SP, Ire., 63/303. 134. Bridges et al., *A perfect narrative*, p. 11.
[104] Bridges et al., *A perfect narrative*, p. 11. Moody and Simms, *The bishopric of Derry*, ii, 404.
[105] This story is told in Heath, *Chronicle*, p. 438. Tyrellan had formerly belonged to the earl of Clanricarde.
[106] Coote's account is in SP, Ire., 63/307. 211 (*Cal. SP, Ire., 1660–2*, p. 423). Bridges et al., *A Perfect Narrative*, p. 11. Ludlow, *Memoirs*, ii, 187. Brayfield had been governor of Athlone during his previous service in Ireland. *Arch. Hib.*, 7, p. 46.

nation to 'stand by that Parliament and those who have declared already at Dublin, no lesse here, or shall hereafter so declare' confirms the description in both its signatories and its substance. The four Coote brothers, their cousin Oliver St George, and Solomon Cambre were the only New English subscribers: the others, headed by Colonel Sadler, Lieutenant-Colonel Moore and George Ingoldsby, were indeed English-Irish.[107] The content had a pronounced professional edge: the army leaders were denounced not only for interrupting parliament, but for having tried 'to involve us all in the same guilt with themselves', and much was made of their cashiering officers and soldiers 'anciently serviceable to the good Cause' without payment of arrears, and their indifference to the 'want of pay' of the soldiers while the treasury was 'Exhausted in large Sallaries to sup the grandeur of themselves'.[108]

In Munster, in two coups manifestly linked with the Dublin conspiracy, Thomas Stanley took command of Clonmel, where he had been governor until the previous summer, and Ralph Wilson seized Limerick on 15 December from John Nelson, his former lieutenant-colonel, with whom Ludlow had replaced him as governor. Nelson, it was claimed, 'was frighted hence by the violence of the souldiers' and the 'Anabaptist Officers decryed and exploded': the townsmen supported the garrison, and the two combined to write to Colonel Ingoldsby in London to invite him to resume his earlier governorship, 'as judging you heartie for a Parliament's interest'.[109] In the Cork area, where the presence of Warden provided a direct link with events in Dublin, there was some initial confusion, not least in the mind of Colonel Wallis who protested that he had not encountered such difficulties 'since first I drew a sword in this

---

[107] Cambre, from a Wicklow settler family, had commanded in Wexford in 1656, where he was a justice of the peace as late as June 1658, and had settled on arrears land in Tipperary. Dunlop, *Commonwealth*, p. 623n; *Arch. Hib.*, 7, pp. 25, 29. Ingoldsby was Henry's brother.

[108] *Declaration of Sir Charles Coot*. In the NLI catalogue this is mistakenly assigned the date 19 January 1659[60].

[109] The twenty signatories included Ben Lucas, a witness to the Articles of Limerick in April 1652 (*Arch. Hib.*, 7, pp. 63–4, 66) and Sampson Toogood, both of whom shortly joined the council of officers in Dublin, Waller's son Richard and the local minister George Burdett. 20 December 1659, Carte MS 67, f. 287. Ingoldsby clearly released the letter to the *Parliamentary Intelligencer*, which paraphrased it, 26 December–2 January.

quarrell'. He reported on 23 December that there were two gatherings of gentlemen, at Mallow and Youghal, some of them former army officers and some of them former royalists, 'yet both uniteing'. He did not see himself as standing for the army against supporters of parliament: 'they declare a concurrance with the late declaration which if true I hope for peace in this countrey' he wrote, but he thought their concern for parliament's interest 'contrary to the grounds and principles they have formerly proceeded on', and professed himself unable to understand 'the reason of so many gentlemen of the country drawing themselves together and forming themselves into troops, appointing officers with other preparacions of hostile manner, surprising the Blockhouse of Youghall and keepeing that towne as a Garrison'. His associated troubles included the mutiny of the foot soldiers in Cork, fomented by those who had 'long waited for our divisions', which was resolved by money and promises of indemnity, and the defection of Axtell's company at Mallow and part of Sir Maurice Fenton's at Youghal.[110] In fact, Youghal was taken by Francis Foulkes, a close associate of Broghill and governor of Dungarvan in the 1650s, who had been one of the prime movers in the defection of Youghal to parliament in 1649.[111] To the east, William Leigh in Waterford and John Puckle in Ross endorsed the Dublin officers. The long-term governor of Cork, Colonel Phayre, and the recently appointed governors of Kinsale and Wexford, Robert Saunders, who had been cashiered from Phayre's regiment by Cromwell and reinstated by Ludlow,[112] and Solomon Richards, Ludlow's regimental lieutenant-colonel, responded alike: each declared for parliament but refused at first to accept the authority of the new regime in Dublin 'to the great disadvantage of the Parliament and public charge of the Nation and the good people thereof'.[113] Within weeks it was alleged that the adhesion of Cork to the Dublin officers had been due to the actions of private soldiers and citizens, though Phayre and Wallis 'laboured much to the contrary',[114] and this pattern of initial

---

[110] *Cal. SP, Ire., 1647–60*, p. 695. SP, Ire., 63/287. 187; 63/306. 49. Fenton was an officer in Waller's regiment. *Cal. SP, Ire., 1647–60*, p. 700.
[111] For Foulkes, see p. 218 below.
[112] Dunlop, *Commonwealth*, pp. 114n, 651. Ludlow, *Memoirs*, ii, 74.
[113] Ludlow, *Memoirs*, ii, 189–90. Articles against Sir Hardress Waller, TCD MS 844, f. 192v.
[114] Bridges et al., *A perfect narrative*, p. 11.

military reserve followed by fairly speedy capitulation to local pressure seems to have been common. The leaders of the coup paid particular tribute to the contribution of the common soldiers and junior officers who had deserted some disaffected commanders and forced others to comply. An alternative view held that the soldiers 'sold their officers, upon some promise of their arrears, some for a barrel of beer, and others for trifles'.[115] If Wallis was representative, the reserve of the officers may have owed less to hostility to parliament than to suspicion of the motives of those who had come to its support.

What he heard of Irish events left Ludlow in a quandary. He could not but approve of the stated purposes of the officers who had secured Dublin Castle and noted that their declaration was signed by his brother-in-law, 'with many others of known integrity'. On the other hand, he deeply distrusted some of those involved, particularly Theophilus Jones, 'who upon all occasions had shown himself a principle instrument of mischief amongst us', and 'Col Bridges and others, who had been very active to support the usurpation of the Cromwells'.[116] In this at least his views resembled those of John Jones who characterized what was taking place both as the realization of earlier fears of 'the Engageing of the English fforces in Ireland, one against another' and, with apparent incongruity, as 'the casting off the English Government and Parliamentary authority in this nation'. His meaning was elucidated by his subsequent accusation that Waller was trying 'to start a Warr betweene the two Nations'.[117] The implication, that the coup was fundamentally a movement by the older settler community against the totality of recent changes, disguised as a defence of the Long Parliament, came to be widely shared by English republicans. In more immediate terms, Jones saw dangers in the taking of arms by unauthorized forces and especially in the movement of troops out of quarters. He believed that promises of three months' pay had been made to bribe the soldiers and could not be honoured: both the soldiers and the citizenry they would have to be billeted on would be alienated, the tories would make free, and there would be 'a new Warr upon the English, and thereby give an entrance to Charles Stuart his confederates'. To avert this, he envisaged an arrangement by which he would resume his

---

[115] *A sober vindication of Lieutenant General Ludlow, and others*, p. 14.
[116] Ludlow, *Memoirs*, ii, 185.   [117] 'Inedited letters', p. 293.

position as deputy commander in chief, acting only on the advice of a committee comprising Waller, the three Warrens, Lawrence and Cooper (or any four of them), until such time as Ludlow's pleasure was known. In the meantime, all strong places should stay in their present hands and troops return to their quarters. Tactically, his plan was that these ideas should be propounded to 'such as are reputed most honest amongst them, and best fixed to the Cause and Interest wee are to maytayne, as to Mr Winter and his people, and by them to Waller'.[118] Very shortly, however, Jones clutched at the insubstantial straw represented by a printed copy of Monck's reply to the letter sent to him on 4 November by the Irish officers.[119] Jones, who claimed never to have received the original, which was dated 11 November, concluded that its proposal that parliament should be restored for an agreed period was entirely faithful 'to the Cause and Interest we have beene ingaged in during all the tyme of the late Troubles in these Three Nations'. On 22 December, he offered Waller his assistance in promoting an accommodation on that basis.[120] In England at the same time, Ludlow was likewise worrying about the consequences of the Dublin coup when his initial doubts as to 'what judgement to make of it' were resolved by word from Kempson, who explained that while he had thought it in the public interest to subscribe to the declaration, 'yet he was so unsatisfied with the spirits and principles of these men, that he was very hardly persuaded to sign it'.[121] Kempson's advice was that Ludlow should hurry over and Ludlow decided to take it. On 24 December he set out for Ireland, to support them if they were honest or reduce them if they were not, as he later phrased it.[122]

In Dublin, little more than a week after the coup, the number of garrisons which had declared support was judged sufficient to assure success and the council of officers requested Broghill and Coote to join them in Dublin with a view to establishing what was in effect a provisional military government operating through the authority vested in Major General Waller, 'that by his hand Orders might pass upon all occasions'. The first priority, in the necessarily circumspect phraseology of the

---

[118] Ibid., pp. 295–6. [119] E 669 f. 22 (38). [120] 'Inedited letters', pp. 296–7.
[121] Ludlow, *Memoirs*, ii, 185. Ludlow reported an exchange in which Warden told Kempson 'that though I thought him a Cavalier, yet I should find him as faithful to the Commonwealth as any man'. Ibid., p. 187. [122] Ludlow, *Memoirs*, ii, 185, 187.

circumstances, was to replace 'disaffected' officers with 'friends to the parliament'.[123] At an early stage, according to Ludlow's thoroughly self-regarding account, a company of foot in Lawrence's regiment, asked to declare for parliament and professing themselves unsure what parliament was meant, had resolved to be faithful to parliament and to Ludlow as commander in chief; this precedent, he claimed, was widely followed.[124] There is some confirmation of this version of events in an early draft of a progress report to the commissioners at Portsmouth in which the officers outlined their difficulties frankly. Ludlow, they explained, was the 'principall propp and hope' of the

> opposeing party among us, who by underhand messages and letters have nowe earnestly sollicited his speedy repaire hither for heading them; and being big-swollene in theire hopes therein they conceale not what they expect from and by him, declareing that then the wheele will turn, and casting out menaces, even to blood, against those now appeareing against them in that cause.[125]

This admission stood in contradiction to the confident tone of the rest of the letter, in which they reported that 'all considerable places' had declared for parliament, that those senior officers who had been unwilling to cooperate had failed to gain the support of their men, and that they now intended to proceed to the 'new modelling' of the army, cautiously serving notice that it would be necessary to remove some officers who had been recently appointed by parliament itself. On second thoughts, they decided not to reveal their fear of the potential strength of the 'adverse party'. Instead, they aggressively attacked Ludlow's recent behaviour, focusing on the evidence of his apparent defection from parliament rather than upon the threat that he posed to themselves. While in Ireland, it was alleged, he had disobliged the parliament's friends, dismissing them from the army without consultation, and consulting instead with 'the very abjects of men and most not of the army' rather than taking the advice of his officers. Having appointed Jones as his deputy, he had culpably neglected to dismiss him when there was mani-

---

[123] Bridges et al., *A Perfect Narrative*, pp. 9, 11, 12.   [124] *Memoirs*, ii, 187.
[125] Deleted portion of a draft of the letter of 24 December, in the hand of Dr Henry Jones. TCD MS 844, f. 188.

fest cause. Subsequently, he had failed to return to his post in Ireland, avoided contact with the commissioners at Portsmouth and the council of state, and stayed among the parliament's enemies. Casuistically insisting that they could not 'judge it safe' to receive him back 'having thus given our thoughts unto your Honours',[126] they assured the commissioners that they would not displace him, 'yet our jealousies of him grow daily on your behalf, and as to a prosperous government of our affairs here'.[127] They sought advice as to whether they should accept him as commander, but they made it clear that in the meantime they were resolved 'not to owne him but to restraine his actings against you to our power'.[128] The letter was drafted on 24 December by Dr Henry Jones and signed by his brother Theophilus and John Warren and on Christmas Day the receiver general of revenue, Robert Wood, a former client of Henry Cromwell, was deputed to take it to England.[129] As verification of the claim that Ireland was under control, he was authorized to tell the commissioners 'that they could, if need be, send over 3,000 or 4,000 men for the service of the parliament'.[130]

On 26 December, these proceedings were regularized by the council of officers which agreed without dissent that Ludlow's conduct since leaving Ireland 'hath given just occasion of suspicion that he is no friend to the parliament' and decided that if he were to return he should not be admitted unless the council of state, the parliamentary commissioners at Portsmouth or parliament itself should signify that this was their wish. The record of that meeting makes it plain that as they began to formalize their proceedings the council of officers continued to include representatives of the junior officers: it was signed by Sir Charles Coote, Colonels Temple, Warden, Cole, Jones, Long, Bridges and Chidley Coote, Lieutenant-Colonel John Warren, Majors Edward Warren and William Meredith (who had commanded a troop of Henry Cromwell's horse and been major to Theophilus Jones in the early 1650s),[131] eight or nine captains, a

---

[126] TCD MS 844, ff. 185–6v.
[127] *HMC Portland MSS*, i, 688–9. Cf. *CJ*, vii, 803.   [128] TCD MS 844, ff. 185–6.
[129] Wood was a mathematician of repute who served in Henry Cromwell's household and seems to have become receiver general of revenue in October 1658. *DNB*. Barnard, *Cromwellian Ireland*, pp. 223–4.
[130] *HMC Portland MSS*, i, 690.
[131] *Regimental history*, pp. 596, 614.

lieutenant, two cornets and two ensigns.¹³² The geographical spread, on the other hand, was not wide. Cole, who lived in Dublin, was the only Ulster representative; Captain George Ingoldsby had come from Connacht with the Cootes and Captain Ben Lucas had arrived from Limerick; Warden and perhaps Captain Fitzgerald, who was still in Dublin, remained the only obvious link with the Munster leadership. Given the ambiguous status of Sir Charles Coote, the only senior officers on the council who held valid commissions were Edward Warren and Meredith, who had been in England with the Irish Brigade.

On 28 December, the council of officers addressed themselves systematically to the consolidation of their position, inside and outside the country. First, they declared a day of public thanksgiving, to be observed in Dublin on 3 January and in the rest of the country two weeks later. The medium for this simple order was a profusely rhetorical outpouring of professed guilt and passionate accusation:

> Had not the powers and policies of hell prevailed far, and laid the very necks of Magistracy and Ministry upon the block of direful Anarchy and Arbytrarie rule?... What ordinance of God was not slighted, opposed, maligned and scorned by specious Pretences and strong Delusions? Were not God's own people very deeply guilty of Apostacie and Hypocrisie, of Unfaithfulness and Breach of Covenant in all Relations?... Were we not hastening to the sad Catastrophe of the German tragedy, and Münster declarations, procured by the like fanatick Spirits, which then obstructed Reformation Work?... Do not the signal returns of His mercy challenge proportionable returns of our duty?[133]

---

[132] There are two variant lists. Ludlow, *Memoirs*, ii, 471; *Cal. SP, Ire., 1647–60*, pp. 695–6. Bridges and Meredith are from the latter, which also includes Capt. Lucas, Ensign Mainwaring, Capt. Dan Lisle, Capt. Sandford, Capt. Geo Ingoldsby and Cornet (*sic*) Robert Fitzgerald. It does not include Joyner, Bond and Cornet Edward and Ensign Thos Harrington. The names in common are the senior officers and Capts. John Frank, Abel Warren, Robert Cooke, Lt. Thompson, Cornet Leigh. Both Frank and Leigh had been co-signatories with Jones and Thompson in a 1657 petition of officers and agents. Petty, *Down survey*, pp. 180–1.

[133] *An account of the affairs of Ireland in reference to the late change in England; with a declaration of several officers of the army in Ireland, holding forth their steadfast resolution to adhere to the parliament* (London, 1659). *Parliamentary Intelligencer*, 16–23 January. Davies argues that

The second document approved for circulation by the officers at this meeting was prosaic by contrast, but beguilingly so, for its thrust was dramatic. It was a letter signed by Waller as major general, 'with the advice and consent of a Council of Officers', and addressed to officials of the counties, cities and principal boroughs: it required those Protestants 'whose good affections to the Parliament in the present change have been testified' to elect representatives 'to be here at the Tholsel in Dublin' on 24 January, 'to consult and deliberate, do and consent to such things as shall be found necessary for the good of the Publick, and the service of the Parliament, to whose pleasure all is to be submitted'. The preamble rehearsed the dangers that arbitrary power had recently presented to God's true religion, to the fundamental laws of the land, and to the liberties and freedom of the people and noted that the danger had been removed 'by the blessing of God on the counsels and endeavors of the Army here in Ireland': 'yet some things remain as yet to be done for preserving the peace of this Nation, for upholding trade, Traffick and Commerce, for the administration of distributive justice, for inspection into the Publick Revenues and Treasury, for the orderly management and distribution thereof, towards supporting and supplying the Army and Publick charge of the Nation'. The names of those chosen were to be returned to Dr Dudley Loftus.[134] This was, at its most narrow, the solution to the financially driven dangers that had worried John Jones: at

the Münster reference indicates Presbyterian leanings. *The restoration*, p. 250. McGuire argues that it shows no more than a general sense of the need for orthodoxy and stability. 'The Dublin Convention', Cosgrove and McGuire, *Parliament and community*, p. 123. Both assume that this is the declaration of 14 December. In February, the analogy was developed at some length by George Pressick in *A breife relation of some of the most remarkable passages of the Anabaptists in High and Low Germany in the year 1521* (London, 1660), which set out to show 'how near these Sectaries and these Nations have advanced both in Doctrine, and practice to these in that in Germany'. The book was dedicated to Broghill, Coote and Jones, 'the three cheif worthyes of Ireland in this blessed work' of suppressing 'their insolent, Tyrannical usurped Authority, which they exercised over God's people in this nation', p. 2.

[134] Borlase, 'History of the execrable Rebellion', with additions by the author, Stowe MS 82, f. 282. The circular was printed, with blanks for the insertion of the appropriate names and numbers. Cork's agent received 'precepts' early in January 'for choosing of two members for each county and one for each town' to assemble as a 'convention'. T. C. Barnard, 'The Protestant interest, 1641–60', in Ohlmeyer, *Independence to occupation*, p. 219. The circular does not use the term convention.

[123]

its broadest, it might seem to point towards that 'casting off of the English government' that underlay his anxiety.

It is probably unnecessary to seek the influences behind so obvious a course of action as the mobilization of general support for the *coup d'état* and the involvement of civilians in the provisional arrangements for government that must necessarily follow it, but there was a proximate precedent and perhaps even a political theory. The precedent had been set by General Monck whose preparations for the possibility that he might need to take the bulk of his army out of Scotland had included the summoning of a convention of representatives of the shires and burghs at Edinburgh on 15 November and another at Berwick on 12 December. He sought money, of course, but also their cooperation in preserving the peace while he answered the 'call from God and his people to march into England' and in the event he decided to entrust Scotland to its nobility and gentry.[135] The theory was provided in a pamphlet written by Robert Chambers, minister at St Patrick's and St Kevin's in Dublin, 'Approved by the Major General and Council of Officers sitting at Dublin, and by them ordered to be forthwith printed and published', which was issued about this time by the official printer, William Bladen. Said on its title page to have been written on 4 November (or, more probably, 14 November), *Some animadversions* was a detailed refutation of the case made for the army in the *Plea for their present practice* of 24 October and its sequel, *The Declaration* of 27 October.[136] The date of composition carries some conviction. These apologias had not reached Dublin by 30 October, but Jones was able to report fully on the reaction to them on 8 November. Chambers was sufficiently abreast with what was happening in England to

---

[135] *Old parliamentary history*, xxii, 19–20. F. D. Dow, *Cromwellian Scotland, 1651–1660* (Edinburgh, 1979), pp. 254–7; Heath, *A chronicle*, p. 432.

[136] The work was issued twice. First, anonymously, under the title *Some animadversions upon the declaration of, and the plea for, the army; together with sixteen queries thence extracted. Or an essay by way of answer to the plea for, and declaration of the army, in reference to their interruption of the parliament's sitting, October the 12. Written November 4. 1659* (Dublin, 1659); second, with a new title page, as by Robert Chambre, under the title *Some animadversions upon the declaration of, and the plea for the army; in reference to their interruption of the parliament's sitting, October the 12. Written Nov. 14, 1659. Some few copies came abroad without the author's name, which is here prefix'd.* (Cashel Diocesan Library: details of publication removed by cropping.)

comment on the non-participation of eight or nine members of the committee of safety and to outline the stance of Ludlow who had arrived in London only on 29 October, but there are no allusions to later developments. Apart from a reference to the effects of taxation upon 'the new planters of Ireland', the tract had no explicit Irish dimension. Chambers spoke well of Ludlow (which tends to corroborate the dating), disparagingly of Vane, contemptuously of Fleetwood and trenchantly of Lambert. His religious and political positions were plainly stated. As to the first, he believed 'that the great interest of Christ lyes chiefly and likelyest between' the Presbyterians and the Congregationalists, and 'that the means to carry it out effectually, must be their agreement upon common principles'.[137] As to the second, it seemed to him obvious that the parliament, 'taking to them such of their fellow Members, as are willing to submit to Commonwealth principles, having not forfeited their right, and filling their vacancyes, with persons not subject to just exception, will prove the most probable basis of the Nations settlement'.[138] He accepted the army's premise, that the 'good peoples interest' was primary, but denied that it had been in danger, excoriated the Machiavellian device of putting the 'mask of religion' on their secret purposes, and listed a series of violations of that interest which began with the original expulsion of the parliament in 1653 and ended with the recent 'taking Romes work out of their hands, teaching Rebellion and deposing Magistrates'. He accepted that a supreme magistrate might be deposed, but not 'knockt in the head by whosoever willed', nor overturned by the army since it had no delegated authority from the people. Ordinarily, the coordinate power 'as between King and Parliament' obviated the difficulty: 'salus populi being suprema lex ; though the King be greater than individuals yet not greater then the whole in their representative, but below them, as the president is inferior to the Council'. Where there was no coordinate power, however, the 'Judges, Justices of the peace, Sheriffs, Mayors (who in the Intervals of Parliaments manage affairs) they may in the behalf of the people stand up in their stations'; where these failed to act, the 'people, as many of them as can conveniently meet, may seize upon the person or persons of such tyrannical Magistrate; and chuse meet persons to try them for their

[137] *Some animadversions*, p. 33. [138] Ibid., p. 28.

male-administrations, and slay them in case of resistance, as you do with other Malefactors': 'for the people, in whom the original of government is, may call a Parliament or appoint such as may be pleased to maintain their cause'.[139] Although this owed a good deal to the early work of William Prynne on *Sovereign Power*, which had been concerned with vindicating parliament in 1643, Chambers developed the argument to a conclusion which hinted at a course of action that might apply to the very different situation of late 1659. His views on recent factional politics seem closest to those of Haselrig, but perhaps only because he had been most resolute in opposing the army, and the inferences that might be drawn from the invoking of Prynne's name are strengthened by the seventh of the sixteen topical questions which he extracted from his text: 'Whether this action, especially the Plea for it (viz) the good peoples interest doth not justify Sir George Booth, at least the good people who joined in that engagement upon the Parliaments going about to destroy the good peoples interest by putting the army into the hands of Anabaptists &c.'[140] His religious concerns, which were with the need to defend the ministry and the tithes that maintained it, were analogically expressed in the citation of St Jude, verse 11 – 'Woe unto them! for they have gone in the way of Cain, and ran greedily after the error of Balaam for reward, and perished in the gainsaying of Corah' – which he read as a now-fulfilled prophecy of the repetition 'under the Gospel' of the sin of Corah and his companions, who had challenged the authority of Moses and Aaron and sought to abrogate their priestly function.[141]

When the dissident army officers wrote to the speaker of the Commons on 15 December 1659 to announce the seizure of Dublin Castle, they concluded their preamble by adapting the words of St Jude to their opponents.[142] When Irish commissioners in London published an apologia about a month later they concluded by explaining that their aim was to rid the army of 'an Anabaptistical and Notional party', which was precisely how Chambers had described the interest that had taken control in the

---

[139] Ibid., pp. 13–14, 15–16.
[140] Ibid., p. 30.
[141] Numbers 16. *Some animadversions*, p. 22.
[142] [Theo Jones et al.], *A letter sent from Ireland dated at Dublin Decemb. 15. 1659 superscribed for the Right Honourable William Lenthall, Esq; Speaker to the Parliament*. London, 1659[60].

summer purges.¹⁴³ The latter was perhaps a commonplace, but the pamphlet's approval by the council of officers is testimony to its reputation and both the specificity of its dating and the absence of updating suggest that it may well have been circulating for some time. It is conceivable that its influence went beyond the provision of allusions and phrases. The invitation to local officers to conduct elections to a parliamentary style assembly filled the constitutional prescription that in the absence of a supreme magistrate tyranny must be confronted by the authority which devolved upon the lower level 'delegated magistrates' or, in the last resort, upon the people themselves. That there was a pronounced community of ideas among the opponents of the regime in December 1659 is clear. All of the statements, implicitly or explicitly, incorporated the assumption that extremist forces were already in control before the expulsion of parliament in October and there was clearly some anxiety lest the reinstatement of parliament should do no more than restore an unsatisfactory status quo. William Petty, writing early in the new year to vindicate himself from the aspersions of Sankey and others who had attacked the honesty and competence with which he had distributed Irish lands, saw the connections in simple terms. His thesis was that almost all of his critics were Anabaptists and sectaries, that their real target had been Henry Cromwell and that they had been complicit in the overthrow of Richard: he welcomed 'the Cheque given them in Ireland, by the wisdom and vigilancy of Sir Hardress Waller, Sir Charles Coote, Sir Theoph. Jones and other good Patriots'.¹⁴⁴ This was not the language of devotion to the rump, and the indications are that it was representative in its view that the immediate source of the problems in Ireland was the restoration of the parliament in May rather than its expulsion in October. Frank opinions as to the true solution of those problems remained as yet outside the limits of public affirmation, but suspicion did not need to observe a similar restraint.

A well-informed republican pamphleteer who wrote *A sober vindication* of Ludlow, and who was undoubtedly of Dublin provenance, was in no doubt that the context was not what it seemed. He provided a good deal

---

¹⁴³ Bridges et al., *A Perfect Narrative*, p. 15.
¹⁴⁴ *Reflections*, pp. 85–7, 124. Petty's post as physician to the army high command had been discontinued by the rump, as he recorded in his will. Lodge, *Peerage*, ii, 354n.

of circumstantial detail to illustrate the real character of what was happening in Dublin, where 'the people made acclamation, for joy, that there should not be an Anabaptist nor a Sectarist left in Ireland'.[145] Sectary, he observed, 'is a name they give to all the Godly and the Parliament's best friends alike (by all judgements, Presbyterians, Independants and Anabaptists)'.[146] He claimed that before the coup there had been talk of religious union and preparations for meetings to propagate brotherly love.[147] After it, no more was heard of reconciliation. John Rogers, arriving 'to preach by Order from the Parliament', had been imprisoned without a hearing and denied bail;[148] Enoch Grey, who was attached to Christ Church,[149] 'dare not stir abroad, being threatened by the Porters and Watermen to be thrown into the water'; Henry Wootton, minister at St Michan's and chaplain to the King's Inns,[150] had been prevented from preaching and confined to his house, Samuel Mather 'discountenanced and discouraged', Dr John Harding[151] put out of his meeting place, and Christopher Blackwood told 'that if he preacht any more at Chichester house his throat would be cut'. Since Robert Chambers and Claudius Gilbert were also being put out, it needed only the removal of Winter and Edward Baines[152] and 'the light of the Gospell will be extinct at Dublin, and what remains but Gross Egyptian darkness?'[153] Of these ministers, only Blackwood and Harding were Baptists. Ultimately the source of this purge was 'the Prelatical, Episcopal Common-prayer-book Party (which are the most numerous)', who joined with the Presbyterians to 'crush and trample

---

[145] *A sober vindication*, p. 10.   [146] Ibid., post-script.   [147] Ibid., p. 11.
[148] His coming had been authorized by parliament in the summer, and finance had been authorized: this assertion constitutes the only evidence that he actually came. Seymour, *Puritans in Ireland*, p. 176.
[149] Ibid., Appendix.
[150] Ibid., Appendix. T. Power, 'The "Black Book" of King's Inns', *The Irish Jurist*, new series, 20 (1985), p. 199. Berry, *The register of the church of St Michan*, p. 13.
[151] A trustee of Trinity College, whose recorded ministry was in Cork. Barnard, *Cromwellian Ireland*, pp. 119n, 199, 210.
[152] St John's, formerly assistant to Chambers in St Patrick's. Seymour, *Puritans in Ireland*, Appendix.
[153] *A sober vindication*, pp. 3, 11, 16. The same treatment, he claimed, had been accorded to Edmund Wells in St Finbarr's in Cork, and William Aspinall (who had recently been appointed minister in Kildare, Seymour, *Puritans in Ireland*, Appendix), neither of whom were Baptists.

upon the Independents, but that being done, they must fall upon the Presbyterians'.[154] There was, of course, a political agenda as well: every soul within the Castle 'was for a parliament', and the coup was a sham. These men were making ready to receive the king 'though that must not be yet mentioned, the design must be first to bring in the Excluded Members in 1648 and then comes in ding dong bells, King, Lords and Commons'.[155] Thus it was that officers who had 'cheerfully declared for Parliament', among them Pretty, Phayre, Wallis, Abbot, Brayfield, Smith, Bennett and Denison, had been summoned to Dublin and 'clapt in prison' while Anabaptists were disarmed, Cavaliers recruited and 'the Native Irish (as the Mayor of Dublin is for one)' empowered 'with the sword'.[156] Extravagant in inference as this undoubtedly is, much of it is entirely consistent with the professions of those who brought about the coup, and descriptively it perhaps catches the mood of a moment of sharp reaction against a detested group whose power had been abruptly ended. The revolution was not at first, it may be suspected, either confined or gentle, though it soon proved wiser to be circumspect. The working alliance between Presbyterians and Episcopalians described by the author of *A sober vindication* ran counter to the association between Presbyterians and Independents which the council of officers had inferentially underwritten in their approval of the publication of *Some animadversions* by the now disfavoured Chambers.

Travelling once again through Beaumaris, Ludlow commandeered the frigate *Oxford* and arrived off Dublin on 31 December.[157] From shipboard he wrote to Waller and the other officers to inform them that parliament had been restored and was to sit on 26 December, which he doubted 'not but they did'. Choosing his words with care, he went on to explain that having 'met with' their declaration he had come to strengthen their hands in the work, hastening over so suddenly that he had not received their account of what had happened 'which I presume I should otherwise have

---

[154] *A sober vindication*, p. 15.   [155] Ibid., p. 3.
[156] Ibid., pp. 2, 3, 11–12. He subsequently added Lowe and Roberts to this list. He was wrong about Wallis who escaped 'unhandsomely' to England with Deane. Broghill to Monck, 7 February 1660, Herefordshire and Worcestershire Record Office, A H 34 (unfoliated).
[157] *Cal. SP, Dom., 1659–60*, p. 317.

done'.[158] The tone of uneasy suspicion was entirely justified. Among the many things that Ludlow did not yet know was that the council of officers in Ireland was reporting to Scotland as well as to London and Portsmouth. Their news had been celebrated by cannonades in Edinburgh and Leith on 26 December, the day after Campbell's arrival at Coldstream, the army had observed a day of thanksgiving, and Campbell, bearing Monck's congratulations and a request for a regiment of horse, was also on his way back to Dublin, by way of Newtownards.[159]

---

[158] Ludlow, *Memoirs*, ii, 187, 449–50.

[159] Nicoll, *Diary of public transactions*, p. 261. Baker, *A chronicle*, p. 738. *Public Intelligencer*, 2–9 January. *Clarke Papers*, iv, 225–6.

5

Setting up for themselves: January to February

The ending of army rule was widely welcomed in England. The restoration of the Long Parliament, however, was welcome only as a means to that end. Once the willingness of the armed forces to submit to civilian authority was assured, the nature of that authority came into question. Ironically, as the rump progressively secured its position by yet another remodelling of the officer corps, it rendered itself correspondingly more vulnerable to political opposition. The first challenge had been immediate. An activist group of secluded members had claimed the right to take their seats on 27 December: though parliament responded by formally expelling them on 5 January, the reconstitution of its membership by undoing the army purge of 1648 remained a well canvassed possibility. The others were that the parliament should either renew its mandate by conducting by-elections to fill the vacant seats or dissolve and allow the question of how England should be governed to be decided by a 'free and full parliament'. Each of these possibilities pointed to a different outcome. Recruitment to the present parliament was designed to preserve the commonwealth. Few questioned that the election of a new parliament would lead to the restoration of the monarchy, though the terms on which this would be done would depend upon how free the elections were. The readmission of the secluded members, though intended as a means of legitimizing the rump, might also serve as a gradualist way of achieving the same result. As the 'rump' set about entrenching itself, the sense of its transience was heightened by the open hostility of influential elements in the city of London and by the enigmatic behaviour of George Monck. Though Monck's declared objective had been achieved on 26 December, he none the less continued his march, entering England on New Year's Day and progressing slowly towards London throughout January. What military justification there was for this advance disappeared with the collapse of Lambert's resistance in the north. Although Monck urged support for parliament and his journey was authorized by it, his intentions could not be guessed, nor his power doubted.[1] It was unsettlingly clear that if he wished to intervene decisively, he could do so.

The 'rump' busied itself with the army, indemnifying against loss of life or estate those involved in the 'late defection' as well as commissioning new officers and recommissioning old ones. It expelled those who had collaborated too closely with the army, enacted a new and larger monthly assessment, and issued a declaration of intent to govern well which gave no indication of what form government would take because that was a subject on which its members could not agree. It was not the only one: an attempt to strengthen the oath of engagement by attaching a clause renouncing Charles Stuart was abandoned. As parliament dithered, opposition mounted, and Monck advanced.

The concerns of the officers who assumed control in Ireland after the *coup d'état* were conditioned, but not determined, by the course of events in England. Initially, while they consolidated their position, they had needed to guard against the possibility of reprisal by allying with the army's opponents in England and Scotland. Thus they reported to the Portsmouth commissioners as the inheritors of parliamentary authority and offered military support if it were needed. When the rump was restored the threat changed, but the priorities were not greatly altered. There was no disposition to relinquish power to those who had unleashed Ludlow and the commissioners upon Ireland. The officers and their civilian associates could not consolidate their position against parliament, however, without its consent, and they needed to convert the anti-army alliance into a partnership by convincing parliament of their good faith and trustworthiness. There were two prime objectives: to underpin their control of force by gaining approval of the alterations in the army command and to secure arrangements for the management of Irish government that did not

---

[1] As John Gorges observed to Broghill on 14 January 1660, 'what he intends is rather imagined than knowne'. Harvard, Orrery MS 18. 22.

challenge the power they had seized. They could not easily dispute parliament's authority, but they could hope to have it delegated to them. It was their misfortune that their relationship with parliament became bound up with the political future of Edmund Ludlow. His disbelief in the sincerity of their commitment to the rump and his determined efforts to defeat their purposes subverted their attempt to ingratiate themselves with parliament. They proceeded partly by lobbying its members, and appointed commissioners to do so systematically, and they relied heavily upon General Monck to argue their case and vouch for their dependability. But as they went deferentially about the business of persuading parliament to endorse them, they encountered a degree of opposition which drove them before long to conclude that only a change of government in England could secure their interests, and to say so publicly.

Ludlow's precipitate arrival on 31 December forced the issue, without fully disclosing its implications. The choice between acknowledging his authority and defying it had already been made formally on 26 December. The considerations were varied, of course: the officers had good reason to resent his previous conduct as commander in chief and they were now in direct competition with him for power, but the proximate justification seemed quite sufficient on its own. On the face of it, Ludlow's activities since leaving Ireland, and especially his active promotion of the army's scheme for a new parliament under a new constitution, raised reasonable doubt as to where his loyalty lay. On the continent, Hyde was puzzled: 'I do not understand Ludlow's part in this Business, nor to which party he is inclined', he wrote on 2 January.[2] In Ireland, evidence was added to inference by an intercepted letter in which Ludlow had reported to John Jones on 17 December that 'We seem to be necessitated to look towards the Long Parliament; 'tis to be feared they will be very high, in case they should be brought in without conditions.'[3] Against that background, his decision to leave London before the parliament actually met was distinctly sinister. The officers responded to his arrival by confirming their earlier decision in the amended form that he should not resume office (or, indeed, leave ship) until parliament confirmed that this was its wish. They

---

[2] Barwick, *Life of Barwick*, p. 477.
[3] *A letter from Sir Hardress Waller and several other Gentlemen at Dublin to Lieutenant General Ludlowe, with his answer to the same.* London, 1660.

also took the precaution of dispersing their prisoners to places of confinement outside Dublin.[4]

It was clear that an external challenge to their exercise of authority remained likely, but from the Commons rather than from the army. To ward off the most obvious threat, the resumption of government by parliament's existing appointees, the officers put the finishing touches to a conversion of the original indictment of Ludlow into articles of impeachment against all of the members of the ousted administration. Collectively, they were charged with having 'joyned with that rebellious part of the army in England'. It was not difficult to make this case against Jones, while Corbet and Thomlinson were involved in his guilt because they had possessed the power to stop him and had not used it:[5] moreover, all three had 'cast off the name of commissioners of parliament, stiling themselves commissioners of the commonwealth'.[6] The case against Ludlow was reinforced by reference to the letters that he had written to various officers in parts of Ireland to promote the sending of agents to 'that Juncto of Officers', the general council of the army,[7] and by the probability that he had been sent into Ireland by Fleetwood.[8] While the articles were being prepared, suspicion was cemented by his conduct in Ireland where he 'menaced such the Parliaments servants even to blood, and hath acted otherwise in hostile manner against them, without expecting the Parliaments pleasure against him and them'.[9]

The officers' decision to withhold obedience to Ludlow's authority was unofficially conveyed to him by Henry Kempson and others who visited him on board the *Oxford* in Monkstown Bay, apparently to warn him that he would be ambushed if he landed. Official notification was brought by

---

[4] Bridges et al., *A perfect narrative*, p. 13.
[5] Article 11.   [6] Article 2.   [7] Article 25.   [8] Article 26.
[9] Article 27. Ludlow, *Memoirs*, ii, 464–70. Articles 17 to 23 of the indictment repeat or develop the charges made in the letter of 26 December. TCD MS 844, ff. 197–200. Two non-military advisers, the baptist minister Thomas Hickes and the lawyer Thomas Fowles were now specially mentioned among Ludlow's confidants (Article 17). Ludlow's last act before leaving London had been to move the council of state to nominate Fowles as attorney general of Ireland. *Cal. SP, Dom., 1659–60*, p. 34. He had served in various capacities, including that of counsel for the commonwealth at the Athlone Commission, justice of assize for west Leinster and Connacht and commissioner for the determination of cases under the act of attainder of 1657. Dunlop, *Commonwealth*, pp. 484–5, 674, 716. Commonwealth State Accounts, *Anal. Hib.*, 15, p. 297.

Captain Lucas, on 2 January, with an assurance that the officers would comply with parliament's ruling and an assertion of their determination to be obeyed in the meantime.[10] Ludlow, turning down Lucas's invitation to appear before the council, replied pugnaciously that his commission from parliament absolved him from obeying 'those who for the most part had no commissions from them', and ordered the officers to forbear. On the same day, the *Oxford* intercepted the pacquet and Ludlow found a letter to Theophilus Jones which mentioned the affairs of the king and continued 'but no more of that till the next summer'. Confirmed in his belief that the plan was 'to bring in the son of the late king', he set out to defeat it.[11] He dispatched messages to a number of trusted garrison commanders and regimental officers assuring them of his own constancy, instructing them not to obey the usurped power of those who were seeking 'to set up for themselves, or some other single person', recommending that they combine forces and asking them to 'draw down' towards Munster any forces that could be spared once the garrisons were secure.[12]

Ludlow selected Munster as his theatre of operations because he believed that there was some ambiguity about the position of a number of garrison commanders in the south and south-east. His information was that Skinner in Duncannon, Phayre in Cork, Saunders in Kinsale and his own lieutenant-colonel of foot, Richards, whom he had appointed to govern Wexford, were unwilling to accept any orders that did not come either from their commander in chief or from parliament itself, and he thought it likely that Leigh in Waterford might be of the same mind since he was a Baptist.[13] Sir Hardress Waller, whose sources of information were better, believed that the only refractory garrisons were Enniskillen in the north, where Arnop finally came into line on 6 January, and Duncannon, 'an obscure nook that can defend nothing but itself, and is easily hindered from doing that'.[14] Skinner, who was a Baptist, had been appointed by Ludlow himself, in place of Colonel Simon Ridgely whose

[10] Ludlow, *Memoirs*, ii, pp. 450–1.
[11] Ibid., 188–92. *Cal. SP, Dom.*, 1659–60, p. 317.
[12] *Cal. SP, Ire.*, 1647–60, p. 704. S.P., Ire., 63/303. 2. Ludlow's later account is not entirely accurate: he did not, as he claimed, inform the officers that parliament was sitting. *Memoirs*, ii, 190. That news seems to have circulated slowly: Colonel Leigh in Waterford had not heard it by 6 January. SP, Ire., 63/303. 7.
[13] Ludlow, *Memoirs*, ii, 192–3. [14] *HMC, Portland MSS*, i, 693.

company captain he had been until he 'laid himself aside out of some pettish discontent'. Ludlow was confident of his loyalty and it was for Duncannon that he set sail on 3 January, the day set aside for public thanksgiving in the city of Dublin.[15] Miles Corbet, who had escaped house arrest and joined Ludlow on board the *Oxford* while it was 'hovering in the Bay of Dublin', transferred to the pacquet boat to return to England. No doubt inadvertently, but revealingly, he lent credence to the stance of the officers by reporting that Ludlow intended to make for Duncannon 'which yet stands for the army'.[16] Ludlow landed without difficulty, though the town was loosely invested by Colonel Temple's horse, and at once wrote to the neighbouring garrisons in Waterford and Ross requiring their assistance and to the more distant commanders, Phayre, Saunders and Richards, encouraging them to defy the authority of the council in Dublin.[17] He had misjudged Leigh, rather surprisingly, since he must have known that Leigh had earlier incurred republican wrath when he had publicly dismissed his ensign for refusing to attend the proclamation of Richard as lord protector, 'not counting him worthy to bear a Colour in his hand, that hath not fidelity in his heart to his Highness service'.[18] Leigh's initial response was politely uncompromising: he wrote that he had no reason to disbelieve the profession of those at Dublin that they were 'only for the old Parliament cause' and that what he had heard of Ludlow's activities in England, where he seemed to associate with Fleetwood rather than with the parliamentarians, was 'grounds of jealousy'.[19] A few days later, he amplified the point, accusing Ludlow of being involved in attempting to set up 'a military parliament, or a Parliament to bee theire creatures' and pointing out that his authority had been superseded both by the appointment of Monck as 'Generalissimo of the three nations' and by parliament's appointment of commissioners to govern the army.[20] From Ross, John Puckle, a former lieutenant-colonel of Law-

---

[15] *Ireland's fidelity*. Skinner had signed a baptist petition in 1657. Herlihy, 'Baptists in Ireland', p. 268. *Publick Intelligencer*, 16–23 January.
[16] Bridges et al., *A perfect narrative*, p. 13. *Cal. SP, Dom.*, pp. 301–2.
[17] Ludlow, *Memoirs*, ii, 194.
[18] *A true catalogue* (London, 1659[60]), p. 23.
[19] *Cal. SP, Ire., 1647–60*, pp. 705–6. SP, Ire., 63/303. 3.
[20] *Cal. SP, Ire., 1647–60*, pp. 707–9. SP, Ire., 63/303. 8. In fact, Monck's appointment had been limited to England and Scotland.

rence's regiment,[21] told Ludlow that 'the full of your Commande' to secure the garrison for parliament had been executed already 'by speciall order from the Maior Generall of theire forces here'; he went on to inform him that 'Duncannon is a Garrison that refused to declare for the now parliament but the othere day', to advise him to go to Dublin, and to assure him that if his commission from parliament was dated after 27 December he would have full obedience.[22] He also forwarded Ludlow's letter to Dublin. Only the garrison at Passage, under the command of Ludlow's recent appointee, Captain Henry Aland, supported him.

At first, if Ludlow is to be credited, there was a sort of truce in the area as the various forces waited to see what would happen. Before long, however, the rumour spread that Coote was coming, hostility developed in Waterford, Leigh made known his support for Dublin, and Lieutenant-Colonel Thomas Scot arrived to reinforce the besiegers with infantry and release Temple to assist Theophilus Jones in making arrangements to take a regiment of horse to Monck.[23] Scot had commanded a troop in Ludlow's regiment until his disbandment in 1655 and from that point the encounter was suffused by an embittered personal note: at one point, acknowledging Ludlow's kindness to his father's wife and 'former respecte' to himself, Scot protested that 'I hope you will not urge private acts of civilitie to envest you in that absolute authoritie you lay claime unto.'[24] On 9 January, the council of officers, significantly reinforced by the arrival in Dublin of Broghill, proclaimed Ludlow a traitor and forbade anyone to assist him.[25] On 10 January, the council wrote to him at length, restating their familiar grounds of objection, now added to by his conduct in Duncannon: they thought it odd that he should have gone to the only

---

[21] *Regimental history*, p. 358. Puckle was one of those appointed by Coote to negotiate the articles concluded at Galway in February 1652 and had been governor of Ross since at least 1655. Dunlop, *Commonwealth*, p. 163. *Arch. Hib.*, 6, p. 194.

[22] *Cal. SP, Ire., 1647–60*, p. 707. SP, Ire., 63/303. 6.

[23] Ludlow, *Memoirs*, ii, 195–6. In reality, Leigh had been uncompromising from the outset and the mayor of Waterford, John Haughton, had been associated with several of his letters, SP, Ire., 63/303. 5, 7. *Clarke Papers*, iv, 226.

[24] *Regimental history*, p. 603. *Cal. SP, Ire., 1647–60*, 712, 713. SP, Ire., 63/303. 13.

[25] *Parliamentary Intelligencer*, 30 January–6 February. The proclamation was signed by Waller, Broghill, Coote, Caulfield, Jones, King, Greene, Owen, Lucas, Lehunt, Cambre, Toogood, Lisle, Jo Maunsel, H. Langrishe, J. Campbell, J. Gregory, Sanford, Jo Harrison, Jo Riding, Simon Garstin, Boyl Maunsell, H. Chatworth, R. Shields and A. Barrington.

place that had not declared for parliament, and, noting his allegation to Puckle that 'we have set up for ourselves', said that they would forbear to say, but nonetheless said, 'that you have set up for yourself'.²⁶ The letter, which contained twenty-nine signatures, only five of them of men who had been present at the original censure of Ludlow on 26 December, was written for publication rather than dispatch.²⁷ More precisely aimed was a further letter written on the following day to the parliament in England denouncing Ludlow's 'actings against the Parliament by a power derived from that the Parliament' and asking for his recall to face the charges against him: they deferred to parliament's judgement in the matter, but urged that a person 'so obnoxious' and 'so distasteful' should not be confirmed in office. They had just learned that Monck no longer needed the horse that had been made ready for him and they offset the bluntness of this message, which was carried to London by Temple, with an offer to put the regiment at parliament's disposal, or a greater force if it were wanted. The letter, unlike that of the previous day, was signed only by senior officers.²⁸

The officers' letter of 10 January reached Ludlow in printed form ten days later.²⁹ Some of the names attached to it must have added to his suspicions, like that of Henry Owen whom he had displaced in favour of Henry Kempson as major of his own regiment of horse, while the totality of the twenty-nine made manifest the extent of recent change, for no more than five were those of men who had been officers when he had held command, and two of those were Waller and Coote.³⁰ Close upon it there followed a letter from the speaker requiring him to attend parlia-

---

²⁶ Ludlow, *Memoirs*, ii, 451–5. *Publick Intelligencer*, 23–30 January.

²⁷ The five were Charles and Chidley Coote, Theophilus Jones, Temple and John Yeoman. The remainder were Jo Salt, Sol Cambre, Rod Mansell, Barry Foulke, Jo Harrison, Geo Pepper, Jo King, Mau Fenton, W. Caulfield, Ric Stephens, Dan Lisle, Tho Hopkins, Hardress Waller, Broghil, Rich Lehunt, Eliah Greene, Henry Owen, Ben Lucas, Jo Frend, Hen Morton, R. Fitzgerald, Sampson Towgood, Jo Maunsell, Will Candler. *A letter from Sir Hardress Waller and several other Gentlemen at Dublin to Lieutenant General Ludlowe, with his answer to the same.* London, 1660.

²⁸ The letter was signed by eleven of those who had signed the letter to Ludlow on the previous day – Waller, Stephens, Lehunt, Cambre, Lisle, Greene, Broghill, Charles and Chidley Coote, Fenton and Temple – together with Thomas Caulfield. *Clarke Papers*, iv, 237–8, 241–3.   ²⁹ Ludlow, *Memoirs*, ii, 455–63.

³⁰ The others were Greene, Frend and Lucas.

ment with an account of Irish affairs, together with what he greeted as the 'astonishing news' that the officers had received from parliament 'an acknowledgement of their service in declaring for them'.³¹ Ludlow had already found time on his way to Duncannon to warn parliament not to take what was happening in Ireland at face value: 'though the parliament's interest be held forth by the officers, another interest is at the bottom', he had assured the speaker.³² The news of what he saw as 'dishonourable compliance' with his and the parliament's enemies convinced him that he must return to London. In a last vituperative exchange, he declined to yield Duncannon on the grounds that it might be required as a landing place for an English force coming to reduce Ireland to obedience, while Scot, he alleged, spoke well of Booth and vilified Haselrig. Ordering Skinner to yield Duncannon only on his instructions or those of parliament, the recalled commander in chief left for London to turn the tables on those who sought to impeach him.³³

The 'dishonourable compliance' was more than two weeks old when Ludlow heard of it, and had preceded his warning. On 31 December, Robert Wood had delivered to Speaker Lenthall the letter addressed to the Portsmouth commissioners and pointed to the offer to 'send over 3,000 or 4,000 men for the service of parliament' as evidence of Ireland's 'good condition'.³⁴ The letters of 15 and 24 December and the declaration of 14 December were read to the House on 4 January and on the following day the Commons approved 'what hath been done', picked out Waller, Coote and Jones by name in its general thanks to the Irish officers for their services, and ordered the commissioners to attend with an account of their management. The council of state was asked to bring forward proposals to establish civil authority, 'to consider how the army in Ireland shall be governed', and to nominate commissioners.³⁵ The antagonism between the officers in Ireland and Ludlow posed problems which parliament only gradually came to understand. The letter of warning written by Ludlow on shipboard on 2 January was forwarded to the speaker by Miles Corbet a week or so after the House had endorsed the officers: at about the same time Lenthall also received a lyrical effusion from Waller, who reported both that the 'undertaking' had been so widely supported 'that I

---

³¹ Ludlow, *Memoirs*, ii, 199.   ³² *Cal. SP, Dom., 1659–60*, p. 310.
³³ Ludlow, *Memoirs*, ii, 200–1.   ³⁴ *HMC, Portland MSS*, i, 690.   ³⁵ *CJ*, vii, 803.

may say a nation was born in a day', and that the only hindrance to its success was the arrival of Ludlow whose landing would have 'put all into blood'.³⁶ On 12 January, the House referred Ludlow's letter to the council of state and demanded that the nominations for commissioners should be brought before it on the following morning, together with draft instructions.³⁷ This direction was evaded: what Scot introduced next day were the names of five men 'fit to be commissioners for governing the army in Ireland' who were to assume the powers formerly exercised by Ludlow. One of the five was Ludlow himself: the others were Steele, Waller, Major Godfrey and Lieutenant-Colonel Walker. It was recommended that the last two, who had come to England with the Irish Brigade, should be appointed to the command of their respective regiments – Allen's horse and Sadler's foot. The house noted Scot's report and agreed to consider it on the following Monday.³⁸ Over the weekend, Lenthall referred Ludlow's allegations to Monck for his comments, and clearly signalled the strategy that lay behind the council of state's proposals when he canvassed the possibility of posting the Irish Brigade to Cheshire in case it should be needed in Ireland.³⁹

The political thrust of the proposals is plain. Both Godfrey and Walker were looked upon by Ludlow as clients who 'would do any honest thing that I should advise'.⁴⁰ However, like Ludlow, they were not immune from suspicion, though from a different quarter. When parliament had resumed, the disposition of the Irish Brigade under their command had given rise to some anxiety and it had been decided to replace them by Daniel Redman and John Brett, both of whom had been victims of the summer remodelling. Independently, Monck had sent the Dublin declaration to the Brigade on 28 December to impress upon its officers that 'unless you join with me in the defence of the parliament, though you should conquer this army, yet you must be necessitated to fight once more for your interests in Ireland': the alternative was to join him, in

---

³⁶ *Cal. SP, Dom.*, *1659–60*, p. 310. *CJ*, vii, 808. *HMC, Portland MSS*, i, 693. Waller was evoking the predicted end of the Babylonian captivity, Isaiah, 66. 8. The same adaptation of the original text had prefaced the address of the army in Scotland to Lenthall after the recall of the rump: 'That a nation may be born in a day, is a truth which this day's experience witnesseth unto us . . .' Whitelock, *Memorials*, iv, 346–8.

³⁷ *CJ*, vii, 808.

³⁸ *CJ*, vii, 811.   ³⁹ *Cal. SP, Dom.*, *1659–60*, p. 310.   ⁴⁰ Ludlow, *Memoirs*, ii, 210.

which case, 'all your interests in Ireland secured'.[41] The horse declared for parliament on 30 December, the foot followed suit next day and both units marched away from Lambert's army towards Lancashire.[42] In the evening, however, Redman and Brett arrived with the speaker's commissions and on New Year's Day they led the Brigade to join the Yorkshiremen who had been assembled by Lord Fairfax on Marston Moor. The handover was not amicable. Godfrey wrote to Haselrig to protest, saying that it was fortunate that the Brigade had parted from Lambert before the arrival of Redman and Brett because they were 'formerly such great sticklers for a Protector, and having received such remarkable favours from one, the officers and soldiers of this brigade did not well resent it'.[43] In the event, the Brigade, which was said to have been 'looked upon as the choicest men in Lambert's Army', acted decisively under its new command. Having required Fairfax, who was suspected of being in favour of a free parliament, to pledge his support for the existing one, the Brigade occupied York peaceably. As a condition of doing so, the officers, Redman with reluctance, first acceded to the demand of the garrison commander that they engage 'to adhere to this present Parliament, as it consists of the Members that sate the Tenth of October, now last past, against a King or any other Single Person whatsoever'. In York, the Brigade received Monck on his march south on 11 January. Since one of Monck's most trusted advisers, Colonel John Clobery, had a brother-in-law, John Otway, who was in turn the brother-in-law of Redman and who worked closely with Dr Barwick, the royalist agent with whom Redman had been dealing since the previous summer, it seems unlikely that Monck was unaware of Redman's connections.[44] He thought well of him nonetheless and soon afterwards, apparently in collusion with the leaders in Ireland, advised the speaker that Redman should be restored to his own regiment 'for you have few better horse soldiers in your service, and he is sober and

---

[41] *Clarke Papers*, iv, 228–9.

[42] *HMC, Portland MSS*, i, 691. *CJ*, vii, 803. Carte MS 67, f. 311. *HMC Leyborne Popham MSS*, p. 140. *Regimental history*, p. 615.   [43] *Cal. SP, Dom., 1659–60*, p. 294; cf. p. 288.

[44] J. Price, *The mystery and method of his majesty's happy restoration laid open to publick view* (London, 1680), p. 73. Ludlow, *Memoirs*, ii, 203. *Publick Intelligencer*, 2–9 January. Barwick, *Life of Barwick*, pp. 161, 162, 187, 189, 223, 224, 231, 496, 498, 506, 523. A. H. Woolrych, 'Yorkshire and the restoration', *Yorkshire Archaeological Journal*, 29 (1958), pp. 494–7. The commander in York was Robert Lilburne.

well-principled'.⁴⁵ He thought less well of Godfrey and Walker, who had attended the general council of the army in December, and set out to thwart the scheme to place control of Ireland in safe republican hands.

Replying to the speaker by return from Ferrybridge, Monck raised no objection to deploying the Irish Brigade to Cheshire but he subverted the council of state's proposals for Ireland by forwarding the articles of impeachment against Ludlow. Assuring Lenthall that the Commons had been misinformed, and counselling them not to be suspicious, he categorically endorsed what had happened in Ireland:⁴⁶ the intention, he affirmed, 'stands upon the same foot with mine and some of your own actings, that is, for the restitution of parliament to its present condition' and for 'the support of those ordinances of God, vizt Magistracy and Ministry, and the preservation of the rights and liberties of all the peoples of these nations'.

Improving the opportunity, and taking Ludlow's removal from office for granted, he went on to propose that parliament should proceed to appoint commissioners for the 'management of their affairs both martial and civil in Ireland' and suggested the names of Broghill, Coote, Waller, Theophilus Jones, Arthur Hill and 'such others as they shall please to join with them'.⁴⁷

Monck's letter was written on the day that the Irish business was to have been dealt with. In fact, the House did not keep to its timetable and the report was not taken until three days later on 19 January. Ludlow's explanation of this delay was conspiratorial. In his memoirs he attributed it to the machinations of his enemies Cooper, Weaver, St John and Reynolds, acting at the bidding of Monck: the object of the stratagem was to allow time for the articles of impeachment to arrive.⁴⁸ The credibility of this allegation is perhaps enhanced by the fact that Ludlow never knew that Monck himself had forwarded the articles during the postponement.

---

⁴⁵ *Clarke Papers*, iv, 252. Ludlow, *Memoirs*, ii, 239. In late January Broghill was involved in mustering men in north Munster to serve under Redman. Francis Armitage to Broghill, 31 January 1660, Orrery MS 18. 22.

⁴⁶ Monck had already had Sir Charles Coote's Declaration published in Edinburgh 'because it is full and clear for the Parliament, and is a great demonstration of the fidelity and honesty of that worthy person, and it is the best thing of its kind I have seen yet extant'. *Parliamentary Intelligencer*, 16–23 January.   ⁴⁷ Ludlow, *Memoirs*, ii, 471–2.

⁴⁸ Ibid., 210. For the internal politics in parliament, see K. H. D. Haley, *The first earl of Shaftesbury* (Oxford, 1968), p. 125.

As it happened, Monck's intervention proved to be unnecessary. The council of state's policy was made untenable by the timely arrival in London of Bridges and two of the Warren brothers, John and Abel, as commissioners representing the army in Ireland, bearing with them the declaration of 28 December, the articles of impeachment and sundry related letters. Parliament received them on 19 January, hearing brief words of reassurance from Bridges on the readiness of the Irish army to obey its commands before the clerk of the house read the material from Ireland in full. Afterwards, by resolution, the powers given to the former commissioners were suspended, and Coote, Waller, Henry Markham and John Weaver were appointed, and Robert Goodwin reappointed, to a new commission 'for Management of the affairs of Ireland', which thus mixed local grandees with experienced outsiders.[49] Markham, one of the commissioners for the management of the Irish revenue since 1654 and already an absentee colonel of foot, had been voted to the vacant command of the deceased Cooper's horse on the previous day. There seems to have been opposition to his nomination, which may have arisen from his reputation as 'an active stickler' for Monck or from his being 'a great acquaintance' of Broghill.[50] John Weaver, a member of parliament and one of its commissioners in Ireland from 1650 to 1653, was his brother-in-law: Weaver, who was also brother-in-law to Samuel Winter, had kept in close touch with Independents in Ireland and encouraged them to oppose the protectorate.[51] The round-up of Irish business was completed by orders that Duncannon and Cork should surrender to Coote and Waller; that those impeached should attend to answer the charges; that the list of nominated officers of the Irish army (which had been brought to England by Temple) should be referred to the commissioners for the army; and that instructions for the new commissioners for Ireland should be prepared forthwith.[52]

The decision to send Bridges and the Warrens to London had been

[49] *CJ*, vii, 815.
[50] Reputedly a Presbyterian, Markham had been appointed one of seven commissioners for the army on 25 December and commander of Windsor Castle on 4 January. His regimental appointment was confirmed by Monck on 25 February. *Regimental history*, pp. 411, 412, 560. Coate, *Mordaunt Letter Book*, p. 155n.
[51] *Regimental history*, p. 412. Barnard, *Cromwellian Ireland*, p. 113.
[52] Ludlow, *Memoirs*, ii, 210–12. *CJ*, vii, 815.

prompted by the need to counter 'disingenuous misinformations' about what was taking place in Ireland. The most damaging of these was the rumour that 'they in Ireland were setting up for themselves, and calling a parliament to govern and manage the affairs of that nation, in opposition to the parliament of England'. The suspicion arose from the summoning of the representative assembly and was given added credence by the choice of 24 January as its date of meeting. This was the date which the committee of safety had announced, on 14 December, for the opening of the parliament agreed upon by the council of officers in England.[53] It can scarcely be doubted that the Irish officers had contrived the coincidence as a gesture of defiance, but in the new situation republican propaganda distorted the symbolism and Ludlow was not alone in concluding that a deliberate challenge to the Long Parliament was intended.[54] In fact, the officers had cancelled the meeting when the resumption of parliament was confirmed. One of the tasks of the commissioners was to dispel suspicion, both by direct representations to parliament and by the publication of *A perfect narrative* of Irish events designed to set the record straight. This pamphlet must have been written in Ireland and published immediately after the arrival of the commissioners in England, for it was on sale in London on January 23. It described the background to the December coup in detail, stressing the constancy of the commitment of the Irish leaders to the cause of parliament, and it paid particular attention to elucidating the context of the decision to summon an assembly, which had been taken at a time when the army was sixteen months in arrears, no parliament was sitting, and there was need to make arrangements for the levy of a contribution 'by way of Loan'. It was also made very clear that steps had been taken to stop the preparations within a few days of the issue of summonses, when news of the restoration of the Long Parliament had been received.[55] Politic as this had been, it meant that an alternative solution to the financial difficulties had to be found and within a week of the publication of *A perfect narrative*, Dr Ralph King, the newly appointed judge advocate, was dispatched to London to request that arrears should be paid and 'that a speedy course may be taken for supplies from thence where the revenue here shall be found short to

[53] Hutton, *The Restoration*, pp. 79–80.
[54] *Cal. SP, Ire., 1647–60*, p. 706.   [55] Bridges et al., *A perfect narrative*, p. 14.

answer the necessary and standing charge of the army and nation'.⁵⁶ Dr King's mission failed before it began: on the day that his instructions were prepared, 26 January, parliament voted to introduce a new assessment which called for a full year's levy to be collected in the six months ending June 24. Ireland's contribution was set at £18,000 per month, double the previous rate. The liability of each county was specified and the responsibility for collection was invested in the new commissioners.⁵⁷

The policy underlying Monck's nominations, that control in Ireland should be left in the hands of the dominant group there, had not been adopted, but he was well pleased with the outcome and commended the commissioners to Broghill (with particular reference to 'your friend Colonel Markham') as 'honest men, and such as I know your lordship will be well satisfied in, for I am confident they are persons of ability and conscience, and such as will act conscientiously in reference to the ordinances of Magistracy and Ministry, and that love and favour such as are for order and discipline in the Church of God'. He attributed the omission of Broghill himself to distrust and promised to 'endeavour to clear all objections (if any be) that shall be made against your Lordship's inclinations and faithfulness to the service of the Parliament'.⁵⁸ His views on the need to combine civil and military authority were strongly endorsed in Ireland. Theophilus Jones, to whom he sent a copy of his letter to the speaker, was deeply suspicious of the intended separation of the two. In a revealing glimpse of the local power balance, writing before the nominations were known, he insisted that Coote's hand needed strengthening, not weakening, 'which we fear is designed'. In another, he not only said bluntly that Steele's predilection for Anabaptists and

---

⁵⁶ Draft [in Henry Jones's hand] of a letter of introduction for Dr King to the council of state, 26 January 1660, TCD MS 844, f. 189. King was one of those whom Forbes identified as an ally of Coote. A former recorder of Londonderry, he had represented Londonderry and Coleraine in all three protectorate parliaments, served as a commissioner for setting forth lands to the army and been appointed prothonotary of the court of common pleas in 1658. Petty, *Down survey*, pp. 227, 276. J. L. J. Hughes (ed.), *Patentee officers in Ireland, 1173–1826* (IMC, 1960).
⁵⁷ *Acts and ordinances*, ii, 1355–403.
⁵⁸ HMC, *Various*, vi (London, 1909), pp. 438–9, MSS of Lord Oranmore and Browne. Monck to Broghill, 27 January 1660.

Quakers made him unacceptable as a commissioner, but hinted broadly that Waller had been uncooperative throughout the 'late actions'.[59] The Irish officers also had reason to be pleased with the outcome. The defeat of Ludlow's faction, which they had worked so desperately to achieve, was indispensable to the consolidation of their position. Whether the alternative arrangements justified Monck's satisfaction was not put to the test, for the decision was never acted upon. Despite a reminder from parliament on 28 January, the council of state never returned with the commissioners' instructions.[60] It had other preoccupations, of course, but within days of his assignment to Ireland Weaver had been appointed a commissioner for the admiralty and navy and soon afterwards Markham was appointed a commissioner for the government of Scotland.[61] Since Goodwin was already a chronic absentee, it seems unlikely that there was any real intention that they should act and it is reasonable to conclude that the council of state had been caught off balance on 19 January and forced into decisions that it was unwilling to execute. The result was that Ireland had no authorized government, civil or military. In practice, the council of officers devolved executive responsibility to two bodies, a committee of safety chaired by the former exchequer court judge Sir James Barry,[62] and an army commission, consisting of Waller, Broghill, Coote, Jones and

---

[59] *Leyborne Popham MSS*, p. 141. [60] *CJ*, vii, 826.
[61] *CJ*, vii, 825. *Regimental history*, p. 560. Nicoll, *Diary*, pp. 277–8.
[62] *A faithful representation of the state of Ireland: whose bleeding eye is upon England for help. Or The horrid conspiracy discovered and most humbly presented to the wisdom of parliament* (London, 1659 [60]). It is possible that the King's Inns accounts, which record meetings involving Barry, Coote, Paul Davis, Gerald Lowther (chief justice of the common pleas, who died early in April) and several others unnamed, provide a clue to its membership. Colum Kenny, *The King's Inns and the kingdom of Ireland* (Dublin, 1992), p. 135, citing the Black Book, ff. 138–45v, 188v. One of the men they may have met at the Inns was Sir Robert Moray, formerly colonel of the Scottish Guards in the French army, who had played an active part in the negotiations between Charles I and the Scots in 1645–6 and been involved in the royalist rising in Scotland in 1653–5. He seems to have resumed his political interests after September 1659 when he left his retreat in Maastricht and went to Paris. There he made contact with Mordaunt who had concluded that France was the most likely source of troops to assist a restoration. Moray's presence in Ireland has not been noticed. He was in Paris in March 1660, when he was collecting testimonies from French Protestant ministers to disprove the allegations that Charles was a Catholic. Alexander Robertson, *The life of Sir Robert Moray* (London, 1922), pp. 98–103. Routledge, *The treaty of the Pyrenees*, p. 96.

John Warren, which was designed to exercise the authority vested in Waller as major general and incorporated him as an essential element in its quorum of three.⁶³ The military arrangement, which had been suggested by Monck, seems not to have been a happy one and, like Jones, Broghill had cause to complain to Monck about Waller.⁶⁴ The practice of making special provision for the command of the forces in Ulster was continued: through Broghill's influence, the firmly Presbyterian John Gorges, who had taken over Smith's command at Carrickfergus after securing Londonderry in December, was appointed 'governor' of the province.⁶⁵

The communications between the officers in Dublin and Monck were conducted not only through Campbell, but also through Colonel Clifton, successively governor of Edinburgh and Leith Castles, Captain James Cuffe, a cousin of the Coote brothers, who was sent to accompany Monck on his march from Newcastle (which he left about 6 January) to London and Sir Joseph Douglas, in whom Monck was said to have reposed trust 'of a great and dangerous Quality', who was sent to Coote from Durham immediately after Cuffe's arrival.⁶⁶ In Munster, Broghill (whose brother Cork had recently moved from Lismore to London) had his own arrangements while Ulster was catered for by both Campbell and Clifton who travelled by way of Newtownards where they had private discussions with Campbell's cousin, Lord Montgomery.⁶⁷ More tantalizing is the fact that Monck's private secretary, Matthew Locke, was the nephew of Sir Paul Davis, former clerk of the Irish Council, who was married to Sir John Barry's sister-in-law.⁶⁸ These cross channel links involved close consultations about the remodelling of the army. Monck, whose fine tuning of his

---

⁶³ Articles against Waller, TCD MS 844, ff. 192v–193.

⁶⁴ Monck to Broghill, 7 February 1659, Rebecca Warner, *Epistolary Curiosities* (London, 1818), i, 53–6.

⁶⁵ John Gorges to Broghill, 14 January 1660, Harvard, Orrery MSS, MS 18. 22.

⁶⁶ Ludlow, *Memoirs*, ii, 209n. Baker, *A chronicle*, p. 743. Price, *The mystery and method of his majesty's happy restoration*, pp. 77–8. Montgomery MSS, p. 224.

⁶⁷ Barnard, 'Land and the limits of loyalty', Barnard and Clark (eds.), *Burlington*, p. 183. Montgomery MSS, pp. 224–5, 249n.

⁶⁸ Aylmer, *The state's servants*, pp. 262–3, 412. Cal. SP, Dom., 1672, p. 531. Locke had served as clerk to the Scottish and Irish Affairs Committee of the council of state in 1650–1. He was appointed clerk of the Irish privy council in September 1661. Hughes, *Patentee officers*.

own forces was continuous, had approved this process from the outset, and had recommended three basic principles. First, to ensure that discipline and order were maintained, the officers should appoint a committee to make appointments to necessary commands, together with a commissary to muster the men, until parliament's pleasure was known. Second, those officers who had been imprisoned should not be released on any account until parliament so ordered. Third, 'As to the cavaliers or Anabaptists that are in the army or nation, it's my sense that none of them be trusted with any forts or strongholds, nor that any be continued in the army but such as are zealous for the Parliament, and have witnessed against that late violence put on the Parliament, and otherwise free from sedition or faction'.[69] These principles were accepted, indeed treated as instructions, but their implementation did not prove easy because Waller was reluctant to share his authority. That there was a good deal of disagreement is plain, but the details and phasing of the remodelling that incensed Ludlow and troubled the council of state are difficult to recover.[70]

The coup itself had been accompanied by the removal, replacement and, in some cases, imprisonment of hostile and suspect officers. The officers claimed that they had 'laid aside' no one who had not either recognized Fleetwood as commander in chief of 'the three Armies' or promoted the election of agents to the general council, and they maintained that they had distinguished between 'those that made the stream, and such who through inadvertencie did swim down in it'. On 9 January, admitting that these proceedings had been irregular, they announced the establishment of a court martial in Dublin to hear the cases of aggrieved field officers and captains, together with local court martials in each county to provide similarly for inferior officers and private soldiers. Appeals were to be lodged before 24 March with Dr Ralph King, who had displaced Kingdon as judge advocate, or with the chief officer in each county, and undertakings were given that appellants 'shall be judged according to the usual Rules and Discipline of War', and that no officer would be judged by his successor in command.[71] Before the second week

[69] *Clarke papers*, iv, 227–8.   [70] TCD MSS 844, Information against Waller.
[71] *A declaration of the Major General and Council of officers in Ireland concerning their late actings there, and for the tryal of such officers and souldiers as finde themselves agrieved for being laid*

of January a new senior command was in place and when Edmund Temple went to England he took with him a list of nominations, including his own, 'for the Approbation of the House'. But the work went on: fresh changes were made 'by reason of New discoveries' and sent to England on 1 February with a covering letter to Lenthall from Colonel Ingoldsby requesting confirmation, so 'that our real Zeal in this good Work may not prove ineffectual, or receive a Discouragement'.[72] This second wave of displacements was regarded with particular suspicion. Since some of those involved had 'declared with the first', it seemed reasonable to infer that lack of commitment to the parliamentary cause was not the deciding factor.[73] The inference was correct: fortified by Monck's third principle, the leaders gave free rein to their aversion to religious radicals and conducted their purge on religious as well as political criteria. Henry Ingoldsby made no bones about this. He assured the speaker that when he had returned to Ireland in January, he had found 'your Armie so modelled, that Rebellion and unruly swords are laid aside, and your most obedient and faithfull servants placed in the Head off Commands': moreover, 'caution has bin also taken not to admit a Cavaleere, nor to continue your late fanatick Antagonists in your Army'.[74]

Ludlow claimed that the Dublin cabal displaced all the field officers, except Colonel Markham and Major Edward Warren, and the evidence suggests that he was right. He may also have been broadly correct in his

---

aside. 9 January 1659 (London, 1659[60]). The declaration was signed by Waller and nineteen others: Coote, Broghill, Jones, Wm Caulfield, King, Greene, Owen, Lucas, J. Gregory, Theo Sandford, Jo Harrison, Jo Reding, Simon Garstin, Boyle Maunsell, H. Clotworthy, R. Shiels, A. Barrington, Ric Lehunt and J. Campbell.

[72] Carte MS 67, f. 312. Printed with minor variations in Zachery Grey, *An impartial examination of vol. 4 of Neal's History of the puritans* (London, 1739), App. 79, pp. 142–3.

[73] *A sober vindication*, p. 2.

[74] Grey, *An impartial examination*, pp. 142–3. Eliah Greene, who ceased to be active after early January, was probably a victim of the second phase. Action against the radicals was not confined to the army. When the news reached Trim that the parliament was again sitting 'and the expectation of those that indeavoured to involve the three Nations in blood is now beene frustrated', the corporation unanimously disfranchised three burgesses 'knowne to be Anabaptists', Colonel Sankey, Gideon Haynes and Ralph Herrick, and agreed 'that none of that sort shalbe hereafter admitted either Burgesses or ffreemen of this said Corporation'. NLI MS 2,292. Assembly book of the borough of Trim, 1659–1720, f. 6 (19 January 1659[60]).

allegation that most of the other officers commissioned by parliament had been removed, if not in the rider that their places had been filled with the most vicious and disaffected persons that could be found.[75] A less rhetorical reading of events was provided by a well-informed republican pamphleteer, writing in late February, who claimed that the leaders of the coup were making a distinction between 'the old Protestants and the New; the old bandying themselves against the others, the new English as they call them, wishing their throats were cut; saying they came to eat the bread out of their mouths (that planted there &c)'.[76] He also alleged that much of the army was in the control of 'old English, Episcopall men', and stressed that one of the features of the new regime that seemed sinister to its critics was the way in which command had been concentrated, with two regiments bestowed on Waller, two more on Sir Charles Coote and one each upon Coote's brothers Richard, Chidley and Thomas, 'so as upon the matter, two men have seven regiments'.[77] To this aggregation Ludlow added the regiment assigned to Coote's cousin, Oliver St George.[78] In fact, it was not unusual for the most senior officers to combine horse and foot commands, as Ludlow himself had done, and there was certainly no shortage of qualified substitutes for those who were cashiered. By 26 December, there were already seven uncommissioned colonels attending the council of officers. At a moment of crisis in mid-February there were fifteen regimental colonels gathered in Dublin, of whom one was based in Munster,[79] two or three in Ulster,[80] and four in Connacht.[81] The 'old Protestants' among them outnumbered the newcomers by eleven to four. All were experienced officers, but only Coote and Waller had official status of any kind. The lieutenant-colonels and majors present were veterans to a man, but none held a current commission. A further dimension was reflected in the presence of three ranking colonels appearing as captains in command of troops or companies. Throughout the country, the changeover at the top of the military establishment had been replicated as retired and cashiered officers took

---

[75] Ludlow, *Memoirs*, ii, 195.   [76] *A faithful representation of the state of Ireland*.
[77] *A sober vindication*, p. 2.   [78] Ludlow, *Memoirs*, ii, 231.   [79] Thomas Stanley.
[80] Lord Caulfield, Gorges and perhaps Cole, who lived in Dublin.
[81] Chidley and Richard Coote, King and Oliver St George. The others were Charles Coote, Ingoldsby, Jones, Owen, Waller, Warden and John Warren.

command of local units and garrisons. In most places this seems to have been a matter of local initiative followed by loose association with the Dublin officers. In Munster, it seems to have been both more tightly directed and more self-contained.

Monck was kept informed of the main outlines of this transformation. He remained approving of the 'honest and sober hands' in which command was put and promised to support what was being done when he reached London. To Broghill, he expressed his pleasure that 'yor Lp: is soe prudently mingled in the mannageing of the military part, wch I thinke to bee in as good hands as can possibly bee, and I shall endeavour to have them soe continued'.[82] His interest was more than cursory: he paid close attention to detail and gave advice that was both politically shrewd and professionally fastidious. Thus he counselled against a proposal to make six troops into a regiment for Theophilus Jones, both 'because it will alter the establishment of Ireland which is settled by act of parliament' and because it might involve 'the making of the dragoons horse, which will increase too much the public charge'.[83] He agreed, and wrote to parliament at Broghill's request to recommend that Temple should have Abbott's regiment of dragoons, and he approved a decision to keep the command of Redman's former regiment open for him, since his command of the Irish Brigade was temporary in kind, and wrote to Lenthall recommending this also, explaining that Redman had been put out of his command by Axtell and Barrow in favour of Allen, who was 'no good friend of yours'.[84] No notice was taken of these recommendations. Apart from the conferring of Cooper's horse upon Markham and a devious proposal, brought forward on 27 January, to appoint Gilbert Mabbott, who was married to the sister of Monck's secretary, as judge advocate,[85] no nominations were brought before the House, and the military revolution in Ireland remained unsanctioned. Parliament's referral to the army commissioners of the list of those nominated to command aroused

---

[82] Monck to Broghill, 7 February 1660, Herefordshire and Worcestershire Record Office, A H 34 (unfoliated).

[83] In fact, as a result of Abbott's importuning of Cromwell, the dragoons in Ireland were paid the same rate as the horse, *Regimental history*, p. 621.

[84] *HMC, Various*, vi, 438–9, MSS of Lord Oranmore and Browne. Monck to Broghill, 27 January 1660.

[85] *CJ*, vii, 825. Dunlop, *Commonwealth*, p. 214n. *DNB*, sub William Clarke.

suspicion in Ireland, no doubt heightened by the submission of Mabbott's name for the place to which Dr King had been nominated. The information which reached the officers, presumably from Temple and the commissioners, was that the local dispositions were to be disregarded and the commands bestowed otherwise 'and in conclusion all revert to the former confusion'.[86]

Grounds for further suspicion were amply supplied by the apparent unwillingness of those in power to take the articles of impeachment seriously. The first hint of this came on 29 January when Corbet and Ludlow were allowed to resume their seats in the Commons.[87] Ludlow was at once directed to render his account, and by inference make a first reply to the charges against him, which was encouraging, though the Irish officers certainly felt that he should do so from the bar of the house rather than from his seat. When the appointed time came, however, the business was deferred until 7 February.[88] Before that day came, Monck had arrived in London and satisfactorily fulfilled his promise to the Irish officers. In his anxiously awaited formal address to the English parliament on 6 February, he confronted unequivocally the delicate, inexplicitly formulated question of whether parliament's allies in Ireland were to be trusted. Having first established basic priorities by reminding the members that what Ireland most needed from them was the passage of the act for settling estates, 'and people will unwillingly pay Taxes for those estates of which they have no legal assurance', he informed them that the remodelling of the army there was needed to undo the effects of recent abuses of the power to nominate officers, and gave them his assurance 'that those now, that have declared for you, will continue faithful, and thereby evince, that as well there as here, it is the sober interest must establish your Dominion'.[89] Despite his effort, the interwoven questions of Ireland and Ludlow remained contentious. At the time appointed for Ludlow's postponed report, the matter was again deferred for a week.[90] He professed to believe that he was being prevented from defending himself:[91] the officers from Ireland believed

---

[86] *Leyborne Popham MSS*, p. 140.   [87] *Publick Intelligencer*, 30 January–6 February.
[88] *CJ*, vii, 829.
[89] *The Lord General Monck, his speech delivered by him in Parliament* (London, 1660), pp. 3–4.
[90] *CJ*, vii, 837.
[91] Ludlow, *Memoirs*, ii, 221.

that he was being shielded from prosecution.⁹² Bridges was particularly incensed to discover two days later that a parliament which professed to be unable to find time to deal with Irish business was not too busy to receive a 'seditious petition' from Praisegod Barebone.⁹³ In outward form at least, the victory went to Ludlow. On 11 February, the House considered a bill designed to reduce Monck's authority by appointing a five-man commission to govern the army in England and Scotland. At the last moment, at Ludlow's prompting, Sir Henry Marten moved an amendment to add the word 'Ireland' and the act passed in that form.⁹⁴ Whether the members had realized it or not, the effect was 'to force the power in Ireland out of the hands of those that had usurped it'.⁹⁵ There was further aggravation on the following day when the council of state was required to report to parliament on the whole question of the imprisonment of officers in Ireland 'upon pretence of being in the last defection'.⁹⁶ The Irish officers reacted angrily to these setbacks. When Thomas Scot waited upon Monck to mollify him with assurances of parliament's goodwill, Bridges interrupted to warn the general not to believe him, for 'their words and their practices agreed not together, as was manifest in their contempt of those his friends in Ireland, who for his sake hazarded themselves in their service'.⁹⁷

In the course of his march from York to London, Monck had publicly opposed the return of the secluded members as unacceptable to the army and divisive to the nation, and had expressed his preference for 'recruiter' elections which would make the parliament, already 'free', 'full' as well. He reaffirmed the point in his address to parliament. Initially, his conduct

---

⁹² Commissioner Jones was 'shipped' from Dublin 'to answer the miscarriages before you' on 1 February, when it was assumed by Ingoldsby that Ludlow was already there 'on the same account'. Grey, *An impartial examination*, App. 79, pp. 142–3.

⁹³ Baker, *A chronicle*, pp. 747, 748. *CJ*, vii, 838. The petition demanded the imposition of an oath of abjuration of monarchy.

⁹⁴ It was agreed that the quorum need not include Monck. *CJ*, vii, 841. Ludlow, *Memoirs*, ii, 223–4.

⁹⁵ Ludlow, *Memoirs*, ii, 224.

⁹⁶ *Parliamentary Intelligencer*, 20–27 January.

⁹⁷ Baker, *A chronicle*, p. 748. Scot thought that Monck was 'too positive in undertaking for the affairs of Ireland, of whose affections to Parliament in the present constitution of it, there was just cause of doubt'. Ibid., p. 746.

in London disappointed those who had expected him to impose his will upon parliament rather than to cooperate with it. Ordered to break the increasingly overt resistance of London to parliament's authority, Monck obeyed with ill grace, and the gates of the city were symbolically burned on 10 February. On the following day, the general and his officers changed tack and wrote to the Commons requiring them to issue writs for new elections within a week and to dissolve the parliament as soon as the House had been filled.[98] The House repaid him by passing the act to place the command of the army in commission, rather than to entrust it to Monck alone. The House, however, did go ahead with the required preparations, and completed arrangements for elections on 18 February. Two days later, Monck again changed course and opted for the simpler way of securing the end of the Long Parliament by permitting the re-entry of the purged members on condition that a dissolution would quickly follow and a new parliament be summoned, that the commonwealth would be preserved, a Presbyterian church settlement concluded, and supreme military authority invested in himself. On 21 February, the secluded members took their seats, comfortably outnumbering the sitting members; on 23 February, they elected a new council of state; on 25 February, they appointed Monck commander in chief with a place on this council.

It was in anticipation of the readmission of the secluded members that Ludlow sought a hearing from the House on 20 February, for he saw it as the last opportunity to gain a sympathetic response. Ostensibly, the hearing was not for himself, but for the officers of Skinner's company in Duncannon who had entrusted him with a remonstrance, defending their refusal to surrender the fort, which served his purpose very well. The allegations made by Skinner and his officers in defence of the 'good ould Causc' against the leaders of the coup were diffuse: apart from their treatment of Ludlow and the commissioners, they had supported the protectorate 'in its dyeing hower by attempting to draw forces to stand up for it', blasphemed like 'the worst sorte of cavillaires', armed Irish converts to Protestantism, 'publiquely declared theire Resolution to root

[98] Baker, *A chronicle*, p. 747. The letter criticized the decision to allow Ludlow and Corbet to sit while under accusation of treason.

out all branded with the name of Sectarists', sent a supporter of Booth to besiege Duncannon and said that the parliament 'was but the rump, faggend or Limb of a Parliament'. The conclusion, however, was sharply focused: the petitioners believed that their aim was 'to root out all of any note that came over since 1649 that so they may be singly on theire owne Account if your Honnors should not answer theire ends'.[99] Introducing the petition, Ludlow not only asked that the conduct of the officers and men in Duncannon be approved, but took the opportunity to denounce the stalemated appointment of Coote and Waller as commissioners on the grounds that they were concerned with neither the English nor the public interest and to demand that more suitable arrangements be made.[100] There followed a sharp exchange with Scot, who declared that at least one of those whom Ludlow denigrated was a faithful servant of parliament, and the speaker intervened to rule that Ludlow could not be heard until the House was satisfied that Duncannon had obeyed its previous order.[101] Ludlow never was heard and the stratagem by which he had hoped to wrest control of the army from the Dublin officers fell with the rump. The army commissioners were disempowered on 21 February, the first day of the new dispensation, and Monck's appointment on 25 February combined the command of the land forces of all three countries.[102] He had already given an assurance that he would 'interpose' with the next parliament to pass an act confirming estates in Ireland.[103] The revised civil arrangements seemed equally to the advantage of the officers in Ireland and their associates. Among the secluded members had been three from New English backgrounds, Arthur Annesley, Sir John Clotworthy and Sir John Temple. Though Clotworthy, who had been elected in 1640, had been by far the most influential of these men in the old parliament itself, Annesley had emerged recently as a leader of the campaign to have the secluded members readmitted and his reward was to be made president of the new council of state, of which Temple was also elected a member, 'by

---

[99] *Cal. SP, Ire., 1647–1660*, pp. 716–17. SP, Ire., 63/303.19.
[100] *Cal. SP, Ire., 1647–1660*, pp. 697–8; SP, Ire., 63/287. 192.
[101] Ludlow, *Memoirs*, ii, 234–5. There is no record of this episode in the journals.
[102] *CJ*, vii, 847, 852.
[103] Baker, *A chronicle*, p. 750.

the friendship and favour' of Monck, it was alleged.[104] Annesley was already in touch with royalist agents and was understood by them to be actively trying to persuade Monck to 'come over'.[105] The opportunity for the council of state to influence Irish events was large. Its instructions required it to 'settle the civil government and public Judicatoryes in Scotland and Ireland, and nominate and appoint commissioners and other officers for the civil government and judges and other officers for the administration of justice there'.[106]

In Ireland, Monck's turnabout had been anticipated by some days, amidst considerable acrimony. The Dublin cabal was less united than Ludlow supposed.[107] The problem at first seemed related to the amour propre of Waller, who was accused of having impeded the orders issued by the council of officers to secure garrisons after the *coup d'état*, refusing to accept the authority of the five-man commission, and issuing orders and commissions in the assumed style of major general of the Parliament's army (rather than of the foot). That principle rather than status was involved became evident when the advice of Monck was invoked to secure his cooperation: 'What is General Monck to me', he said, 'and further said that he had fought against a single person, and that he would take no more notice of His Excellency the Lord General's orders than of any other single person against whom he had engaged.' The struggle which followed centred upon the question of whether or not the claims of the secluded members to readmission should be supported. How the issue arose as a matter of urgency on 15 February is not clearly recorded. It is possible that the trigger was, as a civilian correspondent claimed, provided by the citizens of Dublin: 'we having so unanimously declared against the

---

[104] *History of parliament. The House of Commons, 1660–90* (3 vols., London, 1983), iii, 535. T. P. Courteney, *Memoirs of the life, works and correspondence of Sir William Temple* (2 vols., London, 1836), i, 25. Temple was not an active member: the only task specifically assigned to him, on 27 February, was to report on naval affairs, but he never did so. *CJ*, vii, 854.

[105] Mordaunt to Hyde, 17 February 1660; Mordaunt to King, 17 February 1660, Clarendon MS 69, ff., 166, 170. 'Truly Mr Anslow has served your Majesty so considerably that I may with confidence beg a letter may oblige him.'

[106] *Acts and ordinances*, ii, 1421. They were also to see that the necessary seals were prepared.

[107] Much of what follows is based on the information preferred against Waller, dated 19 February, and brought to England by Dr Ralph King. TCD MS 844, ff. 191–5v.

rump, for a Free and Full Parliament, or the Secluded members to be admitted, we had little reason to expect that the Army of Ireland would have complyed with us'.[108] Against that, the presence of a large number of senior officers in Dublin suggests that there was important business to be transacted and there is no doubt that an appropriate declaration had already been prepared.[109] What is certain is that in an effort to take the initiative Waller presented an 'engagement' opposing readmission, which he wanted the council of officers to subscribe and transmit to England. The officers rejected his proposal and indicated their preference for the return of the purged members. Waller moved the adjournment of the meeting to Dublin Castle, which was under the command of his ally and fellow member of the five-man commission, John Warren. Allegedly, the plan was to seize Coote and other officers, but this was 'discovered on the very point of time wherein it should have been enacted', by Lieutenant Hugh Clotworthy 'whom they sought to inveigle to second them with his troop then in town'.[110] Coote, Jones and other officers 'with about 20 horse and a trumpeter with swords drawn, immediately declared for a free-parliament, by re-admission of the Secluded members'[111] and rode 'up and down the streets of Dublin', followed by a 'rabble'.[112] Waller denounced the officers as 'rebels and traytors' and 'nested himself for the rump'[113] in the Castle with his confederates. The most prominent of these, apart from Warren, were Lieutenant-Colonel Puckle, who had defied Ludlow from Ross, Colonel Thomas Stanley who had secured Clonmel,[114] and Lieutenant-Colonel Henry Flower, who had been displaced in the previous summer as second in command of Fleetwood's foot.[115]

---

[108] *A letter sent from a merchant in Dublin to his friend in London* (London, 1659 [60]).

[109] Warden later claimed to have been 'owning and promoting' the declaration in Kilkenny, 'from whence he marched with Six troopes of horse' to Coote in Dublin where he signed the declaration on 16 February. PRO, SP, Ire., 63/306. 49.

[110] *Leyborne Popham MSS*, p. 155.

[111] *Parliamentary Intelligencer*, 20–27 February. This report includes unattributed quotations from a letter sent by Theophilus Jones to Monck on 19 February.

[112] Ludlow, *Memoirs*, ii, 228–9.

[113] *Montgomery MSS*, pp. 221.   [114] Ludlow, *Memoirs*, ii, 189.

[115] In December, John Jones had suggested to both Fleetwood and Ludlow that Flower should be reinstated. 'Inedited letters', pp. 287–9, 289–91.

On the following day, 16 February, the council of officers formally adopted a declaration calling for a full and free parliament through the admission of the excluded members 'and new ellecions to be made of vacant places', to be conducted on principles that would disqualify those who had assisted the king or rebelled against parliament, and inviting 'all our Brethern in the said nacions, who disdaine to bee made slaves' to join them. This was prefaced by an uninhibited denunciation of the calamitous effects on religion, freedom, prosperity and national reputation of the actions 'of a few inconsiderable persons of annabaptisticall and other fanattique spirits'. The declaration dwelt particularly on the recent introduction of the new assessment and the favouring of Ludlow 'to the astonishment of the people and armey here'. The local consequences of Pride's Purge were trenchantly denounced: for the parliament subsequently to have usurped 'contrary to all Laws, the Supreme Power not only of England, but also of Ireland and Scotland, is a thing that none but tyrants or conquerors would attempt'. First among the elements of the 'happy settlement' that they looked forward to under the fully restored parliament was 'that the true Protestant religion in the pouer and purity thereof, may be established, the Godly Learned and orthodox ministers of the Gospel Mayantayned by their Tythes, and other their accustomed rights', and the list which followed was a comprehensive one. Heresy was to be suppressed, universities and schools cherished, trade fostered, justice administered, the revenues 'returned to their Right and Proper Channels', arrears paid, 'the plantacen of Ireland in the hands of the Adventurers, and souldiers and other English Protestants advanced', impositions removed and 'no charge to be laid upon any of the nations without their own free consent, given by their representatives in their several and respective parliaments'.[116] The declaration was sent to Monck on the same day with fifty-five signatures, among them fifteen colonels, three lieutenant-colonels and four majors. In a covering letter, the officers selected for special emphasis the strength of their objection to the admission to parliament of persons 'who are of fanatic principles, against whom impeachments of treason are exhibited', and the consistency of their present actions with their earlier declaration of 14 December, 'wherein we declared for adhering to the parliament in defence

---

[116] *The declaration of Sir Charles Coote and the rest of the Council of Officers* (London, 1659 [60]).

of its privileges and the just rights and liberties of the people of these nations, which we now clearly see to our great grief are apparently violated by some remaining members now sitting at Westminster'.[117]

Siege had been laid to the Castle, by civilians as well as soldiers. The soldiers within, some 200 foot, 'had each of them a months pay and a red coat to encourage them'. When they refused to accept the declaration, the engineers went to work on the walls. An attempt by Waller to divide his opponents by treating with the mayor was rebuffed on 17 February, and on the following morning Stanley and Captain Thompson submitted.[118] About midday, the soldiers expressed their concurrence with the declaration and 'delivered up their officers, and the Castle; which otherwise, had that day been stormed, the Wall in order thereunto being undermined'.[119] The officers were sent to Athlone for safekeeping.[120] On the same day, an extraordinary assembly of the city of Dublin was held and the declaration was endorsed, 'taking into consideration that a full and free parliament in England is the birthright of the people of England, and in whose prosperity or adversity the said Mayor, sheriffs, commons and citizens are sure to be sharers'.[121] It was decided to print the declaration, with Waller's letter to Mayor Robert Dee and his reply.[122] Shortly afterwards, Dee led the militia to Oxmantown Green where they 'declared their resolution to live and die in defence of what was declared by Sir Charles Coote and the army'.[123]

It appears that the officers in Dublin subsequently dispersed to their commands in the country to secure the widespread adoption of the declaration, which was later said to have been endorsed by the whole army.[124] Certainly, Lord Caulfield wrote to Coote on 20 February to report

---

[117] *Leyborne Popham MSS*, pp. 152–3.
[118] Presumably, the Lieutenant J. Thompson who had been involved in the December coup.
[119] *A letter sent from a merchant in Dublin in Ireland. Parliamentary Intelligencer*, 20–27 January.
[120] On 22 February. *Chief Occurrences*, in *A Declaration of the General Convention of Ireland, with the late proceedings there, newly brought over by a Gentleman* (London, 1659[60]), p. 6.
[121] Gilbert, *Records*, iv, 179–80.
[122] *Parliamentary Intelligencer*, 27 February–5 March. Presumably it was the city of Dublin that sent the declaration to the city of London, with a letter signifying their willingness to justify it. It was considered on 3 March, and an answer drafted. Idem.
[123] *Parliamentary Intelligencer*, 5–12 March. Ormond later assured King Charles that Dee was 'eminently active' in his restoration 'and alwaies right'. Carte MS 68, f. 200.
[124] *A Declaration of the General Convention of Ireland*.

the general concurrence of both horse and foot at Charlemont, where the gentlemen of the country were to meet that day to prepare an address, and where the Anabaptists who 'were very high, and spake big words', were now 'more dejected then ever'.[125] The fragmentary evidence indicates that it was also sent to the towns for their concurrence. In Drogheda, the declaration was proclaimed 'by beat of drum', adopted by a meeting of 'all the inhabitants' and formally entered in the council book.[126] From Nenagh, Henry Whalley wrote to profess his obedience to Coote and to denounce Anabaptists, Quakers and Fifth Monarchists.[127]

The exception to this Dublin based mobilization of opposition was Munster. Apart from Stanley, who joined Waller in the Castle, there was no significant representation from the province in Dublin on 16 February, but two days later, on the day that the crisis in Dublin ended, a parallel declaration was adopted by the army in Munster. Signed by Broghill, Colonel Ralph Wilson, Sir Maurice Fenton, and, in order of rank, by four lieutenant-colonels,[128] four majors, sixteen captains, seven lieutenants, three cornets, six ensigns, a quartermaster and a commissary (in short, by both senior officers and representatives of the junior officers), this repeated the formal declaratory conclusion of the Dublin document word for word, but introduced it very differently. Instead of the polemical denunciations endorsed in Dublin there was a carefully reasoned, epigrammatically composed statement which was concerned to strengthen the argument at two points.[129] Consistency with the December declaration was the first of these, and the reconciliation was oblique: the return of the

---

[125] *Chief Occurrences*, in *A Declaration of the General Convention of Ireland*, p. 7.

[126] Ibid., p. 8. T. Gogarty (ed.), *Council book of the corporation of Drogheda* (Dundalk, 1988), pp. 4–9.

[127] *Chief Occurrences*, in *A Declaration of the General Convention of Ireland*, pp. 7–8.

[128] Including a promoted Ben Lucas.

[129] The opening sentences convey the contrast in style. Dublin: 'Since the authority of Parliamt became openly violated, and that, by theyre owne waged servants of the armey in England, by whome 41 of ye members of Parliamt were torne from ye parliamt house in December 1648...' Cork: 'As the freedom of parliaments is their undoubted right, so are our utmost endeavours for restoring them unto and preserving them in their freedom our undoubted duty. Our interest also is involved in our duty; and if we truly love that, we cannot decline this, since whosoever inquires into the foundations of his own freedom, his posterity's, and his country's, in a free and full parliament, as in a common centre, will find them all to meet.'

secluded members had not been requested then, it was asserted, because it was assumed that the restored members would need no prompting and thought that it would be improper 'to have lessened the beauty of their expected performance' by solicitation. The second point particularly addressed was the contradiction between the respect expressed for the English parliament in its unpurged form and the claim to a separate parliament, which was resolved aggressively by pointing out that not merely were eight parts in ten of the people of England presently unrepresented because of vacant seats, 'but two nations of the three entirely'.[130] A colourful account of the general background to the coordination of these two declarations was supplied by Broghill's contemporary biographer, Thomas Morrice, whose insistence that Broghill had made early approaches to the king is unsupported by the evidence. For what it is worth, Morrice described an agreement by which Coote was to gain control of the north and Broghill of the south as a preliminary to inviting the king to come to Ireland: before the plan could be executed, Coote wrote to tell Broghill 'that their design of declaring for king and free parliament began to take air; and therefore he was obliged to declare before the time agreed on', and to request him to do likewise. Broghill 'was a little troubled at this, fearing such haste would spoil their whole interest; but however his Lordship resolved to declare at the same time, which he did'.[131]

Waller's justification for his actions was that Monck had 'recommended to him the care of preventing – as he said – our declaring for a free parliament'.[132] If this incongruous appeal to Monck's authority was opportunistic, Waller did not dissimulate his view as a regicide that

> the bringing in of the members formerly secluded in 1648 was to bring in a free parliament, and that to bring in a free parliament would be to bring in the king; and that to bring in the king would be to indanger his and all their heads who opposed and cutt off the late king's head, and that if the king was brought in by parliament on any conditions it would be no security to the people.[133]

[130] *TSP*, vii, 817–20. [131] Morrice, *State letters of the first earl of Orrery*, i, 63–5.
[132] *Leyborne Popham MSS*, p. 155.
[133] TCD MS 844, f. 195.

There is little reason to doubt that the claim to have Monck's authority was true. Waller's opposition to the return of the secluded members represented Monck's publicly stated position, and what he said echoed the general's warning to Broghill on 27 January that he should 'discountenance' the 'eager abettors' of the secluded members.[134] Writing to Monck on the day after Waller's capture, Theophilus Jones explained apologetically that the officers had been forced to take the initiative 'in this our declaring, not having first therein advised with Your Excellency' and insisted that the intention was as it had been in December – to free the parliament from force 'which is we doubt not what is intended by Your Excellency, and what is expected from you by the good people of these nations'.[135] Ludlow, who was convinced of Monck's duplicity, was clearly wrong in believing that the leaders in Ireland 'moved not a step without his orders and directions'.[136] Monck's admirers, who wished to believe likewise, seem to have found it difficult to reconcile this episode with their preconceptions and dealt with it confusedly. Thus Baker glossed over the independent initiative in Ireland by ascribing the declaration to the day on which the secluded members resumed their seats. Price, who knew more of the detail, suppressed the contentious issue of the secluded members and focused on the embarrassing contretemps of Douglas: after he had persuaded the

> various interests . . . to confederate quickly into a Declaration for a free parliament . . . the design took effect, even a little with the earliest; for just upon the pinch of them declaring for a free parliament, they were alarmed with the astonishing news of Monck's having broken down the gates of London . . . whereupon [they] expostulated with Douglas as if he had betrayed them. But the next packet from England assured them, that Monck had likewise declared for a free parliament, and so all was right again.[137]

Superficially, the confusion may be explained, here as elsewhere, by the characteristic special pleading of Monck's admirers, who attributed ubi-

---

[134] *HMC Various*, vi, 438–9. On 7 February, Monck told Broghill that he had written to Waller two or three days before he got to London: 'I gave him some smart advice concerning his behaviour to the factious phanaticque part of the Army.' Herefordshire and Worcestershire Record Office, A H 34 (unfoliated).
[135] *Leyborne Popham MSS*, p. 155.   [136] Ludlow, *Memoirs*, ii, 228.
[137] Price, *The mystery and method of his majesty's happy restoration*, p. 78.

quitous control to him, presented his every action as constructively directed towards the king's restoration, and discounted the plain evidence of his protracted opposition to the readmission of the secluded members. The disjunction in this situation, however, was fundamental, for the deference of Coote, at least, towards Monck was feigned and the deepest suspicions of the maligned Waller were well founded. At the very time when Monck was burning the gates of London on 10 February, Sir Arthur Forbes was passing through the city with a message from Sir Charles Coote to the king. As Forbes later told the story, Coote had been disappointed by Monck's failure to respond to the widespread demands for either the readmission of the secluded members or a free parliament which had greeted him on his journey south and had 'resolved to begin the work in Ireland, and to secure all those who were averse to the king's interest, and to invite the king into this kingdom'. Forbes was to seek the king's directions and to say that if the king 'would think fitt to come into Ireland, [Coote] made no question of restoring him to his crown – not knowing, for ought he or I could then conceive, that any other part of the Army in the three kingdoms did intend the same thing'. He asked for some ships and some horsemen's arms, and nothing else: 'if they carried their business, they doubted not of the king's favour; and if they perished, there was no need of conditions'. Forbes consulted with Sir James Cuffe, Coote's agent in London, asked him to advise Coote 'to hasten his declaration for a free parliament and the securing of those persons that had a hand in the murder of the king', and journeyed on.[138] It must have been at about the same time that Coote confided to Garrett Moore, who was leaving for England, a somewhat similar assurance of his willingness to serve the king 'allowing him such conditions that might bear proportion with the consequence of his service': in England, Moore was persuaded of the sincerity of this approach in conversation with 'a bosome friend Sir Charles expressly sent into England to observe the humors and inclinations of the people there and to give him frequent notice thereof to the end he may the better designe his owne busines', who was presumably

---

[138] Forbes to Ormond, Granard Papers, PRONI H/1/5/1. William Montgomery, writing long before this letter was published in 1868 (John Forbes, *Memoirs of the earls of Granard*, pp. 202–6), stated obliquely that Forbes told Lord Montgomery 'on what message he went from Coote to the King'. *Montgomery MSS*, p. 224.

James Cuffe.[139] There are hints of another dimension in this episode. Moore, who was the earl of Clanricarde's son-in-law (and 'a very knoweing man, and of great partes'), had been linked with Sir Robert Talbot as agent for a group of Irish Catholics in the previous summer.[140]

The arrival of Forbes in Brussels was certainly timely. Edward Hyde had no contacts in Ireland, relied entirely on secondhand information relayed through England and seriously misunderstood recent developments. His view of Ireland tended towards the fatalistic, as his unenthusiastic response to a mistaken report that Colonel Redman had gone to Ireland in January suggests: 'somewhat will be done when the work is begun in England; Otherwise I do not suppose that much can be done there to any purpose'.[141] That this was more than a realistic recognition of the inability of the royalists to overcome the practical problems of organizing in Ireland appears from a survey of events there since Richard's overthrow which Hyde sent for briefing purposes to Charles's ambassador in Spain, Sir Henry Bennet, in February. In this, he developed the thesis that whatever happened in England, Ireland followed suit, so that it could be assumed that 'what soever shall be done at Westminster, or rather by Monke will steere them'. The exposition revealed that Hyde had failed to understand that the coup in Dublin had taken place before the recall of the Long Parliament at Christmas. Those in power in Ireland, he wrote at a time when the officers' declaration was already on sale in London, were 'very well contented' with the present situation, 'as they will no doubt [be] with anything that falls out tomorrow'.[142] The difficulties of conspiring at

---

[139] Clancarty to Ormond, 2 April 1660 (NS), Carte MS 214, f. 10. The timing is suggested by the covering note in which Clancarty explained that a previous letter to the same effect had miscarried and commented that Coote was now 'much more able and powrefull' than he had been when 'he communicated those thoughts'. Ibid., ff. 11–11v.

[140] Newsletter, 30 June 1659, Clarendon MS 61, f. 361. In May 1651, Moore, as governor of Sligo, had replied to Coote's call to surrender the fort: 'Had I found an inclination in you to become a good subject, and to fall from those rebellious spirits, who had a hand in the unparalleled murder of our late Soveraine Charles the first – without such a resolution you may not expect any personal conference with me.' H. T. Crofton, *Crofton memoirs*, p. 149. Moore was related to Lord Montgomery. Carte MS 31, ff. 97, 106.

[141] Hyde to Barwick, 12 January 1660, White Kennett, *A register and chronicle ecclesiastical and civil* (London, 1728), p. 1.

[142] Hyde to Bennett, 25 February 1660, Clarendon MS 70, ff. 43–43v.

a distance had in any case been increased by recent events. As the spy Samuel Morland phrased it: 'Of late so irrationall and suddain have been our Changes, and our Governors, of such heterogeneous Interests, that it is not only hard to keep in with all, but very difficult to give a full description of our Government before another come upon the stage.'[143] Though instability created opportunity, the royalists were insufficiently organized to take systematic advantage of it and their disposition was to cultivate dissent as the occasion arose and hope that chaos might open the way for restoration. The advice and predictions that were coming from England were increasingly encouraging. An anonymous correspondent encapsulated many of them in a sentence in late January: 'It is the belief of most sober men that neither will this government last long, nor any other be able to keep out the King.'[144] But it remained true that the opportunity that was emerging was that of defeating the army and constructive planning was all the more necessary. Thus Forbes was able to provide Hyde and others with an encouragingly different view of the potential for support in Ireland, at precisely the time when plans needed to be made. From London, Mordaunt was advising the king to accept offers of assistance from Scotland or Ireland, 'for no warre can now be made at any distance from this place, but it will restore you',[145] and a correspondent who had heard that the king had been invited to Ireland urged him to go, 'for his being on some part of his owne land but one weeke in safetie would doe his business for the people in general are mad for him'.[146] The disadvantages of making use of Ireland remained, however. Lines of communication were long, intelligence was poor, and an Irish based initiative might not prove to be an appropriate way of gathering support in England. Nonetheless, as Ormond later reminded the king, the approach through Forbes was made 'before your Majestie had any addresse out of England or was well assured that your restitution was intended in any of the changes then happening there', and it seems clear that for the first time since Henry's submission the possibility of using support in

---

[143] Morland to Hyde, 6 January 1660, Clarendon MS 68, ff. 511–12.
[144] Morland to Hyde, 30 January 1660, Clarendon MS 69, f. 40.
[145] Mordaunt to King, 17 February 1660, Clarendon MS 69, f. 170.
[146] Heath to Hyde, 2 March 1660, Clarendon MS 70, ff. 64–5.

Ireland was beginning to be considered, however tentatively, before news arrived of the new coup in Dublin.[147]

The struggle between Ludlow and the Irish commissioners in London was carried out in part in a public exchange of pamphlets. The commissioners not only published their apologia in *A perfect narrative* but were presumably responsible for the publication in London of a whole series of declarations of the council of officers. Inevitably, the particular issue that was before parliament became central to the debate. Both the letter sent to Ludlow in Duncannon on 10 January, with his reply, and the Duncannon petition itself were published early in February. They were followed by *A sober vindication of Lt. Gen. Ludlow and others* which argued the legitimacy of Ludlow's position and aggressively accused his opponents both of opposing parliament itself in the interests of the secluded members and of being covert Episcopalians. Shortly afterwards there appeared an unrestrained rebuttal of the 'Cunning Sophistications' of *A perfect narrative*, or 'Errative' as the authors preferred to call it. This *Representation* had been intended for presentation to parliament but was overtaken by the return of the secluded members on 21 February. Its chief contribution to the debate was to revive the suspicions of January. One of the 'sophistications' identified was the statement that the convention had been 'stopped', which the authors, who claimed to have recently left Ireland, countered by observing that the elections had already taken place and the members were 'in a readiness to sit when they please'.[148] Another was that the Irish leaders declared that they were for a parliament 'but never tell us for what parl'. They were quite prepared, the authors maintained, 'to stand upon their own legs (as they say) deeming themselves able to subsist without a dependence upon this Nation'.[149] By the time this pamphlet was published, the implied prediction had been fulfilled. The Irish leaders had decided to summon the convention for 27 February.

[147] *Cal. SP, Ire., 1663–5*, p. 310; S.P., Ire., 63/315. 51. Ormond wrongly remembered the approach as being made in January. Hyde had received a detailed account of the Dublin coup before 10 March, when he wrote to Bennet in Spain. Clarendon MS 70, ff. 137–8.

[148] This was certainly the case in Kinsale, which conducted an election in January. Though the record of this decision was amended by the addition of the words 'said convention superseaded', the choice stood. Caulfield, *Kinsale*, p. 52.

[149] *A faithful representation of the state of Ireland*.

There seems to be no evidence to indicate when this decision was made. One contemporary version was that an original revised plan for a meeting early in February was delayed until the army was remodelled and Hardress Waller out of the way.[150] The strenuous efforts to undo the damage that news of the convention had caused in England makes this extremely unlikely, and the inference that the decision arose from the explicit rejection of existing authority in England on 16 February is easily drawn. Although the practical considerations advanced in December in favour of an assembly remained valid, the purpose served by the revival of the convention device was the acquisition of full national backing for the officers' declaration of 16 February. A report that reached London for publication in early March was surely correct in identifying the purpose of the meeting as being 'to finde out a way (in case England should not agree with them) how the Souldiery might be best provided for there, the Country being unanimously resolved to defend those things conteined in the Declaration of Sir Charles Coot with their lives and fortunes'.[151] The decision was attributed by Edmund Borlase in his published *History of the execrable rebellion* to the 'vigilance and excellent contrivance and industry of Dr Dudley Loftus':[152] in his unpublished revision of the book he added the clause 'who had the seasonable and effectuall advice of Dr Henry Jones, Bp of Clogher, a true Royalist who had long worked for the turn'.[153] An alternative contemporary view was that the council of officers had decided to go ahead with the convention 'under the petition of the Mayor and Aldermen of Dublin'.[154] The two are easily reconciled: Loftus's political connections with Dublin went back at least to 1655 when he had acted for the city in managing a petition requesting that Henry Cromwell should replace Fleetwood as lord deputy.[155] Given his appointment as returning officer, it is evident that Loftus was prominently involved from the outset, but the probability is that there were convergent influences and that the reactivation of the assembly arose out of discussions about

[150] H. R., ' A letter to the author', Cox, *Hibernica Anglicana*, p. 2.
[151] *Parliamentary Intelligencer*, 27 February–5 March.
[152] Borlase, *The Irish rebellion*, p. 316.
[153] Stowe MS 142, f. 242. Jones had contributed a prefatory letter to the published edition.
[154] H. R., 'A letter to the author of the History of Ireland', Cox, *Hibernica Anglicana*, p. 2.
[155] Sir George Ayscough to Henry Cromwell, 4 December 1655, Lansdowne MS 821, f. 46.

how to proceed in the aftermath of a convulsion which involved the adoption of a local political programme as well as public defiance of the English parliament.

The significance of the decision altered very rapidly. When the assembly met at the Tholsel on Monday, 27 February, only to adjourn to the following Friday, 'in expectation of a full confluence of all the Members',[156] it did so in direct challenge to the parliamentary authority that had already been repudiated by the council of officers. Two days later, however, the news that the secluded members had been readmitted and that Monck had been appointed to the command of the armed forces of the three nations reached Dublin.[157] The same post should also have brought the letters which Monck had sent to the regiments on 21 February to tell them of his undertaking to the secluded members that writs were to be issued 'for a future full Representative of the whole commonwealth of England, Scotland and Ireland under such qualifications as may secure our cause'.[158] When the Convention assembled again on 2 March, therefore, the political context was wholly altered. The proximate objective of the officers' declaration had been gained: the legitimacy of parliament had been restored. Moreover, military authority was now in friendly hands. As the Dublin and Cork declarations had made clear, however, the 'Parliament of '48' had an added resonance in Ireland, for that parliament had never asserted the right to tax Ireland. Paradoxically, its reinstatement strengthened the argument in favour of the need for local action to solve local problems and justified the Convention rather than made it redundant.

---

[156] *Chief Occurrences*, in *A Declaration of the General Convention of Ireland*, p. 8.
[157] Ibid., p. 9.
[158] Baker, *A chronicle*, p. 750. Davies, *The restoration*, pp. 289–90. Price, *The mystery and method of his majesty's happy restoration*, pp. 115–16. *Mercurius Politicus*, 16–23 February. It was not evident for some time that parliament intended to disregard the commitment to a three nation parliament. The provision that the constituencies should be those specified in the Instrument of Government was also ignored. The three-member committee which recommended 'how and in what manner' the parliament should be summoned included Annesley. *Old parliamentary history*, pp. 1581–2. To judge by Monck's attitude to Scottish representation, which was actively demanded, he was firmly against the continuation of the parliamentary union. Dow, *Cromwellian Scotland*, pp. 261–2.

6

The election results

I

The representatives who assembled in Dublin at the beginning of March 1660 were drawn from the traditional constituencies, but not in the usual proportions. While each county returned its customary two members, the boroughs and cities were limited to one, with the exception of Dublin and Dublin University. The preferential treatment of the city may have reflected the corporation's part in promoting the meeting, or it may be that the electoral arrangements were influenced by the example of Scotland where boroughs returned one member, except Edinburgh which returned two. Dublin took the opportunity to return influential local figures. The university, by contrast, returned men of national prominence in Broghill and Chidley Coote and its special treatment may have been designed for this purpose. As Broghill's return indicates, this was not strictly speaking a surrogate House of Commons: membership was not restricted by the normal rules of eligibility and the Convention included three peers and a quondam bishop. Fifteen boroughs which would ordinarily have been expected to return members had not done so by the time that the extant list of members was compiled about mid-March:[1] six of these were in Leinster,[2] five in Ulster,[3] three in Connacht[4] and one in Munster.[5] The proportionate representation of the provinces, however, remained roughly the same as in the last parliament. The names of the members returned for two county and three borough seats were omitted from the list. In one case, this was because the member had died since his election; in two, it was because the members had also been returned for another constituency for which they

---

[1] *An account of the chief occurrences of Ireland. Together with some particulars from England. From Monday the 12 of March, to Monday the 19 of March* (Dublin, 1659[60]).
[2] Banagher, Callan, Enniscorthy, Inistiogue, Old Leighlin, Ross.
[3] Ballyshannon, Clogher, Donegal, Dungannon, Limavady.
[4] Castlebar, Roscommon, Sligo. [5] Ennis.

had opted to sit; the probability is that this happened in the remaining two as well.⁶ The optimum outcome was an assembly of 158 members, compared with the 240 who had been summoned to the Commons in 1640:⁷ only 138 are known to have been returned.

ULSTER
ANTRIM

County Sir John Clotworthy, Sir George Rawdon
Belfast Sir Jerome Alexander
Carrickfergus Hercules Davis

Antrim had been one of the original ten counties allocated to adventurers and soldiers but its returns to the Convention were wholly unaffected by recent influences. Both Clotworthy and Rawdon were former members of the Irish parliament, Clotworthy for the county in 1634 and Rawdon for Belfast in 1640. Clotworthy, one of the secluded members, had been elected to the English parliament in 1640 and combined an active part in the politics of the civil war in the Presbyterian interest with command of one of the regiments financed by parliament for service in Ulster in 1642. It was he who had moved the inclusion of Ireland in the Solemn League and Covenant in 1643. After the civil war he was one of the eleven members against whom the army presented charges of impeachment in 1647. He was closely involved in promoting the Adventurers' Act, became a substantial original adventurer, subsequently doubled his interest in the market, and drew more than 11,000 acres in County Antrim, largely comprised of the estates of the earl of Antrim. His wife was Broghill's sister-in-law.⁸ Another of the 'British regiments' had been commanded by

---

[6] Cavan borough; County Waterford and Athlone; County Mayo and Ballinakill, respectively. Armagh Borough had replaced its dually elected member before the list was compiled. County Waterford did so on 15 May.

[7] In 1640–1 the re-enfranchisement of boroughs brought this figure gradually up to 254, two less than the number of members returned to the 1634 parliament.

[8] *DNB*. M. F. Keeler, *The Long Parliament, 1640–41: a biographical study of its members* (Philadelphia, 1954). S. M'Skimmin, *The history and antiquities of the county of the town of Carrickfergus*, ed. E. McCrum (Belfast, 1909), p. 484. Bottigheimer, *English money and Irish land*, pp. 179, 201. *Cal.SP, Ire., 1660–2*, p. 649. Robert Armstrong, 'Protestant Ireland and the English parliament, 1641–1647' (Ph.D., University of Dublin, 1995), p. 107.

Lord Conway, and Rawdon, who had come to Ireland as agent on the Conway estate east of Lough Neagh in 1633 and acquired land in Antrim, Down and Dublin in his own right, became its major. He had campaigned with Monck in 1642 and again in the later 1640s, and remained on friendly terms with him. Indeed, he had visited him in Scotland in the June of 1659, and during the summer Monck's brother-in-law, Dr Thomas Clarges, was lobbying MPs on Rawdon's behalf in relation to his estates and the act of settlement. Throughout the war, and as late as 1651, Rawdon had commanded cavalry in Ulster. He may have withdrawn for a time, since he was later classified as a '49 officer, the term used after the restoration to denote those who had not received satisfaction for pre-1649 arrears in the 1650s, because they had been judged not to have shown 'good affection' to parliament. However, Rawdon was a member of an 'Ulster committee' carrying out parliamentary orders as early as August 1651. A little later, he served as a commissioner for revenue in the Belfast precinct and he represented the north-eastern counties in the union parliament in 1659, but his collaboration with the regime was certainly prudential: Rawdon maintained Jeremy Taylor as chaplain and boasted that his Scots neighbours 'esteem me one of the horns against the Kirk'.[9] Alexander's return must have involved the cooperation of the county's chief settler family, the Chichesters, who controlled Belfast. By his own account, however, his election was managed by Coote and Broghill, 'against my will, and unknowne to me'. He had come to Ireland after being debarred from practising law in England in 1626, transacted business in the area for the Conways, invested £7,000 in the acquisition of land from the Magennis family in County Down, represented Lifford in 1634, and fallen foul of

---

[9] DNB. Barnard, *Cromwellian Ireland*, p. 151. C. J. Stranks, *The life and writings of Jeremy Taylor* (London,1952), pp. 189–201. Kevin McKenny, 'A 17th century "real estate company": the 1649 officers and the Irish land settlements, 1641–1681' (MA, St Patrick's College, Maynooth, 1989), Appendix A. 'A diary of the proceedings of the Leinster army under Gov. Jones', *Ulster Journal of Archaeology*, 2nd series, 3 (1897–8), 154. *Rawdon Papers*, pp. 178, 179–80, 195. *Cal. SP, Ire., 1669–70*, p. 367. Arnold, *The restoration land settlement in County Dublin*, pp. 48–9. Rawdon, who was related to the Hills through his first wife, had married the second Lord Conway's daughter in 1654. Both he and Clotworthy were JPs for County Antrim. Information about individuals who had been MPs in 1640–41 has been drawn from Brid McGrath, 'A biographical dictionary of the membership of the Irish house of commons, 1640–41' (Ph.D., University of Dublin, 1997) in addition to the sources cited.

Lord Deputy Wentworth who dismissed him as a 'scurvy puritan'. In 1642, he subscribed £50 to the original Adventure and later became an active member both of the Committee of Adventurers (a role in which he clashed sharply with Clotworthy) and of the Goldsmiths' Hall committee which was responsible for raising money for the Scots armies in England and Ireland. He seems to have resumed the connection with the adventurers in the 1650s, acting for some time as legal adviser to the committee in London, but he also performed the more lowly duties of clerk of the peace in County Longford. In the early part of the decade, however, he had spent some time on the continent where he had helped to finance royalist refugees, the duke of York among them. His daughter had recently married the eldest brother of Dr Gorges.[10] Hercules Davis, by contrast, belonged to a well-established local merchant family. Little is known of him beyond the fact that he married Lord Montgomery's sister-in-law in the following year, which suggests that his political stance may be reasonably inferred from that of his father, John, who had represented Carrickfergus in parliament in 1640 and was its mayor in 1660. John Davis had been deeply involved in the military supply trade to Ireland in the 1640s as commissary for provisions in the north and had been a close associate of Clotworthy. When he was elected to the union parliament in 1656, however, Thurloe asked Henry Cromwell to prevent him from attending, as 'a most pestilent fellow' who favoured the king, and Henry, whose enquiries revealed that Davis was indeed 'a very naughty man', complied. In 1657, Colonel Cooper objected to Davis's purchase of Clotworthy's house in the town on the grounds that he was unfit to live in a place 'that over-lookes our guards', and a little later one of Dr Jones's informants reported that Davis was 'verie intimat with the Irish, and with the ould adverse party, telling them all newes'.[11]

[10] R. Gillespie, *Colonial Ulster* (Cork, 1985), pp. 79, 126, 140, 172, 176–7. W. G. Neely, *Kilcooley – land and people in Tipperary* (Belfast, 1984), pp. 25, 28, 29. Alexander to Sir Edward Massey, post October 1661, Barwick MSS, No. 3. C. Rogers, 'Notes in the history of Sir Jerome Alexander', *Roy. Hist. Soc., Trans.*, 2 (1873), pp. 94–116. J. P. Prendergast, 'Further notes in the history of Sir Jerome Alexander', ibid., 2, pp. 117–42. F. E. Ball, *The Judges in Ireland* (2 vols., London, 1926), i, 267. Armstrong, 'Protestant Ireland and the English parliament', p. 178. Dublin Statute Staple database (in preparation).

[11] S. Pender, *A census of Ireland, c. 1659* (IMC, 1939), p. 20. *Egmont MSS*, i, 273. *TSP*, v, 398, 443; vi, 219, 454. *Montgomery MSS*, p. 329. M'Skimmin, *Carrickfergus*, pp. 393–4, 412,

ARMAGH

County Sir George Acheson, Edward Richardson
Borough Sir William Gore
Charlemont Edward Rowley

By contrast, in Armagh, which was also one of the original ten designated counties, county representation was shared between old and new settlers. Sir George Acheson's father had combined office as joint secretary of state in Scotland with the acquisition of plantation undertakings in Armagh and Cavan. George, who was born in 1629 and had inherited a Scottish baronetcy, lived at Markethill and was sheriff of both Armagh and Tyrone in 1657. He had served for some years as lieutenant-colonel of Sir William Cole's regiment, but when the Scottish change of sides complicated matters after 1648 he took the royalist side, like many of his compatriots. His first wife had been Sir Charles Coote's sister-in-law. His second, to whom he was married in November 1659, was Lord Caulfield's sister.[12] He was also elected for the borough, but opted to sit for the county seat. Edward Richardson was a veteran of Dungan's Hill and the storming of Drogheda who had come from Worcester to Ireland as a captain in Castle's regiment in 1647. He was disbanded in 1653 with the rank of major, with arrears assigned to him in Meath, but he seems to have continued in command of a 'loose company' for some time thereafter and to have acquired additional arrears land in Waterford and Kilkenny. His principal estate, however, was in Oneilland barony in Armagh and had been acquired by marriage to the heiress of the English undertaker Francis Sacheverall. He was a justice of the peace and had served as sheriff of Armagh in 1655 and of both Armagh and Tyrone in 1656: the completeness of his integration into the county is suggested by the fact that he was returned again in the elections of 1661 and

---

414–16, 432n, 471–2. Dunlop, *Commonwealth*, p. 625. John is said to have visited Charles at Breda early in 1660. Lodge, *Peerage*, iii, 150–1n.

[12] George Hill, *An historical account of the Plantation in Ulster* (Belfast, 1877), p. 472. *Cal. SP, Ire., 1633–47*, p. 250. Dunlop, *Commonwealth*, p. 633n. G. Burtchaell, *Genealogical memoirs of the members of parliament for the county and city of Kilkenny* (London, 1888), p. 78. E. Hamilton, *The Irish rebellion of 1641* (London, 1920), pp. 347, 348. Acheson and Coote had married daughters of Robert Hannay, a Scottish baronet who was appointed clerk of the nichells in Ireland in 1631 and died in Dublin in 1658. Lodge, *Peerage*, vi, 81–2. G.E.C., ii, 335. Hughes, *Patentee officers*. Earl of Belmore, *Parliamentary memoirs of Fermanagh and Tyrone* (Dublin, 1887), p. 362.

appointed a captain in the militia.[13] The borough representatives were both from firmly established colonial backgrounds. The eighteen-year-old William Gore had recently succeeded to the baronetcy associated with the senior branch of a servitor family with estates in Donegal and Fermanagh whose junior branch had flourished in Sligo and formed part of the Coote nexus. His grandfather had represented Ballyshannon in 1613 and his father County Donegal in 1640. He had entered Dublin University three years earlier, after schooling in London. His return for Armagh in place of Acheson may safely be attributed to family ties. Acheson had recently married his mother's sister: their brother, Lord Caulfield, owned former abbey lands in the town.[14] Edward Rowley's grand-father had come to Ulster with his grand-uncle, one of the Irish Society's agents in Londonderry and member of the 1613 parliament for Coleraine County; his father had been killed in 1641. Rowley, who was in his late twenties, lived in the barony of Tiranny in the west of the county close to the Caulfield controlled borough of Charlemont.[15] In a Convention that was sensitive to gradations of social status he was one of only three commoners described as 'gentleman' rather than 'esquire'.

DOWN

County Sir Arthur Hill, Roger West
Bangor John Temple
Downpatrick Sir John Percival
Killelagh James Cuffe
Newtownards Thomas Caulfield
Newry Dr Joseph Waterhouse

---

[13] *Regimental history*, pp. 632–3. *HMC, Ormond MSS*, i, 199; ii, 247–51. *Census of Ireland. Burke's Landed Gentry*. James Stuart, *Historical memoirs of the city of Armagh* (Newry, 1819), p. 638. *Reports of the Irish Record Commissioners* (3 vols., Dublin, 1811–25), Rep. 8, p. 289. Prendergast papers, ii, 446–9, 600–5. Belmore, *Parliamentary memoirs*, p. 362.

[14] *Burke's Landed Gentry*. Lodge, *Peerage*, iii, 281–2. *Complete baronetage*, i, 233–4. *Alumni Dubliniensis*. Hill, *Plantation in Ulster*, pp. 158, 335–6, 514, 525. *Inquisitiones in Officio Rotulorum Cancellarius Hibernica* (Dublin, 1829), ii, Ultonia, Chas II (3). Trimble, *Fermanagh*, pp. 256–7.

[15] Hill, *Plantation in Ulster*, p. 404. P. Robinson, *The plantation of Ulster* (Dublin, 1984), p. 81. T. W. Moody, *The Londonderry plantation 1609–41. The city of London and the plantation in Ulster* (Belfast, 1939), pp. 99–101, 143–7, 154. Lodge, *Peerage*, v, 296.

THE ELECTION RESULTS

In Down, the third of the Ulster counties assigned to adventurers and soldiers, the returns from the boroughs were characterized by an exceptionally hospitable accommodation of outsiders, but the county members were both from local settler families. Colonel Arthur Hill, whose father had come first to Ireland with Essex in the 1570s, was a man of notable influence. A member of parliament in 1634 and 1641[16] and colonel of a regiment throughout the decade, he was said to have laid down his arms in 1649, but he was granted £5,000 by parliament in the following year 'in recompence for his many services in Ireland' and a further £1,000 in 1656. He had served with Rawdon on the 'Ulster committee' in 1651 and as commissioner of the revenue in Belfast precinct and been involved in the survey of forfeited land in Antrim, Armagh and Down. He was also a member of the committee of five which devised the unexecuted arrangements for the transplantation of the Scots in 1653, among them the preparation of a hit list which included Lord Montgomery, and he had represented the north-eastern counties in the union parliament in 1654. In 1656, he was one of the auditors general concerned with the preparation of consolidated accounts for the previous seven years. On the other hand, he sheltered the bishop of Down and Connor and joined Rawdon (with whom he was connected by marriage) in favouring Jeremy Taylor, whose arrival in Ireland evoked much ministerial disapproval and who testified to his orthodoxy. After the restoration, he was among the select group of nineteen men who were pardoned and treated as if they were '49 officers. His sister Frances married Thomas Coote.[17] Roger West's father had come to Ireland with Colonel Thomas Cromwell at the beginning of the century and had represented the Cromwell borough of

---

[16] He was returned in by-elections on both occasions.

[17] *Anal. Hib.*, 15, p. 248. McKenny, 'A 17th century "real estate company"', pp. 200–1. *Cal. SP, Ire., 1660–2*, pp. 198, 316–19; *1647–60*, p. 667; *1669–70*, p. 367. Prendergast papers, ii, 718–25. W. H. Hardinge, 'On manuscript, mapped and other townland surveys in Ireland of a public character, embracing the Gross, Civil, and Down Surveys, from 1640–1688', *RIA trans.*, 24 (1873), Appendix E. Gilbert (ed.), *Facsimiles of the national manuscripts of Ireland*, iv, pt. 2 (London, 1884), Plate lxix. Barnard, *Cromwellian Ireland*, p. 151. Henry Leslie, *A discourse of praying*, p. 1. *Clarendon State Papers*, iv, 664. H. O'Sullivan, 'The Magennis lordship of Iveagh in the early Stuart period', in Lindsey Proudfoot (ed.), *Down: history and society* (Dublin, 1997), p. 189. Hill had acquired Alexander's interest in the Magennis estates, ibid., p. 178.

Downpatrick in 1613. Roger, who had added an estate near Arklow to his inherited property at Ballydugan in Lecale, is said to have fought in England during the civil war and to have reached the rank of major under Fairfax. His associations, however, were in the contrary direction. His wife was a daughter of Sir Henry Tichborne, who had succeeded Parsons as lord justice in 1643, his sister was married to a nephew of Viscount Clandeboye and George Rawdon called him cousin.[18] By contrast, all of the unusually large number of borough members were from outside the county, and most were men of standing. John Temple, a Dublin barrister whose seat was in the gift of the Hamilton family, was the son of the master of the rolls and historian of the rebellion who had recently resumed the seat in the English parliament to which he had been elected in 1646. In 1649, when he was about seventeen years old and attending Gray's Inns, the younger Temple had acquired the adventuring interest of his relative Lieutenant-General Thomas Hammond, partner of John Hampden, and had been allotted land in the barony of Eliogarty in Tipperary.[19] Sir John Percival, whose home was at Kanturk in County Cork and who was married to the daughter of the royalist Robert Southwell of Kinsale, was the heir of one of the previous generation's most successful accumulators of Irish land. His father had been appointed commissary general of victuals for Ireland in April 1642, acted in that capacity in London under parliamentary direction throughout the civil war, and entered the English parliament as member for Newport in

[18] West was appointed poll tax commissioner for Wicklow as well as Down. Edward Parkinson, 'The Wests of Ballydugan, County Down', *UJA*, 2nd series, 12 (1906), pp. 135–41. Brid McGrath, 'The membership of the Irish house of commons, 1613–1615' (M.Litt., University of Dublin, 1985), p. 108. Dunlop, *Commonwealth*, p. 633n. Liam Price, 'The hearth money rolls for County Wicklow', *RSAI jn.*, 61 (1931), p. 168. *Cal. SP, Ire., 1647–60*, p. 496. HMC, *Report 15, App VII, Somerset MSS* (1898), pp. 167–8. Carte MS 68, f. 199. His brother-in-law was married to the daughter of John Bysse, member for Dublin. William Ball Wright, *The Ussher memoirs; or, Genealogical memoirs of the Ussher families in Ireland* (Dublin, 1889), p. 165n.

[19] Both of the members for Bangor in 1640 had been nephews of Viscount Clandeboye. For the Temples see K. H. D. Haley, *An English diplomat in the Low Countries* (Oxford, 1986). The Temples were clients of the Sidney family, and Sir John was a lifelong friend of Algernon. He had been returned to the Long Parliament for Chichester when Algernon was governor. Scott, *Algernon Sidney and the English Republic*, pp. 51, 86. *Cal. SP, Adv.*, pp. 124–5, 345, 349. The younger John became solicitor general in July 1660. Hughes, *Patentee officers*. The 'Census' lists only a Dublin address for him.

Cornwall in 1647.[20] Sir John himself was friendly with Henry Cromwell, whom he had known at Cambridge, and had played a subordinate role to Broghill, Annesley and Clotworthy in the negotiations which led to the amelioration of the treatment of the Munstermen and other Protestants in 1654. After taking up residence in Ireland in 1655 he was restored to his father's posts as clerk of the crown of the court of upper bench and prothonotary of the common pleas and Henry Cromwell knighted him in 1658. Theophilus Jones, a close family friend, had wanted him to take a vacant seat in the 1657 parliament. His failure to secure a seat in Munster may be in part attributable to a dispute about land with Broghill's nephew, Lord Barrymore, and his return instead for a borough which had elected Marcus Trevor in 1640 and was within the area of influence of the Cromwell family sufficiently indicates his leanings in 1660. In the 1640s, Temple's father had been instrumental in laying charges against Sir John Percival's father, largely arising from his alleged support for the 1643 cessation.[21] James Cuffe, Sir Charles Coote's London agent, was a Somerset man who had come to Ireland with his father and brother shortly after the rebellion broke out. Ormonde later testified that Cuffe 'never bore arms against your Majestie' but he served in the 1650s both as secretary to the Loughrea Commissioners, the body responsible for assigning lands to the transplanted Irish in Connacht, and as recorder of Galway. He was a cousin of the Coote brothers, whose mother was the daughter and co-heiress of Hugh Cuffe, a collateral ancestor who had acquired lands in the Munster plantation. One of Cuffe's London contacts had certainly been his wife's brother, Lord Aungier, 28-year-old grandson of both an Irish master of the rolls and an archbishop of Dublin, who had represented the King's County-Longford-Westmeath constituency in the 1659 parliament and was shortly to stand for the English Convention in Surrey as an avowed royalist. That Cuffe's links reached even further beyond the Coote nexus is suggested by his later appointment as clerk of the Munster Council under Broghill's presidency. His seat in Killelagh

---

[20] *Egmont MSS*, i, 175, 188 and passim. An outward show of cooperation in dealing with Ireland was maintained after the outbreak of civil war and Percival continued to transact business with Ormond. Ibid., p. 201.

[21] There is an outline of his career in the introduction to *Egmont MSS*, i, pt i. Jones was his 'mothers confessor', according to his uncle. *Egmont MSS*, i, 581, 589.

was a Hamilton preserve.[22] The apparent stranger in the politically charged company of Down members was Dr Joseph Waterhouse, who had no recorded local associations and was under what ought to have been the disadvantage of being a brother of Oliver Cromwell's household steward, but who was returned for a borough in which the influence of the Hills is likely to have been decisive. Waterhouse, who lived in Dublin, had come to Ireland as the sole physician attending the 1649 expeditionary force and remained an army physician thereafter. He had nurtured grievances about his remuneration and rewards throughout the 1650s and was still reproachfully seeking satisfaction from Henry Cromwell as late as April 1659.[23] Thomas Caulfield, at the house of whose brother Toby, Sir Phelim O'Neill had commenced the rising on 22 October 1641, was both lawyer and soldier, a master in chancery since 1655 and a member of the council of officers which defied Ludlow. Caulfield, whose property was at Donemon in Roscommon, and Viscount Montgomery, who controlled Newtownards, married sisters, daughters of Charles Moore, second Viscount Drogheda.[24]

LONDONDERRY

County Tristram Beresford, John Rowley
Borough John Godbold
Coleraine Michael Beresford

---

[22] HMC, *Report 10*, p. 501. Commonwealth State Accounts, *Anal. Hib.*, 15, pp. 280, 300. Hardiman, *Galway*, App. p. xxi. Lodge, *Peerage*, iii, 375–6; vi, 55–6. DNB, sub Henry Cuffe. 'Gerard Aungier', *Notes and queries*, March 1924, p. 208. *Cal. SP, Ire., 1666–9*, p. 75. Carte MS 68, f. 161. Prendergast papers, i, 193, 451. Both of the members elected for Killelagh in 1661 were clients of the Hamiltons.

[23] Report on the Rawlinson Manuscripts, *Anal. Hib.*, 1 (1930), p. 64. Aylmer, *The state's servants*, pp. 276, 419. R. Sherwood, *The court of Oliver Cromwell* (London, 1977), pp. 33–5, 44. R. W. Ramsey, *Henry Cromwell* (London, 1933), p. 86. Waterhouse to Henry Cromwell, 2 April 1659, Lansdowne MS 823, ff. 282–5. Waterhouse was to become a founding member of the Royal College of Physicians in Ireland in 1667. Lodge, *Peerage*, ii, 353. A Joseph Waterhouse had been lieutenant of Oliver Cromwell's horse troop in 1642. Edward Peacock, *The army lists of the roundheads and cavaliers* (London, 1863), p. 53.

[24] Barnard, *Cromwellian Ireland*, p. 288. Lodge, *Peerage*, ii, 105; iii, 135ff. Caulfield had married Anne Moore in 1657. Herbert Wood (ed.), *The register of S. Catherine's, Dublin, 1636–1715* (Parish Register Society of Dublin, 1908), p. 3. A third sister was married to Thomas's brother, William, Lord Caulfield and a fourth married Hercules Davis in 1661. Montgomery's wife had died in 1655.

Londonderry was one of the additional counties in which forfeited land was allocated to the satisfaction of the arrears of the main body of the Cromwellian army, but representation followed traditional lines. Both county places were taken by descendants of the two original agents of the Irish Society. Tristram Beresford, who was based in Coleraine, took one seat, as his father had done in 1634; John Rowley of Castleroe, who was Beresford's nephew by marriage, took the other, as his father had done in 1640. The 25-year-old Rowley's mother was Sir John Clotworthy's sister, while his father's sister was married to Clotworthy's brother James and Sir John was his guardian. He was a cousin of Edward Rowley, the member for Charlemont.[25] Beresford had played an active part in the defence of Ulster in the 1640s, when he had been lieutenant-colonel of Reeves's regiment, and had campaigned actively outside the province in the early 1650s when he was one of the very few local commanders among the elite group of the council of officers. His brother Michael had unsuccessfully defended Dungiven fort against MacMahon's Ormondist army in 1650. Both brothers had been commissioners in the Londonderry precinct and Tristram had served as a commissioner for the survey of Donegal, Londonderry and Tyrone and had acquired interests in the former estate of the earl of Antrim. Michael had served as sheriff of the county in 1654 and as mayor of Coleraine in 1658–9 and was a justice of the peace for County Antrim. Tristram had been returned for the area to the union parliament in 1656. An initial decision not to allow him and two other members from Ireland to take their seats evoked a successful protest from Henry Cromwell, who assured his father that all three were 'approved of by all the good and sober people here', and Tristram vindicated his judgement by voting in favour of kingship.[26] The odd man out in this company was John Godbold, who had been appointed Recorder of

---

[25] His father Edward had previously represented Coleraine in 1634. John also had a residence in Macosquy, Coleraine barony. Lodge, *Peerage*, v, 296–7. Hill, *Plantation in Ulster*, p. 404. Jennings MSS, Box J2, Notebook A2. Moody, *The Londonderry plantation*, pp. 99–101.

[26] Dunlop, *Commonwealth*, p. 212. [Edward Hogan] (ed.), *The history of the warr of Ireland from 1641 to 1653* (Dublin, 1873), p. 116. Ludlow, *Memoirs*, i, 513. *Cal. SP, Ire., 1647–60*, pp. 623, 687; *1660–2*, p. 649. Lodge, *Peerage*, ii, 296–8. Hardinge, 'On manuscript, mapped and other townland surveys', Appendix E. Moody and Simms, *The bishopric of Derry*, pp. 393–4. *TSP*, v, 477.

Londonderry city (where Sir Charles Coote was among the aldermen) under the new charter of 1657. He was already in the area, having been appointed to a commission to inquire into allegations against ministers in Ulster in the previous year, but no earlier connection with Ireland is recorded.[27]

TYRONE

County Sir Audley Mervyn, Arthur Chichester
Agher Richard Palfrey
Strabane John Moderwell

Tyrone was also assigned to supplement the land available to meet post-'49 arrears and its returns were also unaffected by recent events. Both of the county members were from prominent settler families. Audley Mervyn, who had acquired the plantation estates of his uncle, Lord Castlehaven, and had married Clotworthy's sister as his second wife, had also represented Tyrone in the 1640 parliament. He had played a leading part in the oppositional politics of that assembly, most notably in vigorously arguing the case for the Irish parliament's linked rights of judicature and impeachment. Later, he had commanded one of the British regiments in Ulster through the 1640s. Though he had taken the covenant in 1644 when he was governor of Londonderry, professedly in a bid to retain control of his troops, he had remained loyal until late 1649 when he had come to an arrangement with Sir Charles Coote, who commanded the parliamentary forces in Londonderry. He had recently been admitted to King's Inns as a barrister and been associated with Sankey and Benjamin Worsley as 'Quibler' in their attack on Petty.[28] Arthur Chichester was the

---

[27] Moody and Simms, *The bishopric of Derry*, i, 281. 'Commonwealth records', *Arch. Hib.*, 6, pp. 277–8. It is likely that he was the John Godbold, from Suffolk, who entered Gray's Inn in 1639.

[28] M. Perceval-Maxwell, *The outbreak of the Irish rebellion of 1641* (Dublin, 1994), chapter 7. *Captaine Audley Mervin's speech, delivered in the Upper House to the Lords in Parliament, May 24 1641* (London, 1641). DNB. Petty, *Reflections*, p. 124. J. P. Prendergast, 'Some account of Sir Audley Mervyn', *Trans. Roy. Hist. Soc.*, 3 (1874), pp. 421–49. His sister had married Rory Maguire, and the Confederate general Lord Castlehaven was his cousin. He was later classified as a '49 officer.

grandson of Edward, first Viscount Chichester, who had inherited the estates of his brother, James's long serving lord deputy. His father John, on whom the family's Tyrone estate had been settled, including the whole town of Dungannon, represented that borough in 1640 and died in arms in 1648 when Arthur was less than ten years old. Arthur's mother, Viscount Ranelagh's daughter, was sister-in-law to both Clotworthy and Broghill.[29] Richard Palfrey was a lawyer who had been admitted to the franchise in Dublin in 1649, served as sheriff of the city in 1655–6 and was admitted to King's Inns as an attorney in the following year. Though he lived in Dublin, where he was an active parishioner of St John's under both the old dispensation and its new Presbyterian minister in the 1650s, the indications are that he had some connection with Tyrone. He was appointed to the poll tax commission for the county, as well as for Dublin, and represented Agher again in the 1661 parliament.[30] By contrast, John Moderwell belonged to a family of Scots provenance which had settled in Strabane and the nearby Castlefinn area before 1630.[31] John himself was probably the merchant of that name whose will was proved in 1679.[32]

---

[29] Arthur's father had married in 1638. His uncle, the earl of Donegal, had represented County Antrim in 1640. Arthur succeeded to the earldom in 1674. Peter Roebuck, 'The making of an Ulster great estate: the Chichesters, Barons of Belfast and Viscounts of Carrickfergus, 1599–1648', in *RIA proc.*, 79 C No 1 (1979), pp. 12, 21. Belmore, *Parliamentary memoirs*, pp. 214–15, 232.

[30] Gilbert, *Records*, iii, 487; iv, 81. He was admitted to the franchise as a baker. In the records of St John's, however, he was always referred to as 'Counsellor'. He was so described on his appointment as a churchwarden in 1644. S. C. Hughes, *The church of S. John the evangelist, Dublin* (Dublin, 1889), pp. 23, 95, 121.

[31] They appear to have come from the Renfrewshire-Clyde area. The will of Adam (of Donaghmore, Co Donegal, a parish including Castlefinn and Killygraham), dated 1632, is in G. Thrift (ed.), *Indexes to Irish wills, v: Derry and Raphoe*. Andrew and Robert Moderwell mustered for Strabane in 1630. Adam and Robert did so on the Kingsmill estate in Castlefinn (Add. MSS 4770, f. 184). I am grateful to R. J. Hunter for information about the Moderwells.

[32] PRO, Ire., Beti/51, p. 15 (1a. 44. 6). Sir Arthur Vicars, *Index to the prerogative wills of Ireland, 1536–1810* (2 vols., Dublin, 1897–1914). Moderwell was one of the very few members who were not appointed to the poll tax commission, which may signify non-attendance. He is not mentioned in the Census.

FERMANAGH[33]

County Sir John Cole, William Davis
Enniskillen Robert Cole

Three baronies in Fermanagh had been assigned to post-1649 soldiers, while the remainder of the forfeited land was set aside to meet pre-1649 arrears. The first of these groups made an ambiguous showing in the returns, which included two members of the county's dominant family which had taken the parliamentary side more explicitly than most in the 1640s. Colonel John Cole's father, Sir William, had been a knight of the shire in both 1634 and 1640. A younger son, John had been an officer in his father's regiment before gaining one of his own in 1650: after it was disbanded in 1653, he served as a commissioner in the precinct of Belturbet and as governor of Enniskillen. He sat in the union parliament in 1654 and from 1655 was at least nominally lieutenant-colonel of the absentee Clarke's regiment, which was made up of 'loose companies'. His land in lieu of arrears was located in Tipperary, Waterford and Monaghan, but he lived at Newland in County Dublin. Displaced in the summer of 1659, he had quickly associated himself with the December coup and was a member of the council of officers before the end of the month. He was later pardoned and conferred with the status of a '49 officer. He was married to the sister of his fellow Convention member, Arthur Chichester and his elder brother Michael had married Chidley Coote's daughter.[34] Robert Cole, of Ballymackey near Nenagh, was his cousin. The relationship was a fairly distant one and Robert's side of the family had not come to Ireland, but the two men held neighbouring land in the barony of Lower Ormond. Although the location of Robert's estate suggests that he had been disbanded as a member of the post-1649 army, he had served in Ireland previously and had fought at Ross with Ormond in 1643. He had also signed the petition of Protestant subjects to the king in that year. He had subsequently, according to Ormond, 'served against the

---

[33] The returns for Leitrim, Fermanagh and Kilkenny City were scrambled together in the published list. This seems the most likely reconstruction.

[34] *Regimental history*, p. 636. Belmore, *Parliamentary memoirs*, p. 34. Commonwealth State Accounts, *Anal. Hib.*, 15, p. 254. *Complete Baronetage*, iii, 308. McKenny, 'A 17th century "real estate company"', pp. 200–1. *Cal. SP, Ire., 1660–63*, pp. 198, 316–19. IRC, Rep. 15, pp. 49, 184. Prendergast papers, ii, 599. Lodge, *Peerage*, vi. 48–9.

King'.[35] William Davis, as sheriff of the county in 1659, continued for a second term in 1660 by virtue of the parliamentary order, was the returning officer. He was proprietor of the manor of Knockballymore, the property of his wife's family, the Hattons, who had bought it from the original patentee in 1614.[36]

MONAGHAN

County Richard Blayney, Oliver Ancketil
Borough Thomas Vincent

Monaghan's place in the settlement was similar to that of Fermanagh: one barony had been allocated to post-1649 soldiers and the remainder to earlier arrears. Here, however, new influences surfaced, albeit again ambiguously. Tradition was continued in the return of Richard Blayney, a nephew of the 1640 member who was killed at the beginning of the rebellion and son of Lord Blayney who was killed at Benburb. He had represented the area in the union parliament in 1656 and had been appointed escheator of Tyrone and custos rotulorum of Monaghan in the same year. Early in 1659, he had advanced to the position of escheator of Ulster. When the Convention was elected his brother, the third Lord Blayney, was in London where he was reported in March to be 'cordial and active for the King' and confident of his restoration 'upon honourable conditions'.[37] Thomas Vincent was Richard's father-in-law. A colonial trader, a former master of the Company of Leathersellers, an alderman of the city of London and a close associate of the leaders of London radicalism in the 1640s, Vincent had been the largest individual speculator

---

[35] Belmore, *Parliamentary memoirs*, pp. 40–1, 337, 344. D. F. Gleeson, *Last lords of Ormond: a history of the 'countrie of the three O'Kennedys' during the 17th century* (London, 1938), p. 167. *The true copies of two letters* (London, 1643); *A full and true relation of the late victory* (London, 1643). List of commissioned officers, with comments, 1663. Carte MS 68, ff. 159–63. *Ormond MSS*, new series, ii, 344. He represented Enniskillen again in 1661.

[36] He was elected to parliament in 1661 and died in the following year. Belmore, *Parliamentary memoirs*, pp. 34–5. Davis was appointed a poll tax commissioner for Monaghan as well as for Fermanagh.

[37] Richard succeeded to the title in 1669. Lodge, *Peerage*, vi, 310–14. Commonwealth State Accounts, *Anal. Hib.*, 15 (1944), p. 278. Hughes, *Patentee officers*. *Cal. Clarendon S.P.*, iv, 615. Lord Blayney had been suspected of royalist plotting in 1649. Underdown, *Royalist conspiracy*, p. 25.

in adventurers' lands, raising an initial stake of £300 under the original act and £1,000 under the sea ordinance to an investment with a face value of £11,525 through the purchase of the shares of other adventurers. This he had converted into some 19,000 acres scattered through Queen's County, King's County and Meath. Most of these transactions took place in the 1650s, after he had acquired the Blayney lands from Lord Blayney in 1648 as security for a loan of £6,000 on the Dublin Statute Staple, but Vincent had been a commissioner for the Sea Adventure in 1643, advanced money for Munster in the mid-1640s and was one of the syndicate that financed the war effort there in 1648. He moved to Ireland in 1655 where he became an alderman of Dublin. Two years earlier, Richard Blayney had regained the family estate in a marriage settlement with Vincent's daughter. Vincent had been sheriff of Meath in 1658-9 and presumably continued in office. Since he held land in Meath jointly with Samuel Winter, it seems likely that he was an Independent.[38] The second county member, Oliver Ancketill, had come to Ireland from Dorset as a young man in the 1630s, probably to Tyrone, though his cousin John had settled in Cork. He was a captain in Audley Mervyn's regiment in the 'British Army in Ulster' in the mid-1640s, was serving in Sir John Cole's regiment when it was disbanded in 1653, and settled on arrears land at Glaslough. With Blaney, he was a justice of the peace for the county.[39]

[38] Bottigheimer, *English money and Irish land*, pp. 155–6. Brenner, *Merchants and revolution*, pp. 404, 407, 529. P. Livingston, *The Monaghan story* (Enniskillen, 1980), p. 498. *Cal. SP, Ire., 1647–60*, pp. 382, 768; G.E.C., *Peerage*, ii, 187 (where the sequence of Richard's marriages is incorrect). F. E. Ball, *A history of the county of Dublin* (6 vols., Dublin, 1902–20), iv, 90. Lodge, *Peerage*, vi, 313n. A. B. Beaven, *Aldermen of London* (2 vols., London, 1908–13), i, 222; ii, 83. Keith Lindley, 'Irish adventurers and godly militants in the 1640s', *IHS*, 113 (1994), p. 9; *Popular politics and religion in civil war London* (Aldershot, 1997), p. 331n. *Egmont MSS*, i, 294, 309, 317, 324, 427, 461, 481. Prendergast papers, ii, 939B. Royal Irish Academy, Books of survey and distribution: County Meath, barony of Navan, Trim parish. Vincent was a member of the adventurers' committee appointed by Oliver Cromwell in 1654. *Cal. SP, Adv.*, pp. 382–3. He claimed to have been in possession of the Queen's County land for several years before 9 May 1656. *Cal. SP, Ire., 1663–5*, p. 700.

[39] E. P. Shirley, *History of the county of Monaghan* (London, 1879), pp. 154–60. *Burke's Irish family records. Cal. SP, Ire., 1647–60*, p. 610. W. C. Trimble, *The history of Enniskillen* (3 vols., Enniskillen, 1919–21), ii, 311–12. Oliver was the son of William, and a William Ancketill had been sheriff of Tyrone in 1635. Moody and Simms, *The bishopric of Derry*, i, 202. Monaghan justices of the peace to Henry Cromwell, 6 October 1657, Lansdowne MS 822, f. 198.

CAVAN

County Thomas Coote, Thomas Richardson
Belturbet John Madden

In Cavan, forfeited land had been allotted to the settlement of pre-1649 arrears. This was a county in which the Coote family had substantial interests. Thomas, the youngest of the four brothers, had attended Lincoln's Inn in the late 1630s, represented Trim in the rump of the Irish parliament in the 1640s, commanded a regiment in Ulster in the early 1650s, served afterwards as governor of Coleraine and Belturbet, and represented the combined Cavan–Fermanagh–Monaghan constituency in the 1659 union parliament.[40] Thomas Richardson had been invited by the commissioners to come to Ireland to take up a post as auditor in June 1651, probably at the instigation of John Jones to whom he was already known as 'sometimes a member of Allhallowes Ch.'. He is first recorded in Ireland as one of the commissioners appointed in November 1652 to enquire into the murders and massacres committed against the English: later, he served as a member of the high court of justice in Dublin, commissioner of survey in Clare, auditor of public accounts in Leinster and appraiser under the Galway articles in 1655. By 1660, he was a clerk of chancery, an alderman of Dublin and a member of Winter's Independent congregation. In 1654 he had acquired an estate in Clankee barony by a mixture of purchase and dowry on his marriage to the daughter of Sir Edward Bagshaw of Finglas, County Dublin.[41] John Madden was the son of Thomas Madden, Lord Deputy Wentworth's comptroller, who had represented Dungannon in 1640. In England, in the 1640s, John had taken the parliamentary side, acting as solicitor for parliamentary sequestrations from 1644 to 1649. Though he lived in Kildare, his wife was a niece of the local undertaker, Sir Stephen Butler, whose extensive properties had been confirmed to his heir as the manor of Belturbet; she was also

---

[40] *Regimental history*, pp. xxiii, 620. *Arch. Hib.*, 7, p. 25.
[41] O'Renehan MSS, ii, f. 203. 'Inedited letters', p. 209. Hill, *Plantation in Ulster*, p. 464. Barnard, *Cromwellian Ireland*, p. 83n; T. C. Barnard, 'Lawyers and the law in later seventeenth-century Ireland', *IHS*, 111 (1993), p. 273n. Dunlop, *Commonwealth*, pp. 296, 543, 546. *Anal. Hib.*, 15, p. 320. TCD MS 844, f. 136. Add. MS 19,833. Hardiman, *Galway*, p. 141. Prendergast papers, i, 350. Dublin Statute Staple database (in preparation).

heiress of Castle Waterhouse in the adjourning Fermanagh barony of Knockniny.[42]

DONEGAL

County George Carey, Richard Perkins
Killybegs William Knight
Lifford William, Lord Caulfield

In Donegal, which was reserved for the satisfaction of the arrears of the indemnified Munstermen, no land had been distributed. Electorally, the boroughs of the county played host to a number of prominent outsiders, while the county members were local. George Carey, of Redcastle in Innishowen, where he leased substantial properties on the Chichester estate, was the son of a former recorder of Londonderry who had represented the city in 1613 and the county in 1634. George had been mayor of Londonderry in 1655 and was an alderman under the new charter. He had served as a commissioner for the survey of Donegal, Londonderry and Tyrone. His mother was a sister of the Beresford brothers who sat for Coleraine and County Londonderry.[43] Major Richard Perkins of Lifford, where he held the fort and its supply lands, was descended from the servitor Thomas Perkins who had secured lands in Kilmacrenan and was one of the original corporators of the borough which had been established by his commanding officer, Sir Richard Hansard, whose executor he became. Richard Perkins, who served as provost marshal general in Strafford's 'new army' in 1640, married a daughter of Lord Strabane, son of the first earl of Abercorn. He was a justice of the peace in Monaghan as well as Donegal in the 1650s and

---

[42] Belmore, *Parliamentary memoirs*, pp. 214–15. *Burke's Irish family records*. Hill, *Plantation in Ulster*, pp. 465, 480. Trimble, *Enniskillen*, i, 151–2; ii, 326. P. H. Hore, *History of the town and county of Wexford* (6 vols., London, 1910), iv, 171. PRO, NI, Madden Papers, D.3465/A/2/1–7; B/1.

[43] Lodge, *Peerage*, ii, 291. Brian Bonner, *That audacious traitor* (Dublin, 1975), pp. 220, 223, 227. Dunlop, *Commonwealth*, pp. 633n. Moody and Simms, *The bishopric of Derry*, i, 281. Richard Hayes (ed.), *The register of Derry cathedral, 1642–1703* (Parochial Record Society of Dublin, 1910), p. 36. Hardinge, 'On manuscript, mapped and other townland surveys', Appendix E. *Some funeral entries of Ireland* (Irish memorials of the dead, supplementary vol., 1907–9), p. 99.

sufficiently compliant to have been chosen to inquire into allegations against ministers in two precincts. Previously, however, he had been Ormond's commander in Newry in the mid-1640s: in Ormond's absence he was attached to Kynaston's regiment (though he was 'in prison with the rebels' when it was mustered in May 1648), but he had remained 'a loyal subject' to the end, when he had yielded Lifford to Bishop Heber McMahon on sight of his commission from Ormond in 1650.[44] Like Perkins, William Knight married a Hamilton, in his case a daughter of Sir Claud of Ellistown in Tyrone, the first earl of Abercorn's brother. The family's extensive Ulster interests included a brief lease of the earl of Annandale's proportion, which included Killybegs. A signatory of the 1643 petition of Irish Protestant subjects to King Charles, Knight had fought in Munster and was in command of a regiment in 1647 when he published an attack on Inchiquin which ranged from the lord president's military incompetence to his playing 'at bowls on the Fast day'. In the context of the aftermath of the Lisle expedition, this stance would appear to place him in the Independent camp, but his objections to being commanded by 'the natural Irish' suggest another dimension and he was eventually classified as a '49 officer. Knight, who described himself in his will as residing in Dublin, was a lawyer by profession and was entrusted with government work. He was admitted to King's Inns as an attorney in 1635 and as a member on its revival in 1656, but he had already been favoured with special permission to practise as a counsellor at law in 1653. In the 1650s he had purchased land in Galway.[45] William, fifth Baron Caulfield,

---

[44] Hill, *Plantation in Ulster*, pp. 325, 525. Hunter, 'Plantation in Donegal', *Donegal: history and society*, p. 312. Commonwealth State Accounts, *Anal. Hib.*, 15, pp. 277–8, 278. Belmore, *Parliamentary memoirs*, pp. 172–5. TCD MSS 808, f. 154; 844, f. 46. *Ormond MSS*, i, 178–9; new series, i, 94–5, 96–8. E. H. (ed.), *The history of the warr of Ireland*, p. 123. Prendergast papers, ii, 446–9. John Perkins had been appointed provost marshal of Ulster in 1629, served as MP for Dungannon in the 1634 parliament and commanded the fort there in 1641. R. Lascalles (ed.), *Liber munerum publicorum Hiberniae* (London, 1852), pt. 2, p. 194. W. R. Hutchison, *Tyrone precinct* (Belfast, 1951), p. 57.

[45] His will was proved in 1672. Vicars, *Prerogative wills*. McKenny, 'A 17th century "real estate company"', Appendix A. *Ormond MSS*, new series, ii, 344. *Egmont MSS*, i, 320. George Bennett, *History of Bandon* (Cork, 1869), p. 146. Hunter, 'Plantation in Donegal', *Donegal: history and society*, p. 294. *Burke's Irish family records*, sub Oliver. Prendergast papers, i. 60. Jennings MSS, Box J2, Notebook F. *A letter from Lieutenant Colonel Knight* [BL, E 399 (23)]. William Knight, *A declaration of the treacherous proceedings of Inchiquin*

was a brother of the murdered Toby and of the member for Newtownards. Perkins must have facilitated his return for Lifford, but the two men had conducted themselves very differently in the 1640s when Caulfield had fought on the parliamentary side in the English civil war. A friend of the earl of Essex, he was taken prisoner at the battle of Newbury in 1644, the year in which he succeeded to his brother's title at the age of nineteen, and he was commissioned as a captain of horse in the New Model Army shortly after it was established in the following spring. Late in 1649, he was captured in the act of joining the parliamentary forces in Cork and subsequently exchanged for Ormond's brother. Afterwards he served in Sir Charles Coote's regiment and was disbanded with it in 1655, but he continued to act as commander of the garrison of his family fort of Charlemont on the Armagh–Tyrone border, joined the council of officers in the aftermath of the December coup and signed the February declaration.[46] It seems obvious that he bestowed the Charlemont seat upon Rowley. He was not an outsider to Donegal, in as much as the first Lord Caulfield had acquired lands in all of the plantation counties, but his return for Lifford in particular may be attributable to the fact that the previous generation of the Caulfield and Perkins families had been connected by marriage.[47]

LEINSTER

MEATH

County Dr Henry Jones, Sir William Cadogan
Athboy John Bligh
Kells Henry Ingoldsby

---

against the parliament (London, 1648). *IRC*, Rep. 8, p. 277. It is not clear which regiment Knight assumed command of, but it was probably that of Sir Arthur Loftus. He was appointed a poll tax commissioner for Dublin and Wicklow by the convention, but not for Donegal. He was listed in Dublin in the Census. In 1661, he was returned for Belfast.

[46] *Regimental history*, pp. 103, 107, 617. Dunlop, *Commonwealth*, p. 679. J. P. Prendergast, 'On Charlemont fort', *RSAI Jn.*, 4th series, 6 (1884), pp. 336–7. Carte MS 59, f. 368. Temple, 'Original officer list', *BIHR*, 59, pp. 73, 76. Lodge, *Peerage*, iii, 136–7, 222. Hill, *Plantation in Ulster*, p. 316. His mother was Sir John King's aunt.

[47] Both Thomas Perkins and the first Lord Caulfield's sister Lettice were married to Stauntons, and Caulfield was feoffee in trust for the portions of Thomas Perkins's daughters in 1638. Belmore, *Parliamentary memoirs*, pp. 175–6.

THE ELECTION RESULTS

Navan Henry Pakenham
Trim Alexander Jephson

Meath was one of the four Leinster counties which had formed the core of the original scheme of settlement and was shared between adventurers and the soldiers of the expeditionary force. By contrast with the Ulster counties in the same category, the amount of forfeited land available for settlement was very substantial. The effects were marked in the representation from the Meath boroughs, which was entirely drawn from new elements in the community, while the county members, although they belonged to the traditional establishment, had both been prominent collaborators with the commonwealth regime. Dr Henry Jones, bishop of Clogher, combined local connections with his national prominence. He had acquired an interest in substantial forfeited properties at Summerhill and his brother Ambrose had retained possession of the living at Kells.[48] Sir William Cadogan had been secretary to the master of the rolls, Sir Christopher Wandesforde, in the 1630s and had represented Monaghan borough in 1640. After the rebellion broke out, he was commissioned in Tichborne's regiment, served at the first siege of Drogheda, and spent the war years in Meath, mainly as commander of Trim. There was no ambiguity about his alignment. When he surrendered Trim to Inchiquin in 1649 he exercised the option of joining Colonel Jones with the parliamentary force in Dublin. Subsequently, he became a major in Colonel Foulke's regiment, resumed his governorship of Trim, served as a commissioner for the survey of Antrim, Monaghan, Louth and Meath, acquired some 400 acres in Navan barony as an adventurer's assignee, and represented Meath and Louth in the 1654 union parliament.[49] Given Jones's period as scout master general, Athboy may be said to have returned the only civilian from the county. John Bligh, one of the syndicate which farmed the Irish customs, was a London linen draper of Plymouth origins who had come to Ireland as a merchant and adventurers' agent: he was resident in Dublin by 1654, and had drawn 1,000

---

[48] *DNB*. TCD, MS 844, ff. 176–8. Seymour, *Puritans in Ireland*, p. 43. Henry Jones, *A sermon preached at the consecration of Ambrose, bishop of Kildare* (Dublin, 1667), p. 31.

[49] *Cal. SP, Ire., 1647–60*, p. 782. HMC, *Ormond MSS*, ii, 1–113. *Cal. SP, Adv.*, p. 228. Hardinge, 'On manuscript, mapped and other townland surveys', Appendix E. Richard Butler, *Some notices of the castle and of the ecclesiastical buildings of Trim* (Dublin, 1861), p. 267.

acres in the barony of Moygallion, but he was also part owner with an absentee adventurer of much of the borough. His wife's brother, William Fuller, was to be promoted successively to Irish and English bishoprics after the restoration.[50] The chief associations of Sir Henry Ingoldsby, a Presbyterian who had been active in both England and Ireland in recent months, were with Munster, as former governor and mayor of Limerick, representative of the south-west in all three union parliaments and beneficiary of a 3,500 acre estate which had been 'sett out to him' in Bunratty barony in Clare. Kells, however, was adjacent to the area in which his dragoons had been allotted their arrears when they were disbanded in 1655.[51] Cadogan was portreeve of Navan in 1660 and Henry Pakenham, who came to Ireland from Suffolk with his two brothers in 1642, had been under his command in 1649. Late in that year he was given a troop in Abbott's dragoons. When he was disbanded in 1655 he settled in Westmeath, though his arrears were assigned to him in Wexford. His connections with Meath, however, were marital as well as military. His wife was not only the daughter of a burgess and former portreeve of Trim but a niece of Archbishop James Ussher, who was also Henry Jones's uncle.[52] Cadogan had been portreeve of Trim in the previous year and presumably had something to do with the fact that, despite its recent disfranchisement of Baptists, the town returned a religious radical in Jephson, a distant connection of the Munster family, whose father's property was in Fertullagh barony in Westmeath. Jephson, who joined the army in Ireland and received arrears land in Ardee barony in Louth, was a burgess of the town and lived nearby at Fosterstown. After re-election in 1661, he was executed for his part in the 1663 plot: his scaffold speech, in which he linked

[50] Bottigheimer, *English money and Irish land*, p. 199. *Cal. SP, Adv.*, pp. 11, 68, 146; *Cal. SP, Ire., 1647–60*, pp. 658, 679. Lodge, *Peerage*, ii, 207–8. *Burke's Irish family records*, sub Barrington. IRC, Rep. 15, pp. 147, 172. Fuller became bishop of Limerick in 1664 and of Lincoln in 1667.

[51] Prendergast, *Cromwellian settlement*, pp. 215–16. Prendergast papers, i, 350. Noble, *Memoirs of the protectoral house of Cromwell*, i, 441; ii, 184–5. Burtchaell, *Kilkenny MPs*, p. 623. M. Lenihan, *Limerick: its history and antiquities* (Dublin, 1866), pp. 191, 702. Ingoldsby was the only Meath member not appointed to the poll tax commission for the county, but he was on the Kells panel and on those for the county and city of Limerick.

[52] Pakenham's wife was a daughter of Ellinor and Robert Lill. Wright, *The Ussher memoirs*, p. 83. *Regimental history*, p. 624. Prendergast, *Cromwellian settlement*, p. 216. *Ormond MSS*, ii, 92. Lodge, *Peerage*, iii, 372–3.

anti-Christ, papists and 'the great men of our world' who favoured them, included blessings on both Ormond and the king and he was clearly no republican.⁵³

WESTMEATH

County Sir Henry Piers, William Handcock
Fore William Markham
Kilbeggan Charles Lambert
Mullingar Thomas Long

Westmeath was also one of the core counties in the original scheme, with a high proportion of forfeited land, and the two county seats were shared between newcomers and New English. Sir Henry Piers was the fourth generation of his family to occupy Tristernagh Abbey in Moygoish barony. His grandfather, also Sir Henry, had been secretary to Lord Deputy Chichester, served as a member of the 1613 parliament for Baltimore, acquired plantation land in Cavan, married a daughter of Archbishop Jones of Dublin and converted to Catholicism. His mother was a sister of the antiquarian Sir James Ware, who sat in the convention for St Johnston. Henry had commanded a company in Castle's regiment in the late 1640s, when he was about twenty years of age. Since he had small amounts of post '49 arrears land in both Wexford and Kilkenny, it seems to follow that he remained in arms. He had been sheriff of Longford and Westmeath in 1657 and 1658, was knighted by Henry Cromwell in 1658 and represented the area in the union parliament in the following year. The marriages of his sisters confirm his familiar relationship with the newcomers: Colonels Arnop, Owen and Thomas Scot were his brothers-in-law. Henry himself was complexly connected with Dr Henry Jones, who was both his father-in-law and his brother-in-law.⁵⁴ William Handcock, who was returned for

---

[53] M. O'Dwyer, *The O'Dwyers of Kilnamanagh* (London, 1933), p. 266. Carte MS 68, ff. 574–574v. Butler, *Trim*, p. 267. NLI MS 2,292 Assembly book of the borough of Trim, 1659–1720, ff. 1–2. The assembly book does not record any return to the Convention.

[54] Jones's second wife, to whom he was married in 1646, was Piers's sister Mary. Piers married Jones's daughter Mary some seven years later. NLI MS 2,563, Piers genealogy. *Complete Baronetage*, iii, 308–9. TCD MS 844, f. 45. *Some funeral entries of Ireland*, pp. 92, 114, 118–19. Henry was the author of *A chorographical description of the county of Westmeath*.

Athlone as well as for the county, was an army captain who had amassed lands in Kilkenny, Westmeath and Roscommon, the latter at least by purchase. His military career is unknown, which is characteristic of the select group of Connacht administrators to which he belonged: he had served as receiver of revenue in both the Athlone precinct and in Roscommon and Leitrim and had recently supervised the preparation of the island of Innisboffin as a place of detention for priests 'and other dangerous persons'.[55] William Markham was both a local landowner and a plural officeholder, as chirographer of the court of common pleas and controller of customs in Dublin. He was new to the area and may have been a member of Winter's congregation, but since he was first appointed to office by the king in December 1646 in the dying fall of Ormond's administration he is unlikely to have been new to Ireland. He was already serving the commonwealth by July 1652, was appointed a member of the high court for justice in Dublin at the end of the year and served on a commission to inquire into the authenticity of the conversion of the Irish near Athy in 1654. His standing is suggested by the fact that he was returned to the 1661 parliament for the same constituency.[56] Like Piers, Charles Lambert belonged to an undertaker family and the borough of Kilbeggan was its preserve. His father, who was governor of Dublin under Ormond, had been promoted from a barony to the earldom of Cavan by Charles I in 1646. Charles Lambert himself, at twenty-three, was too young to have a political record.[57] Colonel Thomas Long, who had been active in recent events, had served since bringing a regiment to Ireland in 1647, latterly as the commander of an unregimented company which had been removed from him in the remodelling of 1659. He had an estate in

---

[55] Hughes, *Patentee officers*. Commonwealth State Accounts, *Anal. Hib.*, 15, p. 305. IRC, Rep. 8, p. 272. Add MS 19,833. *Arch. Hib.*, 6, p. 181. R. C. Simington (ed.), *Books of survey and distribution*, i, Roscommon, pp. 112, 115, 120.

[56] Hughes, *Patentee officers*. 'List of warrants for fiants', Carte MS 68, f. 124. Add. MS 19,833. *Arch. Hib.*, 7, p. 63. Dunlop, *Commonwealth*, p. 434. O'Renehan MSS, ii, f. 203. TCD MS 844, f. 136. T. U. Sadleir, 'Kildare members of parliament', *Kildare AS jn.*, 6 (1911), 469–71. A William Markham is recorded in the New Street baptismal register [Unitarian Church, St Stephen's Green, Dublin] as a member of Winter's congregation in the 1650s.

[57] Charles, the fourth son, died in the same year and the borough was represented in the 1661 parliament by two of his brothers. Lodge, *Peerage*, i, 353–7. 'W. H. Welphy's abstracts of Irish Chancery bills', *The Irish Genealogist*, 7 (1987), p. 174.

the county, and properties in Meath, Cork, Kerry and Queen's County as well.[58]

KING'S COUNTY

County Sir George Blundell, Henry Sankey
Philipstown Thomas Gifford

Despite its designation among the original ten, King's County returned only members of the older community, but Henry Sankey was so closely identified with the new regime that his relationship to Colonel Sankey has been presumed. In fact, he was from Edenderry. He was eighteen years old and in England when the rebellion broke out and claimed to have lost property to the value of £300. He was in arms in Ireland by 1644, was with Cromwell at the siege of Drogheda, served for some time as a captain with Theophilus Jones and was actively involved in the negotiations that concluded the war in Connacht in 1652. Subsequently, he served as a commissioner for the survey of King's County and Longford, and was appointed one of the solicitors to the court of claims and qualifications at Athlone and escheator for the province of Leinster. He had acquired lands in both Longford and King's County, where he was a justice of the peace, as well as in Kildare.[59] Sir George Blundell had been returned for Dingle in 1640 but he was a substantial local property owner and had been sheriff in 1657. His father, Sir Francis, had been an Irish privy councillor and, still more influentially, one of the duke of Buckingham's agents in Ireland. Before 1640, George had combined army command with the office of commissioner for customs and excise: after the outbreak of rebellion he commanded a troop in Ormond's regiment, but it must be presumed that he later changed allegiance since he was appointed commissioner of

[58] *Cal. SP, Ire., 1647–60*, p. 609. *IRC*, Rep. 8, p. 278. *Regimental history*, p. 650.
[59] Dunlop, *Commonwealth*, pp. 75n, 236, 253, 260–1. *Cal. SP, Ire., 1647–60*, p. 610; *1660–2*, p. 288. Commonwealth State Accounts, *Anal. Hib.*, 15, pp. 273–4. R. Gillespie and G. Moran (ed.), *Longford: essays in county history* (Dublin, 1991), p. 209. Hughes, *Patentee officers*. TCD MS 814, f. 89v. Prendergast papers, ii, 446–9; iii, 684. Hardinge, 'On manuscript, mapped and other townland surveys', Appendix E. Book of survey and distribution, *Kildare AS jn.*, 10 (1922–8), p. 225. Sankey married a daughter of William Savage of Castle Raban in County Kildare, probably in 1658 when he lent £2,000 to Savage. Thomas Cooke, *The early history of the town of Birr or Parsonstown*, ed. M. Hogan (reprint, Dublin, 1990), p. 68. Dublin Statute Staple database (in preparation).

revenue in the Belfast precinct as early as 1651 and later received arrears land in King's County.[60] His marriage to a grand-daughter of Sir John Gifford of Castle Jordan linked him with Thomas Gifford, who was Sir John's son and heir. The Giffords, who were involved in a celebrated dispute with Lord Chancellor Loftus in the 1630s, were also related by marriage to the Coote and St George families and Thomas's father had represented the Coote controlled borough of Jamestown in 1640. When Thomas sought preferment in 1660, he made his case on the merits of his father, who had spent seven years in gaol in Chester in the king's cause and died shortly after his release, and it is likely that he was too young to have served Charles I.[61]

QUEEN'S COUNTY

County Henry Gilbert, Gilbert Rawson
Maryborough Francis Barrington

All three members elected in Queen's County, the fourth of the original core counties in Leinster, were not only from the older community and native to the area, but former members of parliament. The record of Henry Gilbert, however, perhaps qualified him to represent the newer interest. His father came to Ireland as Constable of Maryborough about 1622, acquired substantial properties and represented the borough in both 1634 and 1640. In the latter parliament, Henry's brother William had been returned for Dublin University. Henry had been joined with his father in his command in 1643 and served in the rump of the Irish parliament as member for Maryborough from 1644. Later, he joined the parliamentary army in Ireland and was disbanded with the rank of captain in Foulke's regiment. His disbandment coincided with the death of his father, whose

---

[60] Dunlop, *Commonwealth*, pp. 40–2. HMC *Ormond MSS*, i, 183, 188, 19, 191. IRC, Rep. 15, p. 213. T. U. Sadleir, 'High sheriffs of the King's County', *Kildare AS jn.*, 8 (1915–17), p. 30. Blundell, whose father had represented Lifford in 1613, was not appointed to the poll tax commission for the county.

[61] *Complete Baronetage*, i, 224–5; iii, 168. *Cal. SP, Ire., 1660–2*, pp. 94, 96, 144. He was appointed constable of Philipstown Castle in 1661. Hughes, *Patentee officers*. In 1662, he married Martha Temple, sister of two fellow members of the convention, and died some days afterwards. G. C. M. Smith (ed.), *The early essays and romances of Sir William Temple* (Oxford, 1930), p. 193.

lands had been sequestered by the Ormond administration in 1649, and he sold out his arrears interest in Ardee, took over the Maryborough command and was appointed high sheriff of the county in 1655. He was father-in-law to the Kilbeggan member, Charles Lambert.[62] Gilbert Rawson of Donoughmore was a former resident of County Kildare who had acquired a substantial interest in Fitzpatrick land in Queen's County shortly before the rebellion as security for loans amounting to £5,650. He had served in the army in Leinster from the beginning of the rebellion and was later credited with an unusually large claim as a '49 officer. He had, however, acted as a commissioner for the survey of County Kilkenny.[63] Francis Barrington of Cullenagh barony belonged to a family which had been settled in the area since the previous century and had supplied one of the borough's members in 1613. Barrington had married Gilbert's sister and both he and Rawson had been fellow members of the truncated Irish parliament in 1647.[64]

LOUTH

County William Aston, Henry Bellingham
Ardee John Ruxton
Carlingford John Slater
Dundalk Arthur Bulkeley
Drogheda William Toxteth

In Louth, a county in which there had been relatively little Protestant landownership before the rebellion, the settlement had been limited in scope but dense. With the exception of the barony of Ardee, the county

[62] 'List of warrants for fiants', Carte MS 68, f. 123. *Cal. SP, Ire., 1647–60*, pp. 387, 510. Sadleir, 'High sheriffs', *Kildare AS jn.*, 8, p. 30. Prendergast papers, ii, 276–7. 'Calendar of petitions to Ormonde in 1649 and 1650', *The Irish Genealogist*, 6 (1983), p. 432.

[63] Rawson, who was a captain in Willoughby's regiment in 1641 and a captain in Oliver Wheeler's in Dublin early in 1647, was in the top 3 per cent of '49 claimants. McKenny, 'A 17th century "real estate company"', pp. 226, 232. *HMC Ormonde MSS*, i, 125, 141, 143, 193, 197. Hughes, *Patentee officers*. Hardinge, 'On manuscript, mapped and other townland surveys', Appendix E. Vicars, *Prerogative wills*. RIA, Books of survey and distribution: Queen's County, barony of Upper Ossory, Bordell parish. Dublin Statute Staple database (in preparation).

[64] *Census of Ireland*. J. O'Hanlon, *History of the Queen's County* (2 vols., reprint, Kilkenny, 1981), pp. 785, 787. *Some funeral entries of Ireland*, p. 46. *CJ Ire.*, i, 357, 368.

had been reserved as additional security for the adventurers in case the ten counties proved insufficient. That eventuality had not come to pass, but Ardee witnessed systematic settlement by soldiers who had served in Ireland before 1649 and half of the members belonged to that group, including those returned for the county.[65] The most prominent was William Aston of Richardstown, a member of the cadet branch of a noble family in Staffordshire, who had come to Ireland in Colonel Hungerford's foot regiment in 1647 and was major of Chidley Coote's horse in the Drogheda area early in 1648. A commissioner of revenue for the precinct, he was disbanded in 1653 and acquired substantial property in the area which he represented in the union parliament in both 1656 and 1659. In the former, he supported the kingship petition; in the latter he contributed vigorously to the debate on the proposal to exclude Irish members, taking the opportunity to argue for the restoration of the Irish parliament so 'that votes may not be imposed upon you here' and insisting that if the right to sit were withdrawn the English parliament should refund the tax that had been collected 'and give us a parliament of our own'. Aston, who had attended Gray's Inn in London before the civil war, held office as 'counsel for the commonwealth' in the court of claims and was admitted to King's Inns in 1658.[66] Henry Bellingham's father Robert had been sheriff of Longford in 1611–12 and later a minor official in the exchequer. Like his brother Daniel, a Dublin alderman who was major of the city militia, Henry was a goldsmith and a freeman of Dublin. He was one of the group of self-styled 'Protestant subjects' who stridently petitioned the king in 1643. He served as lieutenant to Henry Pakenham in Colonel Fenwick's foot, which reached Ireland late in 1646, and added significantly by purchase to his arrears entitlements in Ardee after he was disbanded as a captain in 1653. He too was a commissioner of revenue by 1654 and acted as one of the commissioners for the civil survey in the county.[67] John

---

[65] Harold O'Sullivan, 'Landownership changes in the County of Louth in the seventeenth century' (Ph.D., University of Dublin, 1991), chapter 3.

[66] Ball, *Judges*, i, 268, 271, 341. O'Sullivan, 'The restoration land settlement in the diocese of Armagh', *Seanchas Ard Mhacha*, 16 (1994), p. 43. *Cork HAS jn.*, 2nd series, 7 (1901), p. 215. J. T. Rutt (ed.), *The diary of Thomas Burton* (4 vols., London, 1828), iv, 237. J. B. Leslie, 'Inquisitions concerning the parishes of County Louth', in *Louth HAS jn.*, 7 (1922), p. 38. BL, Add. MS 19,833.

[67] *Ormond MSS*, new series, ii, 344. O'Sullivan, 'The restoration land settlement in the

Ruxton, sheriff of the county, who had also settled in the barony after his disbandment, was of somewhat similar provenance. Originally from Meath, he seems to have arrived in Louth as a junior officer with Colonel Ponsonby who had been in garrison at Athboy and was transferred to Dundalk as governor in 1649.[68] John Slater was the only Louth member who was not appointed a poll tax commissioner and it seems likely that he did not attend the convention. By 1655, he was both storekeeper and collector of the customs at Carlingford, but he had leased tithes in Cooley parish in the early 1650s, before the soldiers' settlement began, and it is possible that he was a civilian.[69] Arthur Bulkeley was a Manchester wool merchant who had acquired corporation properties and purchased land in Ardee barony from Colonel Foulkes, governor of the town. In 1660, he was bailiff of Dundalk. This was a borough in which Mark Trevor had interests, arising from a lease of its lands and properties which he secured from Henry Cromwell as an intriguing farewell present in June 1659, but it is clear that he did not exercise influence on the election for it was Bulkeley who led the resistance against this expropriation.[70] William Toxteth had certainly seen military service, probably with Sir Henry Tichborne, governor of Drogheda during the siege of 1641–2, who was his father-in-law. Tichborne's regiment had split in 1649, shortly before the second siege, at a time when he was in London defending himself against charges of complicity with the royalists. By then, Toxteth was well established in the town, where he was an alderman by the end of the year and mayor in 1650 and 1657. He acquired land in Ferrard barony, presumably by purchase, lived at Beaulieu on the estate held in custodiam by

---

diocese of Armagh', *Seanchas Ard Mhacha*, 16, p. 43. Leslie, 'Inquisitions concerning the parishes of County Louth', p. 38. *Complete Baronetage*, iv, 203. Gilbert, *Records*, iii, 457–8; iv, 33. TCD MS 844, f. 44. Hardinge, 'On manuscript, mapped and other townland surveys', Appendix E. The earl of Cork recorded a transaction with a Henry Bellingham in 1637. A. B. Grosart (ed.), *The Lismore papers*, 1st series (5 vols., London, 1886), v, 1. He was one of the knights of the shire for Louth in 1661.

[68] O'Sullivan, 'Landownership changes in the county of Louth', pp. 66, 69n; 'The restoration land settlement in the diocese of Armagh', 16, p. 43. IRC, Rep. 8, p. 290. TCD MS 844, f. 53. HMC, Rep. 8, p. 529a.

[69] Add. MS 19,833. L. P. Murray, 'Hearth money rolls', *Louth HAS jn.*, 7 (1922), p. 504.

[70] O'Sullivan, 'Landownership changes in the county of Louth', pp. 151, 305ff.; 'The restoration land settlement in the diocese of Armagh', 16, pp. 38, 61. Trevor received a grant of this property in 1661.

Tichborne and served as sheriff of the county in 1656. Both he and Tichborne were later classified as '49 officers and they were grouped together in the allocation of lots. Toxteth's status as the odd man out among the Louth contingent is perhaps confirmed by his subsequent second marriage, to Jane Bramhall, daughter of the archbishop of Armagh.[71]

LONGFORD

County   Adam Molyneux, John Edgeworth
St Johnston   Sir James Ware

In Longford, where the two southernmost baronies had been opened up for the settlement of pre-1649 arrears and the remainder included in the undistributed Munstermen's portion, all three members belonged to well-entrenched official families and had local connections. Adam Molyneux was a third generation settler whose father had been surveyor general of Ireland and member for Mallow in the Irish parliament in 1613 and whose mother was an Ussher. Adam had been a captain of horse in Ormond's army and fought with the king in England, but he had continued in arms with the parliamentarians, served as provost-marshal of Leinster under Henry Cromwell and retained the office under the commissioners. He signed the Dublin declaration of 16 February. Unlike John Edgeworth, his property in Longford had been recently acquired, apparently as pre-'49 arrears, though he may have availed of the opportunities afforded by his position as one of those involved in the survey of forfeited lands in the county to purchase debentures.[72] Edgeworth's father had been a plantation grantee, as well as clerk of the crown and hanaper and

---

[71] Gogarty, *Council Book*, pp. 24–5, 26, 29. Wright, *The Ussher memoirs*, p. 165n. *Census*. Leslie, 'Inquisitions concerning the parishes of County Louth', *Louth HAS jn*, 7 (1922), p. 38. H. O'Sullivan, 'Military operations in County Louth in the run-up to Cromwell's storming of Drogheda', ibid., 22 (1990), p. 203; 'Landownership changes in the county of Louth', p. 69n. McKenny, 'A 17th century "real estate company"', Appendix A. Belmore, *Parliamentary memoirs*, p. 233. IRC, Rep. 15, p. 223. *Cal. SP, Ire., 1647–60*, pp. 604–6. *The works of the most reverend father in God, John Bramhall* (Oxford, 1842), i, cxi, 233. Tichborne was also Roger West's father-in-law.
[72] *Ormond MSS*, i, 148. Hughes, *Patentee officers*. IRC, Rep. 15, p. 132. Carte MS 68, ff. 159–63. Hardinge, 'On manuscript, mapped and other townland surveys', Appendix E. Wright, *The Ussher memoirs*, p. 133. Petty, *Down survey*, pp. 12, 107, 111. Molyneux to Henry Cromwell, 8 July 1657, Lansdowne MS 822, f. 142. *Ormond MSS*, new series, iii, 409.

clerk of the first fruits: his uncle had been bishop of Down and Connor in the 1590s. He himself was returned to the 1640 parliament at a by-election and served as a captain in the regiment of Sir John Borlase in the 1640s, acting for some time as provost-marshal. In 1650, he was a captain in Ormond's horse and he was subsequently classified as a '49 officer. His sister had been married to John King's uncle, who had also served as clerk of the hanaper.[73] The antiquarian Sir James Ware, auditor general and privy councillor before the rebellion, had been returned for Dublin University to the previous two parliaments. His allegiance had been unequivocal. He had been one of the hostages for the treaty by which Dublin was surrendered to parliament in 1647, was banished in 1649 and spent some time in exile in France before returning to London. He came back to live in Ireland in 1658 but he did not resume office, though he collaborated at least to the extent of becoming involved with his brother-in-law, Dudley Loftus, in the plans for the foundation of a new college in the University of Dublin. His father had been one of the original burgesses when St Johnston was incorporated in 1628 and his brother had represented the borough in 1634 and 1640. His sister was the mother of the member for Westmeath, Sir Henry Piers, and his daughter Rose was married to Lord Lambert, father of the member for Kilbeggan.[74]

DUBLIN

County Sir Theophilus Jones, Sir James Barry
Borough John Bysse, William Smith
University Roger, Lord Broghill, Chidley Coote
Newcastle Philip Ferneley
Swords Samuel Bathurst

The county of Dublin, together with Kildare and Carlow, had been retained as government reserve lands. In theory, this resource was int-

---

[73] Hughes, *Patentee officers*. TCD MS 844, f. 50. *HMC Ormond MSS*, i, 239. McKenny, 'A 17th century "real estate company"', Appendix A. *Some funeral entries of Ireland*, pp. 205–6.

[74] *DNB*. Barnard, *Cromwellian Ireland*, pp. 209–10. William O'Sullivan, 'A finding list of Sir James Ware's manuscripts', *RIA proc.*, 97 C no. 2 (1997), pp. 72–3. Ware's sister Cicely was married to Loftus. H. T. Crofton, *Crofton memoirs* (York, 1911), p. 277. *Some funeral entries of Ireland*, pp. 118–19. The office of auditor general was shared by Robert Gorges and Edward Roberts. *Cal. SP, Ire., 1663–65*, p. 470.

ended to yield income, which meant in practice that much of the forfeited land was made available on long-term leases to both Cromwellian and New English beneficiaries. Moreover, a good deal of it was conferred upon favoured individuals by outright grant. The new landholders in Dublin in 1660 included some whose influence was over, or nearly so, including Richard Cromwell and a full hand of regicides (Edmund Ludlow among them), but they also included Charles Coote and Theophilus Jones, and only one newcomer figured in the returns.[75] Jones, whose wife was a member of the Ussher family and a grand-daughter of Archbishop Loftus, had secured the Sarsfield estate at Lucan and had represented the county in the union parliament in 1659.[76] Sir James Barry, formerly second baron of the exchequer, presided over the committee of safety. His father had represented Dublin in all three Stuart parliaments. James, who was married to a daughter of Sir William Parsons, had represented Lismore in 1634. While in England in 1648–9 he served as a member of a subcommittee of the parliamentary committee for Irish affairs, charged with raising money for the prosecution of the war in Ireland. He was not reappointed to his office in the 1650s, but he did perform various quasi-judicial tasks, reporting on Strafford's alteration of land titles in Connacht in 1655 and on a case of murder by witchcraft in Carrickfergus in 1656.[77] John Bysse, recorder of the city, had represented it in the last Irish parliament where he had played an increasingly prominent role in the Protestant opposition group. He had taken the parliamentarian side in 1649 and represented the county in the union parliament in 1656 when, in common with Tristram Beresford, an attempt to exclude him had been foiled by the intervention of Henry Cromwell and he had voted in favour of kingship. He was Edgeworth's brother-in-law.[78] William Smith, by contrast, operated exclusively in the local sphere. He had been a freeman since 1631 and an alderman since 1637, had served three times as mayor in the 1640s, and

---

[75] Arnold, *The restoration settlement*, pp. 34–6.
[76] Prendergast papers, i, 199; iii, 530. Jones had represented the Westmeath–Longford–King's County constituency in the 1654 and 1656 parliaments.
[77] Lodge, *Peerage*, i, 302n. *Cal. SP, Ire., 1669–70*, pp. 355, 357. Jennings MSS, Box J2, Notebooks B, C.
[78] Maxwell, *The outbreak of the rebellion of 1641*, p. 130. Wright, *The Ussher memoirs*, p. 165n. *TSP.*, v, 477. He was appointed chief baron of the exchequer in July 1660. Hughes, *Patentee officers*.

was an active member of the vestry of St John's during the ministry of the Presbyterian Patrick Kerr in the 1650s. In 1660, he was city treasurer.[79] Lord Broghill had some vestigial claim to membership of Trinity College as a former student: Chidley Coote had none. Coote, who had fought throughout the wars, had been an early and open supporter of parliament. In 1644, he had published an anti-cessation pamphlet, subtitled 'A Trap to catch Protestants', and alternated lobbying in Westminster with campaigning in Cheshire.[80] The borough returns were, on the face of it, sharply contrasting. Philip Ferneley, who lived in Newcastle barony, had been both a civil and a military officer before the rebellion, serving as clerk of the Commons since 1628 and chief remembrancer of the court of exchequer since 1636, an office confirmed to him in 1655. In the 1640s, he had served under Ormond, rising from sergeant-major in 1641 to lieutenant-colonel in 1647.[81] Samuel Bathurst had come to Ireland as postmaster in 1658 at the instigation of Secretary Thurloe and had taken up residence in Dublin: he had no connection with Swords and was reputed to be a Baptist. The politics behind his return are elucidated both by Ormond's later report that a number of members of the Irish council 'testified his contributing his endeavours very carefully in that Place in order to his Majesty's restauration' and by an ingenuous account of his conduct of business given later by an assistant who intended to impugn his efficiency and honesty but unmistakably described the routine interception of letters for intelligence purposes.[82] Four of these Dublin members, Broghill,

[79] Barnard, Cromwellian Ireland, p. 84. Hughes, S. John the Evangelist, p. 23. Gilbert, Records, iv, 167. It is likely that he was connected by marriage to Richard Palfrey: Palfrey married Elizabeth Lee in August 1653 and Smith married Dame Elizabeth Lee in the following January. Hughes, Patentee officers, p. 95.

[80] Ireland's lamentation for the late destructive cessation, or, a trap to catch Protestants (London, 1644). Armstrong, 'Protestant Ireland and the English parliament', pp. 156–7, 357–8.

[81] Ormond MSS, i, 125, 133, 141, 143, 149, 163, 181, 187, 188, 193, 197; ibid., new series, iii, 374. Hughes, Patentee officers. John Ferneley had been appointed clerk of pleas in the exchequer in 1610. Philip retained his position as chief remembrancer after the restoration. Cal. SP, Ire., 1666–9, p. 73. He was married to the daughter of a former exchequer court judge, Ursula Blennerhassett, whose sister Dorothy was Edward Richardson's mother-in-law. Some funeral entries of Ireland, p. 95.

[82] Cal. SP, Ire., 1660–2, pp. 682–4; 1663–5, pp. 232–3. PRO, SP, Ire., 63/311. 46, 47; 63/314. 94. Bathurst was not appointed a poll tax commissioner in 1660. A previous association with Ireland is attested by a petition to the Grocers' Hall committee in 1658, in which he complained that he had been unable to recover money invested in Ireland, despite

Coote, Jones and Bysse, were among the select leadership group who were later favoured with a pardon and entitlement to be treated as if they were '49 officers.[83]

KILDARE

County Sir Paul Davis, Sir John Hoey
Borough Francis Peasley
Athy William Scot
Naas Charles Ryves

The returns from Kildare, another of the government reserve counties, were confined to old Protestants. Sir Paul Davis had been clerk of the Irish privy council in the 1630s, represented Enniskillen in the 1634 parliament and County Donegal in 1640, and was a landowner in all three places. He had been one of the delegates sent by Ormond to negotiate with parliament after the civil war and had remained in London for seven years. Like Barry, he served on the parliamentary sub-committee raising revenue for Ireland in 1648–9. General Monck, prompted by his secretary, who was Davis's nephew, recommended that he should be allowed to resume his position as clerk of the council. The recommendation was neither wholehearted nor successful, and Davis was later able to claim that his 'fingers were not defiled with their dispatches', but he was back in Dublin and on the commonwealth payroll by June 1654.[84] Both he and Sir John Hoey, like Barry, had married daughters of Sir William Parsons. Hoey also owned land locally, though his principal estates were in Wicklow and Carlow. He had served as high sheriff of all three in the 1650s. His father had been a sergeant at arms and his mother, Mary Brice, the daughter of a

---

having gone there to get satisfaction. *Cal. SP, Adv.*, p. 395. He does not appear on the list of adventurers. The proximate influence behind his return for Swords may be suggested by the parliamentary elections in 1661 when Sir William Tichborne represented Swords and Bathurst and Sir Henry Tichborne represented Sligo Borough.

[83] McKenny, 'A 17th century "real estate company"', pp. 200–1. *Cal. SP, Ire., 1660–2*, pp. 198, 316–19.

[84] Commonwealth State Accounts, *Anal. Hib.*, 15, p. 252. *Egmont MSS*, i, 540, 542, 554. *Cal. SP, Ire., 1660–2*, pp. 303–4. *Cal. SP, Ire., 1669–70*, pp. 355, 357. His son was appointed attorney general of Munster in July 1660, which suggests that he was on good terms with Broghill. Hughes, *Patentee officers*.

mayor of Dublin. He had attended Lincoln's Inn, represented Carysfort and Wicklow respectively in the last two Irish parliaments, and served the government during the 1640s. He was a captain in Armstrong's regiment in 1648 and was among those who did not revert to their allegiance on Ormond's return; identified as a delinquent by the Ormond administration in 1649, he was already one of the commissioners of revenue in the Athy precinct in 1652 and served as a member of the high court of justice in Dublin.[85] Francis Peasley, of Punchestown in the barony of Naas, was the seventh son in a family which had begun to acquire office in Ireland in the 1620s, perhaps as a result of an association with the secretary of state, Sir George Calvert, and continued to do so under Wentworth. His father, chief sergeant at arms since 1625, had been Wentworth's unsuccessful nominee for Tallow in the 1634 election and had acted as agent for the lord deputy in the purchase of lands in Kildare. Francis was joined with his brother William, second sergeant at arms since 1628, as provost-marshal of Munster in 1639. William had been a member of the 1640 parliament for Agher and Francis was returned for Athboy in 1642. He served with St Leger in Munster at the outset of the rebellion, but soon moved to Dublin, was in command of a company in that area when Ormond left Ireland in 1647 and rejoined him on his return. He sold his interest in the Munster office in 1649 and was later classified as a '49 officer.[86] William Scot, who sat for Athy, was a Queen's County landowner and a colleague of Markham in the Dublin customs. He succeeded his father as searcher, gauger and packer in Dublin in 1643, was appointed customer of Dublin and Wicklow in the same year and was said to have suffered greatly from

---

[85] *Ormond MSS*, ii, 107. Commonwealth State Accounts, *Anal. Hib.*, 15, p. 316. Sadleir, 'Kildare members of parliament', *Kildare AS jn.*, 9 (1918–21), 376–7. Commonwealth records, *Arch. Hib.*, 7, 188. TCD MS 844, ff. 54, 136. Egerton MS 212, A/97.

[86] Sadleir, 'Kildare members of parliament', *Kildare AS jn.*, 8 (1915–17), 197–8. Caulfield, *Kinsale*, p. 420. *Ormond MSS*, i, 128, 191, 195. Hughes, *Patentee officers*. H. F. Kearney, *Strafford in Ireland, 1633–1641* (Manchester, 1959), pp. 47, 173. *Cal. SP, Ire., 1660–2*, p. 349. McKenny, 'A 17th century "real estate" company"', Appendix A. Francis was described as being of Roscrea in his will, proved in 1667. Vicars, *Prerogative wills*. Wentworth, who had managed Calvert's election for Yorkshire in 1620, was already acquainted with the Peasleys. J. P. Cooper (ed.), *Wentworth papers, 1597–1628* (Camden Society, London, 1973), p. 192.

the rebellion. He retained the office of searcher throughout the 1650s.[87] Charles Ryves, a barrister who had been admitted to King's Inns after its revival in 1656, owned property adjoining Naas. The son of Sir William, attorney general in the 1630s and member for Belturbet in the 1634 parliament, he was an official of the court of chancery from 1634, had served under Ormond and was later classified as a '49 officer. He had taken a seat in the rump of the Irish parliament in 1644. Conceded a joint appointment as second examiner in the court when it was revived by the protectorate, he had strenuously maintained his sole right to the office on the strength of his original royal patent.[88]

CARLOW

County William Temple, Richard Andrews
Borough Thomas Reynolds

Like so many other members from the reserved counties, William Temple was the scion of an official dynasty, the eldest son of Sir John and brother of the member for Bangor. William had been born and bred in England, but he spent the last years of the 1650s living on the 1,500 acre estate which his father leased in the county. More than twenty years later he assured his son that 'The native love of my country, and its ancient constitutions, would not suffer me to enter into public affairs till the way was open for the King's happy restoration.' He was, his sister later recalled, elected to the Convention 'without his knowledge'.[89] Richard Andrews belonged to a family which originated with three brothers who had come to Ireland from Northamptonshire at the beginning of the century and occupied both civil and clerical offices in the area, including

---

[87] *Cal. SP, Ire., 1633–47*, p. 387. *Some funeral entries of Ireland*, pp. 200–1. His father's patents dated from the early 1620s. Hughes, *Patentee officers*. Add. MS 19,833. He was still searcher in 1666. *Cal. SP, Ire., 1660–2*, p. 7; SP, Ire., 63/ 303. 57, 58. *Cal. SP, Ire., 1666–9*, p. 76.

[88] *Cal. SP, Ire., 1633–47*, pp. 635, 671; ibid., *1647–60*, pp. 615–16. Hughes, *Patentee officers*. Foster, *Alumni Oxonienses*.

[89] It was to William, who became ambassador in Brussels in 1667, that Dorothy Osborne's celebrated love letters were sent. His life, written by his sister, is in Moore Smith, *The early essays and romances of Sir William Temple Bt*, xi–xvi, 1–31, esp. p. 8. Courteney, *Memoirs of Temple*, ii, 24. Scott, *Algernon Sidney and the English Republic*, p. 231. Haley, *An English diplomat*, pp. 15, 21. Lodge, *Peerage*, v, 239.

the clerkship of the crown and peace and the bishopric of Ferns and Leighlin. Henry Andrews had represented the borough of Sligo in 1613. Richard was later classified as a '49 officer, but he collaborated very fully in the 1650s when he was receiver of revenue in the Athy precinct, a commissioner for the civil survey, storekeeper at Carlow town and a justice of the peace for the county. In September 1659, he was in command of the new county militia force. He had acquired land in the barony of Upper Ormond in Tipperary which was assigned to post '49 arrears, presumably by purchase.[90] Thomas Reynolds was an obscure member of a prominent local family.[91]

WICKLOW

County Sir William Ussher, Richard Kennedy
Borough Robert Hassells
Carysfort Thomas Maule

Wicklow was one of the counties assigned to the Munster claimants and was therefore as yet unaffected by systematic reallocation. Both of the county members were from Dublin based official families with large property interests and both were connected by marriage with Sir Paul Davis. Ussher's grandfather had been Davis's predecessor as clerk of the Irish council and represented the borough of Wicklow (of which he was constable) in 1613 and 1634 and the county in 1640. William, who was appointed prothonotary of the king's bench in 1644, succeeded as his grandfather's heir in 1659. Through the marriages of his sisters, he was John Percival's uncle and brother-in-law of both Theophilus Jones and

---

[90] He was not appointed a poll tax commissioner, and may not have attended. McGrath, 'Membership of the Irish House of Commons', p. 94. *Cal. SP, Ire., 1633–47*, p. 447. Prendergast papers, ii, 446–9. McKenny, 'A 17th century "real estate company"', Appendix A. Add. MS 19,833. *IRC*, Rep. 15, p. 126. Hardinge, 'On manuscript, mapped and other townland surveys', Appendix E. Hughes, *Patentee officers*. Jennings MSS, Box J2, Notebook E.

[91] Thomas was appointed to the poll tax commission for the county, as was Edward Reynolds, who, unlike Thomas, was recorded in the Census. Edward had been appointed to a corn commission for Carlow in 1630 and was involved, as purchaser, in a licence to alienate in 1635. Caulfield, *Youghal*, p. 161. *Inquisitionum in officio Rotulorum Cancellariae Hiberniae* (Dublin, 1826), i, Leinster, Co Carlow (55). The will of John Reynolds of Carlow, merchant, was proved in 1637. Vicars, *Prerogative wills*.

Paul Davis; he had married Elizabeth Parsons, whose sisters Catherine, Jane and Mary had married James Barry, John Hoey and Arthur Hill, while Ann Parsons was Davis's second wife; the wives of Chidley Coote and Adam Molyneux were his cousins, while another cousin was married to Sir Charles Coote's son and heir who was also returned to the Convention.[92] Richard Kennedy of Mount Kennedy was a barrister whose family had lengthy connections with the county and with government office. Educated at Lincoln's Inn, which he entered in 1638, he had joined his father in the rump of the Dublin parliament in its last days in 1647 and served in Kynaston's regiment in the late 1640s. His father was declared a delinquent by the Ormond administration in 1649. Richard acted as Phelim O'Neill's counsel in 1652 and was admitted to King's Inns in 1657. He too was part of the marital web of the Dublin office holders: Davis's third wife was the widow of his elder brother.[93] The provenance of Captain Hassells is uncertain. There is inconclusive evidence to suggest that he was already in Ireland in 1641, but he received post-'49 arrears in Bargy in Wexford, perhaps as a former officer in Ludlow's horse, lived at Kilbride in Wicklow in considerable style in 1660 and was a justice of the peace for the county.[94] Thomas Maule was a Scotsman, now some seventy years of age, who had been notably well connected under the old regime. His family, the Panmures, had supplied two of Charles I's gentlemen of the bedchamber. Thomas had served as secretary to Lord Deputy Falkland and was appointed joint surveyor of the customs in 1627, the year in which he was made a denizen. He secured grants of land in both Wicklow and King's County and was returned to parliament for Sligo in 1634 and Tralee in 1640. Sir Patrick Wemys, a Convention member for

---

[92] Wright, *The Ussher memoirs*, passim. *Some funeral entries of Ireland*, pp. 94–5.
[93] Ball, *Judges*, i, 268, 347. TCD MS 844, f. 46. His father had been second chamberlain in the court of exchequer. *Cal. SP, Ire., 1633–47*, p. 618. Hughes, *Patentee officers*. Sadleir, 'Kildare members of parliament', *Kildare AS jn.*, 8 (1915–17), 197–8. 'Calendar of petitions, 1649–50', *Irish genealogist*, vi (1983), p. 440.
[94] *Cal. SP, Ire., 1647–60*, p. 628. SP, Ire., 63/287.15. Liam Price, 'The hearth money returns for County Wicklow', *RSAI jn.*, 61, p. 169. Prendergast papers, ii, 446–9. There was an officer called Hassall in Coote Sr's regiment in Dublin in December 1641. *Ormond MSS*, i, 131. The name Hassels first appears in Wexford after 1641: D. Gahan, 'The estate system of county Wexford, 1641–1786', in K. Whelan (ed.), *Wexford: history and society* (Dublin, 1987), pp. 208–9. IRC, Rep. 8, p. 274.

County Kilkenny, was his cousin; Coote's father-in-law, Robert Hannay, was a business associate; Stephen Crowe, a Boyle cousin who represented Lismore in 1634 and 1640, was a relative by marriage. Maule had been appointed lieutenant-colonel of Ormond's regiment in 1640, but he did not bear arms during the war, when he moved regularly between Dublin and Chester, and he spent much of the 1650s in England. In a 1663 submission, he claimed that he and his wife 'are and always were protestants and innocent'.[95]

KILKENNY

County Sir Patrick Wemys, Henry Baker
Borough Thomas Evans
Gowran William Warden
Thomastown Thomas Burrell

The five northern baronies in Kilkenny had been used to supplement the land allocated to the post-1649 soldiers in the ten counties, while the five in the south had been assigned to pre-1649 arrears. Between them, the two groups monopolised the returns, though the record of Sir Patrick Wemys was idiosyncratic. A Scotsman and a cousin of Lady Ormond as well as of Maule, Wemys was a former close associate of the marquess, who had secured his return for Gowran in 1640. He had commanded a troop in Ormond's regiment but later defected to the Scots and moved to Ulster, where he fought with them. Later still, he joined Jones's forces in Dublin and fought at Dungan's Hill. In 1653, he had been a member of the commission for setting out arrears land in the county. He was married to the sister of a prominent local Cromwellian leader, Oliver Wheeler, and was appointed an alderman when Kilkenny's charter was restored in 1656.[96] Captain Henry Baker, an activist in the events of recent months,

---

[95] *Cal. SP, Ire., 1625–32*, pp. 327–8, 388, 434, 555; *1666–9*, p. 78. *Egmont MSS*, i, 163, 235, 244, 252–3, 266–7, 270, 293, 303, 311. W. A. Shaw, *Letters of denization and acts of naturalization, 1603–1700* (Huguenot Society of London, 1911), p. 332. Public Library, Armagh, Act of Settlement, 1662: Court of Claims: claims appointed to be heard and determined by His Majesty's Commissioners (IMC, page proofs, 1992), pp. 350–1. Maule retained the surveyor's post after the restoration.

[96] Burtchaell, *Kilkenny MPs*, pp. 38–9, 62–3. *Egmont MSS*, i, 245, 311. Prendergast papers, ii, 581, 583.

had lived in County Louth before the rebellion and subsequently received arrears land at Philipstown in Ardee barony. Nonetheless, when he was disbanded in 1655 he settled in Kilkenny on former Sweetman properties at Earlstown and Castle Eve, which suggests that he had belonged to the foot regiment of Colonel Stubber. In the same year he was among those who petitioned for the restoration of the corporation and he was named as an alderman in the new charter. He had signed the Dublin declaration in February 1660.[97] Thomas Evans, of Kilcreene, was also a city alderman. A Welshman, he had come to Ireland in 1649, probably in Stubber's second regiment to judge by the distribution of his lands in Kilkenny and Queen's County. He had served as a commissioner for the survey of both counties, and also for Waterford, and as a commissioner of the revenue for the Kilkenny precinct. He settled in Kilkenny when he was disbanded with the rank of captain in 1655 and subscribed to the petition for the restoration of the charter. He was a justice of the peace and had been sheriff in 1656. Though he was said to have been lowborn, 'a baker before the war in England', he had a vicarious claim to a share in the Irish parliamentary tradition through his father-in-law who had represented Athy in 1613.[98] Major William Warden had obtained both his pre-'49 and post-'49 lands in the county and lived at Burnchurch in the barony of Gowran.[99] Thomas Burrell was both another former captain in Stubber's regiment and yet another alderman of Kilkenny. Colonel Stubber had campaigned in Munster in 1647–8, was among those dismissed by Inchiquin when he concluded his agreement with the confederates and returned there with a new regiment in 1649: since Burrell was already a captain in Munster in 1646, serving with Jephson and Sterling, he probably joined Stubber in

---

[97] *Cal. SP, Ire., 1633–47*, pp. 561–2. 'Humble petition of the Justices of the peace, etc', *RSAI jn.*, 4th series, 4 (1877), pp. 269–70. Burtchaell, *Kilkenny MPs*, p. 55. Harold O'Sullivan, 'The restoration land settlement in the county of Armagh', *Seanchas Ard Mhacha*, 16, pp. 39, 43.

[98] He married, before 1660, a daughter of Walter Weldon, of St John's Bower in Co. Kildare. He became mayor of Kilkenny in 1660. Burtchaell, *Kilkenny MPs*, pp. 51–3, 253. Prendergast, *Cromwellian settlement*, p. 216; IRC, Rep. 8, p. 265. H. Upton, 'List of High Sheriffs, 1685–6', *Kildare AS jn.*, 11 (1929–32), p. 39. Hardinge, 'On manuscript, mapped and other townland surveys', Appendix E. Prendergast papers, ii, 446–9, 459. Commonwealth records, *Arch. Hib.*, 7, 61–2.

[99] He became sheriff of the county in 1660. Burtchaell, *Kilkenny MPs*, pp. 60–1, 251.

Ireland and he may have belonged to the settler community. The regiments in Munster combined Englishmen with returning refugees and local recruits and no inference is safe, but his appointment as a commissioner of assize at Cork in October 1655 strengthens the probability that he had local connections. He was disbanded in 1655 with arrears allocated to him in the Liberties of Kilkenny and Queen's County, but he also had some property in the Liberties of Thomastown.[100] When Broghill submitted a comprehensive list of Munster candidates for free pardon in 1661, Baker, Burrell and Warden were among them.[101] In the context of the key role of Warden and the active part played by Kilkenny based officers in the Dublin *coup d'état*, the returns from the county strongly suggest both a well-developed political structure centring on Kilkenny corporation and a Munster orientation.

WEXFORD

County Thomas Harte, John Totty
Clonmines Francis Harvey
Fethard Thomas Boyd
Newborough Walter Plunkett

All of County Wexford had been assigned to supplement the shortfall in the ten counties and both of the knights of the shire were former soldiers. Major Thomas Harte had been a captain in the regiment of Sir Arthur Loftus in Munster, probably under the command of William Knight, when Inchiquin abandoned parliament in April 1648. He was in England some months later, helping to collect money to pay the regiment's arrears, and presumably returned to Ireland in 1649 with the main force. He served briefly as a revenue commissioner in the Wexford precinct: in October 1652, however, he was dismissed 'for as much as it hath appeared that he hath abused his Trust, received Bribes, and been in all his Conversation a very prophane person' and was declared 'uncapable' of public employment. In fact, he continued to be appointed to commissions, received land in settlement of post-1649 arrears in Wexford and Tipperary

---

[100] *Regimental history*, pp. 660–2. Prendergast, *Cromwellian settlement*, p. 216. IRC, Rep. 8, p. 253. Burtchaell, *Kilkenny MPs*, p. 55. Prendergast papers, iii, 922. Jennings MSS, Box J2, Notebook A2. *Cal. SP, Ire., 1633–47*, pp. 466, 486.
[101] *Cal. SP, Ire., 1660–2*, pp. 416–19.

and pre-1649 arrears in Sligo, and became a burgess of Wexford which he was to represent in the parliament of 1661. He maintained a substantial residence in Sligo and was appointed to the poll tax commission for that county as well as for Wexford.[102] John Totty was in possession of land in Ballaghkeen barony in Wexford and in King's County, which was subsequently confirmed to him as Alderman Totty. The distribution of his holdings is consistent with that of officers who served in Ireland after 1649, but there seems little doubt that Totty was a Dublin glover who had been admitted to the city franchise, after apprenticeship rather than by grace, in 1647. Whether he subsequently served in the army or acquired his property through the purchase of debentures is unknown. He was an active member of the corporation from 1653, participated as lieutenant of the Dublin Merchant Guild at the second proclamation of Oliver in 1657, served as sheriff in 1657–8 and became an alderman after the restoration.[103] Francis Harvey was a merchant, local in provenance but not in origin. He first appeared in the town of Wexford in the early 1650s, served as mayor in 1658–9, owned some property in Clonmines, and seems to have prospered despite having married a Catholic. His appointment as Mr Francis Harvey in October 1659 to a committee investigating the rogue militia captain, Robert Thornhill, which was otherwise composed of six ranked army officers, suggests that he had no military record.[104] Thomas

[102] *Cal. SP, Ire., 1633–47*, pp. 12, 16, 21; *1660–2*, pp. 82–3. Hore, *Wexford*, ii, 137, 189; iv, 363; v, 308, 310, 312, 337. Hart was one of only eighteen householders in Co. Sligo with more than one hearth in 1662, *Seventeenth century hearth money rolls with full transcript for County Sligo*, ed. E. MacLysaght (IMC, 1667). The name also had New English associations. A possible immediate forebear was Henry Hart of Carrigomane, Co. Clare. Appointed usher in the court of wards in 1626, clerk of the crown and peace in Clare in 1627 and escheator in Munster in 1628, Hart was still in Clare in 1642. Hughes, *Patentee officers*. Dublin statute staple database (in preparation). Hogan (ed.), *Letters and papers relating to the Irish rebellion*, p. 117.

[103] IRC, Rep. 8, p. 294. Gilbert, *Records*, iii, 447; iv, 35, 47, 63–4, 124. John J. Webb, *The guilds of Dublin* (reprint, New York, 1970), p. 168. As mayor in 1672 he opposed the viceroy's attempt to enlarge governmental authority over the city and was described by the earl of Essex as 'a person of as much disloyalty as any about this city'. Gilbert, *Records*, v, vii–xiii. Jacqueline Hill, *From patriots to unionists: Dublin civic politics and Irish Protestant patriotism, 1660–1840* (Oxford, 1997), pp. 50–1, 54.

[104] Hore, *Wexford*, v, 307, 309, 313, 334, 346. Prendergast papers, ii, 457–8. Harvey to Henry Cromwell, 2 April 1659, Lansdowne MS 823, f. 280. Harvey also represented Clonmines in 1661.

Boyd was also a merchant, heavily involved in the transport of 'vagrants' as servants to Barbados, with connections in the Scottish peerage. His original Irish provenance was Whitehouse in County Antrim, but he lived in Wood Quay Ward in Dublin, and it was family connection that brought him to Wexford. In 1653, he had married a daughter of Sir Adam Loftus of Rathfarnham whose brother Nicholas had settled in the area and represented Fethard in both 1613 and 1634. Marriage had brought other influential connections also, for Boyd's wife was a sister of Dudley Loftus.[105] The continuity of traditional interests in the county was more authentically embodied in Walter Plunkett, whose mother was a sister of the Kildare member, Sir John Hoey, and who belonged to one of the dynastic official families which had benefited from the plantation in north Wexford. His father, prothonotary of the court of common pleas, had been one of the original burgesses when Newborough [Gorey] was incorporated in 1618 and had acquired the town from Lord Mountnorris before 1640, when he represented it in parliament. Walter followed this example and, it may be presumed, returned himself. He had been admitted to Lincoln's Inn in 1642 and sat in the Irish parliament from 1644 to the last adjournment. Ormond later testified to his consistent loyalty.[106]

MUNSTER

WATERFORD

County [Roger, Lord Broghill], Richard, Lord Barrymore
Borough William Halsey
Dungarvan Philip Harris
Lismore Sir William Bury
Tallow Boyle Smith

---

[105] *Montgomery MSS*, pp. 139n, 237n. HMC, *House of Lords manuscripts*, new series, vii, 351–2. Sadleir, 'Kildare members of parliament', *Kildare AS jn.*, 6, p. 471. Jennings MSS, Box J2, Notebook A2. R. L. Greaves, *Deliver us from evil: the radical underground in Britain, 1660–1663* (Oxford, 1986), pp. 145–7, 150. He may have been a connection of the Kilmarnock family: his daughter and heiress married William Boyd, second Lord Kilmarnock in 1682. J. B. Paul (ed.), *The Scots peerage* (Edinburgh, 1908), v, pp. 174–5. He was described as gentleman in the returns, but merchant in the poll tax ordinance, where he was appointed to both Dublin and Wicklow panels, but not to Wexford.

[106] Hore, *Wexford*, vi, 612, 616. Hughes, *Patentee Officers. Cal. SP, Ire., 1660–2*, pp. 58–9.

Waterford was one of the three Munster counties included in the original ten assigned to adventurers and soldiers. In the Convention, its representation was shared between members of the Boyle kinship and newcomers. Broghill opted for the Dublin University seat and was not replaced until May. His 30-year-old nephew, Richard Barry, second earl of Barrymore, was Old English in origin but his father had succumbed wholly to the influence of his wife's family. Since 1642, Richard had spent much of his time in England where his aunt, Lady Ranelagh, took charge of him, where John Milton tutored him, and where he had been twice married, on the second occasion to Richard Cromwell's sister-in-law, a daughter of the president of the protectorate council, Henry Lawrence. He had returned to Ireland by 1657 and was in dispute with John Percival about lands at Liscarroll.[107] Captain William Halsey was a prominent newcomer to the county who had been both a commissioner of revenue for the Waterford precinct and an Athlone commissioner, served as second justice in the Munster court until it was abolished in 1655 and was subsequently appointed one of the clerks of the hanaper. He had acquired land in Kilkenny and Tipperary, represented the combined constituency of Waterford and Clonmel in all three protectorate parliaments and voted for kingship in 1657. He was later to become mayor of Waterford in 1661–2 and chief justice in Munster under Broghill's presidency.[108] Philip Harris, one of the three commoners described in the returns as 'gentleman' rather than 'esquire', was presumably another member of Broghill's entourage since he had no recorded local connection and could not have been chosen for Dungarvan except at Broghill's behest. He was an attorney who had been admitted to King's Inns in 1657. He had some land

---

[107] Lodge, *Peerage*, i, 300–2. N. P. Canny, *The upstart earl* (Cambridge, 1982), pp. 47–8. *Egmont MSS*, i, 587, 591. Arising from the dispute, Broghill denied that he held any animus against Percival. Ibid., p. 594.

[108] He had some difficulty getting hold of his clerkship, but claimed that the incumbents had not been faithful to the public since they had stayed in Dublin under Ormond, and one of them had been in the king's quarters in England during the war. *Cal. SP, Ire., 1633–47*, pp. 636–7; *1660–2*, p. 495; *1666–9*, p. 75. Prendergast, *Cromwellian settlement*, pp. 170–5, 275n. Barnard, *Cromwellian Ireland*, p. 274. IRC, Rep. 8, p. 271. Hardinge, 'On manuscript, mapped and other townland surveys', Appendix C, p. 410. He was the subject of a special proviso in the 1657 act of attainder, to cover a delayed claim. *Acts and ordinances*, ii, 1250–62.

dealings in partnership with Colonel Redman in Meath and Kilkenny, but there is no evidence to identify him as a soldier.[109] The former council member, Sir William Bury, who was the only carpetbagger returned in the province, was Broghill's close associate and Lismore was the Boyle family borough. The name borne by Boyle Smith, who was with the army when he was chosen, proclaimed his local provenance, which was Ballynetray, and his family loyalties. His father, who sat for Dungarvan in 1634 and whom he succeeded when he was in his early twenties in 1657, was the late earl of Cork's nephew and Cork was Boyle's godfather. His mother was William Ussher's sister.[110]

TIPPERARY

County Henry Parris, Bartholomew Foulke
Cashel Anthony Ward
Clonmel John Booker
Fethard Nicholas Everarde

The returns from Tipperary, the second of the Munster counties in the original ten assigned to adventurers and soldiers are more problematic than most. Men who actively served the regime formed the majority, but the provenance of both county members is uncertain. Henry Parris, a justice of the peace, had been solicitor and counsellor to the Athlone commissioners, a commissioner of the revenue in the precincts of Limerick and Clonmel and a commissioner for the survey of Waterford. He had recently acquired land to the value of £756 as an adventurer's assignee in several Tipperary baronies and established his residence at Ardmoyle in the barony of Middlethird. He had no previous connections with the area, but John and Thomas Parris had been members of successive generations of the legal profession in Ireland before 1641 so that it is likely that he was of Irish provenance.[111] Bartholomew Foulke was an army captain, probably

---

[109] *IRC*, Rep. 15, p. 130. He was, however, appointed poll tax commissioner for Waterford (as well as for Dublin and Wicklow) which suggests some local connection. The *Census* lists two men of this name, one as a member of the garrison in the town of Mallow, the other in Skinners Row in Dublin. For Harris's work as an attorney after 1660, W. J. Smyth (ed.), *Herbert Correspondence* (IMC, 1963), p. 157 and many other references.

[110] Wright, *The Ussher memoirs*, p. 142. *Lismore papers*, 1st series, iv, 67.

[111] *Cal. SP, Ire., 1660–2*, pp. 367, 469, 592. Commonwealth State Accounts, *Anal. Hib.*, 15, pp.

under Phayre's command, who had been involved both in assigning allotments to soldiers in Ulster and in the civil survey of Meath. He became escheator of Munster, a master in chancery, a probate judge and a freeman of Kinsale. By early January 1660 he had rejoined the army and was a member of the council of officers in Dublin. Since he was returned for Tipperary again after the restoration it is likely that he had developed local interests. His associations are indicated by the fact that the guarantor of his loyalty when he was commissioned in the restoration army was Broghill, which suggests the possibility of a kinship with the Foulke family who were clients of the Boyles in Waterford and active in the wars. This inference is strengthened by the later appointment of Francis Foulke, a member of the Convention for County Cork, as constable of Clonmel Castle in 1661 and his return to parliament for the borough in the same year.[112] Anthony Ward was described in the returns as a burgess of Cashel. The surname does not occur in the area before 1641 and, intriguingly, the only recorded Anthony Ward with local associations was an army preacher who was a schoolmaster in Clonmel in 1653 and was appointed minister in Cashel on the civil list in the following year. He seems to have managed to avoid attracting attention, but he was still resident in the town in 1666 when he was assessed at the lowest rate in the hearth money returns. Since he was not nominated as a poll tax commissioner for either the county or the town of Cashel itself, he is unlikely to have attended the Convention.[113] By contrast, Colonel John Booker was Clonmel's largest property holder and was serving as sheriff of the county in 1660. A drysalter in London and one

---

296, 311. Prendergast, *Cromwellian settlement*, p. 368. Prendergast papers, ii, 446–9; vi, 547. W. P. Burke, *History of Clonmel* (Dublin, 1907), p. 84. Hardinge, 'On manuscript, mapped and other townland surveys', Appendix E. John and Thomas Parris were admitted to King's Inns in 1615 and 1636 respectively. John had been appointed prothonotary of the court of common pleas in 1612. Hughes, *Patentee officers*. A Thomas Parris received adventurers' land to the value of £50 in Queen's County. Bottigheimer, *English money and Irish land*, p. 208. Henry's heir seems to have been called John. *IRC*, Rep. 15, p. 99.

[112] Barnard, *Cromwellian Ireland*, p. 288. Carte MS 68, ff. 159–63. Hughes, *Patentee officers*. Dunlop, *Commonwealth*, p. 399. Caulfield, *Kinsale*, p. 24. Hardinge, 'On manuscript, mapped and other townland surveys', Appendix E. Ramsey, *Henry Cromwell*, p. 112. O'Dwyer, *The O'Dwyers of Kilnamanagh*, p. 271.

[113] He is not listed in the census. Seymour, *Puritans in Ireland*, pp. 222, 226. Jennings MSS, Box J2, Notebook 'Cromwellian Council Orders'. *Cork HAS jn.*, 2nd series, 6 (1899), 203.

of the 'Sunday soldiers' who had defied the king at Turnham Green in 1642, Booker's business had been seriously affected by the civil war and he was excused from paying his assessment in 1643. He took the pro-Essex peace-party side in the quarrels of 1644 and was already a major in the London trained bands when he was nominated by the City's common council to a parliamentary 'committee for Munster' in 1645. He became involved in raising a regiment for service in the province in the following year, lobbied actively on Inchiquin's behalf, and arrived in Munster in October 1646 as lieutenant-colonel to Francis Rowe. In October 1649, he signed the 'Declaration of the Protestant Army in Munster'. Later on, with Parris, he had been a commissioner for the civil survey in the county. The problematic element in his case is that he seems neither to have received arrears land nor to have secured a grant under the acts of settlement and explanation, but was instead classified as a '49 officer.[114] Finally, the return of Nicholas Everarde reflected the unique status of Fethard, which had secured exemption from confiscation and transplantation by virtue of a timely capitulation to Cromwell in 1650. Everarde, a burgess of Clonmel, was perhaps the sole Protestant member of a substantial and well-connected local Old English family which had supplied borough members in 1613 and 1634. He was attending Dublin University when he was confirmed in his estates in 1654, presumably on coming of age, graduated in the following May and entered the Middle Temple in 1656. He was appointed to the poll tax commission for the county, was among those for whom Broghill sought a free pardon in 1661 and was returned to parliament for the borough in 1661, shortly before his death.[115]

---

[114] Lindley, *Popular politics and religion in civil war London*, pp. 320–2. McKenny, 'A 17th century "real estate company"', Appendix A. *Egmont MSS*, i, 320, 328–9, 355–6. Prendergast papers, iii, 922. Armstrong, 'Protestant Ireland and the English parliament', pp. 196, 352. *Calendar of the committee for the advance of money* (3 vols., London, 1888), i, 131. *Cal. SP, Ire., 1633–47*, pp. 408, 410, 449, 451, 455, 456; *1647–60*, p. 691. HMC *Ormond MSS*, i, 215–16.

[115] He was the son of John Everarde whose mother was a daughter of Lord Dunboyne and who married a daughter of David, Viscount Fermoy. *Some funeral entries of Ireland*, p. 163. *Cal. SP, Ire., 1660–2*, pp. 316–19. George, Paul and Thomas Everarde made up a quarter of the burgesses of Fethard in 1660. 'The proprietors of Fethard, 1641–1663', *The Irish Genealogist*, 6 (1980), pp. 5–8; R. H. A. J. Everarde, 'The family of Everarde', ibid., 7 (1989), pp. 507–9. R. C. Simington (ed.), *The civil survey, county of Tipperary*, i, barony of Middlethird, passim, and p. 386.

LIMERICK

County Thomas Southwell, William King
Borough William Yarwell
Askeaton Garrett Fitzgerald
Kilmallock Robert Oliver

In Limerick, the third of the core counties in Munster, representation was mixed. Southwell's family had arrived in Ireland in James's reign, acquired the plantation seignory of Kilfinny before 1640 and supplied a member of parliament for Ennis in 1634. Thomas, who was a nephew of William Lenthall, speaker of the English Commons, and whose son was married to Inchiquin's daughter, had served in the 1640s as major in the regiment of his relative, Sir Hardress Waller, received arrears land in the county and been both a commissioner for the precinct of Limerick and sheriff in the 1650s.[116] Major William King of Hospital, mayor of Limerick in 1656 and a former sheriff of both Limerick and Clare, was one of the signatories of the Munster declaration in February 1660. He had close Boyle connections: his wife was a daughter of John Boyle, bishop of Cork, sister of Michael Boyle, the chaplain-general of the Munster army, and cousin to Broghill. She was also the widow of a former member of parliament for Lismore. King was later to receive preferential treatment in the satisfaction of his claim for arrears in the king's service before 1649. Since the arrangement was negotiated by Broghill, who also benefited, there is no necessary inference of constant loyalty to the royal cause, but it is safe to assume that King had seen service in Munster in the 1640s. He appears to have acquired land in six counties in all three of the available ways: 'in right of a soldier', as an adventurer's assignee, and as a Connacht purchaser.[117] William Yarwell, one of the members of the new corporation of Limerick and its mayor in 1658–9, had served as commissary with the army, was still commissary of stores at Limerick and had received post-'49 arrears in the county. He was one of those who had invited Ingoldsby to

---

[116] *Cal. SP, Ire., 1633–47*, p. 531. Lodge, *Peerage*, vi, 17. *Complete Baronetage*, iii, 318. *Lismore papers*, 1st series, ii, 361. Lenihan, *Limerick*, p. 193.

[117] Carte MS 68, f. 200. IRC. Rep. 8, p. 276; Rep. 15, pp. 109, 247. Petty, *Down survey*, p. 195. James Frost, *The history and topography of the county of Clare* (Dublin, 1883), p. 626. *Cal. SP, Ire., 1660–2*, p. 475. His wife was a daughter of Sir John Brown: her sister had married Lieutenant-Colonel Nelson. Ibid., *1666–9*, p. 86.

return as governor in December 1659.[118] The provenance of Robert Oliver, the member for Kilmallock, is uncertain. He is said to have been descended from the 'clerk of the munitions' at Cork in 1612, but he first came to notice in 1649, when he was among those who defected to Cromwell in Munster. By then, he had been married to the daughter of a pre-1641 Limerick settler, Andrew Ormsby, for at least four years. He later served in Richard Coote's regiment and settled at Castle Oliver near Kilmallock when he was disbanded in 1653. He too was commissioned on Broghill's assurances after the restoration.[119] So also was Captain Garrett Fitzgerald of Ballyrand whose clientage was confirmed by his later appointment as clerk of the Munster council under the presidency of Broghill in 1662. He was probably related by marriage to Major Ralph Wilson whose wife was a Fitzgerald and for whose son he stood as godfather when he was baptised by Samuel Winter.[120]

CORK

County Francis Foulke, Richard Kyrle
Borough Peter Courthorpe
Baltimore Richard Townshend
Bandon Samuel Browne
Clonakilty St John Brodrick
Kinsale Henry Bathurst
Mallow Robert Foulke
Youghal Henry Tint

---

[118] Lenihan, *Limerick*, pp. 192, 703. Dunlop, *Commonwealth*, pp. 208, 713. Add. MS 19,833. He was later 'sent for' to fight against the Dutch and reached the rank of lieutenant–colonel. IRC, Rep. 15, p. 99.

[119] C. M. Tenison, 'Cork MPs, 1559–1800', *Cork HAS jn.*, 2nd series, 2 (1896), 136–7. 'List of the officers who revolted in Munster', Carte MS 68, f. 150; ibid., f. 161. *Regimental history*, p. 620. Wright, *The Ussher memoirs*, pp. 142–3. IRC, Rep 8, p. 284. IRC, Rep. 15, p. 77.

[120] Carte MS 68, f. 161. IRC, Rep. 8, p. 267. H. J. Lawlor (ed.), *The register of Provost Winter* (Parish Register Society of Dublin, 1911), p. 13. He represented Limerick County in 1661 and was one of those for whom Broghill procured a pardon in that year. *Cal. SP, Ire., 1660–2*, pp. 416–19. He was appointed to the poll tax commissions in both Cork and Limerick.

Four baronies in the north and four in the south west[121] of Cork had been assigned to settling pre-1649 arrears; three in the middle had been assigned to widows and maimed soldiers, though it is fairly clear that they were never distributed; nine others, spread throughout the county, had been retained in the government's reserve. The returns from the county, which sent more members to the Convention than any other, departed sharply from the evolved practice of the 1650s when the established settlers had controlled the politics of the county and contested its elections.[122] Nonetheless, five of the nine members belonged to families which had arrived in the county before 1641. Francis Foulke of Camphire, County Waterford, was, in Broghill's words, 'a gentleman of 800 L a yeere, alwayes bred with me'. His father, also Francis, had been lessee of 600 acres in Waterford from the earl of Cork in 1640. Both father and son had joined the army in England in 1642, presumably as refugees, and Francis Jr had accompanied Broghill back to Ireland where he rose to the rank of lieutenant-colonel and served as governor of Dungarvan. With his brother Robert, he was involved in organizing the defection of the Munster towns to parliament in 1649. He was a justice of the peace in Cork in 1654, represented the combined boroughs of Cork and Youghal in the 1659 parliament and signed the Munster declaration of 18 February.[123] Robert Foulke had taken up lands in the barony of Fermoy, at Currahnahency, and was married to a Boyle from Castlelyons, the family seat of the Barrymores. His return for Mallow was undoubtedly managed by Sir John Jephson, who had inherited control of the town from his late brother

---

[121] Not allowing for the division of both east and west Carbery in two parts. David Dickson, 'An economic history of the Cork region in the eighteenth century' (Ph.D., University of Dublin, 1977), pp. 15–16.

[122] Barnard, 'Lord Broghill, Vincent Gookin and the Cork elections of 1659', *EHR*, 88 (1973), pp. 352–9.

[123] Barnard, 'Cork elections of 1659', *EHR*, 88, p. 356; 'The political, material and mental culture of the Cork settlers c. 1650–1700', P. O'Flanagan and C. G. Buttimer (eds.), *Cork: history and society* (Dublin, 1993), p. 339. *TSP*, vii, 597. H.F. Berry, 'Justices of the peace for the county of Cork', *Cork HAS jn.*, 2nd series, 3 (1897), 59. William Nolan and Thomas Power (eds.), *Waterford: history and society* (Dublin, 1992), p. 223. *Lismore papers*, 1st series, v, 27. Peacock, *The army lists of the roundheads and cavaliers*, p. 41. William Cobbett, *The parliamentary history of England* (36 vols., London, 1806–20), iii, 1537. In his consolidated list of the Irish members of Cromwellian parliaments, Scott confused Foulke with the governor of Drogheda, *RSAI jn.*, 23 (1893), pp. 73–9.

William, an active promoter of the kingship petition in the union parliament, and who was himself married to a daughter of the earl of Cork's 'perfideows kinsman', Archbishop Boyle of Tuam. In the familiar pattern, Broghill acted as guarantor for both brothers when they were commissioned after the restoration.[124] Broghill was a member of the corporation of Youghal and may be taken to have influenced the election of Henry Tint of Ballycrenane, whose background was very different. His grandfather had gone to England 'when Munster was quiet' to fight for Charles I and died there in 1646. Henry, who was his heir, had been compelled to compound for his lands. He was, however, married to a Boyle cousin, step-sister of the member for Tallow, and his mother was a daughter of Sir Edward Harris, chief justice of Munster and member of the 1613 parliament, which makes it possible that he was also a Boyle by descent, for his grandfather's second wife was Edmund Spenser's widow.[125] Broghill was also a member of Cork corporation and its representative, Peter Courthorpe of Courtown, a justice of the peace in 1654 and sheriff in 1656–7, had been one of his captains: some time later he was to claim that Courthorpe had been assaulted for praying for Charles I at his execution and had done much to assist the restoration.[126] It is not clear whether Courthorpe was a first generation settler. He was lessee of Belvelly Castle on the Great Island in 1636 and occupied Cahirdangan Castle in 1641, and both of his wives were from Ireland, the second a Gifford. By 1660, he had acquired the greater part of Spenser's Kilcolman property.[127] Henry Bathurst had been recorder of Kinsale since 1656. His appointment had

---

[124] Dunlop, *Commonwealth*, p. 454n. Caulfield, *Youghal*, p. 566. M. D. Jephson, *An Anglo-Irish miscellany: some records of the Jephsons of Mallow* (Dublin, 1964), pp. 52, 72. Carte MS 68, ff. 199, 200. *Lismore Papers*, 1st series, v, 72.

[125] Lodge, *Peerage*, ii, 247n. IRC, Rep. 15. p. 74. Wright, *The Ussher memoirs*, p. 142. *Cal. SP, Ire., 1669–70*, p. 629. It is not possible to establish which of Sir Robert Tint's wives was the mother of his children. 'Pedigree of the Tynte family', *Cork HAS jn.*, 2nd series, 28 (1922), 61. The earl of Cork referred to the Tints as his cousins. *Lismore Papers*, 1st series, v, 106. Henry was elected for County Cork in 1661 and died in 1662, when his place was taken by John Percival.

[126] Barnard, 'Cork elections of 1659', *EHR*, 88, p. 360. H. F. Berry, 'Sheriffs of the County Cork, Henry III to 1660', *RSAI jn.*, 25 (1905), p. 48. *Cal. SP, Ire., 1669–70*, pp. 43–4.

[127] In a 1667 patent he was described as the son of Sir Peter Courthorpe of Bealvealey. IRC, Rep. 15, p. 129. Tenison, 'Cork MPs', *Cork HAS jn.*, 2nd series, 1 (1895), 277; J. C., 'The old castles around Cork harbour', ibid., 21 (1915), 106.

come at a time when Broghill's influence in the borough was uncontested and he was later to serve as attorney general of Munster under Broghill's lord presidency, as well as adding the recordership of Cork to that of Kinsale. He had practised law in the area before the rebellion and was admitted to King's Inns in 1658. With Percival, whose father-in-law lived in the town, he was a member of a small commission charged with setting and letting tithes and glebes in Cork.[128] Richard Townsend of Castlehaven had fought in the west country throughout the civil war and, on Waller's nomination, brought a regiment to the south of Ireland in July 1647, with Phayre as his lieutenant-colonel. He left when Inchiquin changed sides but returned in 1649 and was in command of the Cork garrison when it defected to Cromwell in October.[129] He was accompanied on the second occasion by Richard Kyrle, whose father had been sheriff of Herefordshire and whose brother was an officer in the New Model Army. Kyrle, who had already been in Munster with Blount's regiment in 1647, became a captain in Broghill's regiment, settled at Dromineene in Duhallow when he was disbanded, and married a sister of Sir John Jephson. He had returned to arms after the December coup.[130] St John Brodrick was a 23-year-old Surreyman in Townshend's Cork garrison when it defected to Cromwell: later, he served in the Scottish campaign, came back to Ireland after the battle of Worcester and settled on land in the barony of Kerricurrihy when his troop was disbanded in 1654. He served as Broghill's provost-marshal and became his close

[128] Barnard, 'Cork elections of 1659', EHR, 88, p. 359. Caulfield, Kinsale, pp. 20, 52, 53, 359. Egmont MSS, i, 581–2. Barnard, 'Lawyers and the law in later seventeenth-century Ireland', IHS, 111 (1993), p. 274n. Hughes, Patentee officers. Cal. SP, Ire., 1660–2, p. 496. Vincent Gookin, who sat for Kinsale in all three protectorate parliaments and wrested the borough from Broghill control in 1659, died in January 1660.

[129] Richard and Dorothea Townshend, An officer of the Long Parliament and his descendants (London, 1892), passim. Regimental history, p. 654. W. H. Welply, 'Colonel Robert Phaire, "regicide"', Cork HAS jn., 31 (1926), pp. 31–6. Armstrong, 'Protestant Ireland and the English parliament', pp. 354–5.

[130] C. M. Tenison, 'Cork MPs, 1559–1800', Cork HAS jn., 2nd series, 1 (1895) p. 523; H. F. Berry, 'The parish of Kilshennig and manor of Newberry', ibid., 9 (1905), 35, 59, 60; H. F. Berry, 'The English settlement in Mallow under the Jephson family', ibid., 12 (1906), 3–4. G. Bennett, History of Bandonbridge (Cork, 1869), p. 146. Ormond MSS, new series, iii, 416. He too was undertaken for by Broghill when he was commissioned after the restoration. Carte MS 68, f. 200. He became governor of Carolina in 1682 and died there in 1684.

neighbour with the acquisition of further property in Barrymore barony. By contrast, his older brother Alan was a former secretary of the Sealed Knot, an active royalist conspirator and a client of Edward Hyde, and Ned Villiers was their cousin.[131] It is probable that Lieutenant Samuel Browne was the Lieutenant Browne who had been stationed in Bandon with Blount's Gloucestershire regiment in 1647. Since he did not receive arrears land and was subsequently classified as a '49 officer it may be inferred that he had not remained with the army, a supposition strengthened by his lack of promotion; since he was provost of the town, which belonged to the Boyles, in 1656–7, and Townshend's lieutenant in a Cork militia company in the early 1660s it may also be inferred that there were no ill feelings.[132]

KERRY

County John Blennerhassett, Sir Arthur Denny
Ardfert Thomas Amory
Dingle Lancelot Sands
Tralee John Blennerhassett, Jr

Kerry was one of the supplementary counties allocated to the post-1649 soldiers, 'the refuse County of Munster' in Petty's words.[133] The county members, however, were both from entrenched local families. The original undertaker of the Tralee seignory was Arthur Denny's great-grandfather: John Blennerhassett's father had been the first provost of Tralee town and its member of parliament in 1613, his younger brother had represented it in 1634, and his son did so in the Convention. The elder John had been a captain of foot in the 1640s and acquired forfeited lands in the 1650s. The younger had been an officer in Nelson's regiment in the area in the early 1650s and sheriff of the county in 1658.[134] He married

---

[131] Prendergast, *Cromwellian settlement*, p. 192. *Cal. SP, Ire., 1647–60*, pp. 530–2. Tenison, 'Cork MPs', p. 177. Lodge, *Peerage*, v, 161–2. Hughes, *Patentee officers*. Barnard, 'Cork settlers', O'Flanagan and Buttimer, *Cork: history and society*, p. 338. Underdown, *Royalist conspiracy*, p. 187 and *passim*.

[132] George Bennett, *History of Bandonbridge*, pp. 146, 188n, 546–7. *Cal. SP, Ire., 1633–47*, pp. 526, 528.

[133] *Reflections*, p. 114.

[134] John King, *The history of County Kerry* (London, 1926), p. 30; *Burke's Irish family records*. Prendergast papers, i, 261.

Arthur Denny's sister about 1654, but the careers of the brothers-in-law contrasted sharply. Denny, though born in 1629, had fought with the king in England in the 1640s, was later classified as a '49 officer, and was tersely described by Ormond as 'always right'. He had a Boyle connection, however, through his marriage to the earl of Barrymore's sister. His father had represented the county in 1640.[135] Thomas Amory, a recent settler close to Ardfert in the barony of Iraghticonnor, had been involved in supplying Cromwell's army as one of the victuallers of the navy under Sir Denis Gawden. He was also, more pertinent no doubt to the explanation of his presence and prominence, married to a daughter of Patrick, Lord Kerry, who had lived in London since 1642.[136] Lancelot Sands was a Cumberland man who had been stationed in Kerry as an officer in Colonel Nelson's regiment in the 1650s and had acquired lands both in the east of the county, in Magunihy barony and in Meath. If Sir William Petty, with whom he quarrelled, is to be believed, he was a Baptist.[137]

CLARE

County Thomas Hickman, Nicholas Purdon

Clare was associated with Connacht for the purposes of transplantation, but it continued to be separately administered and the returns indicate that the county retained an identity distinct from that of the other counties west of the Shannon. On his death, seventeen years later, Thomas Hickman offered 'prayers unto God for prosperity and happinesse of the house of Thomond wherein I haue long serued'. He was presumably related to Gregory Hickman, a burgess of Ennis who reported substantial losses in the rebellion, including a number of valuable leases. Thomas, who was in Clare at the outbreak of the rebellion, leased land

---

[135] Dunlop, *Commonwealth*, p. 633n. Carte MS 68, f. 200. King, *County Kerry*, pp. 30, 112. Burke's *Irish family records*. *Cal. SP, Ire.*, 1660–2, p. 300.

[136] Lodge, *Peerage*, ii, 199. King, *County Kerry*, p. 7. He was appointed customer of the port of Galway in October 1660, was described as 'his Majesty's victualler' in 1666, and died in 1667. *Cal. SP, Ire.*, 1660–2, p. 72; 1666–9, p. 25.

[137] Prendergast, *Cromwellian settlement*, p. 132. King, *County Kerry*, p. 287. Sands accused Petty of seeking a bribe. *Reflections*, pp. 43–6, 71–2, 88–9. Both Amory and Sands were returned for the same boroughs in 1661 and served as sheriffs of the county in 1664 and 1665 respectively. Hughes, *Patentee officers*.

from Thomond in Clare, Limerick and Tipperary and was involved in the preparation of the earl's rent roll in 1656. He acquired ownership of a small amount of land in Clare in the 1650s, in Quin parish in Bunratty Upper, and also had a little property in County Galway.[138] Nicholas Purdon, who had acquired a good deal more, was from Tullagh in the east of the county, belonged to a family which had come to Ireland in the early sixteenth century and had Old English connections through his mother, who was one of the Flemings of Slane. He went over to parliament's side with Inchiquin and contemporary accounts ascribed to him the treacherous killing of Alasdair MacColla after the battle of Knockanass in 1647. When Inchiquin concluded his agreement with the confederates, Purdon was imprisoned with other dissenting senior officers. Subsequently he became a major, with William Warden, in the double horse regiment which Cromwell commissioned Broghill to raise in 1650. Though the regiment was disbanded in 1653, Broghill retained a number of loose troops and companies and Purdon commanded one of these. He took up residence at Ballyclough, near Knockanass, and, in common with Richard Kyrle and Thomas Gifford's father, married one of the Jephson sisters. Unlike Warden, whose history was somewhat similar, Purdon had remained with Broghill in recent months and had signed the Munster Declaration of 18 February.[139]

CONNACHT

In the original settlement scheme, Connacht and County Clare were to be reserved for the accommodation of transplanted Catholic landowners, but this arrangement ignored the interests of Protestant landowning families

---

[138] Frost, *County Clare*, pp. 356, 434, 528, 604, 623. R. C. Simington (ed.), *Books of survey and distribution*, iv, Clare, p. 139. Hickman became sheriff of the county in 1672. Hughes, *Patentee officers*. J. Ainsworth, *The Inchiquin Manuscripts* (IMC, 1961), pp. 512–13, 535, 539, 540, 541. Gregory Hickman signed the return for the Ennis by-election in 1634. Brian O Dalaigh (ed.), *The Corporation book of Ennis* (Dublin, 1990), p. 17.

[139] The published returns list George Purdon as the member, but Nicholas is confirmed by a petition in *Cal. SP, Ire., 1660–2*, pp. 195–6. *Regimental history*, pp. 587, 289. David Stevenson, *Alasdair MacColla and the highland problem in the 17th century* (Edinburgh, 1980), pp. 252–3. *Cal. SP, Ire., 1647–60*, pp. 778, 779, 20. Caulfield, *Kinsale*, p. 436. Berry, 'The English settlement in Cork under the Jephson family', *Cork HAS jn.*, 2nd series, iii, 59. *Burke's Irish family records*. He was a lessee of John Percival. 'W. H. Welphy's abstracts of Irish Chancery bills', *The Irish Genealogist*, 7 (1987), p. 170.

in the area who did not wish to make way. It was opposed by those who had fought in the province, particularly in the regiments of the Coote brothers, and were entitled to arrears 'in those quarters where they have served and are best acquainted'. They had the moral advantage of having disregarded the cessation and collaborated with the English parliament during the civil war and pressure brought changes of plan. First, it was agreed that Protestant landowners should remain in possession, rather than be required to exchange their estates for others across the Shannon. Second, by degrees all of Sligo and the barony of Tirawley in County Mayo were withdrawn from the scheme of transplantation and made available to meet pre-1649 arrears, which was the category that most concerned local Protestants. Third, Leitrim was assigned to the satisfaction of the Munster arrears, and remained undistributed in reserve throughout the commonwealth. A good deal of interchange had taken place in the 1640s when the Coote regiments had linked up with the Laggan army in the north, some of the officers of which had been imported from England, and by no means all of those disbanded in Connacht were of local provenance.

SLIGO
County Robert Parke, Richard Morgan

Robert Parke was a well-established settler on the Leitrim–Sligo border near Dromahaire who had been a member of the Irish parliament in 1641 and the union parliament in 1659.[140] He had been embattled throughout the 1640s (partly as a result of a dispute with Sir Frederick Hamilton rather than engagement with the confederates), was placed in charge of distributing soldiers' allotments in both Sligo and Tirawley and served as sheriff in 1651 and 1656.[141] Captain Robert Morgan had settled at Cottlestown in Castleconnor parish. His wife was a great-granddaughter of Archbishop Loftus and a cousin of both the first Lord Blayney and Richard Blaney and

---

[140] He was returned in a by-election before 28 July 1641, probably for Roscommon: in 1659, he represented the combined constituency of Sligo–Leitrim–Roscommon.

[141] *The information of Sir Frederick Hammilton concerning Sir William Cole; with the answer of William Cole. Together with the replication of Sir Frederick Hammilton* (London, 1644). *The answer and vindication of Sir William Cole unto a charge given in by Sir Frederick Hamilton* (London, 1645). Prendergast papers, ii, 375–6.

it is probable that Morgan was the son of Robert Morgan of Dromahaire whose will was proved in 1637. After service as a captain with both Arthur Hill and Audley Mervyn in Ulster, he had taken command of a troop in Richard Coote's horse in succession to Lord Blayney, who was killed at Benburb. Later, he was one of the commissioners charged with setting out the soldiers' lands in Sligo, where he had become a justice of the peace. He had also acquired post-'49 arrears land in Limerick and Kerry.[142]

MAYO

County Arthur Gore

The recorded return of only one member for County Mayo is probably attributable to a dual return. Since it is unlikely that a knight of the shire would have opted for the less prestigious status of borough member and also unlikely that a member would be returned for more than one county, it seems to follow that the member returned was Chidley Coote and that, like Broghill, he preferred the university to the county seat. Colonel Arthur Gore was the second son of Sir Paul Gore who had founded the Donegal–Fermanagh branch of the family which provided the member for the borough of Armagh. Arthur, whose brother Francis was married to Robert Parke's daughter, had interests in Sligo as well as Mayo. Early in the rebellion he had been placed in charge of Banagher, which commanded an important crossing of the Shannon. After serving as a captain in Richard Coote's horse until its disbandment in 1653, he returned to this post, on which the policy of transplantation conferred large importance and which he still held in 1660 when he was appointed to command a regiment in the newly modelled army. Later, he was one of the select nineteen who were pardoned and given '49 officer status.[143]

[142] *Cal. SP, Ire., 1633–47*, p. 616; *1647–60*, p. 748. *Regimental history*, p. 620. *Egmont MSS*, i, 383. ed. MacLysaght, *Seventeenth century hearth money rolls for County Sligo*, p. 73. Dunlop, *Commonwealth*, pp. 397, 633n. *Anal. Hib.*, 15, p. 279. IRC, Rep. 8, p. 281; ibid., Rep. 15, pp. 80, 239. His wife Bridget was a daughter and co-heiress of Robert Blayney of Tregynon, Montgomeryshire. Her cousin, Sir Arthur Blayney, a former royalist commander, had been involved in the preliminaries to Penruddock's rising in 1655. Underdown, *Royalist conspiracy*, pp. 146–7. Richard Coote acted as his guarantor when he was commissioned in the army after the restoration. Carte MS 68, f. 199.

[143] Hill, *Plantation in Ulster*, p. 492. *Cal. SP, Ire., 1633–47*, p. 355. Mary O'Dowd, *Power, politics and land: early modern Sligo, 1568–1688* (Belfast, 1991), p. 139. *Ormond MSS*, i, 186.

ROSCOMMON

County Richard Coote, Charles Coote, Jr
Boyle John King

Like his brothers Charles and Chidley, Richard Coote, who reached his majority in the year in which the rebellion began, had fought throughout the wars and, like them, he was to be favoured with classification as a '49 officer.[144] His regiment of horse appears to have been something of a political nursery. At the time of its disbandment in 1653 it had six officers. Five of these joined Coote in the Convention, including John Cole, Oliver, Morgan and Gore.[145] The fifth was his major, Sir John King, a substantial landowner whose father had represented Boyle in both 1634 and 1640 and whose family connections with the county dated back to the sixteenth century. In 1658, Henry Cromwell had knighted him and recommended that he should be appointed muster master general, a post formerly held by both his father and his grandfather. He was, Henry wrote, a 'very serious and, I hope, religious man'. Sir John, who had won fame for the capture and hanging of the royalist-confederate commander Bishop MacMahon of Clogher after the battle at Scariffhollis, was linked with Broghill through his wife, the daughter of Sir William Fenton, and his Cork interests were reflected in his membership of the commission of the peace for the county in 1654. Through his aunt's marriage, the Caulfield brothers were his cousins. He had signed the Dublin declaration in February, which suggests that he had already resumed his command. In April, Jeremy Taylor was to pick him out as one of the most influential 'of the king's party' and he too was later rewarded with '49 officer status.[146]

McKenny, 'A 17th century "real estate company"', pp. 200–1. *Cal. SP, Ire., 1660–2*, pp. 198, 316–19. The poll tax ordinance named Oliver St George, Gore, Cuffe and Waddington as the members of the Convention on the poll tax commission for the county.

[144] Lodge, *Peerage*, iii, 207–8. McKenny, 'A 17th century "real estate company"', pp. 200–1. *Cal. SP, Ire., 1660–2*, pp. 198, 316–19.

[145] *Regimental history*, p. 620. The odd man out was Francis King.

[146] Broghill's mother was William Fenton's sister. His cousin Maurice Fenton was King's brother-in-law. King's wife inherited the Munster estates of the White Knight, including Mitchelstown Castle, through her mother. Between them, King's father and grandfather had acquired land in almost every county in Ireland outside Ulster (and in Monaghan). R. D. King-Harman, *The Kings: earls of Kingston* (Cambridge, 1959), chapter 1, passim, and pp. 279–80. *Some funeral entries of Ireland*, p. 100. *TSP*, vii, 161–2. *Cal.*

Richard Coote's fellow county member was his nephew, Sir Charles's eldest son, who was married to a granddaughter of the elder Sir William Ussher and was a brother-in-law of Theophilus Jones and Paul Davis.[147]

LEITRIM

County Henry Crofton, Robert Gorges
Carrick George St George
Jamestown Dudley Loftus

Henry Crofton of Mohill, whose father had represented the county in 1634, was a member of a prominent Connacht settler family. He held pre-'49 arrears land in Sligo, though he was only thirty years old, was a justice of the peace, had been among those entrusted to enquire into allegations against a 'scandalous minister' in 1659 and became sheriff of the county in 1660. His mother was one of the Moores of Mellifont and his wife was the daughter of his fellow Convention member, Robert Morgan.[148] Dr Robert Gorges had been Henry Cromwell's secretary throughout his deputyship, and became both auditor general and clerk of the Irish council in its later stages. A Somerset man from the cadet branch of a prominent family and a cousin of Edward Hyde, Gorges had Master's degrees from both Oxford and Cambridge and had attended the Inner Temple, but his doctorate in laws was conferred by Dublin University. His wife, the daughter of Sir Arthur Loftus, was Broghill's niece, and Broghill spoke of him as his nephew. His brother John, who had become governor of Ulster in the new dispensation, had sat in both the 1654 and 1656 parliaments for Somerset. His eldest brother Thomas, who was recorder of Taunton and represented the borough in all three protectorate parliaments, had married Jerome Alexander's daughter and coheiress two years earlier. Both were Presbyterians. Gorges had acquired property at Kilbrew

---

Clarendon SP, iv, 664. McKenny, 'A 17th century "real estate company"', pp. 200–1. *Cal. SP, Ire., 1660–2*, pp. 198, 316–19. Lodge, *Peerage*, iii, 226n.

[147] He was born about 1630, the son of Coote's first wife.

[148] Crofton, *Crofton Memoirs*, pp. 290–3. O'Dowd, *Power, politics and land*, p. 139. Hughes, *Patentee officers*. Commonwealth State Accounts, *Anal. Hib.*, 15, p. 279. E. T. Gray, 'Some notes on the High Sheriffs of County Leitrim', *Irish Genealogist*, 1 (1941), p. 302. IRC, Rep. 15, p. 26. R. C. Simington (ed.), *Books of survey and distribution*, i, Roscommon, p. 84.

in County Meath, but seems to have had no connection with Leitrim.[149] Sir George St George was a cousin of the Cootes. His father, who was still alive, had come to Ireland with his uncle Oliver St John early in the century, acquired land in the Jacobean plantation of the county and controlled the borough of Carrick which he had represented in 1640. George was colonel of a regiment in the 1640s, captain of a company under Sir Charles Coote in the 1650s, sheriff of the county in 1655, a regimental commander again in the newly modelled army, and brother-in-law to both Richard Coote and Arthur Gore.[150] To Jamestown, which was under the control of the Cootes, whose father had founded the borough, went the honour of returning the returning officer, Dr Dudley Loftus, master in chancery, orientalist and professor of public law in Dublin University, who had been returned to the last Irish parliament from Naas in a by-election in 1642. Loftus had stayed with Ormond until the last, but was serving the commonwealth as a commissioner for revenue in the Dublin precinct by the end of 1651. In the following year, he was deputy judge advocate in Leinster and a member of the high court of justice and by 1654 he was judge of the admiralty. He represented the Kildare–Wicklow constituency at Westminster in 1659 where he was actively involved in preparing legislation as a member of the Commons committee for the affairs of Ireland, including an act of union and a bill for 'the settlement of the ministry'.[151]

GALWAY

County Sir Oliver St George, Henry Waddington
City   Sir Charles Coote, Sr

---

[149] J. Foster, *Alumni Oxoniensis*. Fellow of St John's Oxford, MA 1648. Cambridge, MA (inc.) 1652. Tenison, 'Cork MPs', *Cork HAS jn.*, 2nd series, 1, p. 422. *History of Parliament. The House of Commons, 1660–1690*, 3 vols., London 1983. ii, 417. *Cal. SP, Ire., 1660–2*, p. 308. Robert was returned to the 1661 parliament from the Boyle borough of Bandon. He was appointed as a poll tax commissioner for Meath, but not for Leitrim.

[150] Prendergast papers, iv, 884. Gray, 'High Sheriffs of County Leitrim', p. 302. Lodge, *Peerage*, iii, 111. The elder George St George died in August 1660.

[151] *DNB*. Commonwealth State Accounts, *Anal. Hib.*, 15, p. 320. TCD MS 844, f. 136. Add. MS 19,833. Arthur Annesley to Henry Cromwell, 5 April 1659; Dudley Loftus to Henry Cromwell, 19 April 1659; Lansdowne MS 823, ff. 287, 297–8. Both Sir Charles Coote and his father had been members of the original Jamestown corporation.

Athenry Henry Whalley
Tuam Henry Greenaway

Oddly, Sir Charles Coote, who had represented Leitrim in 1640 and Galway and Mayo in all three union parliaments, contented himself with the city seat, leaving the county seats to his lieutenants. Sir Oliver St George, one of Henry Cromwell's knights, was elder brother of George and a fellow officer in the 1640s. He was with the army in Dublin in February, signed the declaration, and joined his father-in-law, Michael Beresford, in the Convention.[152] Henry Waddington represented the other face of the Connacht establishment. High sheriff of the county in 1660, he had served as receiver of revenue in both the Galway and Athlone precincts and become a notable Connacht purchaser, having acquired about thirty of the decrees known as 'final settlements' which were issued to transplanters by the court at Athlone. He was certainly new to Connacht and his military background seems not to be in doubt since he was both credited with a captaincy and received pre-'49 arrears, but his army career is unrecorded apart from his involvement in the logistics of artillery and other supplies between 1649 and 1651.[153] Earlier he had been a commissioner for the civil survey in Longford, Westmeath and Queen's County, in the last two with Henry Greenaway. Greenaway, also a Connacht purchaser, and also a captain whose army service is mysterious, had been a 'Loughrea commissioner' with Charles Coote and James Cuffe and served as recorder of Galway in 1655 and 1656.[154] Henry Whalley was a more exotic importation: a Nottinghamshire cousin of the Cromwells,

---

[152] *Complete Baronetage*, iii, 120, 305. Coote and St George were both among the nineteen men who were subsequently pardoned and treated as if they were '49 officers. McKenny, 'A 17th century "real estate company"', pp. 200–1. *Cal. SP, Ire., 1660–2*, pp. 198, 316–19.

[153] Prendergast, *Cromwellian settlement*, p. 305n. Commonwealth State Accounts, *Anal. Hib.*, 15, 305. Commonwealth records, *Arch. Hib.*, vii, 34. Add. MS 19,833. *Books of survey and distribution*, iv, Clare, p. xlii. *Cal. SP, Ire., 1660–2*, p. 261; *1669–70*, p. 366. Prendergast papers, ii, 1037–9.

[154] Prendergast, *Cromwellian settlement*, p. 147n. Prendergast papers, i, 451; ii, 226. Petty, *Down survey*, pp. 382–3. Hardinge, 'On manuscript, mapped and other townland surveys', Appendix E. Ainsworth, *The Inchiquin Manuscripts*, p. 442. *Books of survey and distribution*, iv, Clare, p. 503. 'Archives of the town of Galway', *HMC, Rep.* 10, App. pt 5 (1885), p. 501. Dunlop, *Commonwealth*, pp. 387n, 389, 521. Commonwealth State Accounts, *Anal. Hib.*, 15, p. 301. *IRC, Rep.* 15, p. 233.

son of an English member of parliament, brother of a regicide major general, former commissary general and judge advocate of the army, he had sat in the 1656 and 1659 parliaments for the Scottish constituency of Selkirk and Peebles. His Irish experience went back to 1647 when he had been a member of the Lisle expedition to Munster, but he had served in Scotland as well as in England in the 1650s, first as judge of the admiralty court and later as advocate-general of the army. His 6,000 acres in adventurers' lots, acquired by purchase, had been drawn in County Down on land for which Lords Clandeboye and Montgomery subsequently compounded and a special act of parliament had been passed in April 1657 to authorize his compensation in Connacht. The town of Athenry had been included in the subsequent grant. In March 1659 he had exchanged offices with Philip Cartaret to become judge advocate in Ireland: in July, he was summarily replaced.[155]

II

How far the 'good people of the nation' actually contributed to the choice of those who represented them in the Convention is a matter for speculation, but there is no doubt that the membership was thoroughly representative in geographical terms. Ninety-five per cent of those who were returned had a personal or family connection with the area in which their constituency was situated and the few exceptions are readily understood in terms of political associations within the locality. The returns, in short, reflected the newly evolving local power structures. They disclose both areas of New Protestant control and places in which new and old influence was balanced, but they chiefly demonstrate the success with which the Old Protestant community had consolidated and extended its influence. At least ninety-eight of the members returned were Old Protestants; at most, forty were newcomers.[156] Moreover, though there were local parvenus among the members, the majority belonged to the traditional

---

[155] Nobile, *Memoirs of the house of Cromwell*, pp. 154–5. *Cal. SP, Ire., 1647–60*, pp. 589–90, 597–9, 614–15. *Cal. SP, Adv.*, p. 23. *Egmont MSS*, i, 366–7. *DNB*, sub Edward Whalley. Prendergast papers, iii, 527; vii, 89. 'Galway archives', *HMC Rep.* 10, pt. 5, p. 502. Whalley to Henry Cromwell, 15, 22 March 1659, Lansdowne MS 823, ff. 253, 267.

[156] The provenance of two members – Burrell and Hassells – is uncertain.

elite: sixty-eight of the Old Protestants, amounting to slightly less than half of the Convention, belonged to families which had provided members of at least one of the last three Irish parliaments; twenty-seven of these had themselves been members.[157] One was the son of a member of the English Commons. Another sixteen were men whose social positions conformed to the norm of the parliamentary classes and had not changed significantly since 1641: they were landowners,[158] office holders,[159] lawyers[160] or townsmen.[161] All but one of the remaining thirteen had become officers in the parliamentary and commonwealth armies, acquired land in lieu of pay and by other means, and settled among their fellow soldiers.[162] Many of the other Old Protestants had been in the army, of course, and more had acquired land: what set these men apart was that their status in 1660 was unrelated to their inherited circumstances. The exception was Parris, who seems not to have seen military service but otherwise conformed to the characteristics of the group. Their backgrounds varied: most were from small landholding or leaseholding stock, Parris was from a professional family and Bellingham was a townsman. Some of them might not have been out of place in earlier parliaments: others had risen socially under the new order. There may have been two more of the same kind: both of the members whose provenance is doubtful are likely to have been socially mobile settlers.

The majority of the newcomers, twenty-seven of the forty, had come to Ireland in the army. Three of these were later able to establish their right to be classified as '1649 (or '49) officers'.[163] Of the rest, seventeen had chosen to settle in Ireland after their regiments had been disbanded and, in most cases, carried out official duties from time to time;[164] three had remained on active service throughout the 1650s, among whom only Dr

---

[157] In the case of Henry Jones, of the House of Lords.
[158] Acheson, William Davis, Fitzgerald, Morgan and Tint.
[159] Ferneley, Hickman (in the Thomond lordship), Markham and Scot.
[160] Bathurst, Knight and Palfrey.
[161] Moderwell, Reynolds, Smith and Totty.
[162] Ancktil, Baker, Bellingham, Courthorpe, the three Foulkes, Jephson, Oliver, Purdon, Ruxton, Sankey and Totty.
[163] Booker, Browne and Toxteth.
[164] Aston, Brodrick, Burrell, Cuffe, R. Cole, Evans, Handcock, Harte, Hassells, W. King, Kyrle, Pakenham, E. Richardson, Sands, Townshend, Warden and Yarwell.

Waterhouse had failed to acquire substantial estates;[165] three had stayed on as provincial administrators in Connacht and Munster and one as a minister in Cashel.[166] The remaining thirteen newcomers were a mixed bag. Three were adventurers, in the sense that they had secured estates as investors under the 1642 act, though only one was an original subscriber.[167] Two had been members of the Dublin administration, one as a councillor and the other as Henry Cromwell's secretary.[168] Four are likely to have been camp followers, in as much as they were merchants and townsmen who either had been involved in supplying the army in Ireland or were presently dealing with the settlers.[169] There were also three lawyers, of whom one was in private practice, one combined public office with an active professional career and the third was a city recorder. Finally, there was an entrepreneur who had arrived in Ireland less than two years before as postmaster general.[170]

Prendergast's characterisation of the Convention as 'composed entirely of Cromwellian officers' is clearly wide of the mark. Narrowly defined, as military newcomers, the Cromwellian officers in the Convention consisted of only ten men who had come to Ireland with Oliver's expeditionary force in 1649 and seventeen who had already served in the earlier campaigns of the 1640s.[171] Less narrowly defined, the group also included fourteen Old Protestants who had assimilated to the new military community. So defined, it constituted 30 per cent of the membership. Both definitions are certainly narrower than the one that Prendergast had in mind, which encompassed all active collaborators, and it must be conceded that a definition that excludes Sir Charles Coote and Lord Broghill, both of whom held army office throughout the 1650s, makes little apparent sense. The extended service of these two men, however, was unusual. Apart from those who were fully integrated into the ethos of the parliamentary forces, like Phayre, Waller and Wallis, relatively few Old

---

[165] The others were Ingoldsby and Long.
[166] Greenaway and Waddington; Halsey; Ward.   [167] Bligh, Vincent and Whalley.
[168] Bury and Gorges.   [169] Amory, Bulkeley, Harvey and Slater.
[170] Harris, T. Richardson and Godbold; S. Bathurst.
[171] Evans, Greenaway, Halsey, Handcock, Ingoldsby, Sands, Waddington, Ward, Waterhouse, Yarwell; Aston, Booker, Brodrick, Browne, Burrell, R. Cole, Cuffe, Harte, Hassells, W. King, Kyrle, Long, Pakenham, E. Richardson, Townsend, Toxteth, Warden.

Protestants continued as officers of the establishment after the war ended: those who had served longest were disbanded earliest and the army of the 1650s was largely composed of the 1649 expeditionary force and its later reinforcements. Following the practice of public policy in the 1650s, however, the definition of an ex-officer might be extended to include those Old Protestants who were judged to have shown 'good affection' and earned the right to be treated on an equal footing with members of the expeditionary forces. There were at least forty-four of these in the Convention, bringing the officer total to eighty-five. Assuming that the adventurers and other newcomers had a common interest with the officers, a notional Cromwellian interest of ninety-eight might be postulated. If civilians are included, however, the twenty-three members who had held civil office under the regime come into the reckoning, as indeed may those who assisted in local administration, which reduces the calculation, not to absurdity, but to circularity: this was, after all, an assembly largely confined by political circumstances to men who had collaborated in the 1650s.

The provincial returns suggest that both the significance of the distinction between New and Old Protestants and the importance of shared military experience were matters of place and situation. The borough of Lifford in Donegal, where the warden, who was returned for the county, had supported the king to the last and the borough representative had opposed the royal cause from beginning to end, in England as well as Ireland, exemplifies the willingness of men who had made different political and military choices in the years of confusion to work together when confusion returned. Throughout Ulster, traditional power had been consolidated, but in a sharply reductionist way. Almost all of the returns reflect well-established local influences and family relationships within the plantation society, but only two of the members were of Scots origin, one an obscure Strabane townsman and the other a prominent planter who had recently married Lord Caulfield's sister and whose first wife had been Sir Charles Coote's sister-in-law. Of the thirty-six members who represented Ulster in the Convention, twenty-nine were from the pre-1641 community. Seven of them had already served in the Irish parliament and eighteen were closely related to men who had done so. More than a quarter were too young to have played any significant part in the events of the 1640s, but half were former army officers who had passed the test of 'good affection'. Of the seven newcomers, the three who had come to Ireland as soldiers fitted comfortably into the Old Protestant community, Cuffe and Cole through prior family connections and Edward Richardson through marriage with a planter's widow. The lawyer and the adventurer, Thomas Richardson and Vincent, had likewise secured their land acquisitions by marriage and Godbold's recordership of Londonderry made him an *ex officio* member of the establishment, so that only Dr Waterhouse was an unqualified exception to the dominant tendency of Ulster constituencies to return members of the English segment of the traditional colony. Only four of those elected had no demonstrable connection with the locality in which their constituencies were situated, all of them in County Down. Three were returned from the cluster of coastal boroughs in which the unequivocally royalist influence of the Montgomery-Hamilton-Trevor-Cromwell network predominated and may safely be presumed to have sent Cuffe, Percival and Temple to the Convention.[172] The two former were men of political substance with important connections in both England and Ireland, as was Temple's father who managed, though himself otherwise engaged, to have his interests represented by two sons in the Convention. Waterhouse's overt associations were Cromwellian, but it is evident both that he could not have been returned for Newry without the patronage of the Hills and that, in common with many other supporters of 'the single person', he preferred restoration to the republican alternatives in the post-Cromwellian era. The pattern of the borough returns from County Down strongly suggests a different dimension of political management from that which is apparent elsewhere, presumably because those with local influence either could not or would not put themselves forward for election. Nevertheless, the management of returns in the other counties was clearly not narrowly local. The Caulfields' arrangements covered four counties, including Down, and Sir John Clot-

[172] Lord Montgomery, who was allowed to return home after the Dublin coup, on the authority of Theophilus Jones, called on his brother in law, Viscount Moore, at Mellifont *en route* and they concerted 'their councils for the king'. Once home, he got in touch with Vere Cromwell, Mark Trevor, Clanbrassil's friends, 'whom he thought true loyalists', and with his own friends 'whom he knew best of all and trusted most'. *Montgomery MSS*, pp. 223–4. Clanbrassil (*antea* Clandeboye) had died in May 1658 and been succeeded by his twelve year old son. Lodge, *Peerage*, iii, 6–7.

worthy's connections made up a well-defined interest, but the elections were conducted within the socio-political framework created by the plantation and only Palfrey, who fits a well-established electoral pattern of Dublin based lawyers seeking borough seats in parts of the country where they were known, seems to have been unconnected with planter families.

Recent developments in Connacht had been very different from those in Ulster, but the character of its representation showed similarities. The two outsiders who were found seats in the province were political insiders, both returned from Leitrim, where the county elected Henry Cromwell's secretary, Dr Gorges, and the Coote family borough of Jamestown returned Dr Loftus. Otherwise, all the Connacht members were local residents and all but Sir Charles Coote's heir were ex-officers who had passed scrutiny and received their arrears land. All eleven members from the old community were connected by kinship and marriage. Three had sat in parliament previously and all of the others were related to someone who had done so. The newcomers, apart from Gorges, comprised two ex-officer functionaries in the provincial administration and Cromwell's speculating soldier cousin, Henry Whalley, who had acquired Athenry and was closely allied with the Coote interest. In a sense, Whalley personifies the twin characteristics of the Connacht returns: the dominance of the Coote connection and the fusion of the traditional elite with selected newcomers. The features which the province shared with Ulster included a significant incidence of ex-officers among the Old Protestant members, the assimilation of incoming officers to the old community, the retention of political control by the traditional elite and the confinement of participation by newcomers to those who were well integrated with or useful to the Old Protestant community. The reasons behind this convergence were obviously very different. In Ulster it reflected the presence of a sufficiently large established Protestant population to withstand the impact of new settlement: in Connacht, it reflected the dominance of a relatively small one which successfully exploited the end of Old English influence. A corresponding difference of political ethos seems evident. In Ulster, the returns were significantly affected by local influences; in Connacht, they were effectively coordinated on a provincial basis.

The Munster returns resembled those from Connacht in their coherence, though the spread was a great deal wider, and the dominant influence was unmistakably that of Broghill.[173] The aim suggested by the spectrum of members was the creation of a patrimonial and political coalition which was either intentionally inclusive or singlemindedly indifferent to considerations of origin and provenance. Though the balance between old and new favoured men who had been in the province before the rebellion, by eighteen to thirteen, the incidence of parliamentary associations among the members from the older community was significantly lower than elsewhere: none had sat in parliament previously and less than half were related to anyone who had done so.[174] This profile reflected the fact that six of the sixteen officer settlers returned from the province belonged to the old colonial community, but not to its elite. They were men whose army service had turned them into landed proprietors living as part of a new officer settler society. The other ten officer settlers were evenly divided between men who had fought in Munster in the 1640s and men who had come in or after 1649. Officers dominated the returns in Cork and Limerick, but they were present everywhere. The breadth of Broghill's political church and the degree of integration in the province are suggested by the inclusion among them of two officers who had not taken parliament's side in 1649.[175] This eclecticism was repeated among the representatives from the old elite, but according to a rigid principle of selection, for it is clear that while traditional influences appeared to survive in parts of the province they did so only to the extent that they were attached to the collaborative interests of Broghill and his brother, the self-effacing earl of Cork. With the exception of an O'Brien family retainer in Clare, all of the Old Protestants belonged to one or more of three categories: they were relatives, former companions in arms or clients of the Boyle family. They combined at least four men who had served against the king with one who had fought for Charles I in England in the 1640s and they included three Protestant members of the Old

[173] Broghill's influence is illustrated by a confident report on the election to be held in Waterford to rectify the position created by his dual return: 'tomorrow the gentry of this county are to meet at Whitechurch to choose a representative which will be Sir Maurice Fenton, he being recommended by my Lord Broghill and Lt-Coll. Foulk to be elected.' L. Gorstelo to Lord Cork, 14 May 1660. Chatsworth House, Lismore MS 31/87.   [174] Seven, including Barrymore.
[175] Booker and Browne, who were later classified as '49 officers.

English community, among them Broghill's nephew, Lord Barrymore. The only undoubted carpetbagger in the province was Broghill's political ally, the Presbyterian Sir William Bury, on whom he conferred the family seat. Apart from the bizarre return of a puritan minister from Cashel (who seems not to have attended), the only odd man out among the ex-officers, administrators and selected traditional landowners who made up Munster representation was an English merchant, Thomas Amory, whose position in the county, like that of Vincent and the two Richardsons elsewhere, had been secured by marriage, to Lord Kerry's daughter.

In crude figures, Old Protestants dominated in Leinster: they accounted for at least forty of the fifty-six members returned and almost half of them were former members of parliament, while ten others were closely related to someone who had previously sat in either the Lords or Commons. But the returns do disclose local variations, including both concentrations of New Protestant influence and areas in which the new and the old were merged, in a pattern roughly related to the density of new settlement and the previous extent of Protestant influence. Old Protestant influence was unchallenged in Longford and in a block of six contiguous counties extending from the sea to the Shannon and comprising Dublin, Wicklow, Kildare, Carlow, King's County and Queen's County. The only newcomers among the twenty-nine members from these counties were the postmaster-general, whose opportunities for gathering intelligence made him a special case, and an officer settler of uncertain origin who had chosen to settle in Wicklow rather than among his fellow officers in Wexford and was returned for a borough traditionally under local Protestant control. The rest were not merely Old Protestants, but predominantly members of a group of closely interlocked, Dublin-based families which, in addition to their extensive landholdings, had traditionally occupied public office and in almost all cases continued to do so under the new regime. Otherwise, apart from the interloping university representatives, there were four established landholders, a Dublin alderman and a provincial townsman. Nine of the twenty-seven were former officers who met the test of 'good affection'.

In the rest of the province settlement had been active, the spread of Old Protestant influence had been correspondingly curtailed and the clarity of the political balances was complicated in places by the participation of men from the old community who had assimilated to the new order. Between them, Kilkenny, Wexford, Meath, Westmeath and Louth returned fourteen newcomers to the Convention – nine officer settlers, an adventurer and four townsmen – and thirteen Old Protestants, of whom five were well integrated members of the new settler communities in Kilkenny and Ardee. Appearances, however, do not suggest that the soldiers and their associates made up a united political force. From Kilkenny, which had contributed so prominently to the surprise of Dublin Castle, came a renegade member of the old elite in Sir Patrick Wemys, whose Scottish sympathies seem to have led him astray in the 1640s, and four officer settlers, one of them an Old Protestant. Three of these men were veterans of the Munster wars, including William Warden who had served as Broghill's major throughout the 1650s and represented him in Dublin in December. Provincial and county boundaries meant little to the officers, not only because the precincts had cut across them and portions of arrears land had been distributed without regard to them, but for companionate reasons also, and it is likely that the Kilkenny settlers found the politics of Munster more congenial than those of Leinster. In Wexford, where settlement was also dense and links with Kilkenny were close, the returns were quite different: one county and one borough seat went to newcomers, of whom only one was an army man, old office holder influence remained strong enough to return non-residents in two boroughs and the second county seat was taken by the Dublin glover John Totty, whose acquisitions in the area had not affected his civic interests. In Meath and Westmeath the distinctions seem blurred and the newcomers do not emerge as a separate interest. In the former, the county seats went to Old Protestants who had been prominently associated with the parliamentary cause, including Henry Jones; the boroughs returned an adventurer and three officer settlers, of whom one was an old Protestant of extreme radical religious opinions and another had married into Jones's Ussher lineage. In the latter, one of the officers returned had been a member of the council that called the Convention and the other was associated with Coote's Connacht provincial apparatus, while the Old Protestant members comprised two Dublin office holders and the son of an intransigent royalist peer who was returned from the family borough. Louth appears as *sui generis*. The county had no traditional Protestant elite and the community introduced by the fortunes of war and the settlement of Ardee barony provided all six members of the Convention. One, Major Aston, was a man of political weight; two were officer settlers who originated in the old community; and three were townsmen, one of whom was later classified as a '49 officer.

The general picture presented by the returns tends to confirm the impression of those contemporaries who saw the politics of the Convention as variously a contest or partnership between Coote and Broghill. They appear as power brokers, each working systematically from a secure provincial base with connections in other provinces and cooperating with one another, as the division of the university seats indicates. Coote's network seems to have been primarily Old Protestant in ethos, with only a small number of well-assimilated newcomers, while Broghill's combined new and old and included a significant number of men who, whatever their views on monarchy in general and the present situation in particular, had fought on the parliamentary side in the civil war, as Broghill himself had done. It seems evident, however, that a third force was operating in Leinster, composed largely of the elite office-holding class who not only monopolized representation in seven counties, but took seats in three others as well. These men were already closely knit by ties of interest, marriage and political activity; they had adapted themselves rapidly to the changes of the 1650s and managed both to retain their historic role in government and maintain their traditional practice of accumulating land and influence outside the capital city. Their stance was conservative and opportunist. In the 1650s they had collaborated with a government that actively sought their support, seemed purposeful and effective, and was increasingly more moderate. Instability and the revival of extremism prompted them to associate themselves quickly with the December *coup d'état*. They cooperated with the officers in seeking to enlarge support, served as members of the committee of safety that assumed responsibility for civil government, supplied the Convention's returning officer and participated enthusiastically in February in the purging of the republicans and the adoption of a conservative programme. Their distinctiveness was neatly expressed in the following September in Robert Fitzgerald's choice of witnesses to the service that he had rendered in Dublin on 13 December: among those who confirmed how much he had contributed 'when we declared for the Happy Restoration of his Majestie' were James Barry and Richard Kennedy as well as Broghill, Clotworthy and Sir John King.[176] They were by no means an enclosed group. Though they intermarried intricately among themselves, they also had extensive connections with the Protestant gentry and some spanned both groups, most significantly, perhaps, the second of the Jones brothers, Theophilus, who was at the centre of both the December *coup d'état* and the rout of the republicans in February and who maintained close relations with the royalists of County Down.

It seems reasonable to connect the Coote–Broghill apposition with disagreements about the need to impose conditions on the king and divergent attitudes towards the issues of the civil war, as distinct from the abolition of the monarchy. As the situation evolved, some of the issues of the 1640s were arising for settlement again. Once Waller and his associates had been disposed of, the restoration of kingship was not a point of division. The nature of that kingship seems not to have been a potential source of disagreement either, for there is no evidence of active concern with the question of how England should be governed in the future. The concern was with the different question of how Ireland should be governed and there was a common view on the need to restore its political and constitutional self-sufficiency. Nonetheless the politics of 1660 were conditioned by the politics of the late 1640s at least to the extent that the restoration raised the question of religious arrangements. Though there was a practical community of interest among those elected to the Convention on secular matters, there was no such unity of purpose on the religious front. A broad agreement on the need to suppress the sects and restore order was accompanied by disagreement about the form of a national church. To put it no more strongly, those who had willingly associated themselves with parliament's cause in the 1640s were likely to be ill disposed towards the restoration of episcopacy. In terms of the totality of politics, their sympathies were with those in England and Scotland who perceived the need for a negotiated return of the king to his thrones. As it happened, the initial balance of advantage appeared to favour those who opposed a full restoration of the ecclesiastical arrange-

---

[176] PRO, SP, Ire., 63/305. 6a.

ments of the pre-civil war period. But, precisely because the question was more than local, disagreement in Ireland was muted and did not preclude cooperation. There was little dissent from the need to cleanse the church of the excesses of recent years. The composition of the Convention, however, with its predominance of the traditional elite over newcomers, its tiny radical component and its complete closing out of the Scottish community in the north, ensured that the weight of divided opinion would lie on the conservative side.

In the background, of course, there was the larger issue of the king's return, about which there were sharp conflicts of opinion, simplified in the later account of a contemporary who recalled that even before the Convention met there were two parties, one 'being for Articling with the King for the confirmation of the estates of Adventurers and soldiers; and the other party being for his Majesty's restoration without any previous condition'.[177] This was a reductionist rendering of the issues, not least because religious conviction also played a part, as the evidence that Colonel Gorges made a 'circuit to cajole the Presbetn Ministers' in Ulster in February suggests.[178] Moreover, the parties could not engage on equal terms. The constraints of the larger political context inhibited the open expression of quasi-Cavalier opinions. It did so because, on the one hand, the pro-monarchy initiative was firmly held by those to whom the conclusion of an agreement between subjects and king would constitute, in effect, a continuation of the negotiations that had been interrupted by Pride's Purge, while on the other it was far from certain that Monck and the army would allow a restoration. The unconditional restoration of Charles was not an objective that could be overtly pursued within the existing political framework, and those who wished to achieve it had to opt for the alternative politics of the court at Brussels. That did not preclude the pursuit of more limited objectives: within the system, those who were intent upon 'articling' the king must be supported against those who wished to preserve the commonwealth. In Ireland, where Waller's last stand had signalled the defeat of the commonwealthmen, that conflict was over. As a matter of practical politics, however, differences needed to

---

[177] H. R., 'A letter to the author', Cox, *Hibernica Anglicana*, p. 3; cf. Thomas Carte's treatment was derived from this account, *The life of James, duke of Ormond* (6 vols., London, 1851), iv, 6–7.   [178] *Montgomery MSS*, pp. 221–2.

be compromised if broad consent was to be secured in the forthcoming Convention, so that a level of cooperation had to be maintained in working out terms that would protect the interests of those who felt threatened by a restoration. Equally, the more immediate need to tackle Irish problems and establish a mechanism of coordinated response to what happened in England united those who were divided on the fundamental question of the manner of the king's return. Thus the dynamics of both local and cross-channel politics favoured the approach of those who wished to bargain with Charles, because those who did not wish to do so were not free to say so.

7

The General Convention of Ireland: March to April

Objectively, the conditions upon which Monck allowed the secluded members to resume their seats appeared to be irreconcilable, for it was universally understood that any representative assembly other than the rump would wish for a return to monarchy. The majority of the members of the restored parliament had no desire to preserve the commonwealth, but they had no real power of decision. Their predicament had two aspects: first, the limits of possibility were still defined by the potential use of force and they were constrained by the uncertainty that surrounded Monck's intentions; second, they could not be confident that the body that they had agreed to summon would share their sense of the need to ensure that the king was restored on terms that protected the gains of the civil war. In parliament, in a probing collaboration with Monck, they did what they could to further a restoration and to prescribe the conditions upon which it should take place. The most promising area of cooperation was in religion, where Monck's condition accorded with their desires. Rapidly, they put together a religious settlement based upon two elements: the adoption of the confession of faith which had been drawn up by the Westminster Assembly in 1646, but never approved by parliament, and the reimposition of the Presbyterian form of church government nominally introduced in both England and Ireland by an act passed in August 1648.[1] Their dual purposes were reinforced by the re-adoption on 5 March of the Solemn League and Covenant of 1643, which combined the rejection of episcopacy with a pledge to uphold monarchy. Side by side with this attempt to prescribe the form of a religious settlement went a thorough review of the militia commissioners which gave significant local authority to many men whose preference for the return of the king was

---

[1] *CJ*, vii, 858, 862, 874. *Acts and ordinances*, p. 1461.

undisguised. The unease of army officers at the thrust of parliament's policies was suppressed by Monck, and the members proceeded with renewed confidence, but with a certain wariness which led them to discard the tempting suggestion that this parliament should bring the king back, rather than go through the process of summoning another to do so.

It was on 8 March that the bill to call a new parliament on 25 April was introduced: it made no provision for the promised representation of Scotland and Ireland. In its final form, it did observe Monck's original condition by denying the right to sit to those who had assisted the king against the parliament. Its passage, however, was accompanied by the rejection of a complementary proposal to restrict the right to vote along similar lines and by an acknowledgement of the right of the House of Lords to be part of parliament, though the right of lords to take their seats was to be confined to those who had supported parliament. On 16 March, the Long Parliament dissolved itself, more than nineteen years after it had been called.

This attempt to ensure that royalists should play no part in the final decision to recall the king, for there was no longer any doubt whatever that that would be the outcome, reflected a determination that had been pursued by intrigue as well as by parliamentary action. The object was to ensure that the discussions with the king on his recall would be based broadly on the propositions which had been presented to his father at the Isle of Wight, which stipulated the reorganization of the church on Presbyterian principles and modifications of both the prerogative powers of the crown and the arrangements for executive government. Efforts to negotiate with Charles on that basis were made, as were attempts to persuade Monck to lend his authority to a transaction of this kind. Monck was uncooperative. Charles had other options to explore, foremost among which was the attitude of Monck himself, for Charles's advice was that no one else in England had the power to keep his word. When parliament dissolved, with elections imminent and a Convention in the offing, it remained clear that Monck's role, that is the role of the army, would be determinative.

The first recorded concern of the members of the Irish Convention when they met at the Four Courts in the cathedral precincts on 2 March was, in the language of the newsbook which had come into being to support as well as to report the momentous events which had begun in mid-February, 'to lay the foundation of their future councils in consulting with the Oracle'.[2] In plainer words, they attended Christ Church to hear a sermon preached by Samuel Coxe, minister of St Catherine's in Dublin, 'a man reputed the soundest presbyterian in Dublin', according to a northern Presbyterian of exacting standards.[3] Coxe chose a tritely appropriate text from the Book of Proverbs: 'Where no counsel is, the people fall: but in the multitude of counsellors there is safety.'[4] What he had to say was less bland and although his main thrust was religious and programmatic he did not eschew the political. Ascribing responsibility for recent events in conventional terms to the desire of fanatics to 'pull down Magistracy and Ministry', and incorporating the stock allusion to the story of Corah, he extolled as the true nobility those who had 'ventured all for the restitution of our Grand Council the Parliament', and made particular mention of 'the Magistrates of this famous City'.[5] He enjoined the people to obedience and the payment of taxes for the support of the army and enjoined the members of the Convention to be godfearing and wise, resolute and unanimous, and mindful of the expectations raised by the declaration of 16 February.[6] He also warned them to maintain a full correspondence with parliament or its representatives and compared Ireland and 'Great Britain' to bottles which would break if they clashed: 'think not that you are able to stand alone; in taking advice with England will be your honour and safety, and a threefold cord is not easily broken'.[7] His own advice on 'what Our Israel ought to do' consisted of an elaborate exposition of the first duty of the Convention, which was to promote 'the reformed Protestant religion according to the written word of God'.[8] The initial prerequisite was the removal of two 'impediments', popery and schismatic error, the former by enforcing the existing laws, the latter by the root and branch suppression of 'the Separate Congregations in the

---

[2] *An account of the chief occurrences of Ireland*, in *A Declaration of the General Convention of Ireland*, p. 9.   [3] Patrick Adair, *True narrative*, p. 233.   [4] Proverbs, 11. 14.
[5] Samuel Coxe, *Two sermons preached at Christ-Church in the city of Dublin, before the honourable the general convention of Ireland* (Dublin, 1660), pp. 9–11.
[6] Ibid., pp. 13–15.   [7] Ibid., p. 23.
[8] Ibid., pp. 23–4.

land'.⁹ He was careful to exclude 'Good old non-conformists' who were 'disgracefully called by the name of Puritans' and should not be hindered from meeting to worship. What was necessary was 'that none be permitted to gather Churches (as they call them) out of our parochial Congregations, or to exercise Acts pertaining to Church-Government in any of their private meetings'.¹⁰ His positive proposals for action repeated the well-rehearsed needs to encourage a Godly, learned and orthodox ministry and to nurture educational institutions, and he spelled out the corollary, that unsuitable pastors who had 'already crept in' must be ejected.¹¹ Much of this was common ground. In broaching the question of church government, however, Coxe opened a subject of probable dispute, though in the hope of forestalling it. His own position was exclusivist: he saw the discipline of church government as 'the fence of God's vineyard', designed to keep the godly in and the ungodly out, and believed that it must be settled in the manner 'which Christ hath appointed to be in his Church'.

His proposal, however, was undogmatic and mirrored the strategy which his fellow Presbyterians were promoting in England: he entreated the Convention 'to walk hand in hand with our Brethern in the other parts of these Dominions, and That all such matters may be concluded of by a Synodical Assembly of the three Nations'. So that the Lord's people should not be deprived of 'Spiritual food' in the meantime, he asked the members to see to it that 'all Christ's Ordinances, even the Sealing Ordinances' should be administered, though only by pastors in their own parishes and only to 'duly qualified persons'. The last was a thoroughly denominational point: months previously, the author of *A sober vindication* had specified the objection to being examined before the sacrament as the mark of the 'common-prayer-book' party.¹² Coxe's endpiece was David's valediction to Solomon:¹³ 'Arise therefore, and be doing, and the Lord be with you.'¹⁴

The warmth of the reception accorded to this sermon is attested less by the routine courtesy of a vote asking Coxe to print it,¹⁵ than by the Convention's request that he should attend every morning to pray with

---

⁹ Ibid., pp. 25–6.   ¹⁰ Ibid., pp. 8, 26.   ¹¹ Ibid., pp. 26–7, 28.
¹² *A sober vindication*, p. 15.   ¹³ 1 Chronicles, 22. 16.   ¹⁴ Coxe, *Two sermons*, pp. 27–8.
¹⁵ The committee appointed to ask him to do so consisted of Paul Davis, Theophilus Jones and Dudley Loftus. The order is printed as prefatory matter in Coxe, *Two sermons*.

the members before the sitting began. Moreover, on the following day the Convention adopted his suggestion that a day of public fast and humiliation for the nation's sins should be observed, decided that this should take place in Dublin on the following Friday and in the rest of Ireland three weeks later, and invited Coxe to preach again. On this occasion he was to be joined by a fellow Cambridge graduate, Stephen Charnock, minister at Wood Street in Dublin, Fellow of Trinity College and lecturer in St Werburgh's, who had been one of Henry's chaplains and was a Presbyterian with Independent antecedents.[16] The committee appointed to prepare a declaration announcing the fast was headed by Lord Broghill and included Dr Henry Jones as well as two committed Presbyterians, Sir William Bury and Sir John Clotworthy.[17] When it reported on the following Tuesday, the declaration, which listed 'breach of Covenant' as one of the nation's sins,[18] was passed 'as the Act of the House', and two additional ministers were appointed to assist in the Dublin ceremony. Of these, Edward Baines was from the same mould as Charnock: a nephew of Daniel Redman, he was a Cambridge graduate ministering at St John's in Dublin and combined Independency with Presbyterian associations:[19] by contrast, Patrick Adair, minister of Carncastle in Antrim and no doubt selected on Clotworthy's recommendation, was a Scottish Presbyterian who was charged by his ministerial brethren when leaving for Dublin 'to endeavour the promoting of the work of reformation' and did his best to oblige them.[20] Like Coxe and Charnock, both men were resolutely opposed to Episcopalianism and were to remain so.

When the sermon was over on 2 March, the members assembled in the Tholsel to 'fall upon the necessary business of their Generation', and it seems to have been in this session that they decided upon their officers. Sir James Barry, who had presided over the *ad hoc* committee of safety, was

---

[16] Charnock was also a former Fellow of New College, Oxford. Phil Kilroy, *Protestant dissent and controversy in Ireland, 1660–1714* (Cork, 1994), pp. 41, 55n.

[17] *Chief occurrences*, in *A Declaration of the General Convention of Ireland*, p. 11. The other members were Paul Davis, Dudley Loftus, William Aston, John Bysse and one of the Temple brothers.

[18] Adair, *True narrative*, p. 233. The declaration appears not to survive, but Adair is a first hand source on this.

[19] Barnard, *Cromwellian Ireland*, pp. 130n, 139, 140; Seymour, *Puritans in Ireland*, pp. 168, 207.   [20] Adair, *True narrative*, p. 234.

chosen as chairman. His first cousin, Matthew Barry, who was a nephew and protégé of Sir Paul Davis and had served as an administrative functionary under the protectorate, was appointed clerk.[21] Sir James's speech of acceptance and the courtesy speeches which followed it were all concerned with reinforcing a point that Coxe had strongly insisted upon, 'to wit, that the benefit of Ireland chiefly lay in subordination to the authority of the parliament now sitting in England'.[22] Other arrangements were agreed on the Saturday, when the house decided that it would go into grand committee each Wednesday afternoon to consider universities and schools and the maintenance of ministers, and each Thursday afternoon to deal with matters relating to trade.[23] Presumably it was at this meeting that standing committees for these subjects were appointed, and perhaps also another to inspect the revenue and expenditure, together with a committee chaired by Sir Paul Davis which was charged with drawing up a declaration to vindicate the summoning of the Convention and state its objectives. Monday, 5 March, was devoted to housekeeping. The house reviewed the returns, and ordered the clerk to issue writs for constituencies disenfranchised by dual elections and to require those that had not sent members to do so 'with speed'.[24] On Tuesday, it was agreed that the committee concerned with the maintenance of ministers, which was chaired by Loftus, should 'send for Ministers out of all parts of the Nation to advise with'.[25] There is no record of business on 7 March, and it is likely that the finishing touches were being put to the proposed declaration, which was presented to the house on the following day by Sir Paul Davis and adopted.[26]

Beyond asserting that it had been the need to find remedies for 'the high extremities of Ireland' that had required it to meet, the Convention did not seek to justify its existence, though it was at some pains to establish that the news of the readmission of the secluded members had not reached Dublin when it met and that it was in ignorance of this 'Great and

---

[21] Among other things, he had been employed in indexing the 'books of discrimination'. *Anal. Hib.*, 15, 256–7. *Cal. SP, Ire., 1660–2*, p. 353. He had lent £1,200 to Charles Coote in 1657 and £400 to William Ussher in 1659. Dublin Statute Staple database (in preparation).

[22] *Chief occurrences*, in *A Declaration of the General Convention of Ireland*, p. 10.

[23] Ibid., p. 11.   [24] Ibid., p. 12.   [25] Ibid., p. 12.

[26] *A new declaration of the general convention of Ireland. March 12* (London, 1660).

Extraordinary Providence of God' that the members had set to work.[27] The declaration associated the Convention unreservedly with the earlier declaration of the council of officers and pledged the cooperation of 'this Nation' with the army, and with those of their brethern in England and Scotland who joined them, 'for the accomplishment of the good and publick ends therein expressed, and to contribute cheerfully and readily to the charges requisite thereunto by all good and lawfull wayes'. The Convention followed the lead of the officers in placing 'the horrid violence' done to parliament in 1648 at the centre of its interpretation of the recent past. That event 'let in all the miseries and calamities in Church and State' which had engulfed the three nations through 'secret designes and great endeavours utterly to extinguish the Reformed Protestant Religion, to eradicate Parliaments, to subvert the Fundamental Laws of the Land, to take away the Rights, Liberties, Freedom and Properties of the People, and to introduce an arbitrary and Tyrannical government over these Nations'. Now that tyranny had been overthrown, the members of the Convention were concerned to make sure that the implications, already forcefully expressed by the officers, were fully understood. Although they were prudently respectful, and resolved 'constantly to adhere to the present Parliament, and future Parliaments of England in the preservation of them in their Fulness and Freedom', they reminded the restored parliament that it did not possess the authority which the rump had arrogated to itself:

> the right of having Parliaments held in Ireland, is still justly and lawfully due and belonging to Ireland, and that the Parliament of England never charged Ireland in any Age with any Subsidies, or other publick Taxes or Assessment, until after the violence offered to the Parliament of England in December 1648, since which time, they who Invaded the Rights of the Parliament of England, Invaded also the Rights of the Parliament of Ireland, by imposing Taxes and Assessment upon them.

They were also concerned to ensure that the wrong inference was not drawn. Attributing to Ludlow and the commissioners the 'callumny' that 'these their necessitated proceedings' were intended to separate Ireland

---

[27] This was true of course only of the first occasion on which the members assembled, on 27 February.

[249]

from England, they declared their resolution 'for ever to adhere to England' and affirmed that 'the Welfare and Interest of England and Ireland are so inseparably interwoven as the good or evil of either, must necessarily become common to both'.

Thereafter, the declaration became programmatic, and prolixity gave way to concision as the Convention listed the local objectives that its members wished to see achieved. Starkly stated, their concerns were with religion and land. They aimed to have a learned and orthodox 'Preaching Ministry of the Gospel and no other', supported by tithes and other legal maintenance, and settled 'only in a Parochial way'. This was a stage beyond what the officers had demanded in February, and more than Coxe had requested on the previous Friday. From the moment when the Irish opponents of the army regime began to speak out in December 1659, the enemy had been consistently identified as that religious extremism which seemed determined to destroy both magistracy and ministry. Both the negative concentration of the attack upon 'annabaptistical and other fanatique spirits' and the complementary desire to establish Protestantism 'in ye pouer and purity thereof' were founded, however, on a conviction that the fundamental threat lay in the repudiation of the traditional values of comprehensiveness, uniformity of both belief and structure, and a dedicated and educated ministry supported by the community.[28] These beliefs underlay the succinct statement in the declaration: though nothing was said about forms of church government, the terms in which the religious settlement was described carried the unmistakable message that its members wished to reintroduce an inclusive established church system admitting of no dissent. The formulation went beyond the discountenancing of the Quakers, Baptists and Sectaries who had featured so largely in the demonology of successive denunciations, and extended to the exclusion of the normative practices of the Independents also. There were different nuances in the aim to have a 'Preaching Ministry of the Gospel'. In the liturgical disputes between Puritan and Arminian, this was a form of words designed to exclude the notion of the ministry as primarily sacerdotal masters of ritual ceremonies. Although these matters bore directly on church discipline rather than on the suppressed question of church gov-

---

[28] The quotation is from the Dublin Declaration of February 16.

ernment, the tone of the declaration plainly pointed towards a preference for precisely the kind of Presbyterianism that the English parliament was, at that very moment, engaged in reenacting.

In seeking the confirmation of possession of forfeited lands the declaration, without comment, separated the interests of the adventurers, who had benefited under the enabling provisions of the act of adventurers of 1642, from those of the officers and soldiers, who could make no claim to due process, let alone parliamentary sanction. The satisfaction of army arrears was also requested, those outstanding from before 5 June 1649 as well as those which had accumulated since, a formulation which protected the interest of all the victims of the tardy administration of the settlement as well as covering current professional grievances.

The text chosen by Coxe to open the proceedings when the Convention assembled in Christ Church on the following day was Jude 19, 'These be they who separate themselves, sensual, having not the Spirit.' The effect, according to the newsbook, was dramatic: 'At the naming of the words presently there fell a kinde of spirit of Prophecie upon all the Auditors, supposing by the very bending of his bow in the text, what the mark was, at present, and partly present, at which he aimed.' His theme was indeed 'the foulest sin of this age, and generation'. 'We are pestered with Anabaptists, Seekers, Quakers, and the like sort of Vipers', he said, 'but they all began in separation', and he urged the Convention to take action against those who set themselves aside, dealing compassionately with those who had been led astray but as roughly as was necessary with the stubborn. If the 'members of this Honourable Convention' were glad to receive his injunction to suppress the sects, there were other aspects of Coxe's presentation that would have pleased some less than others, for it was the abuse rather than the principle of separation that he denounced. He did not deny that it was necessary to separate the godly from the ungodly and believers from unbelievers, and there was no question of the unworthy being allowed promiscuously to take communion, but these were matters for the church to decide. The sin lay in the wilful exercise of private inclination. Still less congenial to some, no doubt, was the nostalgia with which he recalled 'when work of Reformation began to be set on foot among us in these Nations about the year 1640, and the minds of the good people of the lands were much comforted in hopes of unity, and uniformity in the Worship of God in these lands'.²⁹ The tone did not change, for Coxe was followed by Patrick Adair who prayed 'with much ardency of zeal' before making way for Charnock, who spoke chiefly about the universities: 'he seemed to ground on their corruption, an unavoydable danger, that a deluge of error may overwhelme the face of our Nations, especially in these times, where there is more danger threatened by the overflowing of the waters then care taken in the building of an Ark for preservation of common interest'.³⁰ The six-hour session concluded with prayer, led by Baines, who conformed so well to the spirit of what had gone before as to elicit words of ironic praise from the conservatively inclined newsbook: 'in the Pillar of the wildernesse when nothing but the cloud appears he followes his conscience, but when the other face is turned, with light he followes reason'.³¹ The sequel on the following morning was an order that the committee concerned with the maintenance of ministers, whose brief included the question of fitness for office raised by Coxe, should meet on the afternoon of the following Monday, 12 March.³²

The Convention's intentions were rapidly drawn into a coherent policy in a series of interchanges with the maintenance committee chaired by Dudley Loftus. Urgent action against undesirables was implied in a request for recommendations as to which ministers should be allowed to preach in the Dublin area. The earlier agreement to consult ministers from throughout the country was adapted to the purpose of a more general review when the Convention, at the committee's request, authorized it to appoint a panel of advisors made up of two named ministers from each province. Finally, the Convention confirmed that its wish that the ministry should be supported by tithes 'and other legal maintenance in a Parochial way' was a policy rather than an aspiration and should be put into effect 'as soon as might be': once this had been done the existing system of salaries should be ended. Within the week, the committee was

---

²⁹ *Chief occurrences*, in *A Declaration of the General Convention of Ireland*, p. 13. Coxe, *Two sermons*, pp. 31–61.

³⁰ *Chief occurrences*, in *A Declaration of the General Convention of Ireland*, pp. 14–15. His text was Isaiah, 1. 25–6. Payment for his services is recorded in *Ormond MSS*, new series, iii, 386.

³¹ *Chief occurrences*, in *A Declaration of the General Convention of Ireland*, p. 15.

³² Idem.

both ready to begin purifying the ministry and empowered to set about dismantling the Cromwellian arrangements.[33]

The closely related question of university provision also received attention during the second week of the Convention. The matter was referred to three of the Convention's doctors of the University of Dublin, Jones, Loftus and Gorges, who were instructed to review the progress of the plan for the 'late intended New College', to discover the causes of the delay in erecting it, and to recommend a home for Ussher's celebrated library so that the intention of those who had bought and presented it for public use could be fulfilled.[34] The initiative in establishing a second college had been taken by the English parliament in 1650, but despite its endowment with both the earl of Cork's townhouse and Ussher's library it was not until early in 1659 that detailed proposals had been drawn up for a college, modelled on Trinity, and a bill drafted. All three members of the committee had been involved in this business, and the cause of the delay scarcely needed to be ascertained, for it arose from a mixture of unsettled political conditions and the prejudice of the intervening regime: clearly, their task was to bring the project back to life.[35] The rehousing of the library, by contrast, had been a preoccupation of the commissioners: eight days after taking office, Corbet and Steele had appointed a committee to investigate the possibilities and costs, and early in November the commissioners had a comprehensive discussion about the condition of the collection, how it might be 'fitted for public use', the adequacy of its catalogue and, on the prompting of Henry Jones, the possibility of 'publishing some part of the said library or manuscripts'.[36] The inclusion of the library in the committee's terms of reference was designed to reinforce the argument for the new college, whose foundation would rescue it from storage in Dublin Castle.

---

[33] *An account of the chief occurrences of Ireland. Together with some particulars from England. From Monday the 12 of March, to Monday the 19 of March* (Dublin, 1660), pp. 35, 36, 39.

[34] Sir Charles Coote was also a doctor of laws, having been presented by Loftus in his capacity as public professor of the civil laws on the occasion of Henry Cromwell's installation as chancellor. *Mercurius Politicus*, 23–29 August 1655.

[35] Barnard, *Cromwellian Ireland*, pp. 206–12; 'The purchase of Archbishop Ussher's library in 1657', *Long Room*, iv (1971).

[36] Prendergast papers, ii, 471. The commissioners' penultimate order required the attendance of the provost and fellows, presumably to deal with this matter. Egerton MS 212, A/17.

In the old college, the scholars seized the opportunity to present a petition against the provost. Though it seems not to have survived, a sequel some months later indicates that it complained of Winter's 'tyrannicall and arbitrary actings' and of the withholding of rights and privileges. The familiar lineaments of college faction are discernible, but the broader issue of the ecclesiastical aspect of the provostship was inescapable, and Winter's position was no longer tenable. The outcome of the deliberations of the committee which dealt with the matter, 'at the Green Chamber in the Custom-house', was inexorable: Winter was ordered to surrender the college's charter and suspended some two weeks later when he refused to do so.[37]

The need for measures to preserve public order and safeguard the community against the 'common enemy' was given systematic attention on 13 March, when a series of instructions was issued to both civil and military authorities. Care was to be taken to ensure that those who had been transplanted to Connacht stayed there, and that those who had left the province were sent back: 'all dangerous Papists' were to be removed to a distance of 2 miles from cities, garrison towns and forts. An order suppressing unlawful assemblies was set on foot, and directions issued to prevent meetings in the meantime, particularly those of 'Jesuites, Priests, Friars and others'. Miscellaneous as these measures were, they incorporated a clear distinction between the treatment of transplantees, which was remitted to the army, and all other exercises of authority, in which the participation of a civil officer was required. The Convention seems also to have directed its chairman to make representations to England about the inadequacy of the sea guard to keep pirates away from the Irish coast.[38]

The increase in the Convention's work during the second week, which included a lengthy session devoted to compiling the terms of reference of the revenue committee, impeded progress on what may have been intended to be the main business. On the Monday, a committee had been

---

[37] Barnard, 'Trinity at Charles II's restoration in 1660: a loyal address', *Hermathena*, 109 (1969), pp. 44–50.

[38] *An account of the chief occurrences of Ireland*, 12–19 March, pp. 35–6. Barry to Annesley, 20 March 1660, Clarendon MS 70, f. 201. It was later reported that the latter request had been dealt with, and the Commissioners of the Admiralty and navy ordered 'to provide a convenient number of ships for the *Irish* seas'. *Mercurius Politicus*, 29 March–5 April.

appointed 'to consider of matters fit to be represented into England' and ordered to begin work the same afternoon. This involved the preparation of instructions for commissioners who were to be sent to England to present the Convention's declaration and the business had not been concluded by Saturday, 17 March, when Sir Paul Davis, who had been given 'particular care of this affair', reported to the house. Circumstances made the delay politically embarrassing. On the same day, notification was received that on 8 March the council of state had appointed Broghill, Coote, Bury and Clotworthy as commissioners for 'the mannagement of the Affairs of Ireland'.[39] Others were to be sent over to join them in due course, but in the meantime the responsibility belonged to them.[40] The Convention improvised and William Temple was at once deputed to take the declaration to Arthur Annesley, as president of the council of state, with an intimation that 'severall other weightie matters' were under consideration and would be transmitted by other members 'soe instructed as Wee doubt not will render our intentions and Indeavours acceptable unto you in order to the welfare and unitie of theise Nations'.[41]

It is clear that in these early weeks of March there was no communication between Ireland and England. What is not clear is why this was so. Contrary winds were blamed as successive pacquets failed to arrive from Ireland.[42] Writing on 16 March, however, the correspondent of *Mercurius Politicus* in Chester reported confidently that it was policy rather than weather that decreed that 'there be not so free an intercourse with England as heretofore, till they have more fully understood one another at Dublin'. He discounted rumours that the Convention had declared for a king and a free parliament,[43] but warned that Irish support for the

---

[39] *An account of the chief occurrences of Ireland*, 12–19 March, p. 40. Sir Paul Davis subsequently 'gott in' as clerk to the commissioners. Marcus Trevor to Ormond, 7 April 1660, Carte MS 30, f. 559.

[40] *Cal. SP, Ire., 1647–1660*, pp. 862–3.

[41] Barry to Annesley, 19 March 1660, Clarendon MS 70, f. 201.

[42] Morland to Hyde, 16 March 1660, Clarendon MS 70, ff. 166–166v. *Parliamentary Intelligencer*, 5–12 March.

[43] The Scottish agent, Sharp, had reported this rumour on 4 March, adding that he did not believe it. Wodrow's transcript of the 'consultations of the ministers of Edinburgh', Glasgow University Library, MS Gen 210, f. 17. The Venetian ambassador also heard the rumour. *Cal. SP, Ven., 1659–61*, p. 132.

commonwealth was characterized by local concerns: 'as they are Members of the Country of Ireland, which (it seems) some of them would not have so absolutely depending upon England as formerly, and it is believed, they will make Proposals, which will more fully discover their Aims and Intentions'. By the time that this issue was published, on 22 March, news had arrived from Dublin which confirmed that the Convention was indeed sitting, 'after a Parliamentary manner', that it had not declared for Charles, but that 'as members of that nation' they would insist upon 'Parliaments of their own' and satisfaction on certain matters of trade.[44] In fact, an express had arrived in London on 18 March with a copy of the declaration and Samuel Morland, who knew its contents by the following day, was able to say confidently that 'they in Ireland will lett no letters come over'.[45] The delay in the official dispatch of the declaration to England seems to add substance to the suspicion that the Convention did not wish it to reach England ahead of the supplementary statement which Davis's committee was preparing.

The profile of the new commissioners, of whom all but Coote were known Presbyterians, may safely be assumed to have been determined by Annesley. The decision to appoint them was certainly taken in the knowledge that the Convention was in session, for the last news from Ireland was that representatives had met in Dublin 'to consider how to raise monies in an equal manner, for defraying the charge of the public affairs, till order be sent from England to put them into a regular way of Government'.[46] Their authority, a contemporary carefully noted, 'derived from the Council of State which had been appointed by authority of a Parliament of England a little before this'.[47] As the phrasing suggests, though parliament was sitting when the commissioners were appointed, their names were neither submitted for approval nor formally notified to the House. To all intents and purposes, parliament had delegated the conduct of Irish business to the council of state on 2 March when it took note of a number of letters and public dispatches directed to the speaker, which had been brought by Colonel Temple and others. Referring the

---

[44] *Mercurius Politicus*, 15–22 March. The Munster declaration of 18 February came to hand at the same time, and excerpts were published.
[45] Morland to the King, 19 March 1660, Clarendon MS 70, ff. 203v–4.
[46] *Publick Intelligencer*, 27 February–5 March.   [47] Adair, *True narrative*, p. 236.

issues raised to the council, parliament authorised it to act or refer back as it saw fit.⁴⁸ The effect was noted by Lady Mordaunt, who assured Hyde on 9 March that Annesley 'most certainly rules the whole affaires of Ireland'.⁴⁹ The president of the council of state was already briefing her husband, who reported a week later that Annesley had 'taken very kindly' an approach from Ormond, and emphasised his importance: 'I tell your Lordship a Great Truth when I assure you Ireland is steered by this gentleman and that his reputation for parts is great here too.'⁵⁰ Annesley took Irish business to the house on only two occasions. Both of the issues he raised were of long standing, as was his own involvement with the first. On 7 March, he asked that the house should either reduce the taxes assessed on Ireland and Scotland, or authorize the council of state to extend the period of payment, and the house accepted the second of these alternatives five days later.⁵¹ The effect, of course, was to confirm the right to tax Ireland that Annesley's associates in Dublin were now denying. On 15 March, while the House was rushing through its business with the deadline fast approaching, Annesley introduced an act for continuing the terms, processes and proceedings of the courts of justice in Ireland which went through all stages summarily and was passed.⁵² On the same day, a petition was presented by the committee of adventurers, drawing attention to the fact that many of them had not yet received their due and that those who had done so had not been confirmed in their possession. What the adventurers wanted was that this parliament should complete the business it had begun eighteen years before by the passage of the act 'that is before you'. Formally, parliament received the approach favourably and referred the matter to the council to be settled, but the suit was one that only parliament itself could satisfy.⁵³ After the dissolution, the committee persevered, summoning a meeting of adventurers in Grocers Hall on 20 March 'to consider of such things that may tend to their satisfaction and settlement'.⁵⁴

⁴⁸ *CJ*, vii, 860.   ⁴⁹ *Cal. Clarendon SP*, iv, 592. Clarendon MS 70, ff. 118–19.
⁵⁰ Mordaunt to Ormond, 16 March 1660, Carte MS 213, f. 660.
⁵¹ *CJ*, vii, 866, 872.   ⁵² *CJ*, vii, 878.
⁵³ *Cal. SP, Ire., 1647–60*, p. 718. SP, Ire., 63/303. 23. *CJ*, vii, 878. The petition, dated 10 March, suggested that the deficiencies in the available land should be made up from forfeited lands in Louth, Kildare, Carlow and the barony of Imokilly in Cork.
⁵⁴ *Publick Intelligencer*, 12–19 March.

If the absence of news from Ireland did not inhibit Annesley and the parliament, it was extremely frustrating to eager English royalists: already excited by 'the rump being now enlarged to a Gigot', they had noted 'the rout of the rump's party in Ireland'[55] with glee and been enthused by the 'very heigh declaration'[56] which they reckoned 'portends better than it speaks'.[57] When a copy reached him, Hyde concurred with this view: 'though they doe not in termes declare for the King', he wrote on 7 March, 'yet it is evident enough that they believe there is no other way to make them happy'.[58] The considerations in favour of making use of Ireland to advance the king's restoration had been increasing in strength for some time, both because it seemed an effective way of influencing English events and because it was becoming increasingly practical. The news from Dublin confirmed the opportunity, and on 6 March Hyde prepared drafts of two letters for the king's approval, to be taken by Sir Arthur Forbes to Charles and Richard Coote. For Richard, there were assurances of favour. For Charles, there were answers to his invitation and his request, and more besides. He was to proceed with 'this good worke' as he judged best, with the promise 'that as soone as you have declared for me, you shall receave all the supplyes from abroad you can reasonably expect, and if my own presence be necessary I will God willing come to you, except it be more necessary that I go for Englande'. In the meantime, an agent 'enough instructed', would be sent to confer with him. Enclosed were two blank commissions which would sufficiently authorize 'anything that is to be done' until a 'more formal power' could be sent: one left room for the insertion of a number of names, the other space only for one. It was for Coote to decide whether he should use the latter to assume authority himself or incorporate others with him and use the former. Charles was promised an earldom, Richard a barony.[59] The king's letter and commissions to Sir Charles were prepared on the following day.[60] Sir Arthur

[55] *Cal. Clarendon SP*, iv, 572
[56] This description was used by three of Hyde's correspondents in letters written on 24 February – Woods, Massey and Dixon. Clarendon MS 70, ff. 23, 26v, 28v.
[57] Barwick to Hyde, 27 Feb 1660, Clarendon MS 70, f. 48v.
[58] *Clarendon State Papers*, iii, 705. Clarendon MS 70, ff. 160–160v.
[59] Carte, *Ormond*, iii, 6–8. *Cal. Clarendon SP*, iv, 601. Carte MS 30, f. 551. PRO, N.I., H/1/5/1.
[60] Staffordshire County Record Office, D. 1287 (Bradford MSS), P/616. I am grateful to

Forbes was back in Ireland shortly after 24 March, but poor communications remained a problem. On 7 April Mark Trevor, who was unsure whether his letters were reaching Ormond, reported the return of Forbes without comment: on 18 April he did so again, adding that Forbes was anxiously awaiting 'an express promised to be sent after him' and had already written to Ormond twice.[61] Presumably this was the person 'enough instructed to Confer with you upon all particulars' mentioned in the letter to Coote. In Brussels, Hyde was still, as in January, confessing that intelligence from Ireland 'is not what it ought to be'.[62]

The experience of Trevor, who wrote to Ormond from Dublin under an assumed name on 20 March, was a case in point. Trevor, who claimed to be 'engaged herein to most of the considerable persons of this land', represented them as impatiently balanced between confidence and suspicion as they looked forward to the possibility that the king would accept Coote's offer. The constraints were external: 'Much more then is now done heere should have beene executed, but that by advice it was thought fitt to be delayed untill his pleasure was knowne least to much hast heere might have done harme in England.' Nonetheless, everything was ready for the king, who could have either 'a treaty hence' or 'free admission hither', as he pleased, and he would find that 'neither hartes nor handes wilbe wantinge according as he shall direct'. They were both frustrated 'that nothing is put to us, of his will' and becoming fearful that the initiative in approaching him would be taken by men who did not 'intend to serve him, but by their soe sayings would fayn serve and save themselves'.[63] The suspense mounted quickly, and he wrote again four days later with reference to a report that a treaty was being negotiated between the king and the parliament: if that was not what the king really desired, 'then you must send notice, that soe such as affect that waye may be dissuaded from desiring it or procuring it, the other strengthened against it'. If the king wished for 'a General rising', then arms and ammunition would be needed, and 'something from our Master' that could be shown

---

Toby Barnard for helping me to locate this material. The later copy in the Carte MSS, which is certified by Coote, is dated the previous day, 16 March (NS), Carte MS 30, f. 551.

[61] Mark Trevor to Ormonde, 24 March; 7, 18 April 1660, Carte MS 213, f. 676; 30, ff. 559, 573.   [62] Kennett, *Register*, p. 1. *Clarendon State Papers*, iii, 707.

[63] J. Black to Ormond, 20 March 1660, Carte MS 213, f, 669.

to people to gain their support, but 'the mindes of the people are very forward and ready for the major business' and the northern seaports 'are secure for us'.[64] These attempts to secure directions, offer assistance and coordinate action were defeated by logistics. Trevor's first approach had actually been made three months previously, but his messenger had been captured *en route*.[65] His letter of 20 March was delayed in London and did not reach Ormonde until 2 May, while that of 24 March arrived three days later. But direction was lacking also. It was obviously wise for the court to accept that the state of information and communications made it impossible to orchestrate action in Ireland and therefore to delegate decisions, so that it made sense for the king to tell Coote that he would not 'prescribe or advize the methods you are to take for the doing of this good worke, or the steps that you are to make towards it'.[66] But the situation had changed by the time that Coote received his commission and unless he knew whether the king wanted a treaty facilitated or sabotaged, he could not know what course of action to take. The point that had been missed, as Trevor's straying letters made clear, was that effective decisions could be made only on the basis of accurate information about royal policy. Events were moving so quickly, however, that royal policy was largely a matter of improvisation.

Ten days after he drafted the commissions to Coote, Hyde reacted testily to news from London that Villiers had at last sent an express to Broghill, observing that if Broghill 'had that zeale of the king's service, which some of his ffriends think him to have, or that entire confidence in Ned Villiers that hee imagines, sure hee would have sent an Expresse to him in all this time, and not expected one from him'.[67] Villiers himself, however, put the matter in a more subtle light when he explained that the reason why he was reopening his negotiations with Broghill, 'who probably may be of great consideration again', was because 'it's now thought the King is not to be brought in by the sword'.[68] The implication was that

---

[64] Trevor to Ormond, 24 March 1660, Carte MS 213, f. 676.
[65] Black to Ormond, 20 March 1660, Carte MS 213, f. 669.
[66] King to Coote, 7 March 1660, Staffordshire Record Office, D. 1287 (Bradford MSS), P/616.
[67] *Clarendon State Papers*, iii, 707. Hyde to Rumbold, 16 March 1660, Clarendon MS 70, ff. 163–4.
[68] Villiers to Hyde, 2 March 1660, Clarendon MS 70, f. 66.

though Broghill would not fight for the king, he might be persuaded to politick for him. Hyde appears to have taken the point. On 21 March, he drafted a careful letter in which Charles sought graciously 'to break the ice first' with Broghill who, he had heard, was watching an opportunity to express his affection. The message was brief, but plain: Broghill was assured both that the king understood that he had been 'carryed away with that torrent' and attributed no 'malicious purpose' to him and that he would not regret promoting the king's interest.[69] A less guarded letter, modelled on that sent to Coote, was prepared for John King on the same day, promising arms, munitions, and possibly the king's own presence 'if English affairs permitt', and seeking detailed information to assist decision making.[70]

There does seem to have been an opportunist moment during March when Charles and his advisors were tempted by the idea that the smallest tilt might be enough to upset the regime in England and thought that Ireland might provide it. In reality, developments in England had already begun to change the terms of the situation, perhaps more radically than was appreciated in Brussels. With the return of the secluded members, the possibility had arisen that the restoration of the king might be brought about by political means. Although royalist advisors saw the importance of gaining political support, however, they did not see how it could contribute to overcoming the military power of the army and they continued to assume that the issue would be decided by force. Both France and Spain, competitively anxious to benefit from an English restoration, complicated the choices by holding out the possibility of assistance but it was conceivable that reliable aid from Ireland might prove decisive. In London, Mordaunt was confident that 'if there should happen any opposition here they are able to spare 7000 men hither'.[71] The time for contingency planning had clearly come, but only briefly. The need to think in such terms soon passed. A day or two after parliament

---

[69] *Cal. Clarendon SP*, iv, 610 (where the date given is 22 March. Both letters, to Broghill and King, are clearly dated 31 March (NS). Clarendon MS 70, f. 208).

[70] *Cal. Clarendon SP*, iv, 610. The choice of King may have owed something to the information provided by Clancarty from Paris on 9 March that Coote, Theophilus Jones and Jack King 'are the persons that seeme to resume the government and comaunde of that contrey'. Carte MS 213, f. 674.

[71] Mordaunt to Hyde, 21 March 1660, Clarendon MS 70, f. 209v.

ended, Sir John Grenville waited upon his cousin, General Monck, on the king's behalf.

Though he had a commission to treat with Monck, now some eight months old, Grenville's purpose was exploratory, for the royalists were mystified by Monck, and his brief was simply to convey the king's goodwill. The approach proved quite unexpectedly successful. Monck professed to have been 'ever faithful' to Charles and the terms that he laid down were presented as advice rather than as conditions. They amounted to a statement of the minimal concessions that would reconcile the army to the king's return. These were a general pardon, the payment of arrears, the confirmation of titles to former public land and a measure of religious toleration. The concerns of the members of the 'Presbyterian Knot', who had been soliciting Monck's support for their plans to preserve the religious and constitutional provisions that had been negotiated with Charles I at Newport in 1648, were wholly disregarded. There opened up the dramatic prospect of a restoration resting upon the consent of the army and owing nothing to any of the other existing interest groups, including the English royalists. The strategy of those who convened at Breda to convert Monck's counsel into a royal tender for the reinstitution of the monarchy was to shake off all commitments, and they did so by seductively referring each of the issues identified by Monck to the final judgement of parliament, while promising religious toleration in the interim. The declaration, which was signed on 4 April, was not aimed at the electorate and was not published. Grenville was entrusted with five copies, to be delivered to the Houses of Lords and Commons, the army, the fleet and the city of London at the appropriate time. The election returns, which were already coming to hand, left no doubt that the forthcoming Convention parliament would be receptive to restoration, on whatever terms. The 'Presbyterian Knot' laid elaborate plans to seize the initiative and to secure control over parliamentary business. Monck busied himself with the implementation of a scheme to require every officer to give an undertaking to submit to whatever the Convention parliament might decide: at an initial ceremony on 9 April, when selected regiments presented Monck with a model engagement for provincial regiments to copy, the army of Ireland was represented by Colonel Temple. Lambert's escape on the following night raised alarms which were proved unjustified in the event, for the last stand of the anti-monarchical tendency served only to confirm its impotence and he was back in the Tower before the Convention parliament met on 25 April.

By an apt coincidence, on the day after Hyde had expressed his reservations about Broghill, Broghill himself wrote to Thurloe, who had regained his secretaryship under the new government, to try to dispel the rumours that were circulating in England about Irish intentions. They were not, he protested, setting up for themselves, and they did not 'intend to make Ireland a back door to let in Ch Ste into England, and thereby at one blow cut up by the roots the precious rights we have bin soe longe contending for. I profess, Sir, I know nothing further from the thoughts of all my aquaintance and friends; for interest as well as duty will keep us from soe ruinous a wickedness.'[72] These sentiments do not, of course, place Broghill among the opponents of restoration: they locate him with those who had been for the parliament against the king in the civil war and who were not now disposed to overturn its result by an unconditional return to monarchy. Nor does it seem that he was merely maintaining a pretence for Thurloe's benefit, for he was already seeking allies in Scotland in concert with Presbyterians in Ulster. On 12 March, he made an approach to Robert Douglas and a number of other prominent members of the Edinburgh presbytery associated with the loyalist 'Resolutioner' group with whom he had negotiated during his time as president of the Scottish council.[73] Claiming to write on behalf of 'the chief persons in this Nation, both civill and military', he spoke of 'a door of hope opened for such a just and full settlement, as may through mercy establish these poore Nations, upon foundations of righteousness and peace', and asked that either James Sharp or James Wood should be sent to him in Dublin.[74] On the same day, Colonel John Gorges, in his capacity as 'Governor of Ulster' and speaking for 'the wise and godly' of the province, 'being the most considerable

---

[72] *TSP*, vii, 859.
[73] Julia Buckroyd, *The life of James Sharp, Archbishop of St Andrews, 1618–1679* (Edinburgh, 1987), pp. 33–5.
[74] Wodrow's transcripts, Glasgow University Library, MS Gen 210, ff. 39–40.

interest of the Protestants in Ireland', wrote to Douglas to express his concern that 'we may be divided in no thing, but that the great ends of our Covenant may be persued with ane unanimous consent', and sent over a Mr Kennedy (probably Anthony, the minister at Templepatrick) to establish contact.[75] John Gregg, minister of Newtownards, acting in the name of 'severall of the Brethern', contributed a letter of introduction commending Gorges, both as one who had played an important role in the making of the February Declaration and as one whose words and actions evinced his commitment to the covenant.[76]

Douglas and his brethern dealt courteously with the approach from Ulster and took immediate action on Broghill's proposal.[77] James Sharp was their emissary in London and they wrote to him at once, enclosing a letter to Monck in which they not only sought his approval for Sharp to go to Dublin, but suggested that it might be 'for good purpose' if he were to act as a link between Monck and Broghill 'in all things conduceing to the good of Religion'.[78] Against the contingency that Sharp might be unable to make the journey, they sent his brother to London to be ready to act as substitute.[79] Their enthusiasm was stifled by a report from Sharp, which crossed their letters in the post, explaining that his difficulty in lobbying against the appointment of English commissioners to assume authority in Scotland was that Monck feared that 'we may play such a game as Ireland hath done'.[80] The Edinburgh ministers were taken aback by this 'new started exception'. They assumed that it arose from the Irish demand for a separate parliament, and left it to Sharp to decide whether the proposal should be brought to Monck's attention or set aside.[81] Sharp chose to procrastinate. He was already convinced that a restoration of the king 'on Covenant terms' was impracticable, and his deeply pessimistic reports to Scotland were designed to prepare his brethern for the disappointment of

---

[75] GUL MS Gen 210, ff. 40–1. W. Wodrow, *The history of the sufferings of the Church of Scotland from the restoration to the revolution* (Glasgow, 1829–30), i, p. xiv.

[76] GUL MS Gen 210, ff. 41–2. Gregg's influence was attested by Colonel Cooper who remarked in 1657 that the English in Carrickfergus 'have to much a Scotch spirit by reason of mr Gregg's being formerly their minister'. *TSP*, vi, 349.

[77] GUL MS Gen 210, ff. 47–9.   [78] GUL MS Gen 210, ff. 42–5.

[79] GUL MS Gen 210, f. 45.

[80] GUL MS Gen 210, f. 51.

[81] GUL MS Gen 210, ff. 49–50.

their ambitions.⁸² Although he wrote to Broghill about 12 April, presumably in the same despondent terms, it was not until a week or so later that he 'gave the generall as, an ingenuous, so a full account' of the matter and Monck declared himself 'fully satisfied'.⁸³

The Presbyterian network was not the only one that Broghill was exploring. One of Trevor's worries when he wrote on 24 March was that his prophecy that self-seeking approaches would be made to the king had been fulfilled, and he reported that Broghill and Coote 'are in show very well and pretend great kindness to our Master and fayne would nowe owne him and welcome him to which purpose a dispatch goes at this tyme from hence'.⁸⁴ In all likelihood this was the dispatch quoted by Broghill nine years later when he was facing charges of treason in the English House of Lords. The accusations against him included an allegation that he had threatened 'that if the King did not confirm the estates of a party, at that time headed by the said earl, that his Majesty would be compelled to do it, with 50000 swords'. Broghill's reply was largely legalistic in character: he argued that since there was no indication of when this had happened, no specification of which act of treason was applicable and no suggestion that any action had followed, there was no case to answer. Moreover, perhaps disingenuously, he took the allegation to refer to the period after the king's restoration. In the course of his defence, however, he claimed that towards the latter end of February he had combined with what he revealingly described as seven other army officers (though they included Henry Jones as well as Charles and Richard Coote, Theophilus Jones, Arthur Hill, John King and William Warden) to write to Charles in these terms: 'If yore Matie on this humble invitation will be pleased to honor your Protestant Subjects of Ireland by coming into this yore Kingdome, wee solemnly engage ourselves as wee are Chrystians and Gent[lemen] to serve you with our lives and estates against all opposition, and by God's blessing, with the hazard of both to restore

---

⁸² Buckroyd, *Life of James Sharp*, pp. 46–54. Ian Green, *The re-establishment of the Church of England, 1660–1663* (Oxford, 1978), pp. 14–15.

⁸³ GUL MS Gen 210, ff. 82, 89. The account of this episode given in the introduction to Wodrow, *Sufferings of the Church of Scotland*, is incomplete and misleading. Buckroyd, *Life of James Sharp*, p. 133, n. 4.

⁸⁴ Carte MS 213, f. 276.

you to yore Kingdomes...'⁸⁵ Since four of those named by Broghill were still alive and active in 1669, the episode is unlikely to have been an invention.⁸⁶ The timing, however, is more than doubtful since the king and his advisors were certainly unaware of any overture on Broghill's part by 22 March. Some confirmation of both the address and the later date was provided by Villiers, whose informant on Irish matters was Broghill's brother Francis. On 13 April, ten days after Francis had crossed from Ireland, Villiers told Hyde that he believed that Broghill had now made an approach 'by the expresse out of Ireland'.⁸⁷

Francis Boyle had been preceded to England some days earlier by Jeremy Taylor, who had travelled from the north of Ireland by way of Dublin with Arthur Hill's son William, bearing an important message which he conveyed to the royalist agent Dr Morley.⁸⁸ Taylor shared the view of those who believed that the desire of the members 'that sate in 48' to use the Newport propositions as a basis for a settlement 'and all other unworthy dealing with the King' should be frustrated, and he was authorized to offer Irish force to achieve this. He asserted that, though Broghill and Coote were 'greater in name', the real control of the army was in the hands of Arthur Hill, Theophilus Jones 'and his brother the bishop' and that these three had 'given him order' to tell the king that there were in Ireland ten regiments of foot, five of horse and one of dragoons, that they could raise as many more, 'and will be all ready upon the King's command to declare for him if there be cause for it'. He particularly commended 'of the King's Party', Montgomery, Trevor and King, and asked for directions 'for the management of this affayre with as much speed as may be'.⁸⁹ By the time that Morley transmitted this message to Brussels, on 18 April, circumstances had changed.

In Ireland, the commissioners took over in late March and the indications are that they did not defer to the Convention, but 'ordinarily sat and acted for themselves'.⁹⁰ In religious matters their authority certainly replaced that of the Convention, as being 'more seemingly legal', and it

---

⁸⁵ *Cal.SP, Ire., 1669–70*, pp. 46–7. SP, Ire., 63/326. 67. Howell, *State trials*, vi, 914.
⁸⁶ Charles Coote, Hill and Warden had died.
⁸⁷ Clarendon MS 71, f. 253v.   ⁸⁸ SP, Ire., 63/303. 24, 25.
⁸⁹ *Cal. Clarendon SP*, iv, 664. Morley to Hyde, 18 April 1660, Clarendon MS 71, ff. 295–6.
⁹⁰ Adair, *True narrative*, p. 246.

was they who issued the instructions that implemented the decisions that were made.[91] Presumably they likewise took charge of policing matters, on land and sea, and other executive tasks. The Convention occupied itself with completing arrangements to send commissioners to England.[92] The instructions prepared for them by Davis's committee, which were adopted by the Convention on 30 March, ranged more widely and entered into more detail than the declaration had done, except in the matter of religion, which was dealt with first and in almost identical language.[93] There were some very specific elaborations of the request for the confirmation of the estates received by adventurers, officers and soldiers. Among the adventurers, the lands granted to Henry Whalley and Erasmus Smith in Connacht in place of their original grants in the Ards peninsular were singled out, as were lands 'graunted ordered Voated or set out' to Broghill, Sir Charles Coote, Henry Jones and his deceased brother Michael, 'as A spetiall marke of favour for the Eminent and exterordinary merritts and services performed', and also lands granted to the children of the elder Sir Charles Coote in memory of his services. Returning to a point made in the instructions given almost a year earlier to Bury, Jones and Lawrence, the agents were required to seek the confirmation of the transplantation of the Irish into Connacht and Clare, of decrees granted to them and of dispositions of land made by them: the object of course was to protect the interest of those who had purchased land in the province from them. The case of those who had yet to receive their due for services rendered before June 1649 was emotionally stated: they were for the most part those 'that in the beginning of the Rebellion stood in the gapp with the hassard of their Lives and Estates for maintenance of the English Interest in Ireland and whereon many of them lost their Lives and all of them Dured many hardshipps', and the agents were to move for their satisfaction. The concerns of a very different group were also urged. It comprised those Catholic residents of Cork, Youghal and Kinsale who had played no part in the rebellion and who, though required to move to Connacht, had refused to do so for fear of reprisal. Their case had already been sympathetically considered and land had been set apart for them in the baronies of Muskerry and Barrymore in Cork, but the decrees which they had

[91] Ibid., p. 236.   [92] *Cal. SP, Ire., 1647–1660*, p. 719.   [93] BL, Add MS 32,471, f. 82v.

obtained had not been made good.⁹⁴ It was requested that they should be exempted from transplantation and that the undertakings given to them should be honoured.

The work of the Convention's revenue committee⁹⁵ underlay a number of the representations that were to be made, beginning with the general demand that the management of the affairs of state should cost no more than it had in 1640 and ending with the basic principle that no public charges should be levied on Ireland 'but by Authority of this Convention untill A Parliament may be legally called and held in Ireland'. That principle was already being acted upon. On the previous day, the Convention had formed itself into a grand committee to consider the report of the committee on revenue, with particular reference to the conundrum of finding a less burdensome way of raising money than the method used in the assessment.⁹⁶ The agents were to present a full account of income and expenditure for the year ending 25 December 1659, showing that, even with the monthly assessment, the money available fell 'farr short of Answering that Publique Charge'. They were also to produce the figures of the deputy treasurer for wars which showed that over the previous four and a half years the army had fallen into arrears of fifteen months and eleven days pay, and that this was 'altogether occasioned by want of the expected supplies out of England'. They were to demand both that the historic shortfall should be made good and that the current deficit should be funded by supply from England.⁹⁷ They were also to protest against the management of the customs farm, where the yield allegedly fell short of the rent and the farmers demanded abatements: doubt was cast on the farmers' claim that their contract continued until 24 June, and the agents

---

⁹⁴ *Acts and ordinances*, ii, 1260.

⁹⁵ Its brief was to recommend ways of reducing expenditure, increasing revenue, devising less burdensome means of raising it, and recovering arrears; to examine and report upon the accounts of all officers who handled public money and to recommend means of dealing with recalcitrant officials and debtors; and to consider generally what was 'necessary for the well mannaging of the publick Revenue'. *An account of the chief occurrences of Ireland*, 12–19 March, p. 34.

⁹⁶ *Cal. SP, Ire., 1647–1660*, p. 719.

⁹⁷ Accounts presented to the English parliament dealing with the period 25 February–15 May 1660 record the transmission of £20,000 to Ireland 'to pay the supernumaries above what is intended to be kept up in the Establishment'. *CJ*, viii, 30.

were to move that the negotiation of the contract and the 'regulating' of the book of rates 'may be left to this Convention'. The outcome, it was confidently asserted, would be that the full rent would be secured 'with less pressure to the people'.

Other demands suggest the probability of extensive work by a committee concerned with the administration of justice, and reveal a high level of dissatisfaction with recent practice. It was insisted that the governors, whether in the form of councillors or commissioners, should 'containe themselves within their proper bounds in managing affaires of state and not interposing matters Cognizable in the ordinary Courts of Justice': moreover, the three chief justices should be members of whichever form of government was established, whether council or commission. The courts of upper bench, common pleas and exchequer should, as formerly, each have three judges, adequately rewarded and 'of eminent knowledge and learning in the lawes of this land'. Chancery should also have three, so that matters of equity 'may not lye onely in the breast of one Judge', and the allowance paid to masters in chancery should be increased. To prevent this leading to an increase in charges, the chief baron and the two chief justices of the benches should be made custodians of the great seal with the former lord chancellor's fee and a share of the profits. The exchequer was to stop depriving people of the right to trial by jury by acting in cases where there was a common law remedy, as Corbet was alleged to have done. In addition, the presidency courts of Munster and Connacht were to be re-established, as was the former provincial structure of vice-admiralty courts, and probate courts were to be established in each province and required to hold at least four sessions each year in every county.[98]

The instructions approved, it remained not only to choose commissioners but also to decide to whom they should address themselves. According to a later, self-seeking account by Jerome Alexander, who was concerned to show that he had not 'been the least instrumentall in his

---

[98] The Munster presidency court had been revived in 1649 and operated until 1655 despite the absence of a lord president after Ireton's death in 1651. In Connacht the lord presidency had been continued, and Coote's appointment was confirmed in 1655, but neither the presidency court nor the council functioned in the 1650s. Barnard, *Cromwellian Ireland*, pp. 271–2.

Majesties happy return', he had taken his seat in the Convention on this very day and at once opposed the motion that the instructions should be directed to the lord president and council in England, on the principle 'that by the law of this land all our applications ought to bee to the kinge and his counsell in England'. He was opposed by 'they of the upper forme, cryinge me downe, as fast as one could speak after an other', and accusing him of seeking to 'devide the kingdomes', but 'those of the lower forme cryd upp with me'. The motion was deferred, but subsequently carried.[99] The delay was certainly brief. The chosen agents, Sir John Clotworthy and Major William Aston, passed through Chester on 3 April, accompanied by Francis Boyle.[100] The evidence does suggest that the question of to whom they were to present themselves had given rise to difficulty, but the problem was quite different from the matter of obedience to the king which Alexander claimed to have raised. In the event, they were commissioned to deal with the parliament or with the council of state, or with both, a remit which reflected some uncertainty as to whether parliament would dissolve as planned: it was known that petitions had been presented urging that the present parliament 'should rather continue to settle the Nation, than a new one be called' and informed rumour suggested that this view was likely to prevail. The same source reported optimistically on the favourable view taken in England of Irish proceedings. It was not only 'supposed that the Authority in England will not deny Ireland its former privileges of Parliament and taxing themselves', but suggested that Ireland would receive a subvention of £8,000 a month.[101] In fact, the rumours had been too sanguine. What influential English opinion had approved was the action taken in February.

A few days after news of the Convention's activities reached London, a royalist spy reported that lists of officers had been sent from Ireland for approval and conjectured that 'their designe is to bring Ireland into the

---

[99] Alexander to Sir Edward Massey, post October 1661, Barwick MSS, No. 3. Alexander also claimed to have advised the December conspirators 'to declare for a free parliament, which I knew could not be without the kinge' and to have advised Coote 'to call a convention and soe to engage all the kingdome in the businesse for a free parliament'.

[100] *Parliamentary Intelligencer*, 2–6 April. There were those who thought that Shannon was one of the commissioners. Heath, *Chronicle*, p. 440. Lansdowne MS 692, f. 22.

[101] *Cal. SP, Ire., 1647–1660*, p. 719. *An account of the chief occurrences of Ireland*, 12–19 March, p. 40.

same posture as before 49'.[102] By the end of the month another correspondent was including in his enthusiastic round-up of good news the fact that in Ireland 'they play Rex' and had imprisoned Justice Cook and some others.[103] On 6 April, no longer enthusing, he reported that the council of state had sent express orders to Dublin that the Convention should cease,[104] and had ordered that Cook and other prisoners should be sent to England: 'Itt is a peece of unwellcome newes', he concluded. The context in which he placed this intelligence had three distinct elements. The first was a speech delivered in the Convention by Broghill, who was alleged to have said 'that rather then Ireland should bee the least Mote in the Ey of England hee would loose his right hand, but rather then England should be a beame in the ey of Ireland he would loose his head'. The second was the fact that Sir Charles Coote 'hath lost the good esteeme wee had of him, and is, itt is beleived rather inclinable to the phanatick party'. The third was that the Presbyterians in England, who aimed at 'bringing the King in upon conditions', were sobered by the news from Ireland, where it was thought that the Convention proposed to cast themselves at the king's feet.[105] Less than two weeks previously, Dr Barwick, whose sources of information were good (though perhaps not as good as those of the Scottish agent, James Sharp)[106] had confided to Hyde that his opinion of Irish developments was 'that the whole designe was managed with Monkes good liking and that he is willing enough they should goe a little before him to make his worke the more easy'.[107] Now he reported that Monck 'seemes much displeased at the busines of Ireland but how real he is in it I know not. A little time more will discover much.'[108] The account of its affairs that Monck received from the Convention's commissioners on 9 April may have eased

---

[102] *Cal. Clarendon SP*, iv, 617. Morland to Hyde, 23 March 1660, Clarendon MS 71, f. 34. News that the lists had been approved reached Ireland before 25 April. *Leyborne-Popham MSS*, p. 179.

[103] *Cal. Clarendon SP*, iv, 628. Ludlow's reading was that Coote seized Cook 'to make some amends to his sacred Majesty by that sacrifice'. *Memoirs*, ii, 240.

[104] A rumour that this was intended had been conveyed by Morland to Hyde on 23 March, Clarendon MS 71, f. 34.

[105] Miles Barton to Hyde, 6 April 1660, Clarendon MS 71, f. 156.   [106] See p. 264 above.

[107] 30 March 1660, Clarendon MS 71, ff. 108–10.

[108] Barwick to Hyde, 10 April 1660, Clarendon MS 71, f. 280v. The calendared version of these remarks is misleading. *Cal. Clarendon SP*, iv, 629, 647,

his mind about the game that was being played in Dublin.[109] The indications are that his immediate priority in Ireland was the propitiation of Broghill. On 25 April 1660, an encoded correspondent reported to Thurloe that the news of Broghill being made lord president of Munster had been celebrated with bonfires and volleys in Cork.[110]

What influenced the council of state in demanding that the Convention be forborne does not directly appear and beyond the fact that the order had reached Dublin by 7 April the timing is uncertain. The simplest explanation is that the gathering had been a source of unease in England from the time it had been summoned and it must have seemed all the more improper for it to remain in being once parliament itself had referred the issue to the electorate and dissolved. But the continuation of the Convention as a coordinating medium for an independent Irish political response was also sinister. The prospect of a local initiative, whether to welcome the king unreservedly or to seek terms, was a disturbing one. The arrest of Cook, a justice of the upper bench, had alarming implications, for Cook had been the king's chief prosecutor: he was not technically a regicide, but the possibility that the Irish leaders were preemptively moving towards the punishment of those who had killed the king was alarming to a council of state which was set upon dictating terms. Immediately upon hearing the news in early April the council demanded that Cook and the other prisoners, who included the regicide John Jones and the king's gaoler Matthew Thomlinson, should be sent to London.[111] Ludlow may not have been alone in concluding that the intention in Ireland had been that Cook should be sacrificed 'to make some amends to his sacred Majesty'.[112]

---

[109] *An exact accompt of the public transactions of the three nations, with occurrences from foreign parts*, 6–13 April.   [110] *TSP*, vii, 909.

[111] *Cal. Clarendon SP*, iv, 639. Cook was not sent over until 19 May, after a second demand. Ludlow, *Memoirs*, ii, 269, 271.

[112] *Memoirs*, ii, 240. In describing the arrests of the regicides in England later, Ludlow described Coote as 'having opened the bloody scene by the seizure of' Cook, ibid., ii, 268. There may have been a hint of the same concern two weeks previously when the council of state wrote to Broghill, Coote and Jones (presumably as the remaining members of the army committee) to demand an explanation of Waller's confinement in Athlone without just cause and contrary to law (*Cal. SP, Dom, 1659–60*, p. 398), though Ludlow's belief that this was instigated by his cousin, Sir William Waller, is plausible (*Memoirs*, ii, 239). Waller was released on condition that he reported to the council of state in London, which he did on 28 April (*Parliamentary Intelligencer*, 30 Apr –7 May).

Irish extremists did not draw hope to match these fears from the policy of those in authority in Dublin which Trevor believed to be based on the premise that the best way of reaching a speedy settlement was to 'keepe all things upon a very slow motion'.[113] The point was perhaps confirmed from an opposing direction by Dean Nicholas Bernard who was involved in negotiations in London aimed at reconciling religious differences through the promotion of a scheme of moderate episcopacy, and who secretly warned Ormond that 'there are some here who out of an over early zeale do as much put back the service, as others in moderate wayes are advancing it'.[114] Writing to Ormond on 7 April, Trevor claimed that he and Lord Cromwell 'have perpetually beene spurringe these fellowes to doe, what they have done'. Although he was deeply sceptical of the approach that was being adopted, he did not feel free to reject it: he and others, 'not knowing of any command from our Mr what else to do', were prepared to 'see them goe on in this way they are in'. He concluded optimistically by assuring Ormond that the Convention was defying the order to dissolve and 'still proceed in asserting their liberty and non-dependance on Engl. in short, they are all ready for a right impression'.[115] It seems probable that a set of proposals received by Ormond on 17 April originated with Trevor or Cromwell. This was concerned to establish that if a treaty were to be agreed between 'E[ngland]' and the king, 'then we desire the affairs of the Church may be left to a free Parliament in I[reland]': if it were not, then an invasion force of 10,000 foot and 4,000 horse was offered to the king, 'Or if he please he wilbe welcome heere.' If no treaty was agreed, the king should 'make good, the Act of Attainder, Acte of Settlement, Act of Transplantation, all grauntts made by Parlam & Protectors, Protestant estates excepted. That Wynns I[reland].'[116] Trevor

---

[113] Trevor to Ormond, 7 April 1660, Carte MS 30, f. 559.

[114] J. Spurr, *The restoration of the Church of England, 1646–1689* (New Haven, 1991), pp. 31, 143. Green, *The re-establishment of the Church of England*, pp. 13–15. Carte MS 30, f. 580. As early as 2 March, one of Hyde's correspondents had been worried that Ireland 'outgoes Our pace ... but we hope that when they hear of our compliance with them in the mayne matter, which is including the Secluded Members, that they will keep pace with us in the rest'. Cooper to Hyde, Clarendon MS 70, f. 77v.

[115] Carte MS 30, f. 559.

[116] Carte MS 30, f. 564. The endorsement reads 'Phil Carpenters note for CK': there is evidence of Carpenter acting as a go-between for Ormond with Ireland. I take these

[273]

remained confident that force was on the king's side, 'the militia being put into good hands and well armed, the army are right set for the most part'. But on 18 April he warned Ormond that the prerequisite was an assurance 'of pardon and enjoyment of estates, which is the only thing the most perverse of them all barck at'.[117] In a second, conspiratorial letter written under a pseudonym on the same day, he told Ormond 'I think they are tracking of you there very closely although [I] am confident they will not drive as furiously as might be expected with out possitive order from our Master or directions how affairs shalbe manadged for his service.' The endorsement on that letter is yet another eloquent testimony to the impediments to conspiracy: 'Coll Trevor by Coll Cromwell. Dat: 18 Apr. 1660. Opened by my Lord at Bruxelles. 22 May 1660.'[118]

So far as there were difficulties and tensions within the army in Ireland, they came from a very different direction to the one represented by Mark Trevor. In early April, Colonel Edward Warren, Captain Thompson and Captain Shaw were arrested on charges of 'tampering with the soldiers' and seeking to alienate their affections from their officers 'by forging scandalous and malicious reports'. The substance of these was that some of the officers had designs 'to divide from England'. To counteract them, the officers adopted a declaration on 13 April in which they repeated emphatically what they had already 'asserted to all the World' and engaged 'to acquiesce cheerfully in what the present Council of State, or the Parliament of England, or those deriving authority from them or either of them shall determine, in order to a well-grounded peace and general settlement of these Nations'.[119] The fifty-six men who 'gleefully subscribed' this statement included fourteen members of the Convention, among them all three acting members of the commission for government,

---

recommendations to be the 'bills' insistently but obliquely referred to in Trevor's pseudonymous letter of 18 April. Ibid., f. 571. If dragoons are counted as horse, the proposed force corresponds with the information given by Jeremy Taylor to Morley.

[117] Carte MS 30, f. 573.

[118] T. Black [M.Trevor] to Ormond, 18 April 1660, Carte MS 30, f. 571. Vere Cromwell was in Brussels in April and presumably did not receive the letter until his return to London. Mayart to Ormond, 20 April 1660, Carte MS 30, f. 577.

[119] *Parliamentary Intelligencer*, 16–23 April. The text had been published, without report or signatures, on 20 April. *An exact account*, 13–20 April.

for Sir William Bury subscribed, as did Henry Jones.[120] The declaration was circulated to local forces for their endorsement, to the particular satisfaction of Colonel Gorges whose concern was with the 'work of Reformation' and who declared himself content 'whilst England steers us', disapproved of developments in Dublin and distanced himself not only from 'their' Convention but from 'their' army.[121]

That there were divisions within the leadership in Ireland is well attested. From their very different points of view, the Presbyterian minister Patrick Adair and Trevor attributed them to the same cause, rivalry between Broghill and Coote. Writing after the event, Adair traced a simple process by which both men, seeking to ingratiate themselves because they feared the king's displeasure as 'great compliers with the times before', 'resolved to prevent one another by offering the King, though then abroad, all conditions on his return that he could require'.[122] By then, Broghill had long since become a redoubtable supporter of episcopacy but Adair, whose local secular hero was Sir John Clotworthy and who spoke well of Bury, gave no hint of Broghill's earlier position though he must have known of it. On the contrary, the story that he told was that Clotworthy had managed to persuade Coote and Broghill to reconcile their differences and 'to send one for them both to the King, with conditions for Ireland as well as for England on his Restoration. And they both pitched upon Sir John to go on this negotiation. He accordingly went as far as London in his way to Holland; but Monck's actings prevented his further journey.'[123] Clotworthy's movements are consistent with this story, though they do not confirm it: he was in Dublin on 10 March, reported to be in London on 17 March, but back in Ireland again in time to accompany Aston to London as an agent at the beginning of April.[124] In short, he may well have made an abortive expedition, been sent back to assume his place as a member of the newly appointed government commission and recovered his position by having himself

---

[120] The other Convention members were Broghill, Burrell, Sir Charles, Chidley, Richard and Thomas Coote, Thomas Caulfield, Thomas Long, Oliver St George, John King, William King and Theo Jones. A third Jones brother, Oliver, also signed. The description is Coote's, *Leyborne Popham MSS*, p. 179.

[121] GUL MS Gen 210, ff. 98–9. [122] Adair, *True narrative*, p. 232. [123] Ibid.

[124] He was one of the committee appointed to thank the chaplains for their conduct of the fast. Coxe, *Two sermons*.

[275]

appointed as a Convention agent. It is conceivable that his mission supplied the basis of the rumour that Coote had gone over to the 'fanatic party'. Writing to Ormond on 18 April, Trevor likewise described Broghill and Coote as 'not a little jealous of each others actings', but came to the somewhat different conclusion that they were nonetheless at one in awaiting English events: he thought Coote 'much firmer' for the king's interest and believed that 'if any clash happens Lord Broghill will countenance such as are most opposite to the business'.[125]

The accuracy of Trevor's judgement, and the simplistic nature of Adair's, may be inferred from Broghill's report to Thurloe on 24 April of 'odd plots here concerning the King'. The context was provided by his anxiety lest the 'Cavaleir Party' should dominate the English Convention: if that were to be so, 'God only knows what will be the evils', he wrote, finding some consolation in the fact that the lords, 'I mean of 48, do resolve to sit'.[126] That sentiment indicates that Broghill was still with those who were working towards a conditional restoration, for the reinstatement of the House of Lords as it had been constituted in 1648 was a part of the strategy of the 'Presbyterian Knot'. He had already welcomed the move in lavish terms in correspondence with the speaker of the house, the earl of Manchester: 'We would freely have ventured our all to have restored them, and shall as freely venture it to serve and preserve them', he wrote on 2 April.[127] His associations speak even more plainly. It was one of the leaders of the 'Presbyterian Knot', his wife's brother-in-law, the earl of Northumberland, who found him a seat in the forthcoming English Convention for Arundel.[128] Against this background, Broghill's assurance to Thurloe that Munster, most of Ulster and some of Leinster were secure 'against any, that shall be for the King or not for the council of state or parliament', and that the army was 'for the most part fixed, I mean for council of state or parliament', was not disingenuous. Broghill was not

---

[125] Carte MS 30, f. 573. Alexander shared the suspicion of Broghill: 'what his purpose and intente were I know not (but have a shrewd guess) but Coote and he could not well agree uppon the reckoninge'. Alexander to Sir Edward Massey, post-October 1661, Barwick MSS, No. 3.

[126] TSP, vii, 908.

[127] William Drogo Montague, duke of Manchester, *Court and society from Elizabeth to Anne* (London, 1864), i, 396–7.

[128] *History of parliament. The house of Commons, 1660–1690*, i, 702.

pretending to be against a restoration, but aiming to prevent one dictated by royalists. The conspicuous omission of Connacht from his list of secure areas indicates where the danger lay in Ireland, and the implication was reinforced by his confidence that he and Bury 'walke together'.[129] His coolness was a source of embarrassment to Ned Villiers, who was already beginning to distance himself from Broghill on 13 April, when he implied that he had been misled by Francis Boyle whom he had taken 'to be of more solidity than he is'.[130] By 1 May, his reservations about Broghill had become explicit: he wished for 'greater demonstration of his particular affection' and protested that in the 'Feudes' between Broghill and Coote 'I shall be on his side who is most for the King Knowing noe Relation or ffriendship equivalent to that.'[131]

The nature of Anglo-Irish political dynamics, as they were explained to Ormond after the event by Francis, Lord Aungier, perhaps sufficiently explains why Coote's trump card, the king's commission, remained unused. Aungier had succeeded in his bid to represent Surrey as an unconcealed royalist in the English Convention when he first made contact with Ormond in April.[132] If 'Sir Charles Coote and his interest' had not been 'advised the contrary from time to time' by English royalists, he wrote in May

> They had out-runne this Kingdome, in declaring for his Majesty. But we considered here the Humor of the Presbyterian interest, And that if those in Ireland had declared before we had wound up these peevish other unto those ends at which we aymed we might by too much haste (when Lambert was in motion) have beene in danger of to have lost that greate and formidable Party which by stroaking we have joyned, & well cemented to his Majesties interests.

Aungier was in no doubt that the strategy had been successful, and that Ireland 'was no small spurre unto the slowe and heavye paced Presbyters, who therefore hastened to our wisht for End, least they should see themselves cast behind, & in the Reare of Ireland'.[133] According to Forbes,

---

[129] *TSP*, vii, 908. [130] Villiers to Hyde, Clarendon MS 71, ff. 253v–4.
[131] Villiers to Hyde, 1 May 1660, Clarendon MS 72, f. 121.
[132] Aungier to Ormond, 17 April 1660, Carte MS 214, f. 48.
[133] Aungier to Ormond, 11 May 1660, Carte MS 30, f. 657.

however, the commission was brought briefly into play. After making no use of it for some time, he claimed, Coote heard that 'the King's restauration had been retarded, and conditions likely to be put upon his Majesty'. He thereupon filled one of the commissions and ordered Forbes to take charge of Ulster, 'resolving immediately to declare for the King', but 'the next pacquet from England bringing better hopes of the King's affairs there, he suppressed it again'.[134] After the restoration Coote listed those to whom he had made promises on the basis of the king's assurances from Brussels as his brothers Richard and Chidley, Sir John King, Oliver St George, Sir John Cole, Dr Henry Jones and Sir James Shaen: Forbes was not mentioned.[135]

The Convention was concerning itself with money and religion. As to the latter, it was evident from the outset that its collective position was a conservative one in the sense that it was committed to a parochial, tithe-supported inclusive church without provision for derogation and dissent. Neither the officers nor the Convention had expressed any view on the question of church government in their respective declarations, nor should the choice of Presbyterian chaplains be taken as indicating more than a preference for the most conservative option available in the circumstances. In broad terms, the competing possibilities were Presbyterianism or the restoration of episcopacy, but the clarity of the choice was obscured in a number of ways. Most beguilingly, the two were not necessarily incompatible: the revered Archbishop Ussher himself had argued in favour of a middle way and the notion of a 'limited episcopacy' was being actively canvassed in England. Most obviously, there was more than one version of Presbyterianism. The Scottish model verged on theocracy: by contrast, its English rival, which had been enacted by the Long Parliament in the 1640s and was now in the course of reenactment, had been famously condemned by Robert Baillie as a 'lame erastian presbytery'. Most fundamentally, those who regarded the organizational form of the church as divinely ordained denied the possibility of choice. This was the position of the Scottish Presbyterians in Ulster[136] and of some members of the formerly established church. For those who took the view that church forms were of human contrivance, it was possible to

[134] PRO, NI, H/1/5/1.   [135] Cal. SP, Ire., 1660–2, pp. 243, 463.
[136] Adair, True narrative, p. 248.

subordinate preference to the achievement of higher priorities. However distasteful the English variety of Presbyterianism might be, it had the virtue of preserving the prime conservative values of order and uniformity, and there was nothing in principle to prevent many Episcopalians settling for it as second best, if only in the short term. Realistically, indeed, there was no other prudent choice at first, because the political advantage was plainly on the Presbyterian side. There seems little doubt that the members of the Convention were 'most part prelatical', but as a matter of preference rather than of principle, and Adair was probably right in thinking that they held back while there was a possibility that Charles, who had taken the Covenant in 1650, 'would own that side'.[137] A more alarming possibility was that his enemies were right in alleging that he was a Catholic. Before Colonel Bridges returned to Ireland towards the end of March, he arranged to meet Edward Massey, formerly major-general of the army of the Western Association but for some years a royalist activist, whom he wished 'to satisfy him concerning the King, to clear those aspersions cast upon his Majesty'.[138] The aspersions were no doubt the rumours of Charles's inclination to Catholicism but, since Bridges was an Independent and Massey a Presbyterian, the assurances sought are likely to have gone further than a denial of the king's papistry.

The first exploratory steps were denominationally neutral to the extent that both Episcopalians and Presbyterians of either variety could endorse the Convention's objectives with conviction. Outside Ulster, moreover, there was a good deal of common ground between Presbyterians and the more moderate Independents. Men who believed, as the Independents did, 'that ecclesiastical constitutions are alterable and changeable and not to be accounted equal to the Word of God',[139] could reasonably resist conformity, but were logically disposed towards some kind of accommodation. Thus the Convention's declaration, though it rejected congregational organization, did not preclude Independent participation. That was certainly not the intention. The Dublin newsletter, which was published by the official printer and editorially welcomed the imminent return of tithes and parishes, made the point in an irreverent story from London where Henry Cromwell's chief advisor on religious matters, Dr Worth,

[137] Ibid., p. 231.   [138] *TSP*, vii, 866.   [139] Seymour, *Puritans in Ireland*, p. 229.

was alleged to have engaged in disputation with an Independent spokesman from Ireland: as soon as the Independent had finished making his case, rumours of the dissolution of parliament spread among the company and he departed abruptly, giving Worth an effortless victory. The moral of this text was hardly delphic: 'take at the present the Egge, the Cockatrice will appear soon after'. Nor was the sub-text notably subtle: the buffoon-like characterization of Worth, 'dropping as some suppose out of the Clouds' and producing 'a Cross-Commission from the Associated truly called Churches', meditating briefly 'for the hanging his brains again upon the hinges', and 'bending his arm and brows in the dismal posture of a combatant', was patently Episcopalian.[140]

Even those who held Presbyterian government to be of divine origin might ultimately be able to accept that modified 'Episcopacy of a new Make'[141] was compatible with their beliefs. For the moment, however, they were intractable in their insistence on a restoration governed by the terms of the Solemn League and Covenant which required a settlement of religion in all three kingdoms 'according to the word of God and the example of the best reformed churches', a prescription which the Scots found unambiguous. Circumstances seemed to favour them, but they were under the local disadvantage that they 'had not men of note and quality to be leaders in these affairs', or so it was afterwards claimed.[142] Colonel Gorges, who had canvassed the ministers before the Convention and joined Broghill in his approach to the 'Resolutioners', was a conspicuous exception. He kept in touch with the group in Edinburgh and wanted the king restored 'upon the Call of his People in Parliament upon a Covenant account'.[143] Though there may have been relatively few of his persuasion in the Convention, the initial signals certainly suggested that the Episcopalians were reconciled to a form of Presbyterian settlement. The four ministers patronized by the Convention in its first days were Presbyterians of assorted kinds. The representative advisory group appointed on the recommendation of the committee of maintenance, on the other hand, was more mixed in composition. It included Adair, Charnock and Cox, but all the others were to conform and receive preferment after

---

[140] *An account of the chief occurrences of Ireland*, p. 39.
[141] Wodrow, *Sufferings*, i, p. xxxi.   [142] Adair, *True narrative*, p. 229.
[143] Wodrow, *Sufferings*, i, p. xxii.

the restoration: George Burdett, who had supported the coup in Limerick in December and was a former Independent who had become a Presbyterian activist by 1660;[144] Daniel Burston, whose ministry was in the Boyle town of Tallow;[145] Thomas Vesey, whose patron was the Convention member John Rowley and who was one of those who had supported Henry Cromwell's conservative shift at a convention of ministers in Dublin in 1658;[146] John Wilkinson, minister in Sligo, who had done likewise and who was a former chaplain in one of the Coote regiments;[147] and William Portman of whom little is known beyond the fact that he was based at Boyle, but who may safely be assumed to have been a client of the King family who controlled the town.[148]

The first task of the advisory committee was to review the existing incumbents and separate those who conformed to the stipulated criteria from those who did not. This resolved itself into the preparation of two lists, one consisting of undesirables, 'who a little before had ruled all', who were to be deprived of their salaries and denied permission to preach, the other composed of those deemed eligible to have parishes, receive tithes and be inducted into their churches. The initial identification of sheep and

---

[144] *Egmont MSS*, i, 615. He subsequently became chancellor and dean of Leighlin. H. Cotton, *Fasti Ecclesiae Hibernicae* (6 vols., Dublin, 1851–78), ii, 390, 394. Seymour, *Puritans in Ireland*, p. 208. He was a TCD graduate who had been expelled from New England and served as a chaplain in the New Model Army. Anne Laurence, *Parliamentary army chaplains, 1642–1651* (Royal Historical Society, 1990), p. 105.

[145] In 1662 Burston, who admitted that he had 'received Presbyterial imposition of hands' (perhaps by Worth's association), accused the Presbyterians of 'outrageous violence, in extruding of an order of Divine Institution' in a defence of Episcopacy which he claimed to have written about 1658. Daniel Burston, *The evangelist yet evangelising* (Dublin, 1662), pp. 23, 30. He had moved from Tallow to Waterford by July 1660, was appointed praecentor of Lismore in 1663 and dean of Waterford in 1670. Gorstelo to Lord Cork, 23 July 1660, Lismore MS 31/92. Cotton, *Fasti*, i, 140, 156, 174. *Irish Genealogist*, 6 (1982), p. 27n.

[146] Vesey was minister at Coleraine in the 1650s and held the living of Camus Macosquin in 1661. He subsequently became archdeacon of Armagh. *DNB*, entry for his son John, archbishop of Tuam. Moody and Simms, *The bishopric of Derry*, i, 327. Reid, *Presbyterian church*, ii, 360–2.

[147] Laurence, *Parliamentary army chaplains*, pp. 188–9. Wilkinson was appointed a prebendary in the diocese of Elphin in 1636 and retained the position in 1666, when he was also rector of Sligo. Cotton, *Fasti*, iv, 153. Reid, *Presbyterian church*, ii, 360–2.

[148] He was appointed archdeacon of Elphin in 1662 and represented the cathedral chapter in convocation. Cotton, *Fasti*, iv, 110, 141.

goats seems to have proceeded amicably but, according to Adair, whose Scottish Presbyterian views made him the odd man out in this company, the issue of suitability quickly divided the advisory committee from the committee it served and split the advisory committee itself. A blacklist and a complementary schedule of about 160 'sober, orthodox men', more than 60 of whom were Presbyterian ministers in the north,[149] were presented and accepted. The committee of maintenance, however, pressed the claims of an omitted group, described by Adair as 'divers old prelatical men who were corrupt in their doctrine and immoral in their lives, and were generally known to be unworthy of all place in the church'. The terms of reference given to the advisors when they were asked to resolve a dispute between two clerics in Naas in April suggest the problem, for the merits of the case were presented as secondary to the preliminary questions of the abilities of the disputants, 'and whether they be in Orders, and do administer the Sacraments'.[150] It is evident that the criteria were designed to eliminate radicals rather than traditionalists. The advisors, or the majority of them, took it for granted that undue devotion to the Church of Ireland was a disqualification, but the committee of maintenance did not. When the committee refused to accept that the advisors were entitled to exercise a veto and threatened to present the names directly to the commissioners for approval, the majority backed down and 'were drawn to be lax in these things, and would give recommendations to men, with whom the fewest number could not join'.[151] On 7 May, when the Convention stood adjourned, the commissioners intervened directly and laid down a set of guidelines to be followed by the advisory committee: these stipulated that a suitable appointee was one who was willing to accept a parochial charge, baptize children, administer the Lord's Supper in accordance with the directions of the Westminster assembly and 'declare his good affection unto a legal Parliamentary settlement in this nation'.[152]

It was predictable that the dispute about the revision of the list of recognized ministers should have been resolved conservatively in favour

---

[149] Adair, *True narrative*, p. 235.
[150] Seymour, *Puritans in Ireland*, pp. 178–9. One of the disputants, Richard Underwood, was an Episcopalian. Barnard, *Cromwellian Ireland*, p. 152.
[151] Adair, *True narrative*, p. 240.   [152] Seymour, *Puritans in Ireland*, p. 179.

of the unreconstructed clergy who had succeeded in adapting themselves to the arrangements of the commonwealth. The sharper test of the prevailing trend was provided by applications for reinstatement, three of which were dealt with by the commissioners themselves in the second week of April. The first was straightforward inasmuch as it had a strong and topical political flavour. The supplicant was the former minister at Kilcullen in Kildare, Heritage Badcock, who had been ejected in the previous August for opposing the expedition against Booth and was reported to have described himself as 'an enemy to all gathered churches'. On 7 April, the commissioners issued an order restoring him and asked the committee of maintenance, 'to whom matters of this kind were formerly referred', to consider the question of how he was to be maintained. Three days later, retrospective payment of his salary was authorized.[153] The second case had large implications, heavily nuanced by the fact that the claimant was undoubtedly 'prelatical'. Essex Digby, who had been rector of Geashill in King's County in 1641 and had returned there in the June of 1659 after a lengthy exile in Belfast where he was a salaried minister, asked to be settled in his old living and to have the appropriated tithes restored to him. After consultation with the committee of maintenance, his request was granted on 12 April when an order signed by Sir Paul Davis as clerk of the council also allowed him his arrears.[154] The issues raised in the third case were even more fundamental. It arose from a petition originally addressed to the Convention in which fourteen Cork clergy had asked to be restored to benefices from which they had been unjustly and illegally dispossessed. The Convention had appointed a select committee to examine the evidence and the commissioners' cognizance of the matter arose from a supplementary petition in which the clergymen, as they challengingly called themselves, requested that the benefices and tithes which they claimed should be sequestered when the existing leasing arrangements ended on Mayday, so that they would be available in the event of a favourable finding. With the reservation that ministers who were in possession of any portion of the disputed assets should remain undistur-

---

[153] Ibid., pp. 175, 181. Prendergast papers, v, 205, 210, 215. I take the phrasing as a recognition of the committee's standing in these matters, rather than as an indication that its designated business had been completed.

[154] Prendergast papers, v, 216. Seymour, *Puritans in Ireland*, p. 182.

bed, the commissioners granted the petition on 10 April.[155] One of these petitioners had an appointment on the civil list, far away in Elphin, and one was a schoolmaster in Cork who had been employed briefly to preach to the Irish of Connacht in their own language.[156] The other twelve were unknown to the commonwealth church, and the willingness of the Convention to entertain and the commissioners to facilitate what amounted to an application for the reinstatement of debarred Church of Ireland clergy to their livings signalled the increasing confidence of conservative forces.

A prudent discretion on the part of the more traditionally inclined members of the advisory committee may have masked divisions at first, but their deliberations became overtly politicized as time went on. In addition to being required to judge their fellows, they had also been invited to 'consult among themselves anent what overtures might tend to the good of the church'.[157] The poles in the dispute to which that invitation led were provided by Adair, who had brought with him an agenda dictated by his brethern in the north of which the chief priority was to have the Covenant ratified, and his fellow representative from Ulster, Vesey, who was, in Adair's estimation, 'highly prelatical in his heart and not sound in his principles, which was not so well known to the rest'. Adair sought to persuade his fellow ministers to recommend to the Convention the 'owning' of the Covenant 'and thereafter the renewing of it', while Vesey successfully organized opposition among the members of the Convention itself. At the bidding of 'the high Prelatical faction', Sir James Barry 'did openly declare if that Covenant came in before the Convention to be taken into consideration, or any votings passed about it, he would leave the chair and protest against it'. That was sufficient to quash the proposal.[158] The date of this episode is uncertain, but the tendency was running strongly against the Presbyterian alternative, let alone the Scottish form of it, through April, perhaps keeping pace with

---

[155] Prendergast papers, v, 212–14.
[156] Robert Browne and Phelim Fitzsimons. Seymour, *Puritans*, pp. 159, 208. The others were Edward Sipig, Michael Baylie, Richard Baylie, John Ash, Bernard Packington, James Bruce, Thomas Roberts, Killian Hussey, Samuel Jordan, Thomas Blackwell, John Snare and Benjamin Hiram.   [157] Adair, *True narrative*, p. 233.
[158] Ibid., pp. 234–5.

growing 'intelligence of the King's resolutions as to Religion'.[159] A book by Robert Chambers, judged to be 'dangerous and indeede treasonable', was condemned to be burned by the public hangman and he was put 'out of salary' and ordered not to preach 'untill he should publiquely recant it'.[160] The ironic likelihood is that this was the work which had been published by order of the council of officers in December, *Some animadversions*, in which Chambers had sought to persuade Independents and Presbyterians that they should form a united front against Episcopalianism. Conclusive confirmation of the extent of the swing away from a resigned acceptance of the unfeasibility of restoring episcopacy was provided by a report from Dublin on 25 April that five of the eight surviving bishops had been 'put in' and were to receive £200 a year.[161] Maxwell of Kilmore and Henry and John Leslie, who had occupied the sees of Down and Raphoe, were certainly among them,[162] and it is difficult to believe that Henry Jones would have been omitted.[163] Though in practical terms the decision meant only that they were being voted salaries, the acceptance of their fitness to belong to the new religious establishment signified the return of the old one and Adair's gloss, that the salaries were 'till things should be otherwise ordered', needed no hindsight.[164]

The revenue question presented no such difficulties. The outcome showed that George Rawdon had spoken for the rest when he hoped for an easing of the cost to landlords, and the solution combined innovation with intransigence. The customary tax base of lands, tenements and hereditaments was set aside in favour of a ten-point scale of personal charges levied on the entire community, male and female, over the age of fifteen years. The five noble ranks, from marquess to baronet, were matched by five grades of commoner: knight, esquire, gentleman, yeo-

---

[159] Ibid., p. 231.
[160] *TSP*, vii, 909. *Cal. SP, Ire., 1660–2*, pp. 41–3. SP, Ire., 63/304. 27.   [161] *TSP*, vii, 909.
[162] John Leslie and Maxwell are specifically mentioned. Payment to Henry Leslie is recorded. All three had been in receipt of government pensions in the 1650s. Seymour, *Puritans in Ireland*, pp. 55, 183. James McGuire, 'Policy and patronage: the appointment of bishops, 1660–61', in A. Ford, J. McGuire and K. Milne (eds.), *As by law established: the Church of Ireland since the reformation* (Dublin, 1995), p. 113.
[163] The other surviving bishops were Bramhall (Derry), who was with the king, Williams (Ossory), who was in Wales, Baily (Clonfert) and Fulwar (Ardfert).
[164] Adair, *True narrative*, pp. 231, 239.

man/farmer and the rest. The rest included servants, whose contribution might be docked from their wages. Only almspeople, 'hospitalmen', ordained ministers and fellows of Trinity College were exempt. Liability ran from £8 to 30s in the first group, and from £1 to 1s in the second. It was acknowledged that 'a more exact distinction' than this was needed in towns and the tax commissioners were given discretion to refine the scheme appropriately, within the lower range. The attendant arrangements were elaborate. Panels of commissioners for each county and many towns were appointed, with instructions to appoint local sub-panels – of 'able and discreet Protestants', so far as possible – whose task was to prepare lists of the names of residents in the area and assess their tax liability. They were also to appoint a chief collector, to whom the resulting estreats were to be delivered, and local sub-collectors. The process was to be completed and the full amount returned to the treasurer before 1 July. The treasurer was to be the president of the council of state, Arthur Annesley, or his nominated deputy, who was to be responsible for disbursing the money 'for the use of the Army, and defraying of other necessary charges' under the supervision of a management committee consisting of the resident commissioners, Broghill, Bury and Coote. These three were also empowered to nominate two alternative treasurers if Annesley did not accept the post before 1 June. The way for these arrangements had been prepared some weeks before when Adam Loftus, in return for compensation, had relinquished his historic claim on various treasury offices, professing that 'he had rather his Couzen Annesley had the same conferred on him then any person in the world'.[165] The ordinance, which included provision for fines and distraints for fraud and failure to pay, a procedure for appeal against the assessments, performance bonds from the 'High Collectors', and an allowance of a shilling in the pound for expenses, was passed on 24 April, the day before the English Convention was to meet. The preamble was pugnacious. It asserted bluntly that recent taxes and assessments had been both unequal and 'contrary to the fundamental Laws of this Realm, and to the usual and accustomed manner for raising of moneys heretofore upon necessary occasions by Parliament in Ireland', and it adroitly used the present

[165] Surrender of offices of vice-treasurer, treasurer at war and receiver general, received by Captain Shaen, 22 March 1660. Clarendon MS 71, f 17.

irregular proceedings to reinforce the rejection of English parliamentary competence. Since the requirement of 'consent in Parliament in this Realm' could not be met, the taxes which it was in everyone's interest to raise 'as things now stand, cannot be otherwise imposed upon them than by their representatives in this Convention assembled'.[166]

The date of the ordinance's passage was significant, for according to one point of view it was the last possible moment. Opinion was divided on the question of whether the Convention should continue in being once the English Convention met on the following day. Initially, there seems to have been no suggestion that it should continue in session. The question that was moved on 25 April, after 'some high debate', was whether it should dissolve in tardy obedience to the instructions of the council of state or merely adjourn. The debate and its outcome seem to have reflected the exacerbation of longstanding differences, partly in response to the urgency of the moment, but also by two new issues. The first of these was the decision to make Broghill lord president of Munster which excited the fury of Coote's party, one of whom fulminated against the appointment in a letter which was subsequently copied to Ormond without address or signature, 'for he that is false to one will not be true to another; and it is certain he hath jugled for tearms in the Kings businesse. For whatever he pretended, he has all along dureing this Convention underhand dealt with and upheld his Majesty's Enemies.' More specifically, the writer alleged that 'last night he was against the Kings having any beneficiall Bargaines, and you will find him extreamly earnest and busye to putt hard Conditions upon his Majesty' and he warned that Broghill intended to go to England 'where he will prosecute that designe vigourously'.[167] The second source of division was the news that a week or so previously the council of state had nominated Sir William Waller as commander in chief of the forces in Ireland, presumably at the instigation of Annesley.[168] This was a move that had two opposed aspects in the kaleidoscopic politics of these weeks. One was provided by the fact that Annesley was cooperating closely with the royalists: Waller, one of the most prominent Presbyterians to have been closely associated with the

---

[166] Pender, *Census*, pp. 610–27.
[167] Carte MS 48, f. 4. Internal evidence suggests that the letter was written about 25 April, probably to Lord Aungier.   [168] GUL MS Gen 210, f. 89.

'Great Trust' in 1659, at once asked Lord Mordaunt to inform the king that 'he would not dispose of himself without his Majesty's special command'.[169] The alternative aspect, however, was that in reality cooperation between Presbyterians and royalists was rapidly being replaced by competing efforts to influence the nature of the imminent settlement and the decision to send Waller to Ireland was a transparent attempt to consolidate Presbyterian influence there. English royalists were understandably disturbed by his appointment and a correspondent reported to Hyde that 'Sir John Clotworthy leades him by the nose at pleashure and I thinck he is bad enough.'[170] The reaction among Coote's supporters in Ireland was combative. The immediate purpose of the author of the broadside against Broghill was to convey Coote's response to the decision 'to have one of the Presbyterian Gange out of England to command here', which was that if assurances that the king was satisfied with the appointment were not forthcoming 'Sir Charles will never quitt that Place and let the other take his remedye as well as he can. For if the Kings interest should miscarrye by his admitting of Sir William Waller without his Majesty's directions, it would reflect much upon him.'[171]

To the urgency imparted by the imminence of a decision in England was thus added the menace contained in these moves by the Presbyterians to improve their position in Ireland, and the Convention's 'high debate', it seems, encompassed discussion of the underlying issue of the nature of the bargain to be made with the king. The tactical imperatives of the immediate local issue followed logically. On balance, the likelihood that the Irish Convention might mobilize opposition if the 'Presbyterian Knot' were to succeed in its bid to dictate settlement terms suggested that it was in the interests of Broghill's group to have it dissolve and of Coote's group to keep it in reserve. Conversely, if the 'Cavaleir party' were to prevail in England the same logic suggested that the organization of resistance of the kind that Broghill had been contemplating through April would be impeded by the existence of the Convention. In practice, a natural reluctance to relinquish influence may have cut across tactical logic and the initial

---

[169] Mordaunt to Ormond, 25 April 1660, Carte MS 30, f. 582. Underdown, *Royalist conspiracy*, p. 236.

[170] Major Woods to Hyde, 20 April 1660, Clarendon MS 71, f. 343.

[171] Carte MS 48, f. 4.

decision not to dissolve may not have been divisive. In the event, however, the majority not only favoured adjournment, for a period of six weeks until 7 June, but proved to be unwilling that this should take effect at once or without adequate provision for contingencies. It was agreed, probably on the following day, that a vacation committee of twenty-one should sit under the chairmanship of William Knight 'to correspond with their agents in England' and Sir James Barry was empowered to reconvene the assembly 'upon any emergency occasion'. Moreover, notwithstanding these provisions, many members remained reluctant to disband until news came from England and the date of the adjournment was finally put back to accommodate a further meeting on 1 May. This was accompanied by agreement that a fast should be kept in Dublin on Friday, 4 May, and a week later in the rest of the country, 'to seek the Lord for a blessing of the Parliament'.[172]

In the midst of this activity, on 25 April, the day that the English Convention opened, Coote wrote in conciliatory terms to Monck, at a time when he could report a sort of compliance with the council of state's wishes since the Irish Convention was on the point of adjourning. His purpose was to reassure Monck, and no doubt to anticipate unfavourable reports of what was taking place, by explaining that while there was some extravagance of language in the Convention the majority of the members, and of the English in Ireland in general, 'are not so rash and precipitous in their resolutions as perhaps they are represented to you', and were willing to expect a good settlement from the wisdom of the parliament and council in England.[173] When the members convened again on 1 May, their actions belied these words. They were still without certain news from England, but what was known about the election returns and the general climate of opinion strongly suggested that the balance of advantage in the English Convention must favour the king's more enthusiastic supporters. Broghill already knew that 'eminent old patriots' were in the minority there and had heard a 'strange report' by the last post, 'as if there should be a close intended with the kinge, only on an act of indempnity, and a few things of that nature'.[174] In this situation, the majority in the Irish Convention took the opportunity to affirm their stance as plainly as prudence

[172] *TSP*, vii, 909. *Leyborne Popham MSS*, p. 179. *Mercurius Publicus*, 3–10 May.
[173] *Leyborne Popham MSS*, p. 179.   [174] *TSP*, vii, 911.

allowed before adjourning for six weeks. On the motion of Henry Whalley, whose brother was a regicide, they adopted 'by publique vote' a declaration condemning the execution of Charles I 'which by true Protestants can be termed no other than the foulest Murther, and Highest Assassination that Sacred or Profane story hath recorded', among other things because it was a breach of the covenant 'which they themselves hath taken': 'And we heartily beg of God, that he would Silence the Cry of the innocent Blood, and not further punish these Nations for the same, by continnueing them in Confusions and Unsettlement, but in the Riches of his Mercy Restore them to Peace upon the sure Foundations of Truth and Righteousness.'[175] The declaration did not pass without debate. According to Broghill, it had been 'drawne up much more sharpely' when it was presented to the house, and he assured Thurloe that "Twas not to be stopped, when once mooved.' He now explained the reasoning behind the adjournment of the Convention in terms which both elucidate the struggle of the previous week and make the triumph of the Coote faction plain: 'they hope within that time, if things continue quiet in England, we shall have a parliament heere; if unquiet then they will be in a better posture to settle England'.[176] Both the accuracy of this reading of his opponents' intentions and the larger context within which they were acting are confirmed by Lord Aungier's elucidation to Ormond of the strategy of the English royalists, 'that it was fitt to keepe Ireland in reserve, to give a checke to rigorous proceedings hence in case we should find the perversenesse runne so high, as to impose unreasonable and dishonourable tearmes upon his Majesty'.[177] The irony was that this was not far distant from what Broghill himself had been intending.

Broghill's anonymous traducer had been right in reporting that he was anxious to take his seat in the English Convention to play his part, as he put it, in helping to 'keep off one extreme, as well as we have through mercy bin lately freed from another'. 'Wee all hope', he wrote to Thurloe, 'thos pretious rights we have soe longe, and we thinke justly contended

---

[175] Alexander to Sir Edward Massey, post-October 1661, Barwick MSS, No. 3. *A Declaration of the General Convention of Ireland expressing their detestation of the unjust proceedings against the late king in a pretended high court of justice in England. 1 May 1660* (Dublin, 1660).   [176] *TSP*, vii, 911.
[177] Aungier to Ormond, 11 May 1660, Carte MS 30, f. 657.

for, will not be exposed, but provided for.'[178] It was, however, already too late. Just as the game had been lost in Dublin, it had been lost in Westminster. Presbyterian preparations to use the English Convention as a means of achieving a restoration on the basis of constitutional limitations drawn from the treaty terms of the 1640s had been defeated by the election returns and by Monck's refusal to cooperate in the light of the mandate that they clearly bestowed. The predominant mood in the Commons was not merely in favour of the king's return, but unreservedly so, and no effort was made to exclude those avowed royalists and their eldest sons who had been elected in defiance of their ineligibility, and who made up perhaps one fifth of the members. In the Lords, the aim of restricting membership to the politically safe was frustrated by Monck's decision to allow those peers who had come of age in the 1650s to take their seats as of hereditary right. Within three days, the recall of the king without conditions of any kind was certain. All that remained was to stage manage the occasion to ensure that it was Charles rather than the Convention that was in the limelight. A three-day adjournment allowed time for Sir John Grenville to deploy the king's declaration and the accompanying royal letters and on 1 May both Houses received his message joyously and agreed upon a declaration of their own, to the effect 'that, according to the ancient and fundamental Laws of this Kingdom, the Government is, and ought to be, by King, Lords, and Commons'. On the following morning, an address from the army officers confirmed their earlier commitment to accepting the Convention's decision and affirmed their loyalty to the king. The republican interlude was at an end. What restoration entailed was not prescribed. Two things were clear, however. English royalists no longer had any need to fall back on support from Ireland and, conversely, it was too late for Irish force to influence the settlement in England.

[178] *TSP*, vii, 911.

8

Without expectation of resurrection: May–June

The 1 May declaration was as close as the Irish Convention could prudently come to proclaiming its support for the king's restoration without breaching the understanding that England should lead the way 'least to much haste heere might have done harm in England'.[1] That there was no disposition to conceal the realities behind the appearance is suggested by the record in the minute book of the corporation of Dublin which described 4 May not, in the official circumlocution, as a day of blessing for the parliament, but as a day 'putt apart by authoritie, and to be kept and observed as a thanksgiveing day for the restauration of his majestie to his crowne'.[2] Two days later news of the parliamentary votes to end the republic reached Dublin in the pacquet. Bishop Williams of Ossory, who also arrived from Holyhead on *The Harp* early that Sunday morning, went straight to St Bride's where he 'publickly prayed for the King, I am sure the first man in the Kingdom of Ireland'.[3]

The inconvenience of suspending Irish political activity to give the English parliament a clear run became apparent at once, for there was no collective mechanism for receiving and responding to this intelligence. The result was that it was the army which reacted first. The tone it struck was entirely out of step with the public mood that was developing in England, but there is no indication that it was adopting a consciously dissident position or that its stance was unrepresentative of civilian opinion. Events in England moved quickly, news arrived tardily, and the full significance of what had happened was not immediately apparent in Dublin. Replying on 8 May to the account of the Convention's decisions

---

[1] Black [Trevor] to Ormond, 20 March 1660, Carte MS 213, f. 669.
[2] Gilbert, *Records*, iv, 80.
[3] Griffith Williams, *The persecution and oppression of John Bale...and of Griffith Williams...two learned men and right reverend bishops of Ossory* (London, 1664), pp. 15–16.

which Thurloe had written on 1 May, Broghill expressed surprise at the precipitate recognition of the king, which would, he wrote, 'cause a man to wounder as much as at anythinge has happened in this age, which hath bin not unfruitfull in admirable productions'. But he took it for granted that there would be an opportunity 'to ascertayne those just rights by an agreement, which we contended for soe successfully in the war', and spoke of the need to pray for parliament, 'our whole settlement being now to be concluded on; and what is now done will hardly admit of the least amendment, tho' wee might afterwards discover never soe greate an oversight'.[4] In this he echoed the 'humble address' to Monck that the army had adopted the previous day, which was likewise based on the assumption that the parliamentary votes were the forerunners of a negotiated settlement. The address was uninhibited in its condemnation of the recent 'deluge of evils upon Church and State' and fulsome both in its welcome for the way in which 'through the goodness of God, light is now breaking out of darkness, and order out of confusion' and in the 'abundant joy and contentment' with which it greeted the parliamentary votes. Nonetheless, it fell short of recognizing that the king's restoration without terms had been effectively accomplished, interpreting the votes only as showing parliament's 'hearty and joyful sense of his Majesties gracious offer to all his loving subjects'. There was more than a hint of reservation in the undertaking given, 'that we shall observe in all due obedience what commands and orders (conducible to a well-grounded settlement) shall be to us directed from your Excellency', for this phrasing referred back to the preamble's condemnation of the purge of parliament in 1648 'when they were proceeding to a well-grounded settlement'.[5] Broghill, forwarding the address to Thurloe, described it as unanimous, and the possibility that it was in any way controversial seems to be precluded by the choice of Sir John King, upon whom the more conservative could rely to soften its impact, to present it to Monck.[6]

The second institutional response to the news of the king's imminent restoration struck a very different note. When the assembly of the city of Dublin convened on 11 May it focused on the king's declaration from Breda, which had been dispatched throughout the country as soon as it

[4] *TSP*, vii, 912.
[5] *Mercurius Publicus*, 10–17 May.
[6] *Publick Intelligencer*, 14–21 May.

came to hand, with orders that it be made public.⁷ The Convention member William Smith and Alderman Peter Wybrants, a long-established Dutch merchant who had been mayor in the previous year, were appointed as agents to attend the king, with instructions not only to welcome his restoration, but 'to acknowledge his declaration sent unto the two houses of parliament in England to bee a gracious condescension to all his lovinge subjects of this cittie and to manifest their desires to become partakers of his gratious offers to all his lovinge subjects therein contained'. This enthusiasm was somewhat belied by the assembly's other concern: before adjourning for six days, its members guarded against the possibility that Charles's return might quickly upset the city's political balance, by making anticipatory appointments of the city officers for the following year, to take up office at the usual time.⁸ Three days later, Trim corporation met to consider the king's 'gratious and tender offers' and resolved that they would 'Seasonably embrace the good that we owe unto ourselves' and 'with all humilitye and alacritye take hold of his Majestyes favourable and mercifull Declaration and everything therein contained'.⁹ These indications of ready compliance suggest that the initial reaction to the king's declaration in Ireland differed from that of the Convention's agents in England. They had been present when both it and Charles's accompanying letter were read and they were disappointed to find that there was 'no mention at all of Ireland'.¹⁰ To add to their anxiety, parliament also ignored Ireland, though the president of the council of state did not. On 7 May, Annesley issued Broghill's commission as lord president of Munster and appointed John Percival, William Fenton and the adventurers William Penn and William Hawkins as members of his council.¹¹ It was not until the following day, the day on which Charles was

---

⁷ It was published at Kinsale on 11 May. *Council Book*, pp. 53–4. The Dublin meeting had been postponed for a week because the set date coincided with the day of thanksgiving.

⁸ Gilbert, *Records*, iv, 181. The precaution proved unnecessary and appointments were made as usual in October, when two of the three officers appointed in May were confirmed.

⁹ NLI MS, 2,292 Assembly book of the borough of Trim, 1659–1720, f. 8 (14 May 1660).

¹⁰ Clarendon MS 72, f. 91.

¹¹ BL, Egerton MS 2,542, f. 334; 2,551, ff. 69–70. *Egmont MSS*, ii, pt. ii, 611. Broghill's commission was sent to him by the earl of Cork on 11 May. Lynch, *Orrery*, p. 103, citing Burlington, 'Diary', III (Chatsworth). On the same day, Annesley appointed Percival

formally proclaimed King of England, Scotland, France and Ireland, that Irish business was considered in the lower house, and then to purely technical effect. Proceedings in Ireland as elsewhere were henceforth to run in the king's name, and the concern was simply to authorize the continued use of the present seals until they could be replaced. On the following day, the commissioners for managing Irish affairs were instructed to publish the proclamation.[12] In the meantime, the Irish agents had busied themselves in two ways. First, in association with Sir George Rawdon, who appears to have come to London on behalf of the army, they had gathered together three Irish peers – Cork, Meath and Rawdon's brother in law, Viscount Conway – with whom they wrote jointly to Ormond on 4 May.[13] They offered an improbably charitable, but politically significant, interpretation of the king's omission, 'which wee hope was because his Majestie knowing it a peculiar distinct Kingdom, resolv'd therefore to take it in to particular consideration', but the dominant note was one of alarm. Speaking for 'the Protestant body of Ireland', they noted that God had not merely restored the king, but also 'Our Birth right the lawes and liberties of a free-borne People': nonetheless, they feared that they had 'the least visible hopes of reaping the fruit and benefit of it and may therefore probably fall into some Unmerrited Disappointment of their iust expectations therein'. Their preference was that Ormond should use his influence to ensure that 'the like Gracious Acts of favour and respect may be conferred by his Majestie on that Kingdom', but they were careful to leave it to Ormond's judgement to proceed as he thought fit, 'upon conference with our worthy friend Capt Tytus', to whom they entrusted their petition.[14] Already, disagreements were beginning to appear. According to Cork, the petition was accompanied by a draft letter for the king's signature which was not disclosed to Meath or himself but

---

clerk of the crown in the court of upper bench and prothonotary of the common pleas. *Egmont MSS*, p. 611. W. G. Irwin, 'The presidency of Munster, 1660–1672' (MA, University College Cork, 1976), pp. 3–4.

[12] *CJ*, viii, 17, 19.

[13] Conway was a regular attender at the House of Lords, to which he had been admitted as one of the 'young peers' on 27 April.

[14] Clarendon MS 72, f. 91. Captain Silius Titus, a royalist propagandist and agent, seems to have left for the continent on 5 May. Courtney to Hyde, 5 May 1660, Clarendon MS 72, ff. 228–9. For Titus, see *History of parliament. The House of Commons, 1660–1690*, iii, 570–1.

which he understood to be concerned with 'a confirmation of forfeited lands and some other particulars'. On 7 May, he wrote to disassociate himself from this approach which 'ought in my opinion very maturely to be considered, before any such concessions pass from the King, since many persons estates wilbe concluded by them, and some who when heard may I conceave cleer themselves from guilt, and consequently from ruine wilbe by this caution preserved which I heartily wish manye may be'.[15] Behind these Protestant differences was a more sinister development. Catholic Old English aspirants to royal favour, cut off from all means of political expression in Ireland, were now gathering in London, and a group led by the former speaker of the Confederate assembly, Nicholas Plunkett, had already appealed to Ormond to mediate on their behalf.[16] A few days after Cork had expressed his unease, Lord Dillon wrote to Ormond protesting against the 'private application by some of great authority in Ireland', and insisting that 'those that faithfully served the king should receive no prejudice'.[17] The need for a quick and preemptive settlement in the Protestant interest was manifest.

The agents' second course of action had been to address petitions to each of the Houses of the English parliament drawing attention to the need for 'speedy and healing Provisions and Remedies' for Irish concerns and seeking support for a request to the king 'for the calling and holding of a Parliament there, as formerly, for Remedy of the unsettled Condition of that Kingdom'. Both houses approved the petition on 11 May, but the address to the king prepared by the House of Lords and agreed on the following day modified the request significantly by making the implicit explicit: it desired the summoning of a parliament 'to consist of Protestant Peers and Commons'.[18]

The attempt to draw the king's attention to Ireland and to state the strength of the Protestant case was reinforced by Lord Aungier. He wrote to Ormond on 11 May, ostensibly to report the endorsement of the

---

[15] Cork to Ormond, 7 May 1660, Clarendon MS 72, f. 255. Cork had made contact with Ormond by letter on 12 April. Carte MS 30, f. 563.
[16] 'The address of the Irish', Carte MS 30, f. 626.
[17] 11 May 1660, Carte MS 214, ff. 169–70v. Viscount Dillon of Costello Gallen, who had converted to his ancestral Catholicism in 1646, was still nominally joint lord president of Connacht in the royalist interest.
[18] *CJ*, viii, 23–4. *LJ*, xi, 19, 22, 24, 25. *Publick Intelligencer*, 7–14 May.

request for an Irish parliament 'since the care and govt of Ireland is yours', but in reality to extol 'the High Devotion which Sir Charles Coote and his interest (who have now the effective power of Ireland) doe beare unto his Majesty'. His object was to establish that Ireland had as great a claim to credit with the king as had England, and he sought the best of both worlds. On the one hand, he explained that 'those advices which shapt the Careere of Ireland' had been designed not only to keep its potential as a reserve against an attempt to 'impose unreasonable and dishonourable tearmes' upon the king but also to avoid offending the Presbyterians by restraining the 'haste' of Coote and his associates: otherwise, 'they had out-runne this Kingdome'. On the other hand, perhaps not altogether consistently, he argued that the competition from Ireland had prompted the Presbyterians to move more quickly than they would otherwise have done.[19]

It was on the morning of 12 May that the pacquet brought an account of the proclaiming of the king to Dublin, whereupon the Convention's recess committee arranged for the members to reassemble on 14 May. On the intervening Sunday the clergy 'prayed fully and particularly for his Majesty' and on Monday the Convention, rather than following to the letter the parliamentary instruction to publish the proclamation, set about adapting it for local purposes. The substance and much of the wording were left unaltered, but the order of the sentences was rearranged and a reference to 'the Imperial crown of the realm of England, and of all the Kingdoms, Dominions, and rights belonging to the same' was changed to 'the Imperial crowns of England, Scotland, France and Ireland'. Above all, those who acknowledged, published, declared and proclaimed, in terms markedly different from the English original, 'That the said high and mighty Prince Charles the Second immediately from and after the death of his said Royal Father of happy memory, was and is become our onely, lawful, lineal and rightful Liege-Lord', were the General Convention of Ireland, the lords commissioners for government, the commissioners for the army, members of the nobility, the mayor, aldermen, sheriffs and commons of Dublin, the officers and soldiers of the army 'in and about the said city, and other freemen of this Kingdom now present'.[20] When the

[19] Aungier to Ormond, 11 May 1660, Carte MS 30, f. 657.
[20] The English proclamation was in the name of 'the Lords and Commons now assembled in Parliament, together with the Lord Mayor, Aldermen and Commons of the City of

proclamation had been adopted and Ireland's separate response as a 'peculiar distinct Kingdom' thereby established, the 'solemnities' of the occasion were attended to. In the afternoon, the members of the Convention reconvened at the custom house where they were joined by the commissioners, the judges, the officers of state and members of the nobility and gentry before they rode to meet the city dignitaries at Dame's Gate. Led by the city horse, flanked by foot soldiers, with cavalry bringing up the rear, they processed to the Castle Gate, the Town Hall, the Corn Market and the Bridge Gate, at each of which the proclamation was read by the clerk of the council, before returning to the council chamber to sign the proclamation: people cheered, bells were rung, volleys fired, bonfires and fireworks lit, and 'the streets ran with Wine from the Conduits and other places'. In the evening there was enacted 'the Solemnization of the Funeral of a certain Monster they called The Commonwealth, represented by an ugly mis-shapen body without a Head, but with a huge insatiable belly, and a prodigious rump. The deformed Corps attended by Friends in Vizards, instead of mourners, was carried to the grave, and buried without expectation of resurrection.'[21]

On the following days, the members of the Irish Convention got down to business. They began by preparing a declaration 'laying hold of the King's concessions'.[22] Their tactic was firmly to appropriate the Breda declaration, which had 'not only prevented but granted our chiefest desires'. 'All your subiects vertually are in Parliament, and by Parliament you doe gratiously promise to be advised; your Majesty could not grant more, nor your People ask more', they acknowledged, thanking the king for declining to be judge in his own 'deepest concernments', for leaving it to his people to punish the murderers of his father, and for observing the laws while pardoning those who had broken them. They concluded by assuring Charles of the acquiescence of 'this your Army' who 'with their

London, and other Freemen of the Kingdom now present'. *Publick Intelligencer*, 7–14 May.
[21] *Publick Intelligencer*, 21–28 May. Gilbert, *Records*, iv, 572–3. The proclamation was published elsewhere in the following days; for example, in Kilkenny on 19 May (by John Joyner). Burtcheall, *Kilkenny members*, pp. 48–9.
[22] The order of business is suggested by a chronologically arranged list of 'The particulars of the Ordinances Declarations and orders sent by the Commissioners appointed to attend his Majestie', Carte MS 70, f. 23.

hands have subscribed the same, and we are confident if your Service require it would do the like with their blood against all opposers'.[23] They went on to compose a combined address and petition to Charles and to appoint a committee to attend him. The address presented the members as 'necessitated to assemble ourselves in order to your Majesties Returne' and expressed joyful recognition 'that your Majestie is and of meere right ought to be by the lawes of God and of this Realm, our most Rightfull and Soveraigne liege Lord and King'. The petitionary conclusion asked Charles to consider the 'expedients' to be offered by their commissioners towards the 'Resettlement' of the 'Foundations of this your Kingdom of Ireland'.[24]

Their choice of commissioners was both prudently and blatantly unrepresentative. In addition to those already in London (including Sir John King and George Rawdon as well as the two commissioners) they appointed James Barry (who was described by his long defunct office of chief justice of the court of common pleas), Broghill, Coote, Paul Davis, Theophilus Jones, Arthur Hill, Audley Mervyn, Richard Kennedy and, seemingly a little later, Sir Maurice Eustace.[25] Thus, only the fact of Aston's previous employment prevented their delegation from being wholly composed of men who had been in Ireland before the rebellion. The selection of Eustace is strategically telling and may have involved some political sleight of hand. On 17 May, the assembly of the city of Dublin reconvened and, following both the lead that they themselves had given on 11 May and the example set by the Convention, approved an address to the king in which, noting that his declaration had stipulated a response within forty days, they formally laid claim to his offer of 'grace and favour'. They also added Sir Maurice Eustace, a freeman of the city who had married the daughter of a former mayor, to their delegation.[26] It is possible that this was prompted by Eustace's selection as a delegate by the Convention since the Dublin assembly adjourned on 11 May. However, the first report of the Convention's delegates did not include Eustace and he was listed last, after the 'esquires', in the original version of the address to the king, which was otherwise in order of precedence. It seems

[23] Carte MS 30, ff. 670–70v.   [24] Carte MS 30, ff. 675–5v.
[25] *Mercurius Publicus*, 17–24 May; *Publick Intelligencer*, 21–28 May.
[26] Gilbert, *Records*, iv, 182.

more likely that his cooption by the city prepared the way for his inclusion in the Convention's delegation, despite the fact that he was not a member.[27] Eustace was of Old English origin and, like Barry, Davis and Kennedy, a member of the Dublin based office-holding elite. A former fellow of Trinity, he had succeeded Barry as first serjeant in 1634 and served as speaker of the Irish parliament from 1640 to 1647. Thereafter, he spent seven years in jail in Chester before returning to Ireland and resuming his legal practice. Though he was on intimate terms with Annesley, his sudden prominence at this juncture was certainly due to his closeness to Ormond, whose choice for the lord chancellorship he was shortly to become. In office, he was to prove cavalier to the point of embarrassing his patron.[28]

The Convention members were continuously busy. They voted a sum of £20,000 as a gift to the king, £4,000 to the duke of York and £2,000 to the duke of Gloucester, an investment which seems to have absorbed by far the greater part of the money raised under the poll tax ordinance.[29] They ordered that all ministers 'at all meetings for the publique Worship and Service of God' should pray for the king and his 'Royal Progenie' and that the arms of the commonwealth should be taken down and the arms of the king 'sett up instead thereof, as of right they ought to bee'.[30] Following the example of the English parliament, they appointed 24 May as a day of general thanksgiving for the king's 'resettlement', to be observed throughout Ireland, requiring 'that all persons do forbear to labor or exercise their ordinary callings on that day'. Taking the opportunity to nail their religious colours to the mast, they gave Henry Jones responsibility for the

[27] The order of precedence was discreetly corrected in the version of the address presented to the king, certified as a true copy by the secretary to the commissioners, Thomas Kennedy. Carte MS, 44 f. 664. Kennedy was one of the clerks of the Convention. *Cal. SP, Ire., 1660–2*, pp. 100, 119.

[28] Ball, *Judges*, i, 273–6, 344–6. F. W. X. Fincham, 'Letters concerning Sir Maurice Eustace', *EHR*, 35 (1920), p. 254.

[29] Annesley's accounts as receiver general for the year 4 April 1660 to 20 March 1661 record poll tax returns as contributing a little over £29,000 out of a total revenue of £156,000. TCD MS 808, f. 182. The yield of a double poll tax adopted by the Convention during its second session in March 1661 was a little over £77,000. Sean Egan, 'Finance and the government of Ireland, 1660–85' (Ph.D., Dublin University, 1983), pp. 30–8. O'Donoghue, 'Parliament in Ireland under Charles II', p. 26.

[30] Instructions to the commissioners, 25 May 1660, Carte MS 30, ff. 673–674v.

arrangements in Dublin under the proscribed style of 'Lord Bishop of Clogher'.[31] Less combatively, they gave themselves the satisfaction of making an order 'for the suppressing of Anabaptisticall preachers'.[32] To maintain a source of revenue, they issued an order 'that the excise and new impost be paid by all manner of persons whatsoever trading in or to the Kingdom of Ireland' until 29 September, with the proviso that while the farmers should remain responsible until 24 June the function should revert to the crown thereafter.[33] To meet the expenses of the delegation to the king, they ordered 'that the Poll-money be collected a second time'.[34]

Disturbances of two kinds followed the king's restoration, from those who were opposed to it and from those who hoped to benefit from it. On 17 May came news of 'some rebellious spirits being gathered into a body, headed by one Lieut. Colonel Eyres'. Eyres was a leveller republican diehard who had settled in County Galway and was protesting against the 'late happy alterations'. Theophilus Jones marched at once to suppress the outbreak, captured Eyres, and 'no mischief hapned'.[35] At the same time, more ominously, there were reports of attempts by forfeited proprietors to re-possess the estates to which they supposed that the return of monarchy would again entitle them. In anticipation of the likely consequences if this supposition were to become widespread, the Convention issued a declaration 'for preservation of the peace, and quieting possessions' on 20 May and followed it up with an order for 'keeping the Transplanted Irish in Connacht and Clare'.[36] Meanwhile, the commis-

---

[31] *CJ*, viii, 2, 19. The declaration appointing the day is printed as prefatory matter in Henry Jones, *A Sermon preach'd at Christs-Church Dublin before the General Convention of Ireland* (London, 1660), with an order of 14 May deputing him 'to carry on the work' of the day.

[32] Carte MS 70, f. 23.

[33] R. Steele (ed.), *Tudor and Stuart Proclamations, 1485–1714* (2 vols., Oxford, 1910), ii, no. 621. Carte MS 70, f. 23. TCD MS 808, f. 156v.

[34] Carte MS 70, f. 23. The receiver general's accounts indicate that this order was not executed. TCD MS 808, f. 182.

[35] *Mercurius Publicus*, 17–24 May; 31 May–7 June 1660. *Publick Intelligencer*, 21–28 May.

[36] Carte MS 70, f. 23. H. R., 'A letter to the author', Cox, *Hibernia Anglicana*, p. 3. Opportunism had not been confined to Catholics. The author of the Montgomery MSS, who had been in Dublin in December, went back to Down and 'surprised by artifice (without siege) my house of Rosemount and Castle of Quinlinbay' on 12 Feb., and was not disturbed by Gorges who came to 'view the pretended forcible entry'. He did this, he

sioners for government ordered the sequestration of the estates of regicides and others associated with the execution of Charles I and at last complied with the order to send John Cook to England, where he was committed to the Tower of London.[37]

The English parliament had been concerning itself with the preparation of the act of indemnity, which it intended to have ready to present to the king on his arrival in England.[38] This bill became the focus of attention of the Irish commissioners and other interested parties who saw it as an opportunity to achieve their objectives at a stroke and lobbied for the addition of a proviso relating to Ireland. In the form in which it was referred to Ormond for his opinion, the proviso incorporated the standard exclusion of those 'who have had any hand in the plotting contriving or designing the great and heynous Rebellion of Ireland, or in Ayding assisting or abetting the same', which had been regularly demanded in the peace negotiations of the 1640s. It also stipulated that the act should not extend

> to Enure to restore to any person or persons, other than the earl of Ormond and other the Protestants of Ireland, any Estate sold or disposed of by both or either houses of Parliament or any Convention assuming the Stile or name of a Parliament or any person or persons deriving authority from them or any of them, or which was approved and confirmed by them or any of them.[39]

If the suspicions of Lord Cork were correct, the commissioners had already sent a similar suggestion to Ormond for the consideration of the king. The decision to use the alternative political channel substituted aggression for deference. The proviso proposal amounted to a preemptive bid to confront Charles on his return with a bill that would require him to

---

wrote, 'in the cause of his Majesty's restoration'. Colonel Barrow held a lease of the property. *Montgomery MSS*, pp. 203, 221–2.

[37] The regicides were Gregory Clement, Corbet, Hewson, John Jones, Edmund Ludlow, Waller and the late Henry Ireton: the others were Axtell, Barrow, Cook, Henry Hunks, Phayre and Thomas Wogan. *Mercurius Publicus*, 31 May–7 June. Phayre was arrested in Cork on 18 May.

[38] Among those excepted in Section 12 of the act were Waller, Hewson, Corbet, John Jones and Axtell. It was in the context of this business that it was ordered on 14 May that John Cook 'who is now in custody in Ireland' should be sent for. *CJ*, viii, 26.

[39] The proviso. Carte MS 30, f. 669.

give unqualified approval to every transaction affecting land owned by Catholics that had taken place in Ireland during the interregnum.

The reason for this change of approach was elucidated for Ormond by Aungier, who explained that the commissioners,

> being themselves concerned (& particularly Sir John Clotworthy) in the new purchases there, refuse to thinke themselves secure in any Parliament which shall be called in Ireland, except they can exclude out of the Act of Indempnity (which is prepareing now in England) all those who have had any hand in the Rebellion, under which notion they would comprehend promiscuously all those of the Popish Religion, who have beene either sequestered, or in Armes.[40]

The tactics of this are involved, but unmistakable. In essence, it was a matter of restricting the discretion of the restored monarchy, both because of its suspected proclivity towards certain Catholics and because of its undoubted hostility towards usurpers and their collaborators. The logic of the declaration of Breda, and more particularly of the recent request for an Irish version of it, suggested that decisions about Irish estates would ultimately come within the remit of the Irish parliament. Realism suggested that the sequence of events needed to be reversed, for two reasons. First, in the absence of any statutory impediment to Catholic membership, the Irish parliament could not be depended upon to uphold the land settlement unless the confirmation of the settlement had first ensured Protestant control of the parliament. So long as titles were in doubt, parliament was doubtful, for there could be no certainty that elections would be based on present possession without reference to competing claims to ownership. It followed that the question must be settled by statute before the courts reopened in the autumn. Second, as the reaction of Cork and Aungier made clear, this was not an issue on which full Protestant agreement could be taken for granted. Many New English collaborators and all newcomers had a common interest in preserving the Cromwellian land arrangements, but it was reasonable to expect that influence would soon pass to those who had kept faith with the king, lost

---

[40] Aungier to Ormond, 22 May 1660, Carte MS 30, ff. 667–8.

rather than gained during the interregnum, and were likely to be unsympathetic towards those who had done neither. Whether it was better to be prudently cooperative with the new regime or inflexible towards it was a matter for individual judgement. The nuances of this emergent conflict of approach, and its location within the older community of settlers, are suggested by Aungier's emphasis on Clotworthy's purchases rather than Aston's debentures. Ormond saw the matter differently and had already discounted the option of obduracy. In a set of briefing notes for Charles, advising him that he could rely on Sir Paul Davis, 'who is honest and tractable to what he will have him do', and probably upon Barry also, Ormond had suggested that 'great use may bee made' of Hill, Clotworthy 'and the rest of that gange who must all of theire kind be rescuede by hime'.[41] As an active and influential member of the Commons (who had acquired an adventurer's interest in the Clanmelier estate) Aungier was in a position to take practical action.[42] He set himself to secure the amendment of the original wording and to prevent the clause from being incorporated in the act of indemnity until Ormond and the king had been consulted and he claimed to have persuaded the committee to postpone its report until their 'further instructions and alterations' were received.[43] In the event, the bill was not ready when the king arrived and it remained for the Convention's second set of commissioners to seek to redeem the failure of the first.

The king had left Breda for the Hague about 14 May, and sailed for England on 23 May. As his return became imminent, the presence of expectant Catholic supplicants in London demanded action. On 23 May, Annesley, who had been returned for Carmarthen by his royalist relations and retained his position as president of the council of state,[44] introduced a declaration which provided not only for the apprehension of Irish rebels, complementing similar proceedings against regicides and others, but also for the banishment of Irish papists from London, Westminster and the

---

[41] Untitled notes to messenger 'for him', Carte MS 214, f. 221v.
[42] *History of parliament. The House of Commons, 1660–1690*, i, 570–72. He had been appointed to the committee on election and privileges on the second day of the session and though he spoke rarely, if ever, was prominent in committee and conference.
[43] Aungier to Ormond, 22 May 1660, Carte MS 30, ff. 667–8.
[44] *History of parliament. The House of Commons, 1660–1690*, i, 510, 536–7. His father had been returned for the same seat in 1625.

court. Discussion in committee both modified and extended these proposals and in the event two separate declarations were reported. One simply required the laws against papists to be effectively executed. The other required all Irish papists and rebels to leave England, 'or otherwise to be proceeded against according to law', and aggressively (and no doubt collusively) reinforced the Irish Convention's declaration of 20 May. Noting that 'many, deeply guilty' of rebellion in Ireland, had lately committed acts of violence and repossessed estates, recalling the innocent blood spilt in the past and warning 'of new mischiefs of the same kind likely to fall out', the declaration prohibited 'all Irish papists from disturbing the possession of any English Protestant in Ireland, but by course of law'. After further discussion of this supplementary declaration, which was managed for the Commons by Aungier and Sir John Temple, the House of Lords proposed that it would be appropriate to seek the king's approval to have it issued in the form of a royal proclamation. The Commons concurred on 29 May, the day on which the king arrived in London, and the proclamation was formally published in his name on 1 June.[45]

By this stage, the preparation of an answer to the original petition of the agents and the associated peers had made considerable progress. A revised version of the Breda declaration, modified to suit the particular conditions of Ireland, had passed between Hyde and Ormond. Much of the wording was identical to that of the original, and the issues dealt with – indemnity, freedom of conscience, security of estates and army arrears – were the same, as was the strategy of referring each to the decision of parliament. The only original element was the insertion of an undertaking that Ireland would have successive parliaments with the sole right of consent to public taxation. Otherwise the adaptations were that the offer of a general pardon, which would pass under the great seal of Ireland, was confined to 'all our subiects of that Kingdome who have been bred & brought up in the Protestant religion or who have been Protestants on the 23d of October 1641 and so continued ever since, and to all such of the Popish

---

[45] *CJ*, viii, 44–8. *LJ*, xi, 42, 45–6. *Old parliamentary history* (24 vols., London, 1751–62), xxii. 311–13. *Proclamation against the rebels in Ireland. June 1* (Dublin, 1660). Temple had been returned for Tregony in Cornwall, in the Presbyterian interest. *History of parliament. The House of Commons, 1660–1690*, i, 179–80; iii, 535–6.

religion then that have prooved their constant good affection'; the assurance of liberty to tender consciences, pending an act of the Irish parliament, was limited to Protestants; and the section referring the problems arising from grants and purchases of estates to parliament incorporated the following additional clauses:

> and the effectual Settling and Confirming of all and every the Estates of Adventurers, Officers and Souldiers there, and the further provision for such of them as are nott yett satisfied, And all things relating to such Graunts Sales Purchases Estates Settlements Confirmations and Provizions shall be determined and settled in Parliament there which can best provide for the just satisfaction of all interests therein respectively concerned.[46]

The dispatch of this answer was long delayed and it attracted so little attention that Prendergast concluded that it had never been sent, but it was not unknown.[47] Writing to Ormond in 1661, James Murray referred to the provision for tender consciences in the Breda declaration 'which also his Majesty was pleased to declare in his Gracious answer, directed to the General Convention of Ireland', and Ormond himself later reminded the king of promises made in 'the Declarations from Breda'.[48] It was, of course, overtaken by events, at first because the Irish Convention's commissioners judged that certain decisions were better made in England and subsequently because the need for a complementary approach towards Ireland was removed after the Convention accepted the Breda declaration on May 14.

In Ireland, Jones delivered his thanksgiving sermon on 24 May, taking a text which enabled him to draw comparisons between David and King Charles and apply the biblical precedent to the politics of the moment.[49] Recalling that David had practised clemency on his return from exile, he

---

[46] 'For the chairman of the General Convention of Ireland and the representatives of that our kingdom assembled in Dublin', Carte MS 30, ff. 680–2; Clarendon MS 72, ff. 435–7.

[47] Prendergast found a couple of cases in which the benefit of the declaration appeared to have been claimed in submissions to the exchequer, but he later discounted this evidence because of the absence of other references. Prendergast papers, xii, f. 335.

[48] John Forbes, *Memoirs of the earls of Granard*, pp. 209–10. SP, Ire., 63/315. 51.

[49] Psalms 118, 24–6. 'This is the day which the Lord hath made; we will rejoice and be glad in it' etc.

continued: 'David's sufferings, and personal injuries, were, by him, soon forgiven, and forgotten; and all passed over, as it were, by generall Act of Oblivion, and that given by him not demanded of him. Thus was it to the generality of his people who had formerly so opposed him.' He went on, however, to argue that mercy must not occlude justice and to call for the execution of the regicides. Finally, praising the instruments that the Lord had used, he dwelt particularly on the members of the Convention in terms that emphasized his own role as one of their leaders rather than one of themselves: 'You have strengthened our hands here, and the hands of others elsewhere, who have been engaged in this cause with you, you have in your forward, and prudent zeal, stirred up Emulation (I will not say envy) in others, to the quickening and hasting of this work to that perfection in which we see it at this day.'[50]

Thus reassured of its claims to that place in the vanguard which was a vital element in its bargaining position, on that and the following day the Convention adopted a set of instructions for its commissioners. Despite the earlier request for a 'Resettlement, even from your Majesty's owne hand', these built presumptuously upon the Breda declaration, taking it for granted that the king was committed to allowing the Irish parliament to make the decisions that would restore Ireland 'to such a Condicion as will be a high addicion of honour and greatnes to your Majestie and of Comfort and Safetie to your People'.[51] Apart from the formalities of offering the king their congratulations and telling him of the 'joy and gladness' with which he had been proclaimed, the commissioners were to seek a Protestant parliament in Ireland and, 'in order thereto', the quick appointment of a government and the provision of a great seal so that the statutory preliminaries for summoning parliament required by Poynings' Act could be conducted. They were also asked to secure the king's promise that he would accede to a request from the parliament that Poynings' Act should be suspended while it was in session (which would allow bills to be initiated and considered without prior certification in England). They were specifically instructed to request an act of recognition of the royal title and an act of general pardon and oblivion for all Protestant inhabitants. In the case of the latter, both the form and the

[50] Jones, *A sermon*, pp. 11–13, 22.   [51] Carte MS 30, ff. 675–5v.

exceptions were to be subject to the agreement of parliament. There was to be confirmation of all fines, recoveries and judgements made in the courts since the execution of Charles I, as parliament thought fit. Attainders likewise were to be subject to parliamentary concurrence. An act was to be passed for settling the estates of adventurers, soldiers and transplanted Irish; undisposed of land in Muskerry and Barrymore baronies was to be used to satisfy the inhabitants of Cork, Youghal and Kinsale, again 'as the Irish Parliament shall think fitt'. Impropriated tithes and glebelands at the king's disposal were to be granted to the clergy on the recommendation of parliament, while escheated lands formerly excepted from tithe and other payments were to be made liable for payment 'for ever afterwards' to the incumbents. The settling of the customs and the book of rates and the regulation of trade and manufacture were to be left to parliament, and the present farmers were to be required to present their accounts at once. All rents outstanding at Easter 1660, including exchequer rents unpaid before the rebellion as well as those owed by adventurers, soldiers and other grantees of parliament, were to be remitted. Finally, lands bestowed 'by grant of parliament' were to be confirmed by the king, 'by the advice of parliament'. If this was presumptuous, it was not as resolute as the phrasing made it appear: the commissioners, who were left to make what use they thought appropriate of the previous instructions given to Clotworthy and Aston, were given 'the same latitude ... in manadgeing or ordering' their own instructions.[52] Thus, while Clotworthy, Aston and their associates in England had been out of step with the Irish Convention in trying to have the guiding principles of an Irish land settlement incorporated in an act of the English parliament, they were at one with it in the settlement they sought and in their determination to find a way of curtailing the king's freedom of action.

Over the next few days the Irish Convention prolonged the celebrations by designating 29 May, which was the king's birthday, as another day of thanksgiving, to be 'observed with great solemnity'. They also complemented the gifts already made to the king and his brothers by ordering that a sword and spurs of beaten gold, a gold belt and hatband and 'the Best horse their Commissioners can buy in England, with

[52] Carte MS 30, ff. 673–4v.

Capirisons suitable', should be presented to Monck in recognition of his services.⁵³ On 26 May, they charged their commissioners with the additional task of representing 'the necessitated state of the College of Dublin for want of sufficient maintenance for the Provost thereof' and proposed that the Irish parliament should deal with the matter.⁵⁴ Their main concern as they approached adjournment, however, was with the maintenance of law and order. They issued an order 'for suppressing unlawful assemblies' of priests and friars, set in train the investigation of treasonable speeches against the king, and ordered that the laws against 'Sabbeth-breaking, Cursing, Swearing, Drunkenness &c. be put in execution, and commended it to the Mayor &c. to be done accordingly'. Finally, they ordered that the peace was to be kept everywhere, that possession of property was to remain undisturbed until the king's pleasure was known, and that tories, woodkerne and other robbers were to be speedily suppressed. On 28 May, they nominated an adjournment committee under the chairmanship of William Knight and adjourned until 1 November.⁵⁵ On the following day, the session ended as it had begun on 2 March, with the members of the General Convention of Ireland gathering in Christ Church cathedral, where 'Divine Service was read, with great devotion, and much spiritual joy, and thankfulness expressed.' Afterwards, the members dined together, 'where was much civil mirth and friendship' and joy for the king's return. Then they parted, 'all retiring hence to live as his Loyal Subjects', leaving the conditions under which they would do so in the care of those who were due to set forth next day on their mission to court.⁵⁶ Next day brought with it, however, a mundane reminder of the uncertainties of Irish political activity, for the commissioners were unable to sail, 'the wind not being fair', and it was more than a week before they reached London.⁵⁷ They travelled without Sir Charles Coote who, it was reported, 'cannot yet be so well

---

⁵³ *Mercurius Publicus*, 31 May–7 June.
⁵⁴ Carte MS 44, f. 662.
⁵⁵ Carte MS 70, f. 23; 44, f. 662. *Mercurius Publicus*, 31 May–7 June. Steele, *Proclamations*, ii, no. 617 [National Archives, Ire., 1. A. (156)]
⁵⁶ *Mercurius Publicus*, 31 May–7 June. Across the river, on the same day, Sir James Barry's daughter Anne was married to Stephen Butler of Belturbet whose cousin was married to the borough member, John Madden. Berry, *Register of the church of St Michan*, p. 78.
⁵⁷ *Mercurius Publicus*, 31 May–7 June. Ramsey, *Henry Cromwell*, p. 357.

spared... there having been lately some little contests in Ireland which his presence will easily awe'.[58]

The commissioners were formally received by the king on 18 June. By then, their negotiating position on the settlement of religion had altered significantly and they had come to realise that royal concern for 'the just satisfaction of all interests' meant that it was not only Protestants more loyal than themselves that they must contend with. The brief they had received from the Convention had been reticent about religion, in effect continuing the earlier instructions for Aston and Clotworthy, which had repeated the wording of the Convention's original declaration of 9 March. To this remit the Convention had added only a direction that the delegation should seek an assurance that the next parliament would inherit the control over the reconstruction of the parochial arrangements that the Convention was already exercising. Thus the delegation's instructions incorporated an early compromise, designed to meet the requirements of a different political situation, from which the Convention itself had increasingly departed in operational decisions on ecclesiastical matters that revealed an unmistakable preference on the part of the majority of its members for a return to the traditional forms of church organization and worship. The brief could not reflect that gradual shift towards traditionalism, partly no doubt in default of a clear indication of the king's intentions, but also because the need for unity continued to compel respect for Presbyterian opinion, as the characterization of the execution of King Charles as a breach of the covenant on 1 May plainly showed, and the contentious question of church government remained too sensitive to be raised, let alone decided. On the day after the delegation left Ireland, however, the chairman of the Convention's committee on religion, Dudley Loftus, broke ranks. 'In the behalf of the orthodox Protestant clergy', he wrote privately to Ormond to urge 'the preservation of the sacred order of bishops and the use of the liturgy', pointing out that episcopacy was established 'by the laws and constitution of the land which have not received any alteration' and including a list of vacancies and recommendations for filling them.[59]

Unknown to Loftus, his initiative had already received what amounted

---

[58] *Publick Intelligencer*, 4–11 June.   [59] Carte MS 30, ff. 685, 689.

to a royal validation. Two days earlier, Charles had addressed the issue obliquely but encouragingly in a *Gracious Message to all his loving Subjects in the Kingdom of Ireland upon their exemplary return to their Obedience*.[60] His ostensible purpose was to acknowledge that Ireland had been 'early in its dutiful addresses' and to promise a forgiving regime in which treasons and rebellions would be washed away as if they had never been committed, but he included a number of recommendations. One of these adverted to justice, and he counselled his Irish subjects to be sparing of blood, except that of murderers and, curiously, 'Sodomites'. Otherwise he dealt only with religion. Though the tone was bland, a sense of the possible narrowness of the lines of a religious settlement emerged. His emphasis upon the need to preserve university learning and grammar schools was common form; his suggestion that 'oppressed Orthodox Protestant clergy' should be restored to their livings sanctioned the course of action that was already in train; but the gloss that he placed upon the need for true and sincere worship of God contained a clear signal that current speculation about the possibility of a compromise that would incorporate Presbyterians and Episcopalians in a new church establishment did not reflect his intentions. Although Charles presented the centre ground reassuringly as lying between schismatics on one side and superstition on the other, Episcopalians could draw confidence from the concluding adjuration to 'publish and maintain that Protestant Reformation of Religion which we profess, which we have received from our ancestors'.

In England, without doubt, the inference to be drawn from the king's message was made explicit to the delegation, by Ormond and others. At what precise date Charles and his advisors had decided to undertake an exemplary restoration of episcopacy in Ireland does not appear, but preparations were under way very quickly. By 14 June, only four days after the Irish delegation had arrived, the Scots agent James Sharp had already heard 'talk as if there were diverse Nominated to be Bishops in Ireland'.[61] The composition of the delegation was not such as to dispose it to resist a conservative *fait accompli*. Discounting Mervyn, whose acceptance of the covenant appears to have been genuinely insincere,[62] only three of its

[60] London, 1660.   [61] GUL MS Gen 210, f. 138.
[62] M. Perceval-Maxwell, 'The adoption of the solemn league and covenant by the Scots in Ulster', *Scotia*, 2 (1978), pp. 10–13.

members are at all likely to have entertained reservations. Clotworthy certainly did so, and was subsequently under suspicion of inciting resistance to the new order until a viscountcy removed his scruples. Aston's religious views are unknown. His commitment to the parliamentary cause had been of a different order from that of his fellow commissioners, but his pairing with Clotworthy in the first agency to England strongly suggests that he belonged to the other camp and the inference is strengthened by his prompt appointment to a judgeship on Ormond's recommendation. There remained Broghill, whose brother was fitting smoothly into the new order in London and who had made early contact with Sharp and was no doubt well informed about the futility of Presbyterian hopes.[63] He conformed to the trend and abandoned the covenant without recorded regret, and the Irish delegation readily facilitated the plan to reconstitute the hierarchy of the Church of Ireland.

The official report of the audience of 18 June, when the Irish delegates were sandwiched between official groups from London and Scotland, presented the occasion as entirely formal in character. Barry was said to have expressed the nation's sorrow at the death of the king's father and their joy at his own restoration, assured him of the loyalty of his subjects in Ireland and dwelt particularly on the 'large testimonies of their eminent services' given by Broghill, Coote and Theophilus Jones. He then presented the Convention's gift in the form of a bill for £20,000. After Charles had thanked them for their loyalty and assured them of his favour, 'they all kissed his Majesty's hand' before withdrawing.[64] James Sharp's information, which he relayed to Scotland on the following day, was that the meeting had gone beyond these courtesies and the commissioners had taken the opportunity to move 'that Religion might be settled in that Kingdome, as it was in the days of K. James and K. Charles, looking upon that establishment as the only fence against schism and confusion: we may conjecture from this what measure our presbyterian brethern may expect there'.[65]

When the delegation met Charles again on 20 June, it became apparent that religion was not the only area in which they judged it necessary to

---

[63] Barnard, 'Land and the limits of loyalty', Barnard and Clark (eds.), *Burlington*, p. 184. GUL MS Gen 210, f. 138.   [64] *Mercurius Publicus*, 14–21 June.
[65] GUL MS Gen 210, ff. 142–3.

adapt the requests of the Convention to their perception of the realities of court politics and royal intentions. They presented the king with a carefully selected set of the Convention's key requests relating to the reconstitution of due governmental process and the rapid implementation of the means of reaching a settlement: the appointment of a governor or governors and council, the replacement of the great seal and the summoning of a Protestant parliament to pass an act of recognition of the royal title and agree upon the terms of acts of general pardon and attainder. In doing so, they suppressed the request for the suspension of Poynings' Act. More significantly, they departed from their brief in requesting that the act of general pardon, indemnity and oblivion should extend to 'all his subiects of Ireland' rather than its 'Protestant inhabitants'. Although this concession was heavily qualified by the provision that the act should be framed 'in such manner, and with such exceptions as in the said next Parliament in Ireland shall be agreed upon', the amendment signalled the delegation's recognition of the need to accommodate itself to the existence of a competing Catholic interest.[66] On the same day, the privy council appointed a sub-committee to deal with Irish affairs, with Ormond as its dominant member, and it was to that group that the remainder of the 'humble Desires' of the Irish Convention were delivered next day.[67] In preparing these, the delegation had taken advantage of the latitude given to them to manage their instructions. They omitted nothing, but they drew on Aston and Clotworthy's earlier brief to request the reintroduction of the presidency courts, concisely expressed the underlying principle that 'no Taxe, Imposition or other charges whatsoever be layd upon your Majesties subiects of Ireland but by comon consent in Parliament there', and incorporated the request made in May 1659 for the vacation of the Strafford inquisitions in Connacht, Clare and elsewhere.[68] On the religious issue, however, they abandoned their mandate. They took care to incorporate the Convention's stated objectives, tactfully qualified by a provi-

---

[66] 'Part of the humble desires presented to his majestie', TCD MS 808, f. 156.
[67] McGuire, 'The Dublin Convention, the Protestant community and the emergence of an ecclesiastical settlement in 1660', Cosgrove and McGuire, *Parliament and community*, p. 137. 'The further humble Desires', TCD MS 808, ff. 157–8.
[68] The first section of the Act of Explanation (17 & 18 Chas II, c. 2) declared these inquisitions 'to have been null and void, as if the same had never been taken'.

sion making allowance for the liberty to tender consciences promised by Charles from Breda, in seeking 'That Godly, Learned, orthodox, and ordained Preaching Ministers of the Gospell be settled there as speedily as may be in a parochiall way and supported by tythes, Gleabes and other legall maintenance.' In this phrasing, only the requirement for ordination was new and this was a point of elaboration rather than of substance. However, this fidelity to the letter of their instructions was incongruously subjoined to an unequivocal request that removed the ambiguities of the past and repudiated the compromises of the present by repeating what had been said to the king three days earlier: 'That the Church of Ireland be resettled in Doctrine Discipline and Worship, as it was in the time of your Royal father of blessed memory, according to the Lawes then and now in force in that Kingdom.' The logic of this was followed through in the suggestion, for which the delegation had only the most slender warrant, that the provostship of Trinity College should be linked in a 'perpetual union' with the deanery of that other institution dedicated to the Holy and Undivided Trinity, the cathedral 'commonly called Christ's Church'.

On the following day, John Bligh's brother-in-law, William Fuller, dined with his friend Samuel Pepys in the Sun tavern and told him 'how he hath the grant of being Deane of St Patrickes in Ireland'.[69] The day after, Sharp gloomily informed his principals in Edinburgh that

> All is wrong here as to Church affairs; Episcopacy in probability will be settled to the height, no discerning man does question it and their Lands will be all restored, none of the presbyterian way to oppose or do anything safe to complain in secret: We know not the temper of this people to have any thing to doe with them: the bishops in Ireland are all Nominated, Dr Bramble is to be Archbishop of Armangh [sic] and they are to sitt down with the next session of parliament.[70]

The formal reinstallation of the Church of Ireland was delayed until the following January, when the unique collective consecration of twelve bishops dramatized a renewal which was also a return to the 1630s,

---

[69] R. C. Latham and W. Matthews (eds.), *The diary of Samuel Pepys* (London 1995) i, 181.
[70] GUL MS Gen 210, f. 144. By July 7, he knew of Taylor's appointment to Down. Reid, *Presbyterian church*, ii, 249n.

qualified only by the inclusion of Edward Worth.[71] The critical decisions, however, had been made within weeks of the king's return, facilitated in some degree by the willing compliance of the Irish delegation.

It seems unlikely that many of the members of the Irish Convention would have wished fervently for a different outcome. The heavily canvassed alternative was an accommodation with Presbyterianism, but the Presbyterian presence in the Convention was largely of the English variety, founded on preference rather than on a conviction that divine ordinance enjoined that particular form of church government. They might prefer 'an Episcopacy of a new make', but they could make do without it. Convention members who were deeply averse to Episcopalianism perhaps had more to gain from the liberty to tender consciences promised by the declaration of Breda than from an inclusive church settlement catering for Presbyterian interests and repressing dissent. The strength of more fundamentalist Presbyterianism among the Scots in the north had never been expressed in effective influence within the Convention. The northern ministers took independent action, but their attempt to influence events by sending two of their number, one English and one Scottish, to England to demand that their 'Covenanted King' should uphold the covenant received short shrift. Their arrival was 'verie ill-relished' by the commissioners and their reception by their brethern reserved. Annesley, Broghill and Clotworthy took them to see Monck who 'disgusted their address' and their introduction to Charles was postponed until they 'did smooth' their petition into a meek request to be allowed to exercise their ministry.[72] Coote had feared worse. He suspected Clotworthy and the Gorges brothers of promoting a petition about church government and worried about 'the hands the Munster garrisons are in', but the thrust of the petition which finally came to notice, from a group of former army officers in County Tipperary, including the Convention member Barry Foulke, was not sectional. It expressed dissatisfaction with the effectiveness of the efforts that were being made to preserve and advance the Protestant English interest and purported to be directed 'to the strengthening of their hands that are in Authority and doe labour to

---

[71] James McGuire, 'Policy and patronage: the appointment of bishops, 1660–61', in Ford, McGuire and Milne (eds.), *As by law established*, pp. 112–19.
[72] GUL MS Gen 210, ff. 163, 173–4, 178, 181. Adair, *True narrative*, pp. 241–3.

promote the same'.[73] Coote and Bury may have been right in alleging, in an official rebuttal, that the organizers of the petition, had 'some other ends therein', particularly since they included Thomas Stanley who had joined Waller in his defiant stand in Dublin Castle, but the dominant note of the petition itself was fear of being sold out to the Irish, and the immediate source of Coote's anxiety was Clotworthy, who had offensively identified Eustace as 'agent' for the Catholics and called for support for the demand for a Protestant parliament.[74] In reality, the luxury of religious contention was precluded by the politics of the land and parliamentary settlements. Personal and collective interest demanded a unified Protestant front, the risk of exciting royal displeasure and cavalier revenge was considerable and the supplicant disloyal could not resist the king's determination that Protestantism itself would be settled on his terms.

On the secular front, the calculus seemed to be more favourable, and not only because the members of the Convention were at one. They had never disguised their determination to retain property and the power to preserve it. Their tactics were pragmatic, as the incorporation of Eustace in their delegation indicated. The unconditionality of the restoration, however, was in some degree a matter of appearances. Charles had been restored neither by force nor by popular demand, but by the consent of those who controlled force, a point to which the Convention had directly adverted when it had emphasized the concurrence of the army with the declaration 'laying hold of the King's concessions'. Ormond later freely acknowledged this reality when he reminded the king that, even if he had made no promises to Coote and his associates, 'there weare arguments strong enough at that time to enduce your Majesty to give the English Party in Ireland all possible assurance that they should enjoy what they were possessed of as adventurers or souldiers, or compensation for it, if they had not opposed your Restoration, for the power of the kingdome was intirely in their hands'.[75] The readiness of the consent of the members of the 'English Party' was variable, ranging from the enthusiastic promotion of the king's return to resigned acquiescence in the absence of a sustainable alternative. Throughout that range, however, there was a consistent price, common to men who had survived the 1640s and

[73] Carte MS 31, ff. 3, 9, 20, 24; MS 59, ff. 495–6.
[74] Carte MS 31, ff. 4, 22.   [75] SP, Ire., 63/315. 51.

negotiated the 1650s and to men who had barely begun to put down roots, and as indispensable to those whose gains had already been underwritten by the king as to those who had no claim at all upon royal gratitude, or even mercy. Each individual needed to be secured not only in his personal gains but in his membership of a Protestant community with the power to protect its collective interests. Although it was plain that the existing arrangements would have to be modified to accommodate the superior claims of authentic Protestant cavaliers, and the canny were particularly quick to relinquish their interest in property that was rightfully Ormond's,[76] the priority remained what it had been in the 1640s, to exorcise the Catholic threat once and for all. It was essential that the land settlement should survive, in short, not merely because individuals had profited, but because it was the basis of a reconfiguration of power which excluded Catholic competition in a new colonial Ireland. The condition of Protestant survival was that the community should be made invulnerable to the forces that had almost destroyed it in the 1640s. That was the implicit condition of Charles's return and the essential parameter of the prospective negotiations was that he was expected to settle 'the Kingdome of Ireland, upon the firm foundation of Protestant Strength and Interest' and that he was not free to make common cause with a redefined 'common enemy'.[77] The interests of individuals could not be inviolable if they conflicted with the interests of those with superior claims: the interests of the group must be sacrosanct.

That imperative was only slightly altered by the Irish delegation's alarming discovery that the king was prepared to entertain Catholic claims to reinstatement and expected the commissioners to dispute their claims with representatives of Irish Catholics, led by the former speaker of the Confederate assemblies, Nicholas Plunkett. Early in the course of the negotiations which followed, Charles conceded the essential principle at stake by assenting to the act of indemnity in August. The contentious proviso had been significantly modified to allow for the inclusion of Catholic proprietors by the insertion, after 'the Protestants of Ireland', of the words 'and their Heirs, and such other person and persons as in, and by an Act intended hereafter to be Passed, shall be therein named,

[76] Carte MS 30, f. 701 [Francis Gore]; 31, f. 23 [Cadogan].
[77] The phrasing is Broghill's, *The Irish colours displayed*, p. 15.

mentioned, or expressed in that behalf'. But the proscription of those who had been concerned in the rebellion remained intact.[78] Thereafter, the task of the commissioners was to ensure that the leeway that must be yielded to provide for the equitable treatment of innocent Catholics and the satisfaction of obligations of honour should not jeopardise the collective security of Protestants. Although Coote and Eustace dissented in varying degrees from Broghill's proposition that the Protestants of Ireland should be looked upon 'all as one body',[79] the approach that was incorporated in the king's 'Gracious Declaration of 30 November 1660' met the objectives of the Irish Convention as fully as the circumstances permitted: the settlement was to proceed from the fundamental principle, subject to modification in particular cases, that the distribution of land to adventurers and soldiers should be confirmed as it had stood when the rump had reassembled on 7 May 1659.[80] The particular cases comprised the restoration of ecclesiastical land, the satisfaction of the claims of royalist officers whose service before 1649 remained unrewarded and the reinstatement of certain categories of the dispossessed. Whether the principle and the exceptions could be reconciled remained to be tested, but the benchmark of the status quo was set at 1659 rather than 1641 and the essential features of the Cromwellian revolution in Irish landownership were incorporated in the restoration settlement.

The commissioners were at pains to achieve that goal without compromising their view of Ireland as a 'peculiar distinct kingdom'. When Plunkett set a trap, taking advantage of the contradiction that he perceived between their past commitment to the legislative independence of the Irish parliament and their present dependence on the Adventurers' Act as the sole legal foundation of the settlement, and challenged them to comment on the proposition that the act had no legal force in Ireland, they refused to debate the issue. Instead, they constructed a tortuous argument designed to establish for the English parliament a role in the defence of Protestant Ireland which did not raise the issue of competing jurisdictions. Looking to the past, they argued that the land forfeited by rebellion was legally vested in the king and at his disposal; the Adven-

---

[78] 12 Chas II, c. 11. *An act of free and general pardon, indempnity and oblivion.* London, 1660.
[79] Broghill, *The Irish colours displayed*, p. 15.
[80] Arnold, *The restoration land settlement*, pp. 37–41.

turers' Act comprised the terms of a collaboration entered into by the king and his English parliament to validate measures to be taken in England to procure the resources needed to suppress the rebellion in Ireland; the measures taken in Ireland did not derive their authority from the act, but from the king's entitlement to resume and dispose of the lands concerned. Looking to the future, they hypothesized that if a rebellion in Ireland should become so general that the Irish parliament was unable to convene to deal with it, and if the king were constitutionally unable to invite the English parliament to collaborate with him in procuring the resources to suppress it on the security of forfeitable lands, then it followed that in future the Irish could do as they wished with impunity.[81] In short, resort to the king in a crisis would be nugatory if he were legally confined to working through Irish institutions because the reality was that he could take effective action only in cooperation with the English parliament. To reconcile that reality with constitutional precept, to preserve the settlement and to secure the future, it was vital that the Adventurers' Act should stand as a precedent for action, but not as an acknowledged exercise of English parliamentary authority over Ireland. It is not clear whether the commissioners were privy to the 'Disquisition' upholding the legislative independence of the Irish parliament which the new attorney general for Ireland, William Domville, presented to Ormond in July.[82] It is clear that although they did not press the point of legislative independence, they took considerable care not to concede it.[83]

Protestant interest largely prevailed in the early stages of the restoration settlement. That it did not do so in full cast doubt not only on the prudence of insisting upon the constitutional self-containment of Ireland, but also on 'Protestant strength'. The event of the reinstatement of the monarchy appeared to have been satisfactorily managed, inasmuch as the conditions which some had thought it necessary to impose upon Charles beforehand had been largely accepted by him afterwards. The process of

[81] TCD MS 587, ff. 133–65.
[82] 'A disquisition touching that great question whether an act of parliament made in England shall bind the kingdome and people of Ireland without their allowance and acceptance of such act in the kingdom of Ireland', Molyneux Papers, TCD MS, 890.
[83] Aidan Clarke, 'Colonial constitutional attitudes in Ireland, 1640–60', *RIA proc.*, 90 (1990), C, no. 11, pp. 373–5.

restoration, which began with the king's return and developed into an exploration of the feasibility of reconciling his commitment to the support of elements of the old order with his promises to the new one, proved more problematic. The position both of those Protestants who had been the king's enemies and of those who had collaborated with them rested precariously on the decisions and policies of a king whose goodwill was in doubt, and whose inclination to place his trust in those who had been more loyal than they steadily reduced the influence that they had been able to exercise in the period of transition. The unity that the enlarged Protestant colony had forged as the commonwealth disintegrated was founded upon an alliance of interests that was both too narrow and too disreputable to command the ready support of royalists who believed themselves more honourable and more deserving. The beneficiaries of the usurpation remained a force to be reckoned with, but the ethos of restoration Ireland favoured individual self-help through networks of clientage and ingratiation rather than group action, its political relationships developed correspondingly and the cohesive strength which had been forged in the last year of the commonwealth did not for long survive the circumstances that had created it.

Appendix: Members of the General Convention

Names	Constituency	Dates	Pre-41	MP Ir Parliament	MP Union Parliament	Parliamentary family	Pre-49	Post-49	Army	Adventurers	Administration	Merchants	Other	Local	Local connections
Acheson, George	Armagh	1629–1685	X											X	
Alexander, Jerome	Belfast	c. 1598–1670	X	34 40											X
Amory, Thomas	Ardfert	1667						X				X		X	
Ancketil, Oliver	Co. Monaghan	1609–1666	X											X	
Andrews, Richard	Co. Carlow		X			X								X	
Aston, William	Co. Louth	c. 1620–1671		56 59			X		X					X	
Baker, Henry	Co. Kilkenny	1683	X	40										X	
Barrington, Francis	Maryborough		X	34										X	
Barry, James	Co. Dublin	1603–1672	X			X								X	
Barrymore, Richard	Co. Waterford	1630–1694	X											X	
Bathurst, Henry	Kinsale	1676													
Bathurst, Samuel	Swords	1666						X					X		
Bellingham, Henry	Co. Louth	1677	X			X								X	
Beresford, Michael	Coleraine	a 1665	X		56	X								X	
Beresford, Tristram	Co. Londonderry	1771	X		56	X								X	
Blayney, Richard	Co. Monaghan	1670	X			X								X	
Blennerhassett, John	Co. Kerry	1676	X			X								X	
Blennerhassett, John Jr	Tralee	1677	X			X								X	
Bligh, John	Athboy	1617–1666								X				X	
Blundell, George	King's Co	p 1670	X	40				X						X	
Booker, John	Clonmel	1668					X		X					X	
Boyd, Thomas	Fethard Wx		X			X			X					X	
Broderick, St John	Clonakilty	1627						X	X					X	
Broghill, Roger	Dublin Univ	1621–1679	X		56 59	X									
Browne, Samuel	Bandon						X	X	X					X	
Bulkeley, Arthur	Dundalk							X			X			X	
Burrell, Thomas	Thomastown		?			X		X						X	

Names	Constituency	Dates	Pre-41	MP Ir Parliament	MP Union Parliament	Parliamentary family	Pre-49	Post-49	Army	Adventurers	Administration	Merchants	Other Local	Local connections
Bury, William	Lismore	1603–1661						X		X				
Bysse, John	Dublin B	1606–1679	X	40	56								X	
Cadogan, William	Co. Meath	1601–1661	X	40	54								X	
Carey, George	Co. Donegal	1669	X										X	
Caulfield, Thomas	Newtownards	p 1635	X			X								X
Caulfield, William	Lifford	1625–1671	X			X								X
Chichester, Arthur	Co. Tyrone	c. 1639–1678	X			X							X	
Clotworthy, John	Co. Antrim	1665	X	34		X							X	
Cole, John	Co. Fermanagh	1620–1691	X		54	X							X	
Cole, Robert	Enniskillen													X
Coote, Charles	Galway B	1610–1661	X	40	54 56 59		X		X				X	
Coote, Charles Jr	Co. Roscommon	1630–1672	X			X							X	
Coote, Chidley	Dublin Univ	1668	X			X								
Coote, Richard	Roscommon	1620–1683	X			X							X	
Coote, Thomas	Co. Cavan	1671	X	40	59								X	
Courthorpe, Peter	Cork B	1680	X										X	
Crofton, Henry	Leitrim	1630	X			X							X	
Cuffe, James	Killeagh													
Davis, Hercules	Carrickfergus		X			X	X						X	
Davis, Paul	Co. Kildare	1612–1672	X	34 40					X				X	
Davis, William	Co. Fermanagh	1662	X										X	
Denny, Arthur	Co. Kerry	1629–1673	X			X							X	
Edgeworth, John	Co. Longford	1612–1667	X	40									X	
Evans, Thomas	Kilkenny B	1677					X		X				X	
Everard, Nicholas	Fethard Tipp	1634–1661				X							X	
Ferneley, Philip	Newcastle	1673	X										X	
Fitzgerald, Garrett	Askeaton		X										X	
Foulke, Bartholemew	Co. Tipperary	1672	X										X	
Foulke, Francis	Co. Cork	1678	X		59								X	
Foulke, Robert	Mallow	1691	X										X	
Gifford, Thomas	Philipstown	1662	X			X							X	
Gilbert, Henry	Queen's Co.		X	40									X	
Godbold, John	Londonderry B	1665						X				X	X	
Gore, Arthur	Co. Mayo	1697	X			X							X	

Name	Location	Dates	C1	C2	C3	C4	C5	C6	C7	C8
Gore, William	Armagh B	c. 1640–1705	X							X
Gorges, Robert	Co. Leitrim	c. 1628								
Greenaway, Henry	Tuam									X X
Halsey, William	Waterford B				54 56 59					X
Handcock, William	Co. Westmeath								X	
Harris, Philip	Dungarvan					X				X X
Harte, Thomas	Co. Wexford		?							X X
Harvey, Francis	Clonmines		X			X		X		X X
Hassells, Robert	Wicklow B		X							X X
Hickman, William	Co. Clare	1677	X	40	54					X X
Hill, Arthur	Co. Down	1601–1663	X	34 40						
Hoey, John	Co. Kildare	c1611–1664	X		54 56 59	X				X
Ingoldsby, Henry	Kells	1622–1700	X							X X
Jephson, Alexander	Trim	1663	X							X X
Jones, Henry	Co. Meath	1604–1682	X	40						X X
Jones, Theophilus	Co. Dublin	1685	X		54 56 59	X				X X
Kennedy, Richard	Co. Wicklow	c.1620–1684?	X	40		X				X X
King, John	Boyle	1676	X							
King, William	Co. Limerick	1706					X			X X
Knight, William	Killybegs	1672	X				X			
Kyrle, Richard	Co. Cork	1684					X			X X
Lambert, Charles	Kilbeggan	1637–1660	X	40						X
Loftus, Dudley	Jamestown	1694	X		59	X				X X
Long, Thomas	Mullingar		X							
Madden, John	Belturbet		X							X X
Markham, William	Fore		X							X X
Maule, Thomas	Carysfort	c.1590–1673	X	34 40						X X
Mervyn, Audley	Co. Tyrone	1603–1675	X	40						X X
Moderwell, John	Strabane	1679	X			X				X X
Molyneux, Adam	Co. Longford	1623–1674	X							X X
Morgan, Richard	Co. Sligo	1681	X							X X
Oliver, Robert	Kilmallock	1679	X							X X
Pakenham, Henry	Navan	1691				X				
Palfrey, Richard	Agher	1667	X							X X
Parke, Robert	Co. Sligo	1671	X	40	59					X X
Parris, Henry	Co. Tipperary	1663	X							X X
Peasley, Francis	Kildare B	1667	X	40						X X
Percival, John	Downpatrick	1629–1665	X							X X

Names	Constituency	Dates	Pre-41	MP Ir Parliament	MP Union Parliament	Parliamentary family	Pre-49	Post-49	Army	Adventurers	Administration	Merchants	Other Local	Local connections
Perkins, Richard	Co. Donegal		X			X							X	
Piers, Henry	Co. Westmeath	c. 1628–1691	X		59	X							X	
Plunkett, Walter	Newborough	1702	X										X	
Purdon, Nicholas	Co. Clare	1678	X	40									X	
Rawdon, George	Co. Antrim	1684	X	40	59								X	
Rawson, Gilbert	Queen's Co	a 1674	X	40									X	
Reynolds, Thomas	Carlow B		X										X	
Richardson, Edward	Co. Armagh	1690					X						X	
Richardson, Thomas	Co. Cavan	1668						X	X				X	
Rowley, Edward	Charlemont	c. 1633	X			X					X		X	
Rowley, John	Co. Londonderry	1635–1679	X			X							X	
Ruxton, John	Ardee	1616–1663	X										X	
Ryves, Charles	Naas	1604–1665	X	40									X	
Sands, Lancelot	Dingle	1669						X	X				X	
Sankey, Henry	King's Co	c. 1623–1675	X										X	
Scot, William	Athy		X										X	
Slater, John	Carlingford							X					X	
Smith, Boyle	Tallow	c. 1636	X			X							X	
Smith, William	Dublin B	1681	X									X	X	
Southwell, Thomas	Co. Limerick		X			X							X	
St George, George	Carrick		X			X							X	
St George, Oliver	Co. Galway	1695	X			X							X	
Temple, John	Bangor	1632–1704	X			X							X	
Temple, William	Carlow	1628–1699	X			X							X	
Tint, Henry	Youghal	1662	X										X	
Totty, John	Co Wexford		X										X	
Townshend, Richard	Baltimore	1618–1692					X						X	
Toxteth, William	Drogheda	1668					X		X				X	
Ussher, William	Co. Wicklow	1610–1671	X			X			X				X	
Vincent, Thomas	Monaghan B	1666						X					X	
Waddington, Henry	Co. Galway							X	X				X	
Ward, Anthony	Cashel	1692						X	X				X	

Name	Place	Date									
Warden, William Gowran		1667					X		X		X
Ware, James	St Johnston	1594–1666	X	34 40				X			X
Waterhouse, Joseph	Newry	1668					X	X			
Wemys, Patrick	Co. Kilkenny	1661	X	40							X
West, Roger	Co. Down	1621–1686	X			X					X
Whalley, Henry	Athenry	c 1605			56 59			X	X	X	
Yarwell, William	Limerick							X	X		X
			[98]	[27]	[19]	[41]	[17]	[23] [27]	[3]	[4]	[3] [120] [9]

[138]

Select bibliography

MANUSCRIPTS
Belfast

Public Record Office
D.3465/A/2/1–7; B/1. Madden Papers
H/1/5/1: Granard Papers

Cambridge, Mass.

Harvard
Orrery MSS: MS 218. 22

Dublin

Allen Library
Jennings MSS: transcripts from the Commonwealth records
The King's Inns
Prendergast Papers: transcripts and notes from the Commonwealth records
National Archives
MS 4,974. Caulfield MSS. Extracts from the Commonwealth records
National Library of Ireland
MSS 11,959–61. Transcripts from the Commonwealth records
MS 473. Morrice, Life of Orrery
MS 2,292 Assembly book of the borough of Trim, 1659–1720
MS 2,563 Piers Genealogy
Representative Church Body
MS Libr. 20. Seymour's transcripts from the Commonwealth records
Royal Irish Academy
Books of survey and distribution: Taylor set
Trinity College
MS 808 Miscellaneous papers
MS 844 Miscellaneous papers [of Henry Jones]

SELECT BIBLIOGRAPHY

MS 587 Papers relating to the negotiations, 1660
MS 890 Domville's Disquisition
Unitarian Church, St Stephen's Green
New Street baptismal register

Glasgow

Glasgow University Library
MS Gen 210: Wodrow's transcript of the 'Consultations of the ministers of Edinburgh'

Gloucestershire

County Record Office
Sherborne Muniments, D. 678, Barwick MSS, Letters from Jerome Alexander to Sir Edward Massey

Herefordshire and Worcestershire

County Record Office
A H 34: Lord Broghill to George Monck, 7 February 1660

London

British Library
Add. MSS 4,770. Ulster Muster roll, c. 1630
Add. MSS 4,781. Papers relating to the settlement of Ireland
Add. MS 19,833. Irish Civil List, 1654–5
Add. MS 32,471. Petition on the Irish assessment, 1659. Instructions to the Conventions' commissioners
Add. MS 35,102. List of officers, 1656
Egerton MSS 2,541–2. Nicholas Papers
Egerton MS 212. Extracts from the Cromwellian Council Books
Lansdowne MSS 821–4. Letters to Henry Cromwell, 1655–9
Stowe MS 82. Edmund Borlase, History of the Irish rebellion
Stowe MS 142. Miscellaneous papers relating to Ludlow, 1659
Stowe MS 185. Miscellaneous papers relating to Ludlow, 1659
Public Record Office
SP 63/241–319, 344–448. State Papers relating to Ireland, 1625–70
SP 18/203–225. State Papers, Domestic, 1659–60

SELECT BIBLIOGRAPHY

Maynooth

St Patrick's College, Russell Library
O'Renehan MSS ii. Richard Bagwell's transcripts from the commonwealth records

Oxford

Bodleian Library
Carte MSS
Clarendon MSS
Rawlinson MS C,179: Council of state minutes

Staffordshire

County Record Office
D. 1287 (Bradford MSS), P/616. Charles II to Sir Charles Coote, 17 March 1660 [NS]

PRINTED SOURCES

Abbott, W.C. (ed.), *The writings and speeches of Oliver Cromwell.* 4 vols., Cambridge, Mass., 1937–47

Berry, H. F. (ed.), *The register of the church of St Michan, Dublin 1636 to 1685.* Parochial Record Society of Dublin, 1907

Berwick. E. (ed.), *Rawdon Papers.* London, 1819

Birch, Thomas (ed.), *A collection of the state papers of John Thurloe, esq.* 7 vols., London, 1742

Book of survey and distribution, *Journal of the Kildare Archaeological Society*, 10 (1922–8)

Boyle, Robert, *Works.* 6 vols., London, 1772

[Bramhall, John], *The works of the most reverend father in God, John Bramhall.* Oxford, 1842

Calendar of the Clarendon state papers preserved in the Bodleian Library, ed. O. Ogle, W. H. Bliss, W. D. Macray and F. J. Routledge. 5 vols., Oxford, 1869–1970

'Calendar of petitions to Ormonde in 1649 and 1650', *The Irish Genealogist*, 6 (1983)

Calendar of the proceedings of the committee for the advance of money, 1642–56, ed. M. A. E. Green. 3 vols., London, 1888

Calendar of state papers, Adventurers, 1642–59. London, 1903

Calendar of state papers and manuscripts, relating to English affairs, existing in the

SELECT BIBLIOGRAPHY

archives and collections of Venice,1659–61. London, 1931
Calendar of state papers, domestic series, 1640–61. 20 vols., London, 1860–97
Calendar of state papers relating to Ireland, 1615–70. 8 vols., London, 1880–1910
Carte, Thomas (ed.), *A collection of original letters and papers concerning affairs in England, from 1641–1660*. 2 vols, London, 1739
Catterall, R., 'Two letters', *American Historical Review*, 8 (1902–3)
Caulfield, R. (ed.), *The council book of the corporation of Youghal*. Guildford, 1878
    The council book of the corporation of Kinsale. Guildford, 1879
Clarendon, Edward Hyde, earl of, *The history of the rebellion and civil wars in England*. Ed. W. D. Macray. 6 vols., London, 1888
Coate, M. (ed.), *Mordaunt Letter Book*. Camden Society, 1945
'Commonwealth records', *Archivium Hibernicum*, 7, 8 (1917, 1918–21)
Cooper, J. P. (ed.), *Wentworth papers, 1597–1628*. Camden Society, 1973
'A diary of the proceedings of the Leinster army under Gov. Jones', *Ulster Journal of Archaeology*, 2nd series, 3 (1897–98)
Dunlop, Robert (ed.), *Ireland under the commonwealth: being a selection of documents relating to the government of Ireland, 1651–59* . 2 vols. paged as one, Manchester, 1913
Firth, C. H. (ed.), *Selections from the papers of William Clarke*. Camden Society, 4 vols., London, 1891–1901
Firth, C. H. and Rait, R. S. (eds.), *Acts and ordinances of the interregnum, 1642–1660*. 3 vols. paged as one, London, 1911
Gardiner, S. R. (ed.), *The constitutional documents of the puritan revolution, 1625–1660*. Oxford, 1962
Gilbert J. T. (ed.), *Calendar of ancient records of Dublin in the possession of the municipal corporation*. 17 vols., Dublin, 1885–1916
    Facsimiles of the national manuscripts of Ireland, iv, pt. 2. London, 1884
Gogarty, T. (ed.), *Council book of the corporation of Drogheda*. Dundalk, 1988
Grosart, A. B. (ed.), *The Lismore papers*. 10 vols., London, 1886–8
Guizot, F. *History of Richard Cromwell and the restoration of Charles*. 2 vols., London, 1856
Hayes, Richard (ed.), *The register of Derry cathedral, 1642–1703*. Parochial Record Society of Dublin, 1910
Historical Manuscripts Commission
    Egmont MSS
    Hastings MSS
    House of Lords manuscripts, new series, v
    Leyborne Popham MSS

Ormonde, old and new series
Portland MSS
Rep. 10, App. pt. 5. Archives of the town of Galway
    Archives of the Jesuits in Ireland
Various, vi. MSS of Lord Oranmore and Browne
E. H. [Edward Hogan] (ed.), *The history of the warr of Ireland from 1641 to 1653*. Dublin, 1873
Howell, T. B. (ed.), *Collection of state trials and proceedings for high treason*. 33 vols., London, 1809–26
'Humble petition of the Justices of the peace, etc', *RSAI jn.*, 4th series, 4 (1877)
Inquisitionum in officio Rotulorum Cancellariae Hiberniae asservatarum repertorium. 2 vols., Dublin, 1826
Irish Manuscripts Commission
    Act of Settlement, 1662: Court of Claims: claims appointed to be heard and determined by His Majesty's Commissioners (in press)
    Analecta Hibernica, 1 (1930). Report on the Rawlinson Manuscripts
    The bishopric of Derry and the Irish Society
    A census of Ireland, c. 1659
    The civil survey, 1654–56
    Books of survey and distribution
    Herbert Correspondence
    The Inchiquin Manuscripts
    Letters and papers relating to the Irish rebellion between 1642 and 1646
    Patentee officers in Ireland, 1173–1826
    Seventeenth century hearth money rolls with full transcript for County Sligo
    The Tanner letters. Documents of Irish affairs in the sixteenth and seventeenth centuries extracted from the Tanner collection in the Bodleian Library, Oxford
    The transplantation to Connacht 1654–1658
Journals of the House of Commons, 1574–1714, vols. vii, viii. London, 1803
Journals of the House of Commons of Ireland, vol. i. Dublin, 1796
Journals of the House of Lords, vol. xi. London, n.d.
Journals of the House of Lords of the kingdom of Ireland, vol. i. Dublin, 1779
Lawlor, H. J. (ed.), *The register of Provost Winter*. Parish Register Society of Dublin, 1911
Lowry, T. K. (ed.), *The Hamilton Manuscripts*. Belfast, 1867
Meyer, Joseph (ed.), 'Inedited letters of Cromwell, Col. Jones, Bradshaw and other regicides', *Transactions of the Historic Society of Lancashire and Cheshire*, new series, I (1860–1)

Nicolson, M. H. (ed.), *Conway letters*. London, 1930
Latham, R. C. and Matthews, W. (eds.), *The diary of Samuel Pepys*, vol. i. London, 1995
Ohlmeyer, J. H. (ed.), Dublin Statute Staple database [in preparation]
Power, Thomas (ed.), 'The "Black Book" of King's Inns', *The Irish Jurist*, new series, 20 (1985)
Reports of the Irish Record Commissioners. 3 vols., Dublin, 1811–25
Russell, C. N. and Prendergast, J. P. *An account of the Carte collection of historical papers*. London, 1871
Rutt, J. T. (ed.), *The diary of Thomas Burton*. 4 vols., London, 1828
Scrope, R. and Monkhouse, T. (eds.), *State papers collected by Edward, earl of Clarendon*. 3 vols., Oxford, 1767–86
Some funeral entries of Ireland. Irish memorials of the dead, supplementary vol., 1907–9
Statutes at large passed in the parliaments held in Ireland, 1310–1761. 8 vols., Dublin 1765
Steele, R. (ed.), *Tudor and Stuart Proclamations, 1485–1714*. 2 vols., Oxford, 1910
Warner, G. F. (ed.), *The Nicholas Papers, 1657–60*. Camden Society, 1920
Warner, Rebecca, *Epistolary Curiosities*. London, 1818
Wood, Herbert (ed.), *The register of S. Catherine's, Dublin, 1636–1715*. Parish Register Society of Dublin, 1908
Young, R. M. (ed), *The town book of the corporation of Belfast 1613–1816*. Belfast, 1896

Contemporary works

An account of the affairs of Ireland in reference to the late change in England; with a declaration of several officers of the army in Ireland, holding forth their steadfast resolution to adhere to the parliament. London, 1659[60]
An account of the chief occurrences of Ireland. Together with some particulars from England. From Monday the 12 of March, to Monday the 19 of March. Dublin, 1659[60]
An account of the chief occurrences of Ireland [15–22 Feb] & [22–27 Feb]. Dublin, 1659[60].
Act of indemnity
Adair, Patrick, *A true narrative of the rise and progress of the Presbyterian Church of Ireland, 1603–70*, ed. W. D. Killen, Belfast, 1866
An agreement and resolution of the ministers of Christ associated within the city of Dublin and the province of Leinster. Dublin, 1659

SELECT BIBLIOGRAPHY

Ambitious tyranny clearly demonstrated; in Englands unhappy and confused government. [London?] 1659

The answer and vindication of Sir William Cole unto a charge given in by Sir Frederick Hamilton. London, 1645

Assessment of Ireland for six months. At £9,000 the month, commencing 24 March 1658 and determining the 24 September 1659. Dublin, 1659

Baker, Richard, *A chronicle of the kings of England.* London, 1665

Bindon, S. H. (ed.), *The historical works of Nicholas French.* Dublin 1846

Borlase, Edmund, *The history of the execrable Irish rebellion, 1641–1662.* London, 1680

Boyle, Roger [Orrery, earl of], *An answer to a scandalous letter.* London, 1662

The Irish colours displayed in the reply of an English Protestant to a late letter of an Irish Roman Catholique. London, 1662

A breif of proceedings between Sr Hierom Sankey and Dr William Petty. London, 1659

Bridges, John, A. Warren and E. Warren, *A perfect narrative of the grounds and reasons moving some officers of the army in Ireland to the securing of the Castle in Dublin for the parliament.* London, 1659[60]

A brief narrative of the manner how divers members of the house of commons that were illegally and unjustly imprisoned by the armies force etc. London, 1660

Burston, Daniel, *The evangelist yet evangelising.* Dublin, 1662

[Chambers, Robert], *Some animadversions upon the declaration of, and the plea for, the army; together with sixteen queries thence extracted. Or an essay by way of answer to the plea for, and declaration of the army, in reference to their interruption of the parliament's sitting, October the 12. Written November 4. 1659.* Dublin, 1659

Chambre, Robert, *Some animadversions upon the declaration of, and the plea for the army; in reference to their interruption of the parliament's sitting, October the 12. Written Nov 14, 1659. Some few copies came abroad without the author's name, which is here prefix'd.* N.p., n.d.

[Coote, Charles], *Elegies on the much lamented death of the right honourable the earl of Mountrath* (by Jo. Jones). Dublin, 1661

Coote, Chidley, *Ireland's lamentation for the late destructive cessation, or, a trap to catch Protestants.* London, 1644

Cox, Richard, *Hibernia Anglicana.* London, 1679

Coxe, Samuel, *Two sermons preached before the General Convention in Christs Church, Dublin. March 2, March 9 1659.* Dublin, 1660

A declaration by the officers in Ireland concerning their late actings there. London, 1659[60]

A declaration of several officers of the army in Ireland, on behalf of themselves and those

[332]

SELECT BIBLIOGRAPHY

under their commands, holding forth their stedfast resolutions to adhere to the parliament in defence of its privileges; and the just rights and libertyes of the people of these nations as men and Christians. Dublin, 1659[60]

Declaration of Sir Charles Coot Lord President of Connaught, and of the officers and souldiers under his command. [December 1659]. London, 1659[60]

The declaration of Sir Charles Coote and the rest of the council of officers. London 1659[60]

Declaration of Sir Hardress Waller, Major general of the parliament's forces in Ireland and the council of officers there. Dublin Castle, 28 December 1659. London, 1659[60]

Declaration of the General Convention of Ireland expressing their detestation of the unjust proceedings against the late king in a pretended high court of justice in England. 1 May 1660. Dublin, 1660

A declaration of the General Convention of Ireland, for a day of publick Thanksgiving to be observed throughout the kingdom. 15 May. In Henry Jones, *A sermon*

A declaration of the General Convention of Ireland, with the late proceedings there, newly brought over by a Gentleman. London, 1660

A declaration of the general council of the officers of the army agreed upon at Wallingford House, 27 Octob. 1659. London, 1659

The declaration of the Lord Broghil and the officers of the army in Ireland, in the province of Munster. February 18. London, 1659[60]

The declaration of the Major General and council of officers in Ireland concerning their late actings there, and for the tryal of such officers and souldiers as finde themselves agrieved for being laid aside. 9 January 1659. London, 1659[60]

The declaration of Sir Hardresse Waller. 11 January 1659. Dublin, 1659[60]

'England's confusion', *Somers tracts*, ed., Walter Scott. 13 vols., London, 1809–15, vol. vi

A faithful representation of the state of Ireland: whose bleeding eye is upon England for help Or The horrid conspiracy discovered and most humbly presented to the wisdom of parliament. London, 1659[60]

Firth, C. H. (ed.), *The memoirs of Edmund Ludlow*. 2 vols., Oxford, 1894

A full and true relation of the late victory. London, 1643

Gookin, Vincent, *The author and case of transplanting the Irish into Connaught vindicated.* London, 1655

The great case of transplantation in Ireland discussed. London, 1655

Heath, James, *Chronicle of the late intestine war in the three kingdoms.* London, 1661

Hill, George (ed.), *The Montgomery MSS (1603–1706): compiled from the family papers by William Montgomery of Rosemount Esquire.* Belfast, 1869

The information of Sir Frederick Hammilton concerning Sir William Cole; with the answer of William Cole. Together with the replication of Sir Frederick Hammilton. London, 1644

Ireland's ambition taxed. London, 1659

Ireland's declaration, the remonstrance of the generality of good people of Ireland acknowledging Charles and offering to assist his restoration, under certain conditions. 13 March [1660]

Ireland's fidelity to the parliament of England, in answer to a paper, entitled The petition of the officers and soldiers of Duncannon. [8 February]

Jones, Henry, *A Sermon preach'd at Christs-Church Dublin before the General Convention of Ireland.* 24 May. London 1660

The King's gracious message to all his loving subjects of the kingdom of Ireland upon their exemplary return to obedience. 30 May

Knight, William, *A declaration of the treacherous proceedings of Inchiquin against the parliament.* London, 1648

A letter from Lieutenant Colonel Knight. London, 1648

Larcom, T. A. (ed.), *The Down survey by Dr William Petty, 1655–1656.* Dublin, 1851

[Lawrence, Richard], *England's great interest in the well planting of Ireland.* Dublin, 1656

Lawrence, Richard, *The interest of England in the Irish transplantation stated.* London, 1655

Letter from an officer in Ireland to a kinsman in the English army, urging him to return to duty and reason. 14 August [1659]

A letter from Dublin to a friend in London. [18 February]. London, 1659[60]

A letter from Sir H. Waller and several other gentlemen at Dublin to Ludlow [Jan 9], with his answer. London, 1659[60]

A letter sent from Ireland dated at Dublin Decemb. 15. 1659 superscribed for the Right Honourable William Lenthall, Esq.; speaker to the parliament [Theo Jones et al.] London, 1659[60]

A letter sent from a merchant in Dublin in Ireland to his friend in London, declaring the alteration of affaires there, in summoning a convention of estates to sit at Dublin etc [22 February] London, 1659[60]

Lord General Fleetwoods answer to the humble representation of Colonel Morley. [London], 1659

Monck, George, *A letter to the commissioners of the parliament in Ireland, touching his present acting.* London, 1659

Lord General Monck, His speech delivered by him in the Parliament on Munday, Feb. 6. 1659. London, 1660

SELECT BIBLIOGRAPHY

Morrice, Thomas, *A collection of the state letters of Roger Boyle, the first earl of Orrery.* 2 vols., Dublin, 1743

A new declaration and engagement of the army and forces of Ireland. 13 April 1660. London, 1660

A new declaration of the General Convention now assembled at Dublin in Ireland, 12 March 1659. London, 1659[60]

Newsbooks
  An exact account of the daily proceedings in parliament with occurrences from foreign parts
  An exact accompt of the public transactions of the three nations, with occurrences from foreign parts
  Mercurius Politicus
  Mercurius Publicus
  Occurrences from foreign parts
  Parliamentary Intelligencer
  Publick Intelligencer
  Weekly Intelligencer of the commonwealth

Nicoll, John, *A diary of public transactions.* Bannatyne Club, 1836

Ordnance for the speedy raising of moneys towards the supply of the army and for defraying of other public charges. April 24. Dublin, 1660

Petty, William, *Reflections upon some persons and things in Ireland, by letters to and from Dr Petty. With Sir Hierome Sankey's speech in parliament.* London, 1660

Pressick, George, *A breife relation of some of the most remarkable passages of the Anabaptists in Munster in 1525.* London, 1659[60]

Price, John, *The mystery and method of his majesty's happy restoration laid open to publick view.* London, 1680

A proclamation 9 May 1659, commanding all civil and military officers to put down all symptoms of disaffection to the government. London, 1659

Proclamation against the rebels in Ireland. 1 June. Dublin reprint, 1660

A proclamation of the general convention declaring Charles to be lawful king of Great Britain and Ireland, 14 May 1660. Dublin, 1660

[W. P.] *A reply to the Answer.* 1660

The remonstrance and address of the armies of England, Scotland, and Ireland to the Lord General Monck; presented to His Excellency the 9th of April 1660. London, 1660

Rules and orders to be observed in the proceedings of causes in the high court of chancery in Ireland. Dublin, 1659

W. S., *A sermon preached at the funeral of the right honourable Sir Maurice Eustace.* Dublin 1665

A sober vindication of Lt General Ludlow, and others. In answer to a printed letter sent from Sir Hardress Waller in Ireland, and other non-commissioned Officers at Dublin to Lt General Ludlow at Duncannon, commander in chief of all the Parliament's Forces in Ireland. London, 1659[60]

To the Parliament of the Common-wealth of England, Scotland and Ireland, The humble petition and representation of the despoiled protestants of Ireland. London, 1659

A true catalogue. London, 1659

The true copies of two letters. London, 1643

A true narrative of the proceedings in parliament, councell of state, general councell of the army, and committee of saftie; from the 22 Sept. untill this present. London, 1659

The tryall and condemnation of Mr. John Cooke. London, 1660

Ware, James, *His works concerning Ireland*, ed. W. Harris. 2 vols., Dublin, 1739–46

[Warren, Edward], *In Canaan: By grace, not works*. London, 1655

[Weaver, John], *The life and death of the eminently learned, pious and painful Minister of the Gospel Dr Samuel Winter*. London, 1671

Whitelock, Bulstrode, *Memorials of the English affairs*. 4 vols., London, 1853

Williams, Griffith, *The persecution and oppression of John Bale...and of Griffith Williams...two learned men and right reverend bishops of Ossory*. London, 1664

The works of Stephen Charnock. 2 vols. London, 1684.

Later works and unpublished theses

Agnew, Jean, *Belfast merchant families in the seventeenth century*. Dublin, 1996

Armstrong, Robert, 'Protestant Ireland and the English parliament, 1641–1647'. Ph.D., Dublin University, 1995

Arnold, L. J., 'The Cromwellian settlement of County Dublin', *RSAI jn.*, 101 (1971)

'The Irish court of claims of 1663', *IHS*, 24 (1985)

The restoration land settlement in County Dublin, 1660–1688. Dublin, 1993

Aubrey, Philip, *Mr Secretary Thurloe; Cromwell's secretary of state*. London, 1990

Auden, J. E., 'Sir Jerome Zanckey of Balderstone', *Transactions of the Shropshire Archaeological Society*, 1 (1940)

'Gerard Aungier', *Notes and queries*, March 1924

Aylmer, G. E., *The state's servants*. London, 1973

Bagwell, Richard, *Ireland under the Stuarts*. 3 vols., London, 1909–16

Ball, F. E., *A history of the county of Dublin*. 6 vols., Dublin, 1902–20

The Judges in Ireland. 2 vols., London, 1926

Barnard, T. C., 'Trinity at Charles II's restoration in 1660: a loyal address', *Hermathena*, cix (1969)

'The purchase of Archbishop Ussher's library in 1657', *Long Room*, iv (1971)
'Myles Simner and the New Learning in seventeenth-century Ireland', *RSAI jn.*, 102 (1972)
'Lord Broghill, Vincent Gookin and the Cork elections of 1659', *English Historical Review*, 88 (1973)
'Planters and policies in Cromwellian Ireland', *Past & Present*, 61 (1973)
Cromwellian Ireland. Oxford, 1975
'Crises of identity among Irish Protestants 1641–1685', *Past & Present*, 127 (1990)
'Lawyers and the law in later seventeenth-century Ireland', *IHS*, No. 111 (1993)
'The political, material and mental culture of the Cork settlers, c. 1650–1700', in *Cork: history and society*, ed. P. O'Flanagan and C. G. Buttimer. Dublin. 1993
'Land and the limits of loyalty: the second earl of Cork and first earl of Burlington', in *Lord Burlington: architecture, art and life*, ed. T. C. Barnard and J. Clark. London, 1995
'The Protestant interest, 1641–60', in *Ireland from independence to occupation*, ed. J. H. Ohlmeyer. Cambridge, 1995
'Settling and unsettling Ireland: the Cromwellian and Williamite revolutions', in *Ireland from independence to occupation*, ed. J. H. Ohlmeyer. Cambridge, 1995
Barry, J. G., 'The Cromwellian settlement of the County of Limerick', *Journal of the Limerick Field Club*, 1 (1900)
Barwick, P., *The life of John Barwick*. London, 1728
Beaven, A. B., *Aldermen of London*. 2 vols., London, 1908–13
Beckett, J. C., *The cavalier duke. A life of James Butler, first duke of Ormond, 1610–1688*. Belfast, 1990
Beckett, M., *Sir George Rawdon: a sketch of his life and times*. Belfast, 1935
Earl of Belmore, *Parliamentary memoirs of Fermanagh and Tyrone*. Dublin, 1887
Bennett, George, *History of Bandonbridge*. Cork, 1869
Beresford Ellis, Peter, *Hell or Connaught!* London, 1975
Berry, H. F., 'The English settlement in Cork under the Jephson family', *CorkHAS jn.*, 2nd series, 3 (1897)
'Justices of the Peace for the county of Cork', *Cork HAS jn.*, 2nd series, 3 (1897)
'The parish of Kilshennig and manor of Newberry', *Cork HAS jn.*, 9 (1905)
'Sheriffs of the County Cork, Henry III to 1660', *RSAI jn.*, 35 (1905)
'The English settlement in Mallow under the Jephson family', *Cork HAS jn.*, 12 (1906)

Bolton, F. R., *The Caroline tradition of the Church of Ireland*. London, 1958
  'Griffith Williams, bishop of Ossory (1641–72)', *Journal of the Butler Society*, 2 (1984)
Bonner, Brian, *That audacious traitor*. Dublin, 1975
Bottigheimer, Karl, 'Civil war in Ireland: the reality in Munster', *Emory University Quarterly*, 22 (1966)
  English money and Irish land. The Adventurers in the Cromwellian settlement of Ireland. Oxford, 1971
  'The Restoration land settlement in Ireland: a structural view', *IHS*, 69 (1972)
Brenner, Robert, *Merchants and revolution: commercial change, political conflict, and London's overseas traders, 1550–1653*. Cambridge, 1993
Brown, Keith, *Kingdom or Province? Scotland and the Regal Union, 1603–1715*. London, 1992
Buckroyd, Julia, *The life of James Sharp, Archbishop of St Andrews, 1618–1679*. Edinburgh, 1987
Burke, W. P., *History of Clonmel*. Dublin, 1907
Burke's Irish family records. London, 1976
Burtchaell, G., *Genealogical memoirs of the members of parliament for the county and city of Kilkenny*. London, 1888
Burtchaell, G. and Sadleir, T. U. (eds.), *Alumni Dublinenses*, Dublin, 1935
Butler, John A., *A biography of Richard Cromwell, 1626–1712, the second protector*. New York, 1994
Butler, Richard, *Some notices of the castle and of the ecclesiastical buildings of Trim*. Dublin, 1861
J. C., 'Colonel Phaire, the regicide', *Cork HAS jn.*, 2nd series, 20, 21 (1914,1915)
  'The old castles around Cork harbour', *Cork HAS jn.*, 21 (1915)
Canny, Nicholas, *The upstart earl*. Cambridge, 1982
Carte, Thomas, *The life of James, duke of Ormond*. 6 vols., London, 1851
Christie, W. D., *A life of Anthony Ashley Cooper, first earl of Shaftesbury*. 2 vols., London, 1871
Clarke, Aidan, 'Colonial constitutional attitudes in Ireland, 1640–60', *RIA proc.*, 90, C, no. 11 (1990)
  '1659 and the road to restoration', in *Ireland from independence to occupation*, ed. J. H. Ohlmeyer. Cambridge, 1995
Cobbett, William, *The parliamentary history of England*. 36 vols., London, 1806–20
C[ockayne], G. E., *The complete peerage*. 2nd edition, ed. V. Gibbs. London, 1910–59
C[ockayne], G. E. (ed.), *The complete baronetage*. 5 vols., Exeter, 1900–6

Connolly, S. J., *Religion, law and power: the making of Protestant Ireland, 1660–1760*. Oxford, 1992.

Cooke, Thomas, *The early history of the town of Birr or Parsonstown*, ed. Margaret Hogan. Dublin, 1990

Cotton, H., *Fasti Ecclesiae Hibernicae*. 6 vols., Dublin, 1851–78

Cregan, D. F., 'An Irish Cavalier: Daniel O'Neill in exile and restoration', *Studia Hibernica*, 5 (1965)

Crofton, H. T., *Crofton memoirs*. York, 1911

Davies, Godfrey, *The restoration of Charles II*. Oxford, 1955

Dickson, David, 'An economic history of the Cork region in the eighteenth century'. Ph.D., University of Dublin, 1977.

Dow, F. D., *Cromwellian Scotland, 1651–1660*. Edinburgh, 1979

Egan, Sean, 'Finance and the government of Ireland, 1660–85'. Ph.D. Dublin University, 1983

Everarde, R. H. A. J., 'The family of Everarde', *The Irish Genealogist*, 7 (1989)

Fincham, F. W. X., 'Letters concerning Sir Maurice Eustace', *English Historical Review*, 35 (1920)

Firth, C. H., 'Account of money spent in the conquest and settlement of Ireland', *English Historical Review*, 14 (1899)

Firth, C. H. and Davies, G., *Regimental history of Cromwell's army*. 2 vols. paged as one, Oxford, 1940

Fitzmaurice, Edmund, *The life of William Petty*. London, 1895

Forbes, John, *Memoirs of the House of Granard*. London, 1868

Frost, James, *The history and topography of the county of Clare*. Dublin, 1883

Gahan, D., 'The estate system of county Wexford, 1641–1786', ed. K. Whelan. *Wexford: history and society*. Dublin, 1987

Gardiner, S. R., *History of the commonwealth and protectorate*. London, 1903

Gentles, Ian, *The New Model Army in England, Ireland and Scotland, 1645–53*. Oxford, 1992

Gillespie, Raymond, *Colonial Ulster*. Cork, 1985

'The Presbyterian revolution in Ulster, 1600–1690', in *The churches, Ireland and the Irish*, ed. W. J. Shiels and Diana Woods. Studies in Church History, xxv, Oxford, 1989

Gillespie, R. and Moran, G. (ed.), *Longford: essays in county history*. Dublin, 1991

Gleeson, D. F., *Last lords of Ormond: a history of the 'countrie of the three O'Kennedys' during the 17th century*. London, 1938

Gorges, R., *The story of a family through eleven centuries*. Boston, 1944

Gray, E. T., 'Some notes on High Sheriffs of County Leitrim', *Irish Genealogist*, 1 (1941)

Greaves, R. L., *Deliver us from evil: the radical underground in Britain, 1660–1663*. Oxford, 1986

Greaves, R. L. and Zeller, R. (eds.), *Biographical dictionary of British radicals in the seventeenth century*. 3 vols., London, 1982–4

Green, Ian, *The re-establishment of the Church of England, 1660–1663*. Oxford, 1978

Grey, Zachery, *An impartial examination of vol. 4 of Neal's History of the puritans*. London, 1739

Haley, K. H. D., *The first earl of Shaftesbury*. Oxford, 1968

An English diplomat in the Low Countries. Oxford, 1986

Hamilton, Ernest, *The Irish rebellion of 1641*. London, 1920

Handcock, W., *The history and antiquities of Tallaght*. Dublin, 1991

Hardiman, James, *The history of the town and county of the town of Galway*. Galway, 1926

Hardinge, W. H., 'Manuscript census returns of the people of Ireland', *RIA trans*, 24 (1873)

'On manuscript, mapped and other townland surveys in Ireland, of a public character, embracing the Gross, Civil and Down Surveys, from 1640–1688', *RIA trans*, 24 (1873), Appendix E

Herlihy, Kevin, 'The Irish Baptists, 1650–1780'. Ph.D., University of Dublin, 1992

Hill, George, *An historical account of the plantation in Ulster*. Belfast, 1877

Hill, Jacqueline, *From patriots to unionists: Dublin civic politics and Irish Protestant patriotism, 1660–1840*. Oxford, 1997

History of parliament. The house of commons, 1660–90. 3 vols., London, 1983

Hore, P. H., *History of the town and county of Wexford*. 6 vols., London, 1910

Hughes, S. C., *The church of S. John the evangelist, Dublin*. Dublin, 1889

Hunter, R. J., 'Plantation in Donegal', in *Donegal: history and society*, ed. William Nolan, Liam Ronayne and Mairead Dunlevy. Dublin, 1995

Hutchison, W. R., *Tyrone precinct*. Belfast, 1951

Hutton, R., *The restoration: a political and religious history of England and Wales, 1658–1667*. Oxford, 1987

Irwin, W. G., 'The presidency of Munster, 1660–1672'. MA, University College Cork, 1976

'The Irish presidency courts, 1569–1672', *The Irish Jurist*, 12 (1977)

Jephson, M. D., *An Anglo-Irish miscellany: some records of the Jephsons of Mallow*. Dublin, 1964

Kearney, H. F., *Strafford in Ireland, 1633–1641*. Manchester, 1959

Keeler, M. F., *The Long Parliament, 1640–41, a biographical study of its members*. Philadelphia, 1954

Kennett, White, *A register and chronicle ecclesiastical and civil*. London, 1728

Kenny, Colum, *The King's Inns and the kingdom of Ireland*. Dublin, 1992

Kilroy, Phil, *Protestant dissent and controversy in Ireland*. Cork, 1994

King, John, *The history of County Kerry*. London, 1926

King-Harman, R. D., *The Kings: earls of Kingston*. Cambridge, 1959

Laffan, T., 'Fethard, Co. Tipperary: its charters and corporation records', *RSAI jn.*, 36 (1906)

Lascalles, Rowley (ed.), *Liber munerum publicorum Hiberniae*. London, 1852

Laurence, Anne, *Parliamentary army chaplains, 1642–1651*. Royal Historical Society, 1990

Popular politics and religion in civil war London. Aldershot, 1997

Lenihan, M. *Limerick: its history and antiquities*. Dublin, 1866

Leslie, J. B., 'Inquisitions concerning the parishes of County Louth', *Louth HAS jn*, 7 (1922)

Lindley, Keith, 'Irish adventurers and godly militants in the 1640s', *IHS,* 113 (1994)

Livingston, P., *The Monaghan Story*. Enniskillen, 1980

Lodge, John, *The peerage of Ireland*, ed. M. Archdall. 7 vols., Dublin, 1789

Lynch, K. M. *Roger Boyle, the first earl of Orrery*. Knoxville, 1965

MacCuarta, Brian (ed.), *Ulster 1641*. Belfast, 1993

Maguire, W. A., *The Downshire estates in Ireland*. Oxford, 1972

McGrath, Brid, 'The membership of the Irish house of commons, 1613–1615'. M.Litt., University of Dublin, 1985

'A biographical dictionary of the membership of the Irish house of commons, 1640–1'. Ph.D., University of Dublin, 1997

McGuire, James, 'The Dublin Convention, the protestant community and the emergence of an ecclesiastical settlement in 1660', in *Parliament and community: historical studies XIV*, ed. Art Cosgrove and J. I. McGuire. Belfast, 1983

'Policy and patronage: the appointment of bishops, 1660–61', in *As by law established: the Church of Ireland since the reformation*, ed. A. Ford, J. McGuire and K. Milne. Dublin, 1995

McKenny, Kevin, 'A 17th century "real estate company": the 1649 officers and the Irish land settlements, 1641–1681'. MA, St. Patrick's College, Maynooth, 1989

Marshall, Alan, *Intelligence and espionage in the reign of Charles II, 1660–1685*. Cambridge, 1994

Matthews, A. G. (ed.), *The Savoy declaration of faith and order*. London, 1959

Montague, William Drogo, duke of Manchester, *Court and society from Elizabeth to Anne*. London, 1864

Moody, T. W. *The Londonderry plantation 1609–41. The city of London and the plantation in Ulster*. Belfast, 1939

Moody, T. W., Martin, F. X. and Byrne, F. J. (eds.), *A new history of Ireland, III: early modern Ireland, 1534–1691*. Oxford, 1976

Morrill, J. S., *Cheshire, 1630–1660*. London, 1974

M'Skimmin, S., *The history and antiquities of the county of the town of Carrickfergus*, ed. E. McCrum. Belfast, 1909

Murphy, John A., 'The politics of the Munster Protestants, 1641–1649', *Cork HAS jn.*, 76 (1971)

Neely, W. G., *Kilcooley – land and people in Tipperary*. Belfast, 1984

Noble, Mark, *Memoirs of the protectoral house of Cromwell*. 2 vols., London, 1787

Nolan, William and Power, Thomas (eds.), *Waterford; history and society*. Dublin, 1992

O'Dalaigh, Brian (ed.), *The Corporation book of Ennis*. Dublin, 1990

O'Donoghue, F. M., 'Parliament in Ireland under Charles II'. MA, University College Dublin, 1970

O'Dowd, Mary, *Power, politics and land: early modern Sligo, 1568–1688*. Belfast, 1991

O'Dwyer, M., *The O'Dwyers of Kilnamanagh*. London, 1933

O'Hanlon, J., *History of the Queen's County*. 2 vols., reprint, Kilkenny, 1981

Ohlmeyer, Jane, *Civil war and restoration in the three stuart kingdoms: the career of Randal McDonnell, marquis of Antrim 1609–1683*. Cambridge, 1993

Ohlmeyer, Jane (ed.), *Ireland from independence to occupation 1641–1660*. Cambridge, 1995

[Old parliamentary history]. *The parliamentary or constitutional history of England from the earliest times*. 24 vols., London, 1751–62

O'Sullivan, Harold, 'The Cromwellian and Restoration settlements in the civil parish of Dundalk, 1649–1673', *Louth HAS Jn.*, 19 (1977)

'The Trevors of Rosetrevor: a British colonial family in 17th century Ireland'. M.Litt., University of Dublin, 1985

'The plantation of the Cromwellian soldiers in the barony of Ardee, 1651–56', *Louth HAS jn.*, 21 (1988)

'Military operations in County Louth in the run-up to Cromwell's storming of Drogheda', *Louth HAS jn.*, 22 (1990)

'Landownership changes in the County of Louth in the seventeenth century'. Ph.D., University of Dublin, 1991

'The restoration land settlement in the diocese of Armagh, 1660–1684', *Seanchas Ard Mhacha,* 16 (1994)

'The Magennis lordship of Iveagh in the early Stuart period' in *Down: history and society,* ed. Lindsey Proudfoot. Dublin, 1997

O'Sullivan, M. D., *Old Galway: the history of a Norman colony in Ireland.* Galway, 1983

O'Sullivan, William, 'A finding list of Sir James Ware's manuscripts', *RIA proc.,* 97. C. no. 2 (1997)

L. P., 'Hearth money rolls', *Louth HAS jn.,* 7 (1922)

Parkinson, Edward, 'The Wests of Ballydugan, County Down', *UJA,* 2nd series, 12 (1906)

Paul, J. B. (ed.), *The Scots peerage.* Edinburgh, 1908

Peacock, Edward, *The army lists of the roundheads and cavaliers.* London, 1863

Perceval-Maxwell, M., 'The adoption of the solemn league and Covenant by the Scots in Ulster', *Scotia: American-Canadian Journal of Scottish Studies,* 2 (1982)

The outbreak of the rebellion of 1641. Dublin, 1994

'The proprietors of Fethard, 1641–1663', *The Irish Genealogist,* 6 (1980)

'Pedigree of the Tynte family', *Cork HAS jn.,* 2nd series, 28 (1922)

Prendergast, J. P., *The Cromwellian settlement of Ireland.* Dublin, 1922

   'On Charlemont fort', *RSAI jn.,* 4th series, 6 (1884)

   'Further notes in the history of Sir Jerome Alexander', *Transactions of the Royal Historical Society,* 2 (1873)

   'Some account of Sir Audley Mervyn', *Transactions of the Royal Historical Society,* 3 (1874)

Price, Liam, 'The hearth money rolls for County Wicklow' in *RSAI jn.,* 61 (1931)

Ramsey, R. W., *Henry Cromwell.* London, 1933

Reid, J. S., *History of the Presbyterian church in Ireland,* ed. W. D. Killen. 3 vols., Belfast, 1867

Robertson, Alexander, *The life of Sir Robert Moray.* London, 1922

Robinson, P., *The plantation of Ulster.* Dublin, 1984

Roebuck, Peter, 'The making of an Ulster great estate: the Chichesters, Barons of Belfast and Viscounts of Carrickfergus, 1599–1648', *RIA Proc.,* 79, C, no. 1 (1979)

Rogers, C., 'Notes in the history of Sir Jerome Alexander', *Transactions of the Royal Historical Society,* 2 (1873)

Routledge, F. J., *England and the treaty of the Pyrenees.* Liverpool, 1953

Sadleir, T. U., 'Kildare members of parliament', *Kildare AS jn.,* 6, 9 (1911, 1918–21)

   'High sheriffs of the King's County', 8 (1915–17)

Scott, Eva, *The travels of the king: Charles II in Germany and Flanders, 1654–1660*. London, 1907
Scott, W. R., 'Members for Ireland in the parliaments of the protectorate', *RSAI jn.*, 23 (1893)
Scott, Jonathan, *Algernon Sidney and the English Republic, 1623–1677*. Cambridge, 1988
Seymour, St John D., *The Puritans in Ireland, 1649–1661*. Oxford, 1921
Shaw, W. A., *Letters of denization and acts of naturalization, 1603–1700*. Huguenot Society of London, 1911
Sherwood, R., *The court of Oliver Cromwell*. London, 1977
Shirley, E. P., *History of the county of Monaghan*. London, 1879
Simington, R. C., 'A census of Ireland c. 1659'. *Analecta Hibernica*, 12 (1943)
Smith, G. C. M. (ed.), *The early essays and romances of Sir William Temple*. Oxford, 1930
Smyth, Jim, 'The communities of Ireland and the British state, 1660–1707', *The British problem, c. 1534–1707*, ed. Brendan Bradshaw and John Morrill. London, 1996
Smyth, William, 'Society and settlement in seventeenth century Ireland: the evidence of the "1659 census"', in *Common ground*, ed. William Smyth and Kevin Whelan. Cork, 1998
'Some notes on the High Sheriffs of County Leitrim', *Irish Genealogist*, 1 (1941)
Spurr, J., *The restoration of the Church of England, 1646–1689*. New Haven, 1991
Stevenson, David, *Alasdair MacColla and the highland problem in the 17th century*. Edinburgh, 1980
   Scottish covenanters and Irish confederates: Scottish–Irish relations in the mid-seventeenth century. Belfast, 1981
Stranks, C. J., *The life and writings of Jeremy Taylor*. London, 1952
Stuart, James, *Historical memoirs of the city of Armagh*. Newry, 1819
Temple, R. K. G., 'The original officer list of the New Model Army', *Bulletin of the Institute of Historical Research*, 59 (1986)
Tenison, C. M., 'Cork MPs, 1559–1800', *Cork HAS jn.*, 2nd series, 1, 2 (1895, 1896)
Thrift, G. (ed.), *Indexes to Irish wills, v: Derry and Raphoe*. London. 1909.
Townshend, Richard and Townshend, Dorothea, *An officer of the Long Parliament and his descendants*. London, 1892
Trimble, W. C., *The history of Enniskillen*. 3 vols., Enniskillen, 1919–21
Underdown, David, *Royalist conspiracy in England*. New Haven, 1960
Upton, H., 'List of High Sheriffs, 1685–6', *Kildare AS jn.*, 11 (1929–32)

Vicars, Arthur (ed.), *Index to the prerogative wills of Ireland, 1536–1810*. 2 vols., Dublin, 1897–1914

Webb, John J., *The guilds of Dublin*. New York, 1970

Wedgwood, C. V., *A coffin for King Charles*. New York, 1964

Welphy, W. H., 'Colonel Robert Phaire, "regicide"', *Cork HAS jn.*, 29, 30 (1924–5)

'W. H. Welphy's abstracts of Irish Chancery bills', *The Irish Genealogist*, 7 (1987)

White, B. H., 'Thomas Patient in England and Ireland', *Irish Baptist Historical Society Journal*, 2 (1969–70)

Widdess, J. D. H., *A history of the Royal College of Physicians of Ireland, 1654–1963*. Edinburgh, 1963

Wodrow, W., *The history of the sufferings of the Church of Scotland from the restoration to the revolution*. Glasgow, 1829–30

Woolrych, A. H., 'Yorkshire and the restoration', *Yorkshire Archaeological Journal*, 29 (1958)

Wright, William Ball, *The Ussher memoirs; or, Genealogical memoirs of the Ussher families in Ireland*. Dublin, 1889

Young, J. R., *The Scottish parliament, 1639–1661: a political and constitutional analysis*. Edinburgh, 1996

Index

Abercorn, first earl of, *see* Hamilton, James
Abbott, Col. Daniel   61, 66, 94n, 129, 151, 190
Acheson, Sir George   173, 174, 231n
acts of Parliament   40, 57, 80–1, 99, 101
  adventurers' (1642)   170, 251, 318–19
  against recusancy (1657)   37
  appointing commissioners (1659)   44
  establishing presbyterianism (1648)   243
  for collection of customs (1659)   45
  for commission to govern the army (February 1660)   153, 154
  for commissions of Oyer, Terminer etc. (1659)   80
  for confirmation of estates, progress   33, 44, 57–8, 67, 68, 83–4, 152, 155, 171, 257, 308
  for continuation of legal proceedings (1659)   22
  for continuation of sheriffs and JPs (1659)   79, 183
  for continuing courts of justice, (1660)   257
  for Dublin University (1649)   87
  for Henry Whalley (1657)   230
  for hue and cry (1634)   90
  for new parliament/convention (1660)   244
  of attainder (1657)   212n, 273
  of explanation (1665)   215, 313n
  of general pardon, requested (1660)   262, 274, 305, 307, 313
  of indemnity and general pardon (1659)   40, 56–7, 76n
  of indemnity (1660)   289, 302–3, 304, 317–18
  of oblivion, requested (1659)   34, 36, 44; (1660)   307, 313
  of recognition of the royal title (1660)   307, 312;
  of satisfaction (1653)   5, 34
  of settlement (1652)   11, 12, 13, 81, 273
  of settlement (1663)   215
  of union, proposed   40, 51, 228
  Poynings' Act (1494)   90, 307, 313
  voiding patents, grants etc. (1659)   87, 99
Adair, Patrick, minister   247, 252, 275, 279, 280, 282, 284, 285
adventurers for Irish lands   4, 5–6, 7, 9, 33, 35, 42, 58, 83, 84, 87, 105n, 112, 158, 170, 172, 175, 184, 189, 190, 196, 212, 213, 216, 230, 232, 233, 238, 241, 251, 267, 304, 306, 308, 316, 318
  London committee   33, 172, 257
Agher, Co. Tyrone   180, 181, 203
Aland, Capt. Henry   15, 78n, 106, 137
Alexander, Jerome   109, 170, 171–2, 175n, 227, 269–70, 276n
Allen, Col. William   61, 62, 105, 140, 151
Amory, Thomas   222, 232n, 237
Anabaptist, 25, 28, 43, 62, 79, 85n, 110, 115, 116, 123n, 126, 127, 128, 129, 145, 148, 149n, 160, 251, 301
  see Baptist

Ancketil, John 184
Ancketil, Oliver 184, 231n
Ancketil, William 184n
Andrews, Henry 205
Andrews, Richard 204–5
Anglo-French alliance 47
Anglo-Scottish treaty 92, 104, 106
Annandale, first earl of, *see* Murray, John
Annesley, Arthur, first earl of Anglesey 82, 84n, 155–6, 168n, 177, 255, 256, 257, 258, 270, 286, 287, 294, 300, 304, 315
Annesley, Francis, first Baron Mountnorris 82, 211
Anti-christ 191
Antiscripturism 85
Antrim, Convention members 170–2
Antrim county 5, 81, 171, 175, 179, 189, 211, 247
Antrim, Randall McDonnell, second earl of 170, 179
Ardee, Co. Louth, barony 190, 195, 196, 197, 208, 238, 239
Ardee, town 105, 197
Ardfert, Co. Kerry 221, 222
Ardfert, bishop of *see* Fulwar, Thomas
Ardglass, first earl of, *see* Cromwell, Wingfield
Ardmoyle, Co. Tipperary 213
Ards, Co. Down 267
Ards, third Viscount, *see* Montgomery, Hugh
Arklow, Co. Wicklow 176
Armagh, archbishop of, *see* Bramhall, John and Ussher, James
Armagh, Convention members 173–4, 225
Armagh, county 5, 173, 175, 188
Armagh, town 170n, 173, 174, 281n
Arminian 85, 250
Armorer, Nicholas 48
Armstrong, Col. John 203
army, in England 1, 18, 21, 22, 28, 56–7, 87–8, 170, 243–4, 261, 262, 291
army, in Ireland 6–7, 8, 14, 16, 21, 28, 104, 143, 144, 159, 179, 274–5, 276, 295, 298–9, 316
  disbandment 6–7, 8, 63, 64, 67, 69, 71, 106, 137, 173, 182, 184, 188, 190, 194, 196, 197, 201, 209, 217, 220, 223, 224, 225, 226, 231, 233
  establishment 8–9, 59–60, 88n
  loose companies 8, 63, 71, 89, 173, 182, 192
  garrisons 9, 78, 101, 112, 114, 135, 156, 315
  private soldiers 78, 117–18, 148, 159
  musters 66, 75, 76
  purge 76–8, 127
  pay 5, 36, 75, 76, 95, 116, 118
  condition 101, 102–3
  representatives to general council 104–6;
  see army officers; arrears; Irish brigade; new modelling
army, Scots 12, 21, 22, 28, 92, 140n
army council, of England 24, 88, 91, 94–5, 96
  declaration 95, 96, 99–100, 124
  Plea for their present practice 99n, 124
army officers in Ireland May–December, 1659 46, 67, 76
  response to English events, May 1659 5, 25, 27, 29, 50–1
  'old officers' petition 25, 33
  appointments reviewed 58, 59
  nomination 3, 58, 59–66, 76–8, 88, 149, 151–2, 270–1
  absentees 33, 45, 53, 58, 59, 62, 66, 143
  cashiered officers 75, 76, 95, 101, 106, 112
  response to English events, October 1659 88, 93–6, 97, 98, 99

[347]

INDEX

army officers in Ireland (*cont.*)
  letter to Monck 98, 104, 119
  see council of officers
Arnop, Lt.-Col. William 62, 64, 94n, 115, 135, 191
arrears 5, 6–7, 8, 11, 35, 36, 40, 75, 76, 78n, 116, 118, 144, 158, 173, 179, 184, 190, 194, 195, 196, 205, 209, 215, 216, 221, 224, 235, 268, 305
  English 7, 57
  Munster 12, 35, 186, 198, 205, 224, 267
  pre-1649 6, 35, 171, 182, 183, 185, 198, 207, 208, 210, 218, 224, 227, 229, 251, 267
  post-1649 7, 180, 182, 183, 191, 206, 207, 208, 209, 216, 225, 251
articles of war 37
articles of Limerick 116n
Arundel, Sussex 276
Aske, Capt. Thomas 105
Askeaton, Co. Limerick 216
Aspinall, William, minister 128n
assessments, parliamentary 16, 81, 145, 158, 215, 249, 257, 268
Aston, William 196, 231n, 232n, 239, 247, 270, 275, 299, 304, 308, 310, 312, 313
Athboy, Co. Meath 188, 189, 190, 197, 203
Athenry, Co. Galway 229, 230, 235
Athlone, Co. Westmeath 69, 70, 78n, 115, 159, 170n, 192, 193, 229, 272n
Athy, Co. Kildare 105, 192, 202, 203, 205, 208
attorney general, of Ireland 42, 134n, 204, 319
auditor general 175, 199, 227
Aungier, Francis, third Baron Longford 177, 287n, 290, 304, 305
  letters to Ormond 277, 296–7, 303
Axtell, Col. Daniel 61, 73, 88, 99, 117, 151, 302n

Badcock, Heritage, minister 283
Bagshaw, Sir Edward 185
Baillie, Robert 278
Baily, William, bishop of Clonfert 285n
Baines, Edward, minister 128, 247, 252
Baker, Richard 162
Baker, Henry 207–8, 209, 231n
Ballaghkeen barony, Co. Wexford 210
Ballinakill, Queen's Co. 170n
Ballinasloe, Co. Galway 15, 86
Ballyclough, Co. Cork 223
Ballycrenane, Co. Cork 219
Ballydugan, Co. Down 176
Ballymackey, Co. Tipperary 182
Ballymartyr, Co. Cork 110
Ballynetray, Co. Waterford 213
Ballyrand, Co. Limerick 217
Ballyshannon, Co. Donegal 169n, 174
Baltimore, Co. Cork 191, 217
Banagher, King's Co. 169n, 225
Bandon, Co. Cork 217, 221, 228n
Bangor 174, 204
Baptists 16, 38, 39, 51, 58, 59, 61, 63, 65, 66, 67, 68, 78, 85, 86, 96, 98, 105, 106, 135, 136n, 149n, 158, 190, 201, 222, 250
  see Anabaptist
Barbados 211
Barebone, Praisegod 153
Barebone's Parliament 5, 64n
Bargy barony, Co. Wexford 206
Barnard, T, C. 69n
Barrett, Major John 62, 98
Barrington, A. 137n, 149n
Barrington, Francis 195
Barrow, Col. Robert 63, 84n, 91, 92n, 94, 95, 96, 97, 99, 100, 108n, 151, 302n
Barry, Sir James 146, 147, 200, 202, 206, 240, 247–8, 254, 284, 289, 299, 300, 304, 309n, 312
Barry, Mathew 248
Barry, Richard 200

[348]

Barry, Richard, second earl of
    Barrymore   177, 212, 218, 222,
    236n, 237
Barrymore barony, Co. Cork   221, 267,
    308
Barwick, Dr John   45, 61n, 141, 271
Basil, William   42
Bathurst, Henry   219–20, 231n
Bathurst, Samuel   201, 232n, 237
Baxter, Richard   109n
Beaulieu, Co. Louth   197
Beaumaris, Anglesey   45, 72, 129
Belasyse, John, first Baron   49n
Belfast, Co. Antrim   114, 170, 171, 175,
    188n, 194, 283
Belfast, first Baron, *see* Chichester,
    Arthur
Belfast, first Viscount, *see* Chichester,
    Edward
Bellingham, Daniel   196
Bellingham, Henry   196, 231n
Bellingham, Robert   196
Belturbet, Co. Cavan   182, 185, 204,
    309n
Belvelly Castle, Co. Cork   219
Benburb, battle of   183, 225
benefices   283
Bennett, Major John   62, 129
Bennett, Sir Henry, first earl of
    Arlington   164
Beresford, Michael   179, 186, 229
Beresford, Tristram   179, 186, 200
Bernard, Nicholas, dean of Ardagh   273
Berwick   100, 124
Bingley estate   42
Blackwell, Capt. John   105
Blackwood, Christopher, minister   128
Bladen, William   124
Blayney, Edward, first baron of
    Monaghan, 224
Blayney, Edward, third baron of
    Monaghan   183
Blayney, Henry, second baron of
    Monaghan   183, 184, 225
Blayney, Richard, fourth baron of
    Monaghan   183, 184, 224
Blennerhassett, John Jr   221–2
Blennerhassett, John Sr   221
Bligh, John   189–90, 232n, 314
Blount, Col. Charles   220, 221
Blundell, Sir Francis, 193
Blundell, Sir George   193
Bolton, Major Francis   61, 73
Bond, Capt. William,   109, 112n, 113n
Bonnell, Major Samuel   63, 73
Book of Common Prayer   82n
book of rates   83, 269, 308
Booker, John   214–15, 231n, 232n, 236n
books of discrimination   248n
Booth, Sir George   54, 68, 70, 73, 82,
    102, 106, 126, 139, 155, 282
'Booth's rising'   68, 75, 87
    counter-measures in Ireland   69–72
    see Irish brigade
Borlase, Dr Edmund   167
Borlase, Sir John   199
Boyd, Thomas   210–11
Boyd, William, second Lord
    Kilmarnock   211n
Boyle, Co. Roscommon   226, 281
Boyle, Francis, first Viscount Shannon
    49, 266, 270, 277
Boyle, John, bishop of Cork   216
Boyle, Michael, dean of Cloyne   216
Boyle, Richard, archbishop of Tuam
    219
Boyle, Richard, first earl of Cork   23,
    213, 218, 219
Boyle, Richard, second earl of Cork   23,
    123n, 147, 236, 253, 295–6, 302, 303,
    312
Boyle, Roger, first Baron Broghill and
    first earl of Orrery   1, 12, 23–4, 25,
    27, 29, 30, 32, 49, 50, 53, 106, 109,
    110, 112, 117, 119, 123n, 132n, 137,
    138n, 142, 145, 146, 147, 149n, 151,

Boyle, Roger, first Baron Broghill (*cont.*)
  160, 162, 169, 170, 171, 177, 181, 201, 202n, 209, 212, 213, 214, 215, 216, 217, 218, 219, 220, 223, 225, 226, 227, 232, 236, 238, 239, 240, 247, 255, 260, 266, 267, 272n, 286, 289, 290, 299, 312, 315, 318
  meeting with commissioners 71–2
  and Munster declaration 161–2
  approach to Scots Presbyterians 263–5, 280
  approach to king 265–6
  speech in Convention 271
  appointed lord president of Munster 272, 287, 294
  rivalry with Coote 275–6, 277, 287–9
  view of situation 276–7
  criticism of 287–8
  response to restoration 292–3
Brabazon, Edward, second earl of Meath 45–6, 295
Bramhall, Jane 198
Bramhall, John, bishop of Derry and archbishop of Armagh 198, 285n, 314
Brayfield, Col. Alexander 58, 62, 78n, 94n, 105, 115, 129
Breda 262, 304
  declaration 262, 291, 293–4, 298–9, 299, 303, 306, 314, 315
  Irish version 295, 303, 305–6
Brereton, John, minister 85n
Brereton, Sir William 73
Brest 72
Brett, Lt.-Col. John 63–4, 140–1
Brice, Mary 202
Bridges, Col. John 109, 113n, 118, 121, 143, 153, 279
Bristol 50, 81
British regiments in Ulster 11, 170–1, 180, 184
Brodrick, Alan 221
Brodrick, St John 220–1, 231n, 232n

Broghill, first Baron, *see* Boyle, Roger
brotherly association 84
Brown, Sir John 216n
Browne, Samuel 221, 231n, 232n, 236n
Brussels 72, 164, 241, 259, 261, 266, 274, 278
  treaty of 17
Buckingham, first duke of, *see* Villiers, George
Bulkeley, Arthur 197, 232n
Bunratty baronies, Co. Clare 190, 223
Burdett, George, minister 116n, 281
Burke, Ulick, first marquess of Clanricarde 23, 69, 115n, 164
Burnchurch, Co. Tipperary 208
Burrell, Thomas 208–9, 230n, 231n, 232n, 275n
Burston, Daniel, minister 281
Bury, Sir William 38, 39, 43n, 57, 79, 213, 232n, 237, 247, 255, 267, 275, 277, 286, 316
Butler, Elizabeth, marchioness of Ormond, 31, 50, 207
Butler, James, first marquess of Ormond 10–11, 13, 17, 22, 31, 38, 69, 72, 82n, 86, 159n, 165, 166n, 177, 182, 187, 188, 191, 192, 193, 195, 198, 199, 201, 202, 203, 204, 206, 207, 211, 222, 228, 257, 259, 273–4, 277, 287, 290, 295, 296, 300, 302, 304, 305, 306, 310, 311, 312, 313, 316, 317, 319
Butler, Sir Stephen 185
Butler, Thomas, earl of Ossory 31
Bysse, John 82n, 176n, 200, 202, 247

Cadogan, Sir William 189, 190
Cahirdangan, Co. Cork 219
Callan, Co. Kilkenny 169n
Calvert, Sir George 203
Cambre, Solomon 116, 137n, 138n
Cambridge University 177, 227, 247
Campbell, John [Charles] 114, 130, 137n,

[350]

147, 149n
Camphire, Co. Waterford   218
Camus Macosquin, Co. Londonderry   281n
Candler, William   138n
Carey, George   186
Carlingford, Co. Louth   195, 197
Carlow, castle   114
Carlow, Convention members   204–5, 237
Carlow, county   75, 199, 202, 257n
Carlow town   58, 105, 204, 205
Carmarthan, Wales   304
Carncastle, Co. Antrim   247
Carpenter, Philip   273
Carrick, Co. Leitrim   227, 228
Carrick, Co. Tipperary   22
Carrickfergus, Co. Antrim   9, 62, 63, 103, 115, 147, 170, 172, 200, 264n
Carteret, Dr Philip   105, 230
Cary, Henry, first Viscount Falkland   206
Carysfort, Co. Wicklow   203, 205
Cashel, Co. Tipperary   105, 213, 214, 232, 237
Castle, Major James   63, 173, 191
Castlebar, Co. Mayo   169n
Castleconnor parish, Co. Sligo   224
Castle Eve, Co. Kilkenny   208
Castlefinn, Co. Donegal   181
Castlehaven, Co. Cork   220
Castlehaven, first earl of, *see* Touchet, Audley
Castlehaven, third earl of, see Touchet, James
Castle Jordan, Co. Meath   194
Castlelyons, Co. Cork   218
Castle Oliver, Co. Limerick   217
Castle Raban, Co. Kildare   193n
Castleroe, Co. Londonderry   179
Castle Waterhouse, Co. Fermanagh   186
Catholics   10–11, 16–17, 74, 103, 164, 191, 210, 223, 254, 267, 279, 296, 303, 304–5, 305–6, 313, 316, 317
  innocent   5, 318
  proprietors   4, 317
  residents of Cork, Youghal and Kinsale   267
Caulfield, Thomas   138n, 178, 188, 226, 234, 275n
Caulfield, Toby, first Baron Charlemont   188
Caulfield, Toby, third Baron Charlemont   178, 188
Caulfield, Sir William   42
Caulfield, William, fifth Baron Charlemont   137n, 138n, 149n, 150n, 159, 173, 174, 178n, 187–8, 226, 233, 234
cavaliers   70, 100, 102, 106, 114, 119n, 129, 148, 149, 154, 241, 276, 288, 317
Cavan, Convention members   185–6
Cavan, county   6, 170n, 173, 191
Cavan, first earl of, *see* Lambert, Charles
'census of 1659'   *see* poll tax
cessation of 1643   11, 12, 177
Chambers, Robert   124–6, 128, 285
Charlemont, barons of, *see* Caulfield
Charlemont, Co. Tyrone   160, 173, 174, 179, 188
Charles I   1, 10, 11, 12, 13, 17, 19, 43, 44, 53, 65, 109, 129, 146n, 164n, 182, 187, 192, 194, 198, 206, 219, 222, 236, 244, 262, 290, 298, 302, 308, 312
Charles II   4, 10, 13, 16, 19, 29, 30, 31, 32, 45, 47, 49, 50, 61, 68, 70, 72, 100, 101, 118, 132, 135, 146n, 158, 159n, 161, 165, 172n, 183, 191, 226, 240, 256, 258–62, 263, 265–6, 270, 272, 273–4, 275, 276, 278, 279, 285, 288, 291, 292, 293, 294, 295, 296, 298–9, 299, 302, 303, 304, 305, 306, 310–11, 314, 315, 316–17, 318–20

INDEX

Charles II (*cont.*)
  conditions to be imposed on   17, 240–2, 263, 266, 271, 272, 275, 276, 287, 288, 290, 291, 316, 319
  invited to Ireland by Coote   163–4
  commission to Coote   258, 277–8
  proclaimed king in England   294–5
  proclaimed king in Ireland   297–8
  issues *Gracious message*   311
  proclamation against re-possession of lands   305
  receives Irish commissioners   310, 312–13
  Gracious declaration (November 1660)   318
Charnock, Stephen, minister   247, 252, 280
charters, town   14, 91, 180, 186, 207, 208
Chatworth, H.   137n
Cheshire   54, 68, 72, 140, 142, 201
Chester   50, 103, 194, 207, 270, 300
Chichester, Arthur   180–1, 182
Chichester, Sir Arthur, first Baron Belfast   181, 191
Chichester, Edward, first Viscount Carrickfergus   181
Chichester, John   181
Chichester family   171, 186
Chichester House, Dublin   86, 128
Chirk Castle   73
church government   14–16, 246, 250–1, 278–9, 310, 315
church lands   36, 76, 318
Church of Christ   51, 86
Church of Ireland   14, 278, 282, 284, 312, 314–15
churches
  Christ Church cathedral   128, 244, 245, 251, 309, 314
  All Hallows   185
  New Street   192n
  St Bride's   292
  St Catherine's   245
  St Finbarr's   128n
  St John's   128n, 181, 201, 247
  St Kevin's   124
  St Michan's   128
  St Patrick's   85n, 124
  St Patrick's cathedral   314
  St Werburgh's   247
  Wood Street   247
civil war, England   3, 10, 13, 17, 19, 73, 176, 188, 196, 202, 215, 220, 224, 239, 240, 243, 263
Clanbrassil, first earl of, *see* Hamilton, James
Clanbrassil, second earl of, *see* Hamilton, Henry
Clancarty, first earl of, *see* MacCarthy, Donough
Clandeboye, second Viscount, *see* Hamilton, James
Clankee barony, Co. Cavan   185
Clanmelier estate   304
Clanricarde, first marquess of, *see* Burke, Ulick
Clare, Convention members   222–3, 236
Clare, county   5, 36, 74, 185, 190, 222, 223, 267, 301, 313
Clarges, Dr Thomas   171
Clarke, Col. John   33, 58, 64, 182
Clement, Gregory   302n
Clifton, Col. Richard   147
Clobery, Col. John   61n, 141
Clogher, Co. Tyrone   169n
Clogher, bishop of, *see* Jones, Dr Henry
Clogher, Roman Catholic bishop of, *see* MacMahon, Heber
Clonakilty, Co. Cork   217
Clonfert, bishop of *see* Baily, William
Clonmel, Co. Tipperary   58, 61, 77, 105, 116, 157, 212, 213, 214, 215
Clonmines, Co. Wexford   209, 210
Clotworthy, Hugh   149n, 157

Clotworthy, James 179
Clotworthy, Sir John, first Viscount
    Massereene 155, 170, 171n, 172,
    177, 179, 180, 181, 234–5, 240, 247,
    255, 270, 275–6, 288, 303, 304, 308,
    310, 312, 313, 315, 316
Coldstream 130
Cole, Sir John 64, 112, 113n, 121, 122,
    150n, 182, 184, 226, 278
Cole, Michael 182
Cole, Robert 182–3, 231n, 232n, 234
Cole, Sir William 173, 182
Coleraine, county 174
Coleraine, Co. Londonderry 27, 145n,
    178, 179, 185, 186, 281n
colonists 4, 8, 13, 19–20
    see English-Irish; newcomers; new
        English; new Protestants; old
        English; old protestants; Scots
        settlers
commander in chief 22
    England 59, 92, 154, 155, 168
    Ireland 58, 61, 66, 67, 75, 80, 97, 98,
        111, 120, 133, 139, 155, 168, 287
    Scotland 59, 92, 97, 155, 168
commissioners, England
    admiralty 64, 146, 254n
    army (1659) 87, 97, 136
    army (1660) 143, 151, 153, 157
    for nomination of officers 22, 58, 88
    see Portsmouth; 'nine', the
        commissioners, Ireland
    Athlone 64n, 193, 196, 212, 213
    customs and excise 193
    for defective titles 36
    for determining civil causes 80
    for management of the Irish
        revenue 143
    for ministers in Ulster 180, 187
    for oyer, terminer etc. 80
    for setting out soldiers' land 207,
        214, 224, 225
    for setting tithes in Cork 220

Loughrea 177, 229
of survey 179, 185, 186, 189, 193,
    195, 196, 198, 205, 208, 213, 214,
    215, 229
to consider the public revenue 82
to enquire into the conversion of the
    Irish 192
to enquire into murders and
    massacres 38, 185
to govern the army 146, 156, 272n,
    297
see Poll tax
commissioners, Irish, in England
    (1659) 38, 39, 40, 44, 45, 57–8
    petition 34–7, 44, 57–8
commissioners, Irish, in England
    (January 1660) 126, 143, 144, 152,
    153, 166
commissioners, Irish, in England (April
    1660) 255, 269–70, 271–2, 275–6,
    289, 294–6, 299, 302–3, 304, 305,
    306
    instructions 267–9, 310
commissioners, Irish, in England (June
    1660) 4, 299–300, 301, 304, 308,
    309, 315
    instructions 307–8, 309, 311–12
    received by king 310, 312–13
    religious proposals 312, 313–15
    negotiations 313–14, 317–19
commissioners, parliamentary, for
    Scotland 146, 264
commissioners, parliamentary, in
    Ireland (1650) 42, 67, 143, 185
commissioners, parliamentary, in
    Ireland (1659) 1, 51, 68, 71–2, 75,
    76, 79, 80, 81, 84, 88, 95, 97, 102,
    106, 108, 132, 134, 139, 198, 249,
    253
    appointment 41–3, 44, 57
    instructions 44, 57
    revenue proposals 82–3
    religious policy 84–7

commissioners, parliamentary, in
  Ireland (1659) (*cont.*)
  legislative proposals   90–1
  instructions to Ludlow,   90
  seizure   110
  impeachment   134, 143, 152, 158
commissioners, parliamentary, in
  Ireland (January 1660)   139, 140,
  142, 143, 146, 155
commissioners, parliamentary, in
  Ireland (March 1660)   255, 266–7,
  274, 282, 283–4, 286, 295, 297–8,
  302
committee of safety, English (May,
  1659)   22, 26, 28, 67
committee of safety, English (October
  1659)   88, 92, 97, 100, 125, 144
committee of safety, Irish   146n, 200,
  239, 247
common enemy, the   25, 30, 57, 91, 94,
  99, 101, 102, 104, 112, 254, 317
'common prayer book' party   128, 246
commonwealth   2, 9n, 13, 18, 19, 21,
  35, 45, 71, 76, 83, 119n, 125, 131,
  134, 154, 189, 192, 202, 224, 241,
  243, 256, 283, 284, 298, 300, 320
communications between Ireland and
  the court   259, 260, 274
communications between Ireland and
  England   22, 50, 100, 255
communion, admission to   15, 246, 251
composition fines   7, 12, 14, 36–7, 84n,
  219, 230
  ordinances   12, 13
confederate Catholics   10, 11, 180n,
  208, 223, 224, 226, 296, 317
confession of faith   37
Congregationalists   125
Connacht   5, 10n, 23, 36, 65, 69, 70, 71,
  89, 103, 115, 122, 169, 177, 192, 193,
  200, 222, 223, 224, 227, 232, 238,
  254, 267, 269, 277, 284, 301, 313
Connacht, Convention returns   223–30,
  235
Connacht, lord president of   296n;
  see Coote, Sir Charles
Connacht purchasers   216, 229, 267
conservators of liberty   107
Convention, Irish see General
  Convention of Ireland
Convention, Scottish   124
Conway, Wales   91
Conway, Edward, third Viscount
  Conway and Kiltullagh   39, 43,
  171, 295
Cook, John   90, 270, 272, 302
Cook, Robert   112n
Cooley, Co. Louth   197
Cooper, Sir Anthony Ashley, first earl of
  Shaftesbury   97, 142
Cooper, Col. Thomas   33, 58, 60, 62,
  69, 94n, 97, 98, 99, 100, 103,
  114–15, 119, 143, 151, 172, 264n
Coote, Sir Charles, first earl of
  Mountrath   10n, 23, 24, 30, 31, 32,
  45, 53, 65, 69, 70, 71, 89, 92, 97, 98,
  109, 112, 113, 115, 119, 121, 122,
  123n, 127, 137, 138, 139, 142, 143,
  145, 146, 149n, 150, 155, 157, 159,
  160, 161, 164n , 171, 173, 174, 177,
  180, 188, 200, 207, 226, 227, 228,
  229, 232, 233, 235, 238, 239, 240,
  248n, 253n, 255, 256, 258, 259, 261,
  265, 266, 267, 271, 272n, 275, 286,
  287, 288, 289, 290, 297, 299, 309–10,
  312, 315–16, 318
  declaration of Coote and his officers
    115–16, 142n
  and Dublin declaration   161, 163, 167
  sends Forbes to king   163
  commission from king   258, 260,
    277–8
  rivalry with Broghill   275–6, 277,
    287–9
  and English royalists   277
  comments on convention   289

[354]

INDEX

Coote, Charles Jr   70, 206, 227, 235
Coote, Sir Charles Sr   206, 228n, 267
Coote, Chidley   70n, 116, 121, 138n, 150, 169, 182, 196, 201, 202, 206, 225, 226, 275n, 278
Coote, Richard, first earl of Colloney   70n, 116, 150, 217, 225, 226, 227, 228, 258, 265, 275n, 278
Coote, Thomas   116, 150, 175, 185, 275n
Coote family   122, 147, 177, 185, 194, 224, 228, 235, 281
Corbet, Miles   28, 42, 43, 44, 46, 51, 52, 110, 134, 136, 139, 152, 154n, 253, 269, 302n
Cork, city   86, 98, 117, 135, 143, 217, 219, 267, 272, 308
Cork, clergy, petition   284
Cork, Convention members   217–21, 236
Cork, county   6, 53, 59, 82, 110, 116, 168, 184, 188, 193, 209, 217, 218, 226, 257n, 284
Cork, first earl of, *see* Boyle, Richard
Cork, second earl of, *see* Boyle, Richard
Cornwall   177, 305n
Cottlestown, Co. Sligo   224
council chamber   1, 110
council of officers, Ireland (post-December 1659)   116n, 119–24, 127, 129, 130, 136, 156, 157, 166, 167–8, 178, 182, 188, 214, 229, 250, 285
   declaration of 14 December   111–12, 117, 118, 129, 135, 139, 140, 158, 160, 166
   letter to speaker   113, 126, 139
   letter to Monck   113
   declaration of 28 December   122, 143
   summon convention   123–4, 127
   post-coup objectives   132–3
   relations with Ludlow   120–1, 133–5, 137–9
   remodel army   120, 148–52
   commission to govern army   146, 156, 272n, 297
   devolve powers   146
   declaration of 16 February   158–9, 160, 162, 164, 167, 168, 188, 198, 208, 226, 245, 249, 264, 278
   declaration of 13 April   274–5
   humble address of 7 May   293
   response to restoration   292, 293
council, of Scotland   24, 106n, 263
council of state, English, commonwealth (1649–53)   147n
council of state, English, commonwealth (1659)   22, 33, 34, 40–3, 50, 53, 54, 56, 67, 72, 76, 80, 88, 92, 107, 121, 140, 142, 143, 146, 148, 153
   Irish affairs committees   41, 42, 44, 80
   sub-committee for Irish nominations   59–66, 67, 77
council of state, English, commonwealth (1660)   154, 155, 156, 255, 256–7, 270, 271, 272, 274, 276, 286, 287, 289, 294
council of state, English, protectorate   42, 212
council of state, Irish, protectorate   23, 28, 38, 42, 43, 213, 227, 232
council of state, Scotland   24
coup d'etat, of December 1659   1–3, 108–11, 112, 113, 124, 129, 144, 148, 156, 164, 182, 188, 209, 220, 239, 240
   reaction outside Dublin   114–18
court in exile   48, 50
   and Ireland   164–7, 241, 258–61
Courthorpe, Peter   219, 231n
courts martial   148
Courtown, Co. Cork   219
courts of justice   14, 36, 38, 75, 79, 80, 257, 269, 303

[355]

courts of justice (cont.)
  admiralty and vice-admiralty 228, 269
  chancery 185, 204, 269
  common pleas 145n, 146n, 177, 192, 211, 269, 299
  exchequer 42, 146, 196, 200n, 201, 206n, 269
  high court , 1653 185, 192, 203, 228
  Munster 212
  presidency 269, 313
  probate 214, 269
  upper (king's) bench 42, 177, 205, 269, 272
covenant *see* solemn league and covenant
covenanters 12
Coxe, Samuel, minister 245–7, 248, 250, 251–2, 280
Crofton, Henry 227
Cromwells 2, 30, 51, 53, 56, 60, 66, 77, 118, 229
Cromwell, Catherine 42
Cromwell, Henry 7n, 14, 16, 23, 29, 30, 31, 32, 34, 38, 39, 40, 42, 43, 44, 45–6, 48, 49, 50, 51, 53, 55, 58, 59, 60, 61, 62, 63, 66, 67, 74, 79, 81n, 82n, 84, 85, 86, 96, 101, 109n, 115, 121, 127, 165, 167, 172, 177, 178, 179, 191, 197, 198, 200, 226, 227, 229, 232, 235, 247, 253, 279, 281
  response to Richard's overthrow 24–7, 28, 32–3, 47
  recall and resignation 41, 46–7
  return to England 52, 54
Cromwell, Oliver 6–7, 12, 13, 14, 17, 18, 19, 24, 25, 30, 31, 38, 40, 52, 53, 55, 56, 58, 59, 60, 61, 62n, 63, 64, 71, 76, 82n, 112, 151n, 178, 179, 184n, 193, 215, 217, 220, 223, 232
Cromwell, Richard 17, 18, 19, 21–2, 24, 25, 26, 27, 28, 30, 32, 38, 39, 47, 51, 55, 60, 62n, 63, 76, 78, 127, 136, 200, 210, 212, 222
Cromwell, Col. Thomas 175
Cromwell, Vere, fourth earl of Ardglass 69, 70, 273
Cromwell, Wingfield, second earl of Ardglass 32, 70, 273
Cromwellians 18, 99, 200, 232, 234
'Cromwellian settlement' 4, 5–8, 9, 11–12, 13–14, 14–16, 35, 170, 173, 175, 179, 180, 182, 183, 185, 186, 189, 191, 193, 194, 195–6, 198, 199–200, 202, 205, 207, 209, 212, 213, 216, 218, 221, 223–4, 251, 318
  religious 14–16
Crowe, Stephen 207
crown lands 76
Cuffe, Hugh 177
Cuffe, James 70n, 147, 163–4, 177, 226n, 229, 231n, 232n, 234
Cullenagh barony, Queen's Co. 195
Cumberland 222
Currahnahency, Co. Cork 218
custodiams 8
custom house 1, 110, 298
customs 193, 197, 203, 206, 308
customs duties 35, 45, 82–3, 268, 301
customs farmers 35, 83, 189, 268–9, 301

Dancer, Theo 112n, 113n
Davis, John 115, 172
Davis, Hercules 170, 172, 178n
Davis, Sir Paul 36n, 82n, 146n, 202, 205, 206, 227, 247, 248, 255, 267, 283, 299, 300, 304
Davis, Major Thomas 65, 94n
Davis, William 183, 231n
Deane, Major Joseph 60, 69, 74, 94n, 105n, 129n
debentures 7, 10, 11, 35, 198, 210
Dee, Robert, mayor of Dublin 159
delinquents 14, 57, 203, 206
Dennison, Major John 64, 129

Denny, Sir Arthur   221, 222
deputy treasurer for wars   268
Derby petition   87, 88, 89, 104
Derry, bishop of *see* Bramhall, John
Desborough, Major John   15, 66, 78n, 86, 114
Desmond, Co. Kerry   65
Devereux, Robert, twentieth earl of Essex   188, 215
Dieppe   30
Digby, Essex, minister   283
Dillon, Thomas, fourth Viscount Costello-Gallen   296
Dingle, Co. Kerry   193, 221
directory of worship   82n
Disquisition, A   319
Dixon, William   82n
Dobson, Lt.-Col. Isaac   64, 92, 96–7, 115
Dodson, William, customs farmer   83n
Domville, William   319
Donegal, Convention members   186–8
Donegal, county   12, 42, 174, 179, 188, 202
Donegal, town   169n
Donemon, Co. Roscommon   178
Donoughmore, Queen's Co.   195
Dorset   184
Douglas, Sir Joseph   147, 162
Douglas, Robert, minister   263–4
Down, county   5, 31, 81, 103, 171, 174, 175, 230, 234, 240, 301n
Down, Convention members   174–8
Down and Connor, bishop of   199; *see* Leslie, Henry
Downpatrick, Co. Down   174, 176
Drogheda, Co. Louth   78n, 85, 86, 114, 160, 173, 189, 193, 195, 196, 197
Drogheda, second Viscount, *see* Moore, Charles
Dromahaire, Co. Leitrim   224
Dromineene, Co. Cork   220
Drury, John, customs farmer   83n

Dublin, city   9, 10, 15, 22, 23, 24, 31, 35, 38, 42, 46, 51, 67, 68, 69, 70, 81, 82, 84, 86, 88, 93, 95, 96, 102, 113, 114, 115, 116, 119, 122, 124, 127, 128, 130, 134, 137, 156, 160, 167, 169, 171, 176, 178, 181, 184, 185, 187, 192, 196, 199, 200, 202, 203, 205, 207, 210, 228, 235, 238, 245, 247, 252, 255, 256, 257, 258, 263, 264, 272, 275, 281, 285, 291, 292, 297, 301
  aldermen   167, 184, 185, 196, 200, 210, 237, 293, 297
  citizens   26, 111, 156–7
  council   26, 74, 112, 159, 292, 293–4, 299
  delegation to king   294, 299
  mayor   129, 159, 167, 200, 202, 293, 297, 299
  militia   26, 69, 89, 112, 159, 196
  support for December coup   111, 112
Dublin, county   43, 60, 181, 182, 185, 188n
Dublin, Convention members   199–202, 237
Dublin Castle   1, 51–2, 71, 102, 109, 129, 160, 253, 316
  surprisal   1, 108–11, 118, 126, 238
  occupied by Waller   157–9
Duckenfield, Lt.-Col. John   62, 66
Duhallow, Co. Cork   220
Duncannon, Co. Wexford   78n, 135, 136, 137, 139, 143, 166
  petition   154–5, 166
Dundalk, Co. Louth   195, 197
Dungannon, Co. Tyrone   169n, 181, 185, 187n
Dungan's Hill, battle of   173, 207
Dungarvan, Co. Waterford   117, 211, 212, 213, 218
Dungiven, Co. Londonderry   179
Dunkirk   22, 27, 64n, 70n
Durham   81, 147

Dutch 294

Earlstown, Co. Kilkenny 208
Eastern Association 63
Edenderry, Co. Kildare 193
Edgeworth, John 198, 200
Edinburgh 92, 124, 130, 142n, 147, 169, 263, 280
Edmonds, Capt. Richard 70n
elections 3, 127, 131, 148, 153–4, 166, 169–242, 244, 248, 262, 289, 291, 303
Eliogarty barony, Co. Tipperary 176
Ellistown, Co. Tyrone 187
Elphin, diocese 281n, 284
engagement, oath of 65, 76, 77, 90, 132
engagement, against readmission of secluded members 157
England 2, 3, 5, 12–13, 16, 17, 25, 26, 32, 34, 35, 36, 43, 47, 48, 50, 51, 54, 56, 62, 63, 65, 66, 68, 73, 81, 83, 88, 89, 94, 100, 102, 105, 111, 121, 124, 131, 132, 148, 163, 164, 165, 167, 171, 172, 176, 190, 193, 200, 204, 207, 209, 219, 224, 233, 234, 240, 245, 246, 248, 249, 250, 254, 255, 261, 263, 265, 268, 271, 272, 275, 287, 288, 289, 290, 292, 295, 297, 302, 304, 311
English events 21–2, 56–7, 68, 87–8, 92–3, 106–8, 131–2, 136, 243–4, 262–3
English-Irish 115–16
English party 316
Ennis, Co. Clare 169n, 216, 222
Enniscorthy, Co. Wexford 169n
Enniskillen, Co. Fermanagh 115, 182, 202
episcopacy 15, 240, 243, 273, 275, 278–9, 285, 310, 311–12, 314, 315
limited 273, 278, 280, 281n, 311
Episcopalians 15, 129, 150, 166, 247, 279–80, 285, 311, 315
Essex, twentieth earl of, *see* Devereux, Robert
Estates, confirmation of 6, 29, 33, 34–5, 40, 44, 57, 152, 241, 251, 257, 265, 267, 296, 305, 306, 308; *see* acts of parliament
re-possession of 301, 305
Eustace, Sir Maurice 299–300, 316, 318
Evans, Thomas 208, 231n, 232n
Everarde, Nicholas 215
excise 45, 82–3, 193, 301
expeditionary force, 1649 1, 6, 13, 25, 178, 189, 209, 232, 233
Eyres, Col. William 301

Fairfax, Thomas, Lord 141, 176
Falkland, first viscount, *see* Cary, Henry
fast, days of 85, 247, 289
Fenton, Sir Maurice 112, 113n, 117, 138n, 160, 226n, 236n
Fenton, Sir William 226, 294
Fenwick, Col. Roger 196
Fermanagh, Convention members 182–3
Fermanagh, county 6, 7, 42, 64, 103, 174, 185
Fermoy, Co. Cork 218
Ferneley, John 201n
Ferneley, Philip 201, 231n
Ferns and Leighlin, bishopric of 205
Ferrard barony, Co. Louth 197
Ferrybridge, Yorkshire 142
Fertullagh barony, Co. Westmeath 190
Fethard, Co. Tipperary 74, 213, 215
Fethard, Co. Wexford 209
Fifth Monarchists 60, 160
Finch, Lt.-Col. Simon 64
Finglas, Co. Dublin 185
Fitzgerald, Garrett 217, 231n
Fitzgerald, George, sixteenth earl of Kildare 1, 110

INDEX

Fitzgerald, Robert   1, 110, 122, 138n, 239–40
Fitzmaurice, Patrick, twenty-eighth Baron Kerry   222, 237
Fitzpatrick family   195
Flanders   72
fleet, the   21, 27, 28, 45, 54, 56, 92, 107, 222, 262
Fleetwood, Charles   14, 15–16, 22, 26, 27, 29, 47, 54, 56, 60, 61, 62, 66, 73, 79, 87, 88, 89, 94, 97n, 101, 102, 107, 108, 125, 134, 136, 148, 157, 167
Fleming family   223
Flower, Lt.-Col. Henry   24, 25, 31, 62, 157
Forbes, Sir Arthur   30–1, 69, 70, 145n, 258, 259, 277–8
  attends king   163–5
Fore, Co. Westmeath   191
forfeited lands   5, 6–7, 11, 12, 16, 35, 175, 179, 182, 185, 189, 191, 198, 200, 221, 251, 296, 318
forfeiture   8, 12, 34
forty-nine ('49) officers   171, 175, 180n, 182, 187, 195, 198, 199, 202, 203, 204, 205, 215, 221, 222, 225, 226, 229n, 231, 236, 239
Fosterstown, Co. Meath   190
Foulke, Bartholomew   138n, 213–14, 231n, 315
Foulke, Francis Jr   117, 214, 218, 231n, 236n
Foulke, Francis Sr   218
Foulkes, Col. John   189, 194, 197
Foulke, Robert   218, 231n
Four Courts   244
Fowles, Thomas   134n
France   17, 45, 47, 72, 146n, 199, 261, 295, 297
  ambassador in London   28, 29, 39
Frearer, J.   113n
'free parliament'   3, 115, 131, 153, 156–7, 158, 159, 161, 163, 255, 270n, 273
friars   254, 309
Friend, John   60n, 138n
Fuenterrabia, treaty negotiations   72
Fuller, William, bishop of Limerick   190, 314
Fulwar, Thomas, bishop of Ardfert   285n

Galway, city   63, 66, 70, 115, 137n, 177, 185, 222, 228
Galway, Convention members   228–30
Galway, county   23, 63, 81, 112, 187, 223, 228, 229, 301
Galway, governor   63, 115
Garstin, Simon   137n, 149n
Gawden, Sir Denis   222
Geashill, King's Co.   283
General Convention of Ireland   3, 4, 144, 292, 294, 297, 304, 306, 308, 310, 313, 316, 318
  summoned   123–4, 166–8
  cancelled   144, 166
  composition   169–70
  election returns   170–242, 248
  army members   231–3, 234, 236, 238, 239
  office holders in   239–40
  political complexion   239–42
  religious issues   240–1, 250–1, 252–3, 266–7, 278–85, 310, 315
  convenes   168
  opening ceremony   244–7
  appoints officers and committees   247–8
  proclaims fast days   247, 275n, 289
  declaration of 8 March   248–51, 255, 256, 258, 278, 279, 310
  public order measures   254, 301, 309
  instructions to commissioners, March 1660   267–9
  appoints commissioners   269–70

[359]

General Convention of Ireland (*cont.*)
  ordered to dissolve   271, 272, 273, 287
  poll tax ordinance   285–7, 300, 301
  adjournment debate   287, 288–9, 290
  declaration condemning the execution of Charles I   290, 292, 310
  reconvenes   297
  proclaims Charles as king   296–7
  post-recess business   298–301, 307–9
  declaration laying hold of the king's concessions   298–9
  appoints commissioners to attend king   299
  instructions to commissioners, May 1660   307–8, 309
  declaration for preservation of the peace   301, 305
  adjourns   309
General Convention of Ireland, committees
  advisory committee to committee for maintenance of ministers   248, 252, 280–2, 284
  for commissioners' instructions   254–5, 256, 267
  for maintenance of ministers   248, 252–3, 280, 282, 283, 310
  for new college   253–4
  for revenue   248, 254, 268
  for the administration of justice   269
  for trade   248
  grand committees   248, 268
  to prepare March declaration   248
  vacation   289, 297
general council of the army   92, 104, 106–7, 134, 142, 144, 148
general of the ordnance   23
Gibbon, Col. Robert   64
Gifford family   219
Gifford, Sir John   194, 223
Gifford, Thomas   194, 223

Gilbert, Claudius, minister   128
Gilbert, Henry   194–5
Gilbert, Sir William   194–5
Gilbert, William   194
Glaslough, Co. Monaghan   184
Gloucester   81, 221
Gloucester, Henry, duke of   300
Godbold, John   179–180, 232n, 234
Godfrey, Major John   61, 73, 140, 142
Goldsmith's Hall committee   172
'good affection'   11, 36, 171, 233, 234
'good old cause'   18, 25, 52, 154
Goodwin, Robert   42, 143, 146
Gookin, Vincent   16, 221n
Gore, Arthur   225, 226, 228
Gore, Francis   70, 225
Gore, Sir Paul   225
Gore, Sir William   174
Gorey, see Newborough
Gorges, Col. John   61, 115, 132n, 147, 150n, 199n, 227, 241, 263–4, 275, 280, 301n, 315
Gorges, Dr Robert   61, 103, 172, 227–8, 232n, 235, 253, 315
Gorges, Thomas   172, 227
Gowran, Co. Kilkenny, barony   208
Gowran, town   207
Gracious message, A   311
Graham, James, first marquess of Montrose   31
grandees   57
Gray's Inns   176, 180n, 196
Great Britain   245
Great Island, Co. Cork   219
Great Trust, the   18, 48, 68, 288
Greenaway, Henry   229, 232n
Greene, Major Elias   61, 137n, 138n, 149n
Gregg, John, minister   264
Gregory, J.   137n, 149n
Grenville, Sir John   262, 291
Grey, Enoch, minister   85, 128
Grocers Hall committee   201n, 257

Hague, The   49, 304
Halsey, William   212, 232n
Hamilton, Claude, first Baron Strabane   186
Hamilton, Sir Claud   187
Hamilton, Sir Francis   30–1, 69
Hamilton, Sir Frederick   224
Hamilton, Hans   69
Hamilton, Henry, second earl of Clanbrassil   234n
Hamilton, James, first duke of   41
Hamilton, James, first earl of Abercorn   186, 187
Hamilton, James, second Viscount Clandeboye and first earl of Clanbrassil   176, 230, 234n
Hamilton Family   176, 178, 187, 234
Hammond, Lt.-Col. Thomas   176
Hampden, John   176
Hand, James   112n, 113n
Handcock, William   191–2, 231n, 232n
Hannay, Robert   173n, 207
Hansard, Sir Richard   186
Harding, Dr John, minister   59n, 128
Harp, The   22, 292
Harris, Sir Edward   219
Harris, Philip   212–13, 232n
Harrison, John   137n, 138n, 149n
Hart, Henry   210n
Harte, Thomas   209–10, 231n, 232n
Harvey, Francis   210, 232n
Haselrig, Sir Arthur   67, 88, 107, 126, 139, 141
Hassells, Robert   206, 230n, 231n, 232n, 237
Hatton family   183
Haughton, John   137n
Hawkins, William   58, 294
Haynes, Gideon   149n
Heath, James   2
Henrietta Maria, Queen   48
Herbert, Sir Thomas   53n
Herefordshire   220

Herrick, Ralph   149n
Hewson, Col. John   33, 38, 52, 58, 62, 63, 66, 302n
Hickes, Thomas, minister   86, 134n
Hickman, Gregory   222
Hickman, Thomas   222–3, 231n
Hill, Sir Arthur   103, 142, 171n, 175, 178, 206, 225, 234, 265, 266, 299, 304
Hill, Frances   175
Hill, William   103n, 171n, 178, 234, 266
Hillsborough, Co. Down   103
History of the execrable rebellion   167
Hodges, John   72
Hoey, Sir John   202–3, 206, 211
Holland   275
Holland, first earl of, *see* Rich, Henry
Holyhead   22, 72, 73, 292
Hopkins, Thomas   112n, 113n, 138n
Horton, Col. Thomas   61
Hospital, Co. Limerick   216
Howard, Thomas   49
Hungerford, Col. Anthony   196
Hunks, Henry   302n
Hurd, Lt.-Col Humphrey   114
Hyde, Sir Edward, first earl of Clarendon   17, 29, 31, 133, 166n, 221, 227, 257, 258, 260–1, 263, 266, 271, 288, 305
  response to Richard's overthrow   47–50, 54
  and Booth's rising   72
  view of the Irish situation   164

Imokilly barony, Co. Cork   257n
imperial crown   297
Inchiquin, first earl, *see* Morrogh O'Brien
indemnity   12, 305
  see acts of parliament
Independents   15, 41, 42, 43, 51, 52, 84–5, 86, 128–9, 143, 184, 185, 187, 247, 250, 279–80, 281, 285
Ingoldsby, George   116, 122

Ingoldsby, Henry   30, 52, 63, 64, 65, 68, 116, 149, 150n, 153n, 190, 217, 232n
Ingoldsby, Richard   68
Inistiogue, Co. Kilkenny   169n
Inner Temple   227
Innisboffin, Co. Galway   192
Innishowen, Co. Donegal   186
inquisitions, plantation   36, 44, 313
instrument of government   168n
Iraghticonnor barony, Co. Kerry   222
Ireton, Henry   62, 302n
Irish brigade   73, 77, 85, 88, 102, 103–4, 105, 107, 114, 122, 140–1, 142, 151
Irish natives   25–6, 74, 76, 90, 103, 129, 154, 172, 177, 187, 192, 267, 284, 301, 316, 319
  proposals for control   90–1
Irish papists   25–6, 70, 78, 89, 112, 254, 304–5
Irish rebels   304–5
Irish Society of London   174, 179
Irish soldiers   17
Isle of Wight   106
Isreal   111, 245

Jamaica   65
Jamestown, Co. Leitrim   194, 227, 228
Jenner, Edward, minister   85
Jephson, Alexander   190–1, 231n
Jephson, Sir John   208, 218–19, 220
Jephson, William   46n, 219
Jesuits   57, 254
Jones, Ambrose, minister   189
Jones, Catherine, Viscountess Ranelagh   212
Jones, Lt.-Col. Henry   52, 62, 86, 94n, 98, 105, 109, 110
Jones, Dr Henry, bishop of Clogher   1, 38–9, 57, 70n, 98n, 109, 120n, 121, 145n, 167, 172, 189, 190, 191, 231n, 238, 247, 253, 265, 266, 267, 275, 278, 285, 300–1
  thanksgiving sermon   306–7

Jones, Col. John   34, 41, 42, 62, 67, 68, 71, 86, 89, 90, 91, 95, 96, 98, 99, 105, 106, 108, 110, 120, 133, 153n, 157n, 185, 272, 302n
  appointed deputy commander in chief   93
  comments on army declaration   99–100
  criticism of Ludlow   104
  impeachment   134
  view of situation   100–1, 102, 106, 118–19, 123–4
Jones, Lewis, bishop of Killaloe   1, 38
Jones, Col. Michael   38, 51, 189, 207, 267
Jones, Oliver   275n
Jones, Roger, first Viscount Ranelagh   82n, 181
Jones, Sir Theophilus   1, 38, 67, 69, 70n, 98, 109, 110, 113, 118, 121, 123n, 127, 135, 137, 138n, 139, 142, 145–6, 147, 150n, 157, 162, 177, 193, 200, 202, 205, 227, 240, 261n, 265, 266, 272n, 275n, 299, 301, 312
Jones, Thomas, archbishop of Dublin   177, 191
Joyner, Capt. John   1, 109, 110, 113n
judge advocate
  England   105, 112, 230
  Ireland   66, 105, 112, 144, 148, 151, 230
  Scotland   112, 230
  Leinster   228
judges   80, 125, 156, 269, 298, 312; see courts of justice
justice, administration of   38, 79–81, 90, 93, 123, 156, 158, 257, 269, 311
justices of the peace   14, 22, 37, 78, 79, 125, 173, 179, 184, 186, 193, 205, 206, 208, 213, 218, 219, 225, 226, 227

Kanturk, Co. Cork 176
Keane, Lt.-Col. William 63
Kells, Co. Meath 188, 189, 190
Kempson, Major Henry 60, 98, 105, 111, 112, 118, 119, 134, 138
Kennedy, Anthony, minister 264
Kennedy, Richard 206, 240, 299, 300
Kennedy, Robert 206
Kennedy, Thomas 300n
Kerr, Patrick, minister 201
Kerricurrihy barony, Co. Cork 220
Kerry, Convention members 221–2
Kerry, county 7, 65, 193, 221, 222, 225
Kerry, twentieth-eighth Baron, see Fitzmaurice, Patrick
Kilbeggan, Co. Westmeath 191, 192, 195, 199
Kilbrew, Co. Meath 227
Kilbride, Co. Wicklow 206
Kilcolman, Co. Cork 219
Kilcreene, Co. Kilkenny 208
Kilcullen, Co. Kildare 283
Kildare, Convention members 202–4, 237
Kildare, county 15, 74, 85, 128n, 185, 193, 195, 199, 203, 211, 228, 257n, 283
Kildare, town 202
Kildare, sixteenth earl of, see Fitzgerald, George
Kilfinny, Co. Limerick 216
Kilkenny, city 1, 61, 109, 114, 157n, 207, 208, 298
Kilkenny, Convention members 182n, 207–9, 238
Kilkenny, county 1, 6, 7, 25, 71, 72, 74, 75, 173, 191, 192, 195, 208, 212, 213, 238
Killaloe, bishop of, see Jones, Lewis
Killelagh, Co. Down 174, 177
Killybegs, Co. Donegal 186, 187
Kilmacrenan, Co. Donegal 186
Kilmallock, Co. Limerick 216, 217

Kilmore, bishop of see Maxwell, Robert
King, Francis 226n
King, Sir John, first Baron Kingston 137n, 138n, 149n, 150n, 188n, 199, 226, 239, 261, 265, 266, 275n, 278, 281, 293, 299
King, Dr Ralph 27, 70n, 144–5, 148, 152, 156n
King, William 216, 231n, 232n, 275n
Kingdon, Richard 66, 105, 148
kingship party 129
kingship vote (1657) 16–17, 52, 60, 63, 109, 179, 196, 200, 212, 219
king's party, the 266
King's County, Convention members 193–4, 237
King's County 5, 75, 177, 184, 193, 206, 210, 283
King's Inns 128, 146n, 180, 181, 187, 196, 204, 206, 212, 220
Kinsale, Co. Cork 24, 117, 135, 166n, 176, 214, 217, 219, 267, 295, 308
Knight, William 187, 209, 231n, 289, 309
Knockanass, battle of 223
Knockballymore, Co. Fermanagh 183
Knockniny barony, Co. Fermanagh 186
Kynaston, Col. John 187, 206
Kyrle, Richard 220, 223, 231n, 232n

Laggan army 224
Lagoe, Waldine 66
Lambert, Charles 192, 195, 238
Lambert, Charles, first earl of Cavan 192, 199, 238
Lambert, Maj. Gen. John 41, 68, 92, 93, 97n, 104, 125, 132, 141, 263, 277
Lancashire 68, 70, 141
land see church land; estates; Cromwellian settlement; leases; Restoration settlement

land grants 8, 35, 40, 83, 87, 206, 267, 306
Langrishe, H. 137n
law and security 90–1
Lawrence, Henry 212
Lawrence, Col. Richard 38, 39, 57, 58, 59, 62, 63, 64, 65, 84n, 89, 94n, 98, 105, 109, 110, 119, 120, 136–7, 267
Lawson, John, vice-admiral 107
leases of government land 35, 200
leathersellers, company of 183
Lecale, Co. Down 176
Lehunt, Richard 137n, 138n, 149n
Leigh, Col. William 117, 135, 136, 137
Leinster 5, 42, 84, 114, 169, 185, 193, 198, 228, 276
Leinster, Convention returns 188–211, 237–9
Leith 130, 147
Leitrim, Convention members 182n, 227–8, 235
Leitrim, county 109, 224, 227, 228, 229
Lenthall, William, speaker of the House of Commons 22, 30, 46, 52, 67, 74, 87, 97n, 107, 112, 126, 138–9, 140, 141–2, 145, 149, 151, 216, 256
Leslie, Henry, bishop of Down and Connor 103, 175, 285
Leslie, John, bishop of Raphoe 285
levellers 61, 301
life guard 1, 38, 67, 69, 77
Lifford, Co. Donegal 42, 171, 186, 187, 188, 194n, 233
Lill, Robert and Lill, Ellinor 190n
Lilburne, Col. Robert 141n
Limavady, Co. Londonderry 169n
Limerick, city 30, 74, 103, 116, 122, 216, 281
Limerick, Convention members 216–17, 236
Limerick, county 5, 36, 52, 190n, 216, 223, 225
Limerick, governor 63, 65, 70, 116, 190

Lincolnshire 38
Lincoln's Inn 185, 203, 206, 211
Liscarroll, Co. Cork 212
Lisle, Capt. Daniel 109, 113n, 114, 137n, 138n
Lisle, Lord, *see* Sidney, Philip
Lismore, Co. Waterford 147, 200, 207, 211, 213, 281n
Littleton, Sir Charles 48, 50
Liverpool, Lancashire 50
Locke, Matthew 147, 202
Loftus, Adam, archbishop of Dublin 200, 225
Loftus, Adam, first viscount Ely 194
Loftus, Sir Adam 211, 286
Loftus, Sir Arthur 188n, 209, 227
Loftus, Dr Dudley 123, 167, 199, 211, 228, 235, 247, 252, 253, 310
Loftus, Nicholas 211
London 9, 21, 22, 26, 27, 28, 29, 30, 41, 43, 45, 53, 54, 67, 68, 72, 79, 81, 88, 92, 96, 104, 107, 116, 125, 130, 131, 133, 138, 139, 143, 144, 147, 151, 152, 153, 154, 159n, 162, 163, 165, 166, 167, 174, 176, 177, 183, 189, 196, 197, 199, 202, 214, 215, 222, 262, 264, 272, 273, 275, 279, 296, 302, 304, 305, 312
Londonderry, city 27, 69, 115, 145, 147, 174, 178, 180, 186
Londonderry, Convention members 178–80
Londonderry, county 7, 178, 179
Londonderry, governor 61, 115, 147, 180
Long, Col. Thomas 51, 121, 192–3, 232n, 275n
Longford, Convention members 198–9, 237
Longford, county 6, 12, 172, 177, 191, 193, 196, 229
long parliament see parliament of England

lord chancellor   269, 300
  of England, see Hyde, Sir Edward
  of Ireland, see Steele, William
lord chief baron of Ireland see Corbet,
    Miles
lord lieutenants of Ireland   34
lord protector, see Cromwell, Oliver;
    Cromwell, Richard
Lords, House of, England   100, 265
Lough Neagh   171
Loughrea see Commissioners
Louth, Convention members   195–8,
    238, 238–9
Louth, county   6, 27, 189, 190, 197, 208,
    257n
Lowe, Major William   63, 129n
Lowther, Sir Gerald   146n
Lucan, Co. Dublin   200
Lucas, Capt. Ben   116n, 122, 135, 137n,
    138n, 149n, 160n
Ludlow, Edmund   34, 41, 51, 59, 60, 71,
    74, 75, 79, 85, 86, 87, 88–9, 92n, 93,
    95, 96–7, 99, 101, 103–4, 104, 105,
    106, 111, 113, 114, 115, 116, 117,
    119, 120, 125, 132, 140, 144, 146,
    148, 149, 156, 157, 158, 162, 166,
    178, 200, 206, 249, 271n, 272, 302n
  appointed commander in chief   67,
    74
  arrival in Ireland   68
  addresses Irish problems   75–7
  purge of army   76–8, 88
  return to England   88–91, 93
  at extraordinary general council   107
  response to Dublin coup   118, 119
  return to Ireland   119, 129–30, 133
  criticized by council of officers
    120–1
  impeachment   134, 142, 152–3
  opposition to officers   135–9
  recalled by speaker   138–9
  leaves Ireland   139
  comments on remodelling   149–50

  resumes place in parliament   152
  presents Duncannon petition   154–5

Mabbott, Gilbert   151–2
MacCarthy, Donough, first earl of
    Clancarty   164n
MacColla, Alasdair   223
McDonnell, Randall, second earl of
    Antrim   170, 179
McGuire, James   15
McMahon, Heber, Roman Catholic
    bishop of Clogher   179, 187, 226
Macosquy, Co. Londonderry   179n
Madden, John   185–6, 309n
Madden, Thomas   185
Magennis family   171, 175n
magistracy   22, 91, 122, 142, 145, 245,
    250
Maguire, Rory   180n
Magunihy barony, Co. Kerry   222
major general of foot see Waller, Sir
    Hardress
Mallow, Co. Cork   117, 198, 217, 218
Manchester   197
Manchester, second earl of, see
    Montagu, Edward
Markethill, Co. Armagh   173
Markham, Col. Henry   62, 64, 105, 143,
    145, 146, 149, 151, 192
Markham, William   192, 203, 231n
Marston Moor   141
  battle of   31
Marten, Sir Henry   67, 153
Maryborough, Queen's Co.   194, 195
massacres of 1641   38
masters in chancery   178, 214, 228,
    269
Massey, Sir Edward   279
Mather, Samuel, minister   51, 85, 128
Maule, Thomas   206–7
Maunsell, Boyle   137n, 149n
Maunsell, John   137n, 138n
Maunsell, Rod   138n

[365]

Maxwell, Robert, bishop of Kilmore   285
Mayo, Convention member   225
Mayo, county   7, 23, 36, 63, 170n, 224, 225, 229
mayors   1, 77, 109, 112, 115, 125, 179, 186, 190, 197, 200, 203, 210, 216
Mazarin, Cardinal   48
Meath, Convention members   188–91, 238
Meath, county   5, 27, 65, 173, 184, 188, 189, 193, 197, 213, 214, 222, 228
Meath, Anthony MacGeoghegan, Roman Catholic bishop of   29
Meath, second earl of, see Brabazon, Edward
Mellifont, Co. Louth   227
Mercurius Politicus   110
Meredith, Major William   60n, 121, 122
Mervyn, Sir Audley   109, 180, 184, 225, 299, 311
Middle Temple   215
Middlethird barony, Co. Tipperary   213
militia
   county   76, 78, 80n, 174, 205, 221, 274
   English   57, 90, 243
   see Dublin
Milton, John   212
Minehead, Somerset   24
ministers   15, 16, 37, 44, 57, 78, 84, 86, 158, 186, 214, 227, 232, 237, 241, 248, 252, 280, 281–2, 300, 314, 315
   recognition   281–3
   reinstatement   283–4, 311
ministry   22, 111, 122, 126, 142, 145, 228, 245, 246, 250,
Moderwell, John   181, 231n
Mohill, Co. Leitrim   227
Molyneux, Adam   198, 206

Monaghan, Convention members   183–4
Monaghan, county   6, 7, 182, 185, 186, 189
Monaghan, town   183
monarchy   3, 4, 5, 13, 15, 17, 19, 20, 68, 125, 131, 239, 240, 241, 243, 262, 263, 301, 303, 319
   abolition of   5, 15, 17, 57, 240
Monck, George   27, 28, 30, 31n, 32–3, 54, 61n, 78, 87, 88, 92, 98, 99, 102, 124, 133, 136, 137, 138, 140, 141–3, 144, 146, 147, 153, 156, 158, 164, 202, 241, 243–4, 261, 264, 271–2, 275, 289, 291, 293, 309, 315
   letters from   97–8, 98–9, 104, 106, 114, 119, 142, 144, 161, 162–3, 168, 171
   letters to   98, 113, 119
   comes to England, 131–2
   advice on army remodelling   147–8, 149, 151
   address to parliament   152, 153
   readmits secluded members   153–4, 156
   proposal to king   262
   view of Irish situation   264, 271
Monck, Henry   32–3, 96, 98
Monkstown   134
Montagu, Edward, second earl of Manchester   63, 68, 276
Montagu, Edward, Admiral   28, 45
Montgomery, Hugh, third viscount of the Ards   31–2, 69, 70, 103, 109, 110, 114n, 147, 163n, 164n, 172, 175, 178, 230, 266
Montgomery, William   32, 70, 110, 114n, 163n
Montrose, first marquess of, *see* Graham, James
Moore, Charles, second Viscount Drogheda   178
Moore, Garrett   163–4

Moore, Lt.-Col. William   65, 94n, 112, 116
Moore family   227
Moray, Sir Robert   146n
Mordaunt, Elizabeth, Lady   257
Mordaunt, John, first Viscount Avalon   18, 29, 87, 146n, 165, 257, 261, 288
Morgan, Major Anthony   13n, 27, 60
Morgan, Robert   224–5, 226, 227, 231n
Morland, Samuel   165, 256, 271n
Morley, Dr John   266, 274n
Morrice, Thomas, biographer of Broghill   71, 161
Morrice, Thomas, customs farmer   83n
Morton, Henry   138n
Mount Kennedy, Co. Wicklow   206
Mountnorris, first Baron, *see* Annesley, Francis
Moygallion, Co. Westmeath   190
Moygoish barony, Co. Westmeath   191
Mullingar, Co. Westmeath   191
Munroe, Daniel, 69
Münster   122, 123n
Munster   1, 5, 9, 11–12, 16, 50, 53, 71, 116–17, 122, 135, 147, 151, 160, 169, 177, 187, 190, 203, 208, 209, 214, 215, 216, 219, 220, 221, 230, 232, 238, 269, 276, 315
   council   177, 217, 294
   lord president   49, 187, 212, 220, 272, 294
   ordinance of indemnity   36, 177
   defection to parliament, 1649   117, 215, 217, 218
   declaration of February 18   160–1, 168, 216, 218, 223, 256n
   see arrears; courts of justice
Munster, Convention returns   211–23, 235–7
Murray, James   306
Murray, John, first earl of Annandale   187

Muskerry barony, Co. Cork   267, 308
Naas, Co. Kildare   202, 203, 204, 228, 282
Navan, Co. Meath, barony   189
Navan, town   190
Nelson, Lt.-Col. John   65, 74, 94n, 116, 216n, 221, 222
Nenagh, Co. Tipperary   160, 182
'new army' (1640)   186
Newborough (Gorey)   209, 211
Newbury, battle of   188
Newcastle, Co. Dublin   199, 201
Newcastle, Yorkshire   147
newcomers   8, 9–10, 16–17, 18, 150, 155, 191, 230, 231–2, 234, 235, 236, 237, 238, 303–4
New England   85, 281n
new English, 10, 13, 16–17, 18–19, 25, 36, 51, 64, 65, 118, 150, 155, 191, 200, 303–4
Newland, Co. Dublin   182
New Model Army   13, 51, 53, 61, 62, 64, 188, 220, 281n
new modelling   3, 53, 55, 59–66, 75, 76–8, 88, 95, 108, 120, 131, 140, 147–52, 167, 192
Newport, Cornwall   176
Newport, Isle of Wight   17, 262, 265
new protestants   233, 237
new royalists   102
Newry, Co. Down   174, 187, 234
newsbook, Dublin   245, 251, 252, 279
Newtownards, Co. Down   114n, 130, 147, 174, 178, 187, 264
Nicholas, Sir Edward   17
'nine', the   92, 101, 107
non-conformists   246
Northamptonshire   204
Northumberland, fourteenth earl of, *see* Percy, Algernon
Norwich   81

[367]

Nottinghamshire 229
Nugent, Richard, second earl of Westmeath 45, 69
Nun, Richard 112n

O'Brien, Henry and Barnabas, sixth and seventh earls of Thomond 222-3, 236
O'Brien, Murrough, first earl of Inchiquin 1, 11, 187, 189, 208, 209, 215, 216, 220, 223
officeholding elite 14, 82, 233, 237, 239-40
old English 150, 212, 215, 223, 235, 236-7, 296
Old Leighlin 169
old Protestants 16, 23, 150, 202, 230-1, 232, 233, 234, 235, 236, 237-8
Oliver, Robert 217, 226, 231n
O'Neill, Sir Phelim 178, 206
Oneilland barony, Co. Armagh 173
ordinances 34, 57, 87
  assessment (1654) 81
  doubling 4
  of indemnity and composition (1654) 12, 36, 84n, 177
  sea 184
  see Poll tax
Ormond, Lower, barony, Co. Tipperary 182
Ormond, Upper, barony, Co. Tipperary 205
Ormond, first marquess and duke, *see* Butler, James
Ormond, Lady, *see* Butler, Elizabeth
Ormond peace, second 36n, 69
Ormondist 179
Ormsby, Andrew 217
Ormsby, Capt. 115
Orrery, first earl of, *see* Boyle, Roger
Osborne, Dorothy 204n
Ossory, bishop of *see* Williams, Griffith
Ossory, dean of, *see* Warren, Edward

Ossory, earl of, *see* Butler, Thomas
Otway, John 61n, 141
Owen, Major George 64
Owen, Major Henry 60, 137n, 138, 149n, 150n, 191
Oxford, The 129, 134, 135, 136
Oxford University 227, 247n
Oxmantown Green 159

pacquet 22, 135, 136, 255, 278, 292, 297
Page, Thomas 31
Pakenham, Henry 190, 196, 231n, 232n
Palfrey, Richard 181, 201n, 231n, 235
Papists 191; *see* Irish papists
Paris 28, 48
Parke, Robert 224, 225
parliament, of England, 318-19, *see* Barebone's parliament; ; 'free parliament'; Pride's Purge; secluded members
parliament, of England (1640-53) 3, 5, 10, 11, 12, 19, 21, 98, 125, 168, 175, 176, 199, 201, 209, 224, 249, 253, 278
  acts to have force in Ireland 57, 90
  committee for Irish affairs (1648) 200, 202
  Munster committee 215
parliament, of England (1659-60) 2-3, 18, 21-2, 26, 33-4, 39, 41, 43, 50, 52-3, 54, 56-8, 59, 67, 74, 75, 77, 79, 80, 81, 82, 83-4, 85, 87-8, 89, 91, 93, 99, 100, 101, 102, 104, 107-8, 112, 115, 117, 118, 121, 123, 125, 127, 129, 131, 133, 144, 153-4, 158, 164, 248, 261, 318
parliament, of England (February to March 1660) 131, 132, 142, 143, 144, 146, 151, 152, 154, 155, 157, 166, 167, 243, 249, 256-7,176, 241-2, 251, 257, 261, 270, 274

parliament (convention), of England (1660)   3, 168, 177, 262–3, 276, 277, 286, 287, 289, 290, 291, 292, 296, 300, 303
  Commons   262, 291, 296, 305
  Lords   244, 262, 276, 291, 295n, 296, 305
  vote for restoration   291, 293
  act of indemnity   302–3, 304
  declarations against papists etc.   304–5
parliament, of Ireland   14, 144, 158, 161, 196, 268, 286–7, 302, 303, 305–6, 307–8, 309, 313, 318–19
  see taxation
parliament, of Ireland (1613)   174, 176, 186, 191, 194n, 195, 196, 198, 200, 205, 208, 211, 215, 221
parliament, of Ireland (1634)   170, 171, 175, 179, 182, 186, 187n, 194, 199, 200, 202, 203, 204, 205, 206, 207, 211, 213, 215, 216, 221, 226, 227
parliament, of Ireland (1640)   82, 169, 170, 172, 174, 175, 177, 179, 180, 181, 182, 183, 185, 189, 193, 194, 199, 200, 202, 203, 205, 206, 207, 211, 219, 222, 224, 226, 228, 229, 249, 300
  rump   185, 194, 195, 204, 206, 211, 258
parliament, of Ireland (1661)   174, 178n, 181, 183n, 190, 192, 197n, 210, 215, 217n, 219n, 222n, 228
  request to summon   296, 307, 312
parliament, union   14, 24, 42 168n
parliament, union (1654)   101n, 175, 189, 190, 212, 221n, 227, 229
parliament, union (1656)   16–17, 172, 177, 179, 183, 190, 196, 200, 212, 221n, 227, 230
parliament, union (1659)   18, 21, 23, 24, 30, 63, 82, 109, 171, 185, 190, 191, 196, 200, 212, 218, 221n, 224, 227, 228, 230
  committee for Irish affairs   228
parochial system   246, 250, 252, 278, 279, 281, 282, 310, 314
Parris, Henry   213, 215
Parris, John   213
Parris, Thomas   213
Parsons, Sir William   176, 200, 202, 206
Passage, Co. Wexford   78n, 106, 137
Patient, Thomas, minister   66
Peasley, Francis   203
Peasley, William   203
Penn, Sir William   294
Pepper, George   138n
Pepys, Richard   43
Pepys, Samuel   314
Percival, Sir John   176, 205, 212, 219n, 220, 223n, 234, 294
Percival, Philip   176
Percy, Algernon, fourteenth earl of Northumberland   276
Perfect Narrative, A   144, 166
Perkins, John   187n
Perkins, Richard   186–7, 188, 233
Perkins, Thomas   186, 188n
Petty, Sir William   6, 25, 26, 27, 28, 46, 127, 180, 221, 222
Phayre, Col. Robert   52–3, 64, 98, 117, 129, 135, 136, 214, 220, 232, 302n
Philipstown, King's Co.   193
Philipstown, Co. Louth   208
Phoenix, the   51
Piers, Sir Henry   191, 199
Piers, Sir Henry Sr   191
pirates   254
plantation   36, 44, 158, 172, 177, 180, 188, 191, 198, 211, 216, 228, 233–5
Plunkett, Nicholas   296, 317, 318
Plunkett, Walter   211
Plunkett, William   211
Plymouth   189
poll tax   285–7, 300, 301

poll tax commissioners 181, 188n, 190n, 194n, 197, 201n, 205n, 210, 211n, 213n, 214, 215, 217n, 226n, 228n
poll tax returns 300n
Ponsonby, Col. John 197
Popery 85, 245
Portman, William, minister 281
Porter, Henry, 66
Portsmouth 92, 130
  commissioners at 107, 112, 120, 121, 132, 139
post master, *see* Bathurst, Samuel
precincts 9, 14
  revenue commissioners 171, 175, 179, 193–4, 196, 203, 205, 208, 209, 212, 213, 216, 228, 229
prelacy 85
Prendergast, J. P. 232, 306
Presbyterianism 15, 251, 278–9, 315
Presbyterians 12–13, 14–15, 17–18, 23, 31, 38, 58, 68, 85n, 106, 123n, 125, 128–9, 143n, 147, 154, 170, 181, 190, 201, 227, 237, 241, 243, 244, 245, 246, 247, 256, 263, 271, 277, 278–81, 282, 284, 285, 287, 288, 291, 297, 305n, 310, 311, 312
'Presbyterian Knot' 262, 276, 288
Pressick, George 123n
Pretty, Col. Henry 33, 58, 61, 62, 74, 94n, 106, 114, 129
Price, John 162
Pride, Col. Thomas 60
Pride's Purge 3, 17, 19, 22, 52, 106n, 131, 158, 241, 293
priests 192, 254
privy council, English, Irish sub-committee 313
privy council, Irish 147, 201, 202, 205
privy councillors 193, 199
proclamations
  of lord protector 136, 310
  forbidding unlawful assemblies, etc. 25
  requiring priests to leave 70
  expelling Catholics from Limerick 74, 103
  for continuation of justices etc. 100
  for weekly day of prayer 101–2
  against Irish papists 305
  of king in England 295, 297
  of king in Ireland 297–8
  against disturbing the possessions of Protestants 305
protectorate, Cromwellian 6, 13, 16, 18, 22, 33, 47, 52, 67, 99, 101, 143
  constitution 16–17, 24, 37
Protestant community in Ireland 2, 4, 8, 10–17, 19–20, 316–20
Protestantism 14–15 *see* communion; church government; Episcopalianism; Prebyterianism
Protestants 10–17, 13–15, 19–20, 31, 36, 38, 43, 44, 74, 81, 82, 84n, 123, 158, 177, 195, 215, 223–4, 240, 245, 264, 273, 286, 295, 296, 302, 303, 305–6, 307, 310, 313, 316; *see* Anabaptists; Baptists; Episcopalians; Independents; Presbyterians; Quakers
Protestant subjects, petition of (1643) 182, 187, 196
proviso to the act of indemnity 302–4, 317–18
provost marshals 66, 186, 187n, 198, 199, 203
Prynne, William 126
Puckle, Col. John 78n, 117, 136–7, 138, 157
Punchestown, Co. Kildare 203
Purdon, George 223n
Purdon, Nicholas 71–2, 223, 231n
Purefoy, Lt.-Col. William 63
puritans 15, 246, 250

Quakers 33, 53, 59, 60, 68, 79, 85, 98,

INDEX

146, 160, 250, 251
Queen's County 5, 75, 103, 184, 193, 203, 208, 229
Queen's County, Convention members 194–5, 237
Quin, Co. Clare 223

Radicals 1, 14, 42, 106, 183, 241
    religious 15–16, 37, 84, 87, 149, 190, 238, 282
    see Baptists, Quakers, Fifth monarchists, Seekers, sects
Raleigh, Sir Walter 59
Ranelagh, Viscountess, *see* Jones, Catherine
Ranelagh, first Viscount, *see* Jones, Roger
Raphoe, bishop of *see* Leslie, John
Rathdown barony, Co. Dublin 86
Rathfarnham, Co. Dublin 211
Rawdon, Sir George 43, 170–1, 175, 176, 285, 295, 299
Rawlings, Major William 61, 73
Rawson, Gilbert 195
Read, Major John 61
rebellion of 1641 4, 10–11, 35, 176, 177, 178, 189, 193, 195, 199, 203, 204, 220, 222, 226, 236, 267, 299, 302, 303, 318
receivers 83, 121, 192, 205, 229
recorders 177, 179, 200, 219, 220, 229
recusants 37, 78
Redcastle, Co. Donegal 186
Reding, John 149n
Redman, Col. Daniel 61, 140–1, 142n, 151, 164, 213, 247
Reeves, Col. William 65, 179
reformation, religious 22, 91, 122, 247, 251–2, 275, 311
regicides 17, 38, 42, 51, 68, 101, 161, 200, 230, 272, 290, 302, 304
remodelling *see* new modelling
rents 36, 308

Representation, A faithful 166
representation (of 5 October) 95
republicans 2, 13, 18, 40, 57, 118, 127–8, 136, 142, 144, 150, 191, 234, 239, 240, 291, 301
resolutioners 263–4, 280
restoration, of Charles II 3, 70, 163, 183, 201, 204, 219, 240, 243, 258, 261, 262, 264, 265, 277, 280, 291, 292, 293, 294, 301, 312, 316–17
restoration settlement
    religious 310–12, 313–16
    secular 316–20
revenue 75, 82, 90, 123, 144–5, 158, 192, 268, 285–7, 301 *see* precincts
Reynolds, Edward 205n
Reynolds, John 205n
Reynolds, Robert 34, 142
Reynolds, Thomas 205, 231n
Rich, Henry, first earl of Holland 41
Richards, Lt.-Col. Solomon 61, 78n, 117, 135, 136
Richardson, Edward 173–4, 201n, 231n, 232n, 234, 237
Richardson, Thomas 185, 232n, 234, 237
Richardstown, Co. Louth 196
Ridgely, Simon 135
Riding, John 137n
Ringsend, Co. Dublin 22
Roberts, Edward 59, 66, 129n, 199n
Rogers, John, minister 128
Rokeby, Capt. Fulke 10n
Rome 29
Roscommon, Convention members 226–7
Roscommon, county 36, 109, 178, 192, 224, 226
Roscommon, town 169n
Ross, Co. Wexford 78n, 117, 136, 157, 169n, 182
Rowe, Col. Francis 215
Rowley, Edward 174, 179, 188

[371]

Rowley, John   179, 281
royalism   19, 23
royalists   2, 10, 11, 12, 17–18, 19, 20, 25, 28, 45, 47, 48, 49, 50, 61, 69, 100, 117, 141, 156, 164–5, 167, 172, 173, 176, 177, 197, 221, 226, 234, 238, 240, 244, 258, 262, 265, 277, 279, 288, 290, 291, 318, 320
    rising in England   17–18, 47, 49, 54, 68
rump *see* parliament of England
Rutland   81
Ruxton, John   197, 231n
Ryves, Charles   204
Ryves, Sir William   204

Sacheverall, Francis   173
Sadler, Col. Thomas   63, 70, 94n, 96, 115, 116, 140
St Albans   67
St George, George   70n, 194, 228, 229
St George, Sir Oliver   70n, 109, 116, 150, 194, 226n, 229, 278
St John, Oliver   142
St John, Oliver, first Viscount Grandison   228
St Johnston, Co. Longford   191, 198
St Leger, Sir William   203
Salt, John   138n
Salway, Richard   44
Sandford, Theophilus   112n, 113n, 137n, 149n
Sands, Lancelot   222, 231n, 232n
Sankey, Henry   193, 231n
Sankey, Col. Hierome   28, 33, 58, 59, 61, 73, 84n, 87, 88, 89, 104, 105, 127, 149n, 180, 193
Sarsfield estate   200
Saunders, Col. Robert   117, 135, 136
Savage, Sir William   193n
Scariffhollis, battle of   226
Scot, Thomas Jr   77n, 101, 137, 139, 191

Scot, Thomas Sr   92, 101, 140, 153, 155
Scot, William   203–4, 231n
Scotland   2, 3, 12, 13, 14, 16, 20, 21, 24, 27, 28, 31, 32, 33, 34, 35, 36, 51, 54, 56, 65, 87, 92, 94, 98, 100, 102, 105, 106, 114, 124, 130, 132, 146n, 156, 165, 168n, 169, 173, 220, 230, 240, 244, 249, 263, 264, 295, 297, 312
Scots   10, 12–13, 58, 103, 114, 146n, 181, 206, 207, 211, 280
Scots settlers   12, 30, 31, 59, 69, 73, 171, 175, 233, 241, 278, 315
Sea Flower   77
seal, Irish   75, 269, 295, 305
Sealed Knot, the   17–18, 48n, 49, 68, 221
secluded members   2–3, 22, 82, 100, 129, 131, 153–4, 155, 156, 157, 158, 160–1, 162, 163, 166, 168, 243, 248, 261, 273n
sects   15–16, 85, 128, 155, 240, 250, 251
Seekers   85, 251
Selkirk and Peebles   230
separatists   245–6, 251
Shaen, Sir James   278, 286n
Shannon, first Viscount, *see* Boyle, Francis
Shannon river   222, 224, 225, 237
Sharp, James   255n, 263–5, 271, 311, 312, 314
Shaw, Captain   274
Sheers, Samuel   60n, 105
Shepherd, Capt. Thomas   105
sheriffs   14, 22, 26, 77, 78, 79, 83, 103, 125, 173, 181, 183, 184, 191, 193, 195, 196, 197, 198, 202, 208, 210, 214, 216, 219, 221, 222n, 223n, 224, 227, 228, 229
Shields, R.   137n, 149n
Sidney, Algernon   34, 44, 176n
Sidney, Philip, Viscount Lisle   34, 187, 230

'single person', the   18, 21, 41, 76, 78, 79, 111, 141, 156, 234
Skinner, Capt. William   78n, 135–6, 139, 154
Slane, Co. Meath   223
Slater, John   197, 232n
Sligo, Convention members   224–5
Sligo, county   6, 7, 36, 109, 174, 206, 210, 224, 225, 227
Sligo, town   169n, 205, 281, 281n
Smith, Boyle   213, 219
Smith, Col. Brian   115, 129, 147
Smith, Erasmus   267
Smith, William   200–1, 231n, 294
Sober Vindication, A   127, 129, 166, 246
Socinianism   85
soldiers   5, 6, 7–8, 9, 11, 15, 33, 35, 36, 73, 77, 78, 80, 83, 84, 95, 106, 107, 110, 112, 115, 116, 117–18, 141, 148, 159, 170, 175, 182, 183, 189, 196, 197, 207, 209, 212, 213, 214, 218, 221, 224, 225, 231, 234, 238, 241, 267, 274, 297, 298, 308, 318
solemn league and covenant   13, 180, 243, 247, 264, 278, 280, 284, 290, 310, 311, 312, 315
Some animadversions   124–7, 285
Somerset   51, 177, 227
Southwell, Robert   176
Southwell, Thomas   216
South Werburgh Street, Dublin   1, 110
Sovereign Power   126
Spain   17, 47, 60, 72, 74, 164, 261
speaker, English House of Commons, *see* Lenthall, William
speaker, English House of Lords, *see* Montagu, Edward, earl of Manchester
speaker, Irish House of Commons, *see* Eustace, Sir Maurice
Spenser, Edmund   219n
Staffordshire   70, 196
Stanes, Dr William   105

Stanley, Col. Thomas   23n, 116, 150n, 157, 159, 160, 316
staple towns   83
Staples, Major Alexander   63
Steele, William, lord chancellor   28, 41, 42, 44, 46, 51, 52, 78, 88, 89, 97, 140, 145–6, 253
Stephens, Richard   138n
Sterling, Sir Robert   32, 208
Stillorgan, Co. Dublin   86
Stopford, Capt. James   69
storekeepers   197, 205, 216
Strabane, Co. Tyrone   180, 181, 233
Strabane, first Baron, *see* Hamilton, Claude
Strafford, first earl of, *see* Wentworth, Thomas
Stubber, Col. Peter   208
Suffolk   180n, 190
Summerhill, Co. Meath   189
Surrey   177, 220, 277
surveyor general of Ireland   238
Sweetman family   208
Swords, Co. Dublin   199, 201
synod, proposed   246

Talbot, Sir Robert   164
Tallaght, Co. Dublin   15
Tallow, Co. Waterford   203, 211, 219, 281
Taunton, Somerset   227
taxation   16, 75, 82, 125, 152, 168, 196, 245, 249, 257, 268, 270, 305
  principle of consent   158, 249, 257, 268, 270, 286–7, 305, 313
  see assessment; poll tax
Taylor, Jeremy, bishop of Dromore   69n, 103, 171, 175, 226, 266, 274n, 314n
Temple, Col. Edmund   46, 53, 60n, 112, 113n, 114, 121, 136, 137, 138, 149, 151, 152, 256

Temple, John   176, 177, 194n, 204, 234, 247
Temple, Sir John   156, 176, 177, 204, 234, 305
Temple, Martha   194n
Temple, William   194n, 204, 247, 255
Templepatrick, Co. Antrim   264
thanksgiving, days of   122, 130, 136, 292, 300–1, 306–7, 308
Tholsel, Dublin   123, 247
Thomastown, Co. Kilkenny   207, 209
Thomlinson, Col. Matthew   43, 89, 110, 134, 272
Thomond, *see* O'Brien, Henry and Barnabas, earls of
Thompson, Lt. John   109, 111n, 113n, 159, 274
Thornhill, Capt. Robert   76, 210
Thurloe, John   172, 201, 263, 272, 276, 290, 292, 293
Tichborne, Sir Henry   176, 189, 197, 198, 202n
Tint, Henry   219
Tint, Sir Robert   219, 231n
Tipperary, Convention members   213–15, 315
Tipperary, county   5, 36, 74, 77, 81, 116n, 176, 182, 205, 209, 212, 213, 223, 315
   officers' petition   315–16
Tiranny barony, Co. Armagh   174
Tirawley barony, Co. Mayo   224
tithes   44, 57, 126, 158, 220, 278, 279, 281, 283, 308, 314
Titus, Silius   295
toleration, religious   57, 105, 111–12, 262, 305–6, 314, 315
Tomlins, Edward   66
Tonson, Major Richard   64
Toogood, Sampson   105, 116n, 137n, 138n
tories   74, 90, 118, 309
Totty, John   210, 231n, 238

Touchet, Audley, first earl of Castlehaven   180
Touchet, James, third earl of Castlehaven   180n
Tower of London   16, 107, 302
towns, proposed reforms   91
Townshend, Richard   220, 221, 231n, 232n
Toxteth, William   197–8, 231n, 232n
trade   16, 35, 45, 83, 123, 158, 308
Tralee, Co. Kerry   206, 221
transplantation, of Catholics   5, 26, 38, 177, 222, 223–4, 225, 254, 267, 268, 273, 301, 308
transplantation, of Scots   13, 175
Trap to catch protestants, A   201
treasurer   286
treasurer at war, England   76
treasurer at war, Ireland   105, 286n
Trevor, Mark   31, 32, 48, 50, 69, 70, 103, 109, 177, 197, 259–60, 275
   reports on Irish affairs   259–60, 265, 266, 273–4, 276
Trim, Co. Meath   105, 149n, 185, 189, 190, 294
Trinity College Dublin, see University of Dublin
Tristernagh Abbey, Co. Westmeath   191
Tuam, archbishop of *see* Boyle, Richard
Tuam, Co. Galway   229
Tullagh, Co. Clare   223
Turnham Green, London   215
Twigg, Charles   115
Tyrellan, Co. Galway   115
Tyrone, Convention members   180–2
Tyrone, county   7, 173, 179, 180, 183, 184, 186, 187, 188

Ulster   5, 12–13, 24, 31, 32, 58, 63, 64, 69, 98, 103, 114, 122, 147, 169, 171, 175, 179, 180, 183, 185, 187, 189,

INDEX

207, 213, 233, 263, 264, 276, 277, 278, 284
Ulster, Convention returns   170–88, 225, 233–5
Ulster, governor   147, 227
union   51
  proposed act of   40, 228
universities   87, 111, 158, 248, 252
University of Dublin   52, 58, 85, 86–7, 90, 128n, 169, 174, 194, 199, 201, 215, 227, 228, 247, 253, 281n, 286, 300, 309, 314
  chancellor   52, 86
  new college   253
  petition of scholars   254
  provost *see* Winter, Samuel
University of Dublin, Convention members   169, 212, 237
unlawful assemblies   25, 254, 309
Ussher, James, archbishop of Armagh   190, 278
  library   253
Ussher, Sir William Jr   82n, 205–6, 213, 248n
Ussher, Sir William Sr   205, 227
Ussher family   198, 200, 238

Vane, Sir Henry   93, 125
Venetian ambassador   39, 41, 107n, 255n
Vernon, John   68
Vesey, Thomas, minister   281, 284
Villiers, Edward   49, 50, 221, 260, 265, 277
Villiers, George, first duke of Buckingham   193
Vincent, Thomas   183–4, 232n, 234, 237

Waddington, Henry   226n, 229, 232n
Wales   14, 73, 208
Walker, Col. William   63–4, 73, 104, 107n, 140, 142
Waller, Sir Hardress   31n, 51, 52, 61, 64, 65, 67, 89, 90, 94n, 97, 98, 99, 108, 111, 112, 113–14, 116n, 117n, 119, 123, 127, 135, 137n, 138, 139–40, 142, 143, 146, 146–7, 148, 149n, 150, 155, 160, 161–2, 163, 167, 216, 220, 232, 240, 241, 272n, 302n, 316
  opposes return of secluded members   156–8, 159
Waller, Sir William   272n, 287–8
Wallingford House group   21, 96–7
Wallis, Col. Peter   33, 59, 60, 94n, 105, 116, 118, 129, 232
Wallop, Henry   42
Wandesford, Sir Christopher   189
Ward, Anthony   214, 232n
Ward, William   113n
Warden, Col. William   1, 71–2, 109, 110, 113n, 116, 119n, 121, 122, 150n, 157n, 208, 209, 223, 231n, 232n, 238, 265, 266n
Ware, A.   113n
Ware, Sir James   191, 199
Ware, Sir John   199
Ware, Rose   199
Warren, Abel   108, 113n, 119, 143
Warren, Edward, dean of Ossory   60
Warren, Major Edward   1, 60, 94n, 98, 108, 110, 113n, 119, 121, 122, 149, 274
Warren, Lt.-Col. John   108–9, 113n, 119, 121, 143, 147, 150n, 157
Waterford, Convention members   211–13, 236n
Waterford, county   5, 74, 170n, 173, 182, 207, 211, 213, 218
Waterford, town   24, 25, 85n, 117, 135, 136, 137, 211, 212, 281n
Waterhouse, Dr Joseph   178, 232, 234
Waterhouse, Nathaniel   178
Weaver, John   142, 143, 146
Wells, Edmund, minister   129n

[375]

Wemys, Sir Patrick   206, 207–8, 238
Wentworth, Sir Thomas, first earl of Strafford   36, 44, 171, 185, 186, 200, 203, 313
West, Roger   175–6, 198n
Western Association, army of   279
Westmeath, Convention members   191–3, 238
Westmeath, county   5, 177, 190, 191, 192, 199, 229
Westmeath, second earl of, *see* Nugent, Richard
Westminster   14, 16, 159, 164, 201, 228, 291, 304
Westminster Assembly
  catechisms   85
  confession   84, 243
Westminster Hall   61
Wexford, Convention members   209–11, 238
Wexford, County   7, 74, 76, 116n, 190, 191, 206, 209, 210 211, 237
Wexford, town   78n, 117, 135, 210
Whalley, Henry   78n, 112, 113n, 160, 229, 232n, 235, 267, 290
Wheeler, Lt.-Col. Francis   64
Wheeler, Oliver   195n, 207
Whitehouse, Co. Antrim   211
Whitelock, Bulstrode   34n, 50, 96n
Wicklow, Convention members   205–7, 237
Wicklow, county   12, 74, 76, 176n, 188n, 202, 203, 211, 228

Wicklow, town   205
Wight, Isle of   244
Wilkinson, John, minister   281
Williams, Griffith, bishop of Ossory   285n, 292
Wilson, Lt.-Col. Ralph   65, 116, 160, 217
Wilton, George   110–11
Winckworth, Capt. Thomas   104
Windsor Castle   143n
Winnington bridge, battle of   68
Winter, Samuel   43, 51, 52, 84, 85, 86, 109, 119, 128, 143, 184, 185, 192, 217, 254
witchcraft   200
Wogan, Thomas   302n
Wood, James   263
Wood, Robert   121, 139
Wood Quay ward, Dublin   211
Wootton, Henry, minister   128
Worcester, battle of   64, 220
Worcestershire   48, 173
Worsley, Benjamin   66, 105, 180
Worth, Edward, minister   86, 279–80, 315
Wybrants, Peter   294

Yarwell, William   216–17, 231n, 232n
Yeoman, John   138n
York   141, 153
York, James, duke of   172, 300
Youghal, Co. Cork   117, 217, 218, 219, 267, 308